LINCOLN'S MELANCHOLY

Lincoln's Melancholy

How Depression
Challenged a President
and Fueled His
Greatness

Joshua Wolf Shenk

HOUGHTON MIFFLIN COMPANY
BOSTON · NEW YORK
2005

For information about permission to reproduce selections
from this book, write to Permissions, Houghton Mifflin Company,
215 Park Avenue South, New York, New York 10003.

Visit our Web site: www.houghtonmifflinbooks.com.
Also visit: www.lincolnsmelancholy.com.

Library of Congress Cataloging-in-Publication Data

Shenk, Joshua Wolf.
Lincoln's melancholy : how depression challenged a
president and fueled his greatness / Joshua Wolf Shenk.
p.   cm.
Includes bibliographical references and index.
ISBN-13: 978-0-618-55116-3
ISBN-10: 0-618-55116-6
1. Lincoln, Abraham, 1809–1865 — Psychology.
2. Presidents — United States — Biography. I. Title.
E457.2.S47 2005
973.7'092 — dc22   2005009653

Printed in the United States of America

Book design by Robert Overholtzer

QUM 10 9 8 7 6 5 4 3 2 1

For Joanne Wolf Cohen and Richard L. Shenk

Contents

A NOTE ON THE TEXT

This book is drawn from primary sources, many of which depart from modern standards of punctuation and spelling. Quotations from letters and other period documents are given as in the original.

The inclination to exchange thoughts with one another is probably an original impulse of our nature. If I be in pain I wish to let you know it, and to ask your sympathy and assistance; and my pleasurable emotions also, I wish to communicate to, and share with you.

— ABRAHAM LINCOLN
February 11, 1859

Prelude

A YEAR BEFORE HE DIED, Leo Tolstoy told this story to a reporter for the *New York World:*

"Once while travelling in the Caucasus," he said, "I happened to be the guest of a Caucasian chief of the Circassians, who, living far away from civilized life in the mountains, had but a fragmentary and childish comprehension of the world and its history. The fingers of civilization had never reached him nor his tribe, and all life beyond his native valleys was a dark mystery."

Tolstoy told them of his work and of the industries, inventions, and schools of the outside world. But only when he turned to the subject of warriors and generals and statesmen did he arouse the interest of his tall, gray-bearded host, the chief. "Wait a moment," the chief said. "I want all my neighbors and my sons to listen to you."

"He soon returned," Tolstoy continued, "with a score of wild looking riders and . . . those sons of the wilderness sat around me on the floor and gazed at me as if hungering for knowledge. I spoke at first of our Czars and of their victories; then I spoke of the greatest military leaders. My talk seemed to impress them deeply. The story of Napoleon was so interesting to them that I had to tell them every detail, as, for instance, how his hands looked, how tall he was, who made his guns and pistols and the color of his horse. It was very difficult to satisfy them and to meet their point of view, but I did my best."

When Tolstoy finished, the chief lifted his hand. "But you have not told us a syllable about the greatest general and greatest ruler of the world," he said gravely. "We want to know something about him. He was a hero. He spoke with a voice of thunder; he laughed like the sunrise and his deeds were as strong as the rock and as sweet as the fragrance of roses. The angels appeared to his mother and predicted that the son whom she would conceive would become the greatest the stars had ever seen. He was so great that he even forgave the crimes of his greatest enemies and shook brotherly hands with those who had plotted against his life. His name was Lincoln and the country in which he lived is called America, which is so far away that if a youth should journey to reach it he would be an old man when he arrived. Tell us of that man."

"Tell us, please," shouted one of the others, "and we will present you with the best horse of our stock."

"I looked at them," Tolstoy said, "and saw their faces all aglow, while their eyes were burning . . . I told them of Lincoln and his wisdom, of his home life and youth. They asked me ten questions to one which I was able to answer. They wanted to know all about his habits, his influence upon the people and his physical strength. But they were astonished to hear that Lincoln made a sorry figure on a horse and that he lived such a simple life."

After telling them all he knew, Tolstoy said that he thought he could procure a photograph of Lincoln. He rode off to the nearest town, accompanied by one of the young riders. He found a photograph and gave it to him.

"It was interesting," Tolstoy said, "to witness the gravity of his face and the trembling of his hands when he received my present. He gazed for several minutes silently, like one in a reverent prayer: his eyes filled with tears. He was deeply touched and I asked him why he became so sad."

The young man answered with a question of his own. "Don't you find," he said, "judging from his picture, that his eyes are full of tears and that his lips are sad with a secret sorrow?"

Introduction

IN EARLY MAY 1860, a week before the Republican party held its national convention in Chicago, the delegates from Illinois met in Decatur, a small town in the center of the state. They met in what they called a "wigwam," a kind of urban barn, built over a vacant lot with a canvas roof held up by wood beams. When the Decatur convention opened, on May 9, three thousand men packed inside. After an initial round of huzzahs, at the start of the afternoon session, a thirty-five-year-old politician named Richard Oglesby took the stage. "I am informed," he said, "that a distinguished citizen of Illinois, and one who Illinois will ever delight to honor, is present and I wish to move that this body invite him to a seat on the stand." The crowd waited to hear the man's name, but Oglesby paused — as though, observed a man in the crowd, "to tease expectation to the verge of desperation."

At that moment, Abraham Lincoln was crouched on his heels at the back of the hall, just inside the entrance. A fifty-one-year-old lawyer and a veteran of the state legislature, Lincoln had left his last political office, as U.S. representative, eleven years before. After one middling term in Congress, he mostly stayed away from politics for five years. Then, in 1854, an old debate over slavery took a new turn with the repeal of the Missouri Compromise, which, Lincoln wrote, "aroused me again." Pressing his argument against the extension of slavery, and for its eventual extinction, he helped build the new Republican party in Illinois. In 1858, he challenged Stephen Douglas for his Senate seat, losing the race but gaining a national reputation from the campaign debates. In February 1860, he dazzled a crowd at New York City's Cooper Union with an antislavery speech the *New York Tribune* called among "the most convincing political arguments ever made in this city."

Lincoln came to the Decatur convention in May as a rising star. When Oglesby called his name from the stage of the wigwam, the delegates and onlookers broke into thunderous applause. A half-dozen men seized Lincoln and tried to push him to the front of the room. When that didn't work — the room was too full — they lifted him up on their shoulders and passed him, not unlike in a mosh pit today, over the mass of people to the stage. The crowd roared its approval.

Still, those in the wigwam knew that Lincoln stood a slim chance to take the national nomination the following week at Chicago. Most Republicans expected that the honor would fall to Senator William Seward, the party's leading man. Lincoln, by contrast, failed to rate a mention on preconvention scorecards of seven, twelve, even twenty-one candidates. Lincoln couldn't even count on the backing of his own state convention at Decatur, which he badly wanted. "I am not in a position where it would hurt much for me to not be nominated on the national ticket," he wrote, "but I am where it would hurt some for me to not get the Illinois delegates."

Richard Oglesby, the young politician who was managing the convention, knew Lincoln's position and wanted to improve it. An ambitious and energetic man — he would become a major general in the Union army and, soon afterward, governor of Illinois — Oglesby wanted to deliver the state's delegates for him. Not some, but all; not in a tepid fashion, but with a rousing cheer.

Oglesby had decided that Lincoln needed something to distinguish himself — a catch phrase like "Log Cabin and Hard Cider," which had helped elect William Henry Harrison in 1840. So before the convention, Oglesby had gone to see a white-whiskered old farmer named John Hanks. Hanks was Lincoln's mother's cousin and had lived with the Lincoln family when they first came to Illinois in 1830. Oglesby asked what kind of work Lincoln had done in those days. "Not much of any kind but dreaming," Hanks replied. Then he told the story of how he and Lincoln had once cleared fifteen or twenty acres of black walnut and honey locust trees, built a cabin, and mauled rails for fences.

"John," Oglesby asked, "did you split rails down there with old Abe?"

"Yes, every day," Hanks answered.

"Do you suppose you could find any of them now?"

Hanks said he had seen that old fence about ten years before, and he took Oglesby there the next day. While Oglesby waited in his buggy, Hanks chipped away at the fence with a knife. When he came up with shavings that were black walnut and honey locust, he declared, "They are the identical rails we made."

The rails were just what Oglesby wanted: symbols of free labor, solid character, triumph over the crude frontier, humble origins, and the strength to rise. He and Hanks took two of them, tied them to Oglesby's buggy, and brought them to town. Then, on the first day of the state convention, Oglesby introduced Lincoln with a flourish. This was John Hanks's cue. As Lincoln reached the stage, Hanks burst into the wigwam carrying the rails. A banner hanging from them explained that Lincoln had split them and announced, in large letters:

ABRAHAM LINCOLN
The Rail Candidate
FOR PRESIDENT IN 1860

The crowd went wild. Delegates and onlookers threw hats, books, and canes into the air. The wigwam shook so much that its canvas exterior became detached from the wood beams. "The roof was literally cheered off the building," declared an early account of the maelstrom. The energy of the crowd foreshadowed Lincoln's success. The state's delegates soon resolved to back Lincoln unanimously. Buoyed by the "rail-splitter" image, Lincoln would vault into place as William Seward's main rival for the Republican nomination. On that stage, then, Lincoln stood at the peak of three hard decades in politics. "Lincoln's name was in every mouth," recalled Joseph G. Cannon, who later became Speaker of the House of Representatives, "and in those stirring times everything was on fire."

Yet, to the wigwam audience in Decatur, Lincoln presented a strange figure. He didn't seem euphoric, or triumphant, or even pleased. To the contrary, said a man named Johnson, observing from the convention floor, "I then thought him one of the most diffident and worst plagued men I ever saw."

The next day, the convention closed. The crowds dispersed, leaving behind cigar stubs and handbills and the smell of sweat and whiskey. After the wigwam had emptied, the lieutenant governor of the state, William J. Bross, walked the floor. He noticed his state party's choice for president sitting alone at the end of the hall. Lincoln's head was bowed, his gangly arms bent at the elbows, his hands pressed to his face. As Bross approached, Lincoln noticed him and said, "I'm not very well."

Lincoln's look at that moment — the classic image of gloom — was familiar to everyone who knew him well. These spells were common. And they were just one thread in a curious fabric of behavior and thought that Lincoln's friends and colleagues called his "melancholy." He often wept in public and recited maudlin poetry. He told jokes and stories at odd times — he needed the laughs, he said, for his survival. As a young man he talked of suicide, and as he grew older, he said he saw the world as hard and grim, full of misery, made that way by fates and forces of God. "No element of Mr. Lincoln's character," declared his colleague Henry Whitney, "was so marked, obvious and ingrained as his mysterious and profound melancholy." His law partner William Herndon said, "His melancholy dripped from him as he walked."

Many people are surprised to hear that any aspect of Lincoln could remain largely unknown, let alone something as significant as a lifelong melancholy. It's an old refrain. "There can be no new 'Lincoln stories,'" the journalist Noah Brooks said in 1898. "The stories are all told." In fact, we continue to learn about him, for several reasons. First, the sheer volume of "Lincoln stories" — first-person accounts by people who knew him — makes for a huge trove of basic information. Second, the distinguished scholarly work of each generation often facilitates new discoveries by generations that follow. Lincoln once noted how the printing press spread knowledge by making works widely available that had previously been the province of a privileged few. The same is true when primary sources are collected, transcribed, and published; when exhaustive reference works are produced; when scholars leave published books and carefully organized research files; and when interest in a subject grows to the point that entire institutions — libraries, journals, and museums — are devoted to assisting its students. The main problem with studying Lincoln is not finding sources, but choosing which sources to follow.

A third reason we continue to learn about Lincoln is that, faced with a wealth of material — documents to read and parse, references to follow, contexts to study so that a mere shard can be seen as a piece of a whole — historians must choose interpretive frameworks. And in this they are inexorably subject to the fancies and suppositions of the times they live in. As times change, so do popular dogmas and curiosities. Therefore our approach to history changes as well. This is not to say that history is merely subjective, but that objective and subjective realities interact to create a foundation of accepted truth. "What happens over and over," J. G. Randall wrote in 1945, introducing the first volume of his biography *Lincoln the President,* "is that a certain idea gets started in association with an event or figure. It is repeated by speakers and editors. It soon becomes a part of that superficial aggregation of concepts that goes under the heading 'what everybody knows.' It may take decades before a stock picture is even questioned as to its validity."

In the late nineteenth and early twentieth centuries, Lincoln's melancholy was widely accepted by students of his life, and it became a mainstay of popular culture. But by the late 1940s, the subject began to disappear. The stock picture of Lincoln became one of stoicism, strength, and reserve. There were a number of reasons for this shift. Those curious about the historiography will find a fuller treatment in the Afterword. Here, a summary will suffice.

In the decades after Lincoln's death, two emotional crises he had as a young man became central aspects of his popular persona. For real drama, the agreed-upon facts need no embellishing. But melodrama has its own purposes. The story of Lincoln's love for Ann Rutledge and that of his agonizing courtship of Mary Todd became overblown. Then, in the 1920s and 1930s, they reached absurd heights.

In a sharp response to such pulp, scholars emerging from rapidly expanding Ph.D. history programs fashioned themselves as "scientific historians," whose authority over the evidence of history was supreme. They dismissed oral history in favor of court records and census data and other "hard" evidence. Prominent among these arbiters was J. G. Randall, the leading Lincoln scholar of his age. With his wife and partner, Ruth Painter Randall, he cut the legs out from under the evidence of Lincoln's melancholy in the mid-1940s. The Randalls decided that firsthand reports of Lincoln's two suicidal breakdowns as a young man were only so much "gossip" and innuendo. The effect was profound. In the 1960s and 1970s, graduate students learned that Lincoln's first suicidal breakdown was a "myth." His second episode, during a fascinating, crucial period of his life, was reduced to a few sentences even in full-scale biographies. Scholars of Lincoln largely abandoned the study of his inner life.

The movement away from discussion of Lincoln's melancholy took hold in a culture that was increasingly divided on matters of psychology and human suffering. In the mid-twentieth-century United States, the theories of Sigmund Freud and Emil Kraepelin — the founders, respectively, of psychoanalysis and biological psychiatry — flourished, creating both devoted adherents and sharp critics. History became one front in the war. Inspired by Freud himself, psychoanalysts eagerly put Lincoln on the couch, examining his life through the lens of childhood traumas and sexual conflicts. Many historians found this absurd, especially since much of the evidence in psychobiographies was exaggerated or outright invented.

What resulted was deeply ironic, if not tragic. Serious scholars tended to dismiss both the specific evidence and the broad importance of Lincoln's melancholy, leaving the field entirely to psychoanalysts of the Freudian school, in whose hands it would remain until the end of the twentieth century.

Eventually, changing conditions led to a reappraisal. The buttoned-up culture of the 1940s, which had influenced the Randalls and their followers, gave way to the open, confessional culture of Donahue and Oprah. A tradition of viewing past leaders as stony heroes gave way to one that eagerly sought to see them as human beings, warts and all. And mental illness drew increasing attention.

In the area of Lincoln studies, in the 1980s and 1990s, a group of emerging scholars began, independent of one another, to look anew at original accounts of Lincoln by the men and women who knew him. These historians — including Douglas Wilson, Rodney Davis, Michael Burlingame, and Allen Guelzo — had come of age in an era when the major oral histories were treated, as Davis has noted, "like nuclear waste." But they found to their surprise that such sources were more like rich mines that had been sealed off and left unexplored. First in journals and then in books, they began to reassess some of the most important Lincoln stories. In the process, they brought a number of crucial oral histories to the attention of other scholars and raised again the topics so often discussed in those histories, including Lincoln's melancholy.

Describing what had led to his own work, J. G. Randall explained just what happens when the wheel of scholarship turns: "Evidence is then unearthed, some of it being first discovered, or brought to light after having been forgotten or neglected. Discoloring is corrected, partisan misrepresentation — perhaps accepted unawares by the public — is exposed, predilections and presumptions stripped away. Historical insight cuts through with a new clarity. In this process the historian does not claim to arrive at perfection, but he does hope by fresh inquiry to come nearer to past reality."

In 1998, I came upon a chance reference to Lincoln's melancholy in a sociologist's essay on suicide. I was intrigued enough to investigate the subject and discovered an exciting movement in the field of Lincoln studies. The aforementioned scholars had built a foundation on which new inquiries could rise. Within a year or so, I had begun to gather together all of the basic primary evidence on Lincoln's inner life, intent on studying its meanings and mysteries.

It is significant, of course, that I did this work in a time of relative openness on the subjects of depression and mental illness. When Lincoln was thirty-two, he wrote, "I am now the most miserable man living." Ruth Painter Randall found this a "ridiculous" example of how in Lincoln's time it was "considered quite fashionable to dwell on one's emotions without restraint." Today, more and more people recognize the value of such frank confessions and want to know about the experiences that lay behind them.

But while this book springs from an interest in psychology, it is not a psychobiography. The distinction may seem abstract, but in fact it is crucial. The hallmark of psychobiographies is that they begin with a theory — usually some derivative of Freudian theory — and seek to buttress it with evidence. This book takes the opposite approach. It is the product of a long effort to establish the credible reports of how Lincoln lived, what he felt, and how he grew. This evidence suggests some clear lessons, but also raises challenging questions, for which answers have been sought in modern psychological research, the history of medicine, and the popular and intellectual culture of Lincoln's lifetime. The goal has been to see what we can learn about Lincoln by looking at him through the lens of his melancholy, and to see what we can learn about melancholy by looking at it in light of Lincoln's experience.

Necessary as it is to acknowledge the plain facts and where they lead, it is also important to acknowledge the limits of what we can know. Those of us who are familiar with melancholy well know its elusive nature. It operates in deep recesses of thought and feeling, hidden not only from the view of an observer but, often, from the melancholic as well. The goal is not to know Lincoln's melancholy perfectly, but to know it as best we can, and to see what story emerges.

In broad terms, that story is fairly straightforward. From a young age,

Lincoln experienced psychological pain and distress, to the point that he believed himself temperamentally inclined to suffer to an unusual degree. He learned how to articulate his suffering, find succor, endure, and adapt. Finally, he forged meaning from his affliction so that it became not merely an obstacle to overcome, but a factor in his good life.

This is a story for our time. Affecting more than 100 million people a year, depression is the world's leading cause of disability. In 2000, about a million people worldwide killed themselves — about equal to the number of deaths from war and homicide that year put together. Adjusting for population growth, unipolar depression is ten times more prevalent than it was fifty years ago. When we face this reality, the suffering of a prominent man in history takes on new poignancy, especially as it illuminates not only the nature of suffering but also the way it can become part of a productive life.

As I worked on this book, I heard three main questions about Lincoln's melancholy. First, was it a "clinical depression"? Part One investigates how Lincoln's melancholy manifested itself in his early life and young manhood and how it fits — and challenges — the diagnostic categories of modern psychiatry. Second, what kind of treatment did he undergo? Part Two shows what Lincoln did in response to his melancholy, the strategies he used to heal and help himself. Third, in what way did the melancholy contribute to his work as a public figure? Part Three addresses how Lincoln's melancholy became intertwined with his mature character, ideas, and actions.

This is the story of a man who joined great pain and great power. From his early letters lamenting the "peculiar misfortune" of his temperament, to poetry he wrote on subjects such as suicide and madness, Lincoln's life sprang from a search for meaning that explained, and even ennobled, his affliction. As president, Lincoln urged his countrymen to accept their blessing and their burden, to see that their suffering had meaning, and to join him on a journey toward a more perfect Union.

PART ONE

CHAPTER 1

The Community Said He Was Crazy

IN THREE KEY CRITERIA — the factors that produce depression, the symptoms of what psychiatrists call major depression, and the typical age of onset — the case of Abraham Lincoln is perfect. It could be used in a psychiatry textbook to illustrate a typical depression. Yet Lincoln's case is perfect, too, in a very different sense: it forces us to reckon with the limits of diagnostic categories and raises fundamental questions about the nature of illness and health.

Though great resources in research and clinical science have been devoted to depression in the past few decades, we can neither cure it nor fully explain it. What we can do is describe its general characteristics. The perverse benefit of so much suffering is that we know a great deal about what the sufferers have in common. To start, the principal factors behind depression are biological predisposition and environmental influences. Some people are more susceptible to depression simply by virtue of being born. Depression and other mood disorders run in families, not only because of what happens in those families, but because of the genetic material families share. A person who has one parent or sibling with major depression is one and a half to three times more likely than the general population to experience it.

The standard way to investigate biological predisposition is simply to list the cases of mental illness — or mental characteristics suggestive of potential illness — in a family. With Lincoln, such a family history suggests that he came by his depression, at least in part, by old-fashioned inheritance. His parents, Thomas and Nancy Lincoln, came from Virginia families that crossed the Appalachian Mountains into Kentucky in the late eighteenth century. They married in 1806 and had three children: Sarah, born February 10, 1807; Abraham, born February 12, 1809; and Thomas, born about 1811. Though our information is imperfect, to say the least, both parents had characteristics suggestive of melancholy. Nearly all the descriptions of Nancy Lincoln have her as sad. For example, her cousin John Hanks said her nature "was kindness, mildness, tenderness, sadness." And Lincoln himself described his mother as "intellectual, sensitive and somewhat sad." Tom Lincoln, a farmer and carpenter, was a social man with a talent for jokes and stories, but he, too, had a somber streak. "He seemed to me," said his stepgrandson, "to border on the serious — reflective." This seriousness could tip into gloom. According to a neighbor in Kentucky, he "often got the 'blues,' and had some strange sort of spells, and wanted to be alone all he could when he had them." During these spells he would spend as much as half a day alone in the fields or the woods. His behavior was strange enough to make people wonder if Tom Lincoln was losing his mind.

Perhaps the most striking evidence of mental trouble in Abraham Lincoln's family comes from his paternal relations. His great-uncle once told a court of law that he had "a deranged mind." His uncle Mordecai Lincoln had broad mood swings, which were probably intensified by his heavy drinking. And Mordecai's family was thick with mental disease. All three of his sons — who bore a strong physical resemblance to their first cousin Abraham — were considered melancholy men. One settler who knew both the future president and his cousins spoke of the two "Lincoln characteristics": "their moody spells and great sense of humor." One of these Lincoln cousins swung wildly between melancholia and mania and at times had a tenuous grip on reality, writing letters and notes that suggest madness. Another first cousin of Lincoln's had a daughter committed to the Illinois State Hospital for the Insane. After a trial, a jury in Hancock County committed thirty-nine-year-old Mary Jane Lincoln to the hospital, noting that "her disease is of thirteen years duration." At the hospital, an attendant observed, "Her father was cousin to Abraham Lincoln, and she has features much like his."

What is striking about the case of Mary Jane Lincoln is that the jury, charged with answering the question of whether insanity ran in her family, concluded that "the disease is with her hereditary." According to a family historian who grew up in the late nineteenth century, the descendants of Mordecai Lincoln "suffered from all the nervous disorders known. Some were on the ragged edge." One family member who had frequent spells of intense mental trouble referred to his condition as "the Lincoln horrors."

Three elements of Lincoln's history — the deep, pervasive sadness of his mother, the strange spells of his father, and the striking presence of mental illness in the family of his uncle and cousins — suggest the likelihood of a biological predisposition toward depression. "Predisposition" means an increased risk of developing an illness. As opposed to traditional Mendelian inheritance — in which one dominant gene or two recessive genes lead to an illness or trait — genetic factors in psychiatric illnesses are additive and not categorical. "The genes confer only susceptibility in many cases," explains the psychiatrist S. Nassir Ghaemi, in *The Concepts of Psychiatry,* "not the illness. That is, they only increase the likelihood that fewer or less severe environmental factors are required for the illness to develop, compared with someone who has fewer disease-related genes."

What tips a person from tendency to actuality? For centuries, philosophers and physicians emphasized climate and diet. Today's experts focus on harsh life events and conditions, especially in early childhood. Lincoln's early life certainly had its harsh elements. His only brother died in infancy in Kentucky. In 1816, Abraham's eighth year, the family moved to southern Indiana. Two years later, in the fall of 1818, an infectious disease swept through their small rural community. Among those affected were Lincoln's aunt and uncle, Thomas and Elizabeth Sparrow, and his mother, Nancy Lincoln. Eventually, the disease would be traced to a poisonous root, eaten by cattle and then ingested by humans in milk or meat. But when Abraham watched his mother become ill, the disease was a grim mystery that went by various names, from "puking fever" to "river sickness" to "fall poison." Later, it became known as the "milk sick." "No announcement strikes the members of a western community with so much dread as the report of a case," said a newspaper of the time. A physician described the course of the illness: "When the individual is about to be taken down, he feels weary, trembles more or less under exertion, and often experiences pain, numbness and slight cramps." Nausea soon follows, then "a feeling of depression and burning at the pit of the stomach," then retching, twitching, and tossing side to side. Before long, the patient becomes "deathly pale and shrunk up," listless and indifferent, and lies, between fits of retching, in a "mild coma." First the Sparrows — with whom the Lincolns were close — took sick and died. Then Nancy

Lincoln went to bed with the illness. Ill for about a week, she died on October 5, 1818. She was about thirty-five years old. Her son was nine.

In addition to the loss of his mother, aunt, and uncle, a year or so later Abraham faced the long absence of his father, who returned to Kentucky to court another bride. For two to six months, Tom Lincoln left his children alone with their twenty-year-old cousin, Dennis Hanks. When he returned, the children were dirty and poorly clothed. Lincoln later described himself at this time as "sad, if not pitiful."

The one constant in Abraham's life was his sister, Sarah. She was a thin, strong woman who resembled her father in stature, with brown hair and dark eyes. Like her brother, Sarah Lincoln had a sharp mind. She stayed with the family until 1826, when she married, set up house, and quickly became pregnant. On January 28, 1828, she gave birth to a stillborn child and shortly afterward died herself. "We went out and told Abe," recalled a neighbor. "I never will forget the scene. He sat down in the door of the smoke house and buried his face in his hands. The tears slowly trickled from between his bony fingers and his gaunt frame shook with sobs."

In the emotional development of a child, pervasive tension can be just as influential as loss. Lincoln's relationship with his father — the only other member of his nuclear family who survived — was so cool that observers wondered whether there was any love between them. The relationship was strained by a fundamental conflict. From a young age, Abraham showed a strong interest in his own education. At first his father helped him along, paying school fees and procuring books. "Abe read all the books he could lay his hands on," said his stepmother. "And when he came across a passage that struck him he would write it down . . . then he would re-write it — look at it — repeat it." But at some point Tom Lincoln began to oppose the extent of his son's studies. Abraham sometimes neglected his farm work by reading. Tom would beat him for this, and for other infractions.

To men who had been born and expected to die on farms, book learning had limited value. A man ought to be able to read the Bible (for his moral life) and legal documents (for his work life). Writing could help, too, as could basic arithmetic. Anything more was a luxury, and for working folks seemed frivolous. For generations, Lincoln men had cleared land, raised crops, and worked a trade. So when this boy slipped away from feeding livestock and splitting logs to write poetry and read stories, people thought him lazy. "Lincoln was lazy — a very lazy man," remembered his cousin Dennis Hanks. "He was always reading — scribbling — writing — ciphering — writing poetry &c. &c."

Later, Lincoln's self-education would become the stuff of legend. Many parents have cited Lincoln's long walks to school and ferocious self-discipline to their children. But Lincoln pursued his interests in defiance of established norms. Far from being praised, he was consistently admonished. He may well have paid an emotional toll. Many studies have linked adult mental health to parental support in childhood. Lower levels of support correlate with increased levels of depressive symptoms, among other health problems, in adulthood. After Lincoln left home in his early twenties, his contact with his father was impersonal and infrequent.

When reviewing the facts of Lincoln's childhood, we should keep in mind some context. For example, in the early nineteenth century, one out of four infants died before their first birthday. And about one fourth of all children lost a mother or father before age fifteen. Of the eighteen American presidents in the nineteenth century, nine lost their mother, father, or both while they were children. None of Lincoln's contemporaries, nor Lincoln himself, mentioned the deaths of his siblings and mother as factors contributing to his melancholy. The melancholy was unusual, but the deaths were not. In the same vein, while we ought not to ignore Lincoln's conflict with his father and discount its possible emotional aftereffects, we risk missing more than we gain if we look at it exclusively through the lens of modern psychology. In fact, such a conflict between ambitious young men and their fathers was not uncommon in the early nineteenth century, a time of broad cultural and economic change.

Abraham was not evidently a wounded child, but signs point to his being sensitive. He spent a lot of time alone. He was serious about his studies and reading, and uncommonly eager to explore imaginative realms, which psychologists often observe in sensitive children. He also took up a popular cause among sensitive people, the welfare of animals. Some boys found it fun to set turtles on fire or throw them against trees. "Lincoln would Chide us — tell us it was wrong — would write against it," remembered one of his neighbors. His stepsister remembered him once "contending that an ants life was to it, as sweet as ours to us."

At the same time, Lincoln was a winsome child. Others sought him out, followed him in games, and applauded him when he mounted a stump and performed for them, pretending to be a preacher or a statesman. By the time he was a teenager, grown men would flock around him, eager to hear his jokes and stories. He was well liked.

Lincoln was not depressed in his late teens and early twenties — at least not so far as anyone could see. When he left his family, at age twenty-one, he had no money or connections. His chief asset — perhaps his only real asset — was his golden character. Settling as a stranger in New Salem, a small village on a river bluff in central Illinois, he soon was among the best-liked men around. A gang of rough boys developed a fierce attachment to him after he made a stellar showing in a wrestling match, displaying not only physical strength but a sense of fairness. Others were impressed with Lincoln's wit and intelligence, noticing, for example, how when he recited the poetry of Robert Burns, he nailed the Scottish accent, the fierce emotion, and the devilish humor. Though Lincoln looked like a yokel — tall and gangly, he had thick, black, unruly hair and he wore pants that ended above his ankles — he had good ideas and a good manner. "He became popular with all classes," said Jason Duncan, a physician in New Salem.

After less than a year in New Salem, Lincoln declared himself as a candidate for the Illinois General Assembly. He was twenty-three years old. He lost the race but got nearly every vote in his precinct, which, said another candidate, was "mainly due to his personal popularity." When he volunteered for a state militia campaign against a band of Native Americans under Chief Black Hawk, a part of the bloody Black Hawk War, his company elected Lincoln captain. Nearly three decades later — as a veteran of Congress and his party's nominee for president of the United States — Lincoln wrote that this was "a success which gave me more pleasure than any I have had since."

In his first four years in New Salem, Lincoln struck his new friends and neighbors as sunny and indefatigable. "I never saw Mr Lincoln angry or desponding," said a fellow soldier in the Black Hawk War, "but always cheerful." Indeed, "the whole company, even amid trouble and suffering, received Strength & fortitude, by his bouancy and elasticity." Once Lincoln stopped at the house of a neighbor, Elizabeth Abell, after working in the fields. He was scratched all over from briar thorns. Abell fussed over him, but Lincoln laughed about it and said it was the poor man's lot. "Certainly," she said years later, "he was the best natured man I ever got acquainted with." Asked by a biographer whether the Lincoln she knew was a "sad man," Abell answered, "I never considered him so. He was always social and lively and had great aspirations." Crucially, his liveliness and sociability served him well in politics. Campaigning again for the state legislature in 1834, he went out to a field where a group of about thirty men were working the harvest. A friend of Lincoln's, J. R. Herndon, introduced him. The men said that they couldn't vote for a man who didn't know how to do field work. "Boys," Lincoln said, "if that is all I am sure of your votes." He picked up a scythe and went to work. "I dont think he Lost a vote in the Croud," Herndon wrote.

Lincoln won the election easily. When a mentor in the legislature recommended that he study law, he took the challenge. It would be a good profession to accompany politics, in particular the politics of the Whig party, which drew its strength from the growing number of urban and industrial professionals. In the early nineteenth century, attorneys commanded a kind of awe, embodying the stately Anglo-Saxon tradition of common law and domestic order. Gaining "the secrets of that science," explained the poet-author William Allen Butler, would give a person a perpetual glow, for the law, "more than all other human forces, directs the progress of events."

It is a mark of Lincoln's soaring ambition that, four years from the fields, he sought to join such ranks, at a time when all but five percent of the men in his area did manual work for a living. It was a sign of his pluck that he did it virtually all on his own. While other young men learned the law at universities — or, more commonly, under the tutelage of an established attorney — Lincoln, as he noted in his memoir, "studied with nobody." This was hardly the only mark of his ambition. A lawyer named Lynn McNulty Greene remembered Lincoln telling him that "all his folks seemed to have good sense but none of them had become distinguished, and he believed it was for him to become so." This language suggests that Lincoln had, more than a personal desire, a sense of calling. "Mr. Lincoln," explained his friend O. H. Browning, "believed that there was a predestined work for him in the world . . . Even in his early days he had a strong conviction that he was born for better things than then seemed likely or even possible . . . While I think he was a man of very strong ambition, I think it had its origin in this sentiment, that he was destined for something nobler than he was for the time engaged in." In his first published political speech, Lincoln wrote, "Every man is said to have his peculiar ambition. Whether it be true or not, I can say for one that I have no other so great as that of being truly esteemed of my fellow men, by rendering myself worthy of their esteem."

But there were cracks in Lincoln's sunny disposition. "If the good people in their wisdom shall see fit to keep me in the background," he said in that same speech, "I have been too familiar with disappointments to be very much chagrined." At times, his faith in personal progress gave way and his familiarity with disappointments shone through. Back from the militia campaign, Lincoln and a partner opened their own store, buying the stock on credit. When the store failed, Lincoln was in serious financial jeopardy. Seeing him despondent, his new friends got him a crucial political appointment, as New Salem's postmaster. Later, he was made deputy surveyor, too. These jobs, Lincoln noted, "procured bread, and kept soul and body together." Nevertheless, his debt soon caught up with him: a creditor seized his surveying equipment — including his horse, his compass, and his chain — and put it up for auction. An older man named James Short saw Lincoln moping about and heard him say he might "let the whole thing go." Short tried to cheer him up. Then he went and bought the equipment for $120 (about $2,500 in modern dollars) and returned it to Lincoln.

These streaks of sadness and worry may have been minor depressions. But it wasn't until 1835 that serious concern emerged about Lincoln's mental health. That summer, remembered the schoolteacher Mentor Graham, Lincoln "somewhat injured his health and Constitution." The first sign of trouble came with his intense study of law. He "read hard — day and night — terribly hard," remembered Isaac Cogdal, a stonemason. At times, Lincoln seemed oblivious to his friends and surroundings. "He became emaciated," said Henry McHenry, a farmer in the area, "and his best friends were afraid that he would craze himself — make himself derange."

Around the same time, an epidemic of what doctors called "bilious fever" — typhoid, probably — spread through the area. Doctors administered heroic doses of mercury, quinine, and jalap, a powerful purgative. According to one recollection, Lincoln helped tend to the sick, build coffins for the dead, and assist in the burials — despite the fact that he was "suffering himself with the chills and fever on alternate days." He was probably affected mentally, too, by the waves of death washing across his new home — reminiscent, perhaps, of the "milk sick" that had devastated his family in his youth.

Among the severely afflicted families were Lincoln's friends the Rutledges. Originally from South Carolina, they had been among the first to settle in New Salem, opening a tavern and boarding house, where Lincoln stayed and took meals when he first arrived. He knew the family well and had become friends with Anna Mayes Rutledge, a bright, pretty young woman with flowing blond hair and large blue eyes. In August 1835, Ann took sick. As she lay in bed in her family's cabin, Lincoln visited her often. "It was very evident that he was much distressed," remembered a neighbor named John Jones. She died on August 25. Around the time of her funeral, the weather turned cold and wet. Lincoln said he couldn't bear the idea of rain falling on Ann's grave — and this was the first sign people had that he was in the midst of an emotional collapse. "As to the condition of Lincoln's Mind after the death of Miss R.," Henry McHenry recalled, "after that Event he seemed quite *changed*, he seemed *Retired*, & loved *Solitude*, he seemed wrapped in *profound thought, indifferent*, to transpiring Events, had but Little to say, but would take his gun and wander off in the woods by him self, away from the association of even those he most esteemed, this gloom seemed to deepen for some time, so as to give anxiety to his friends in regard to his Mind."

Indeed, the anxiety was widespread, both for Lincoln's immediate safety and for his long-term mental health. Lincoln "told Me that he felt like Committing Suicide often," remembered Mentor Graham, and his neighbors mobilized to keep him safe. One friend recalled, "Mr Lincolns friends . . . were Compelled to keep watch and ward over Mr Lincoln, he being from the sudden shock somewhat temporarily deranged. We watched during storms — fogs — damp gloomy weather . . . for fear of an accident." Another villager said, "Lincoln was locked up by his friends . . . to prevent derangement or suicide." People wondered whether Lincoln had fallen off the deep end. "That was the time the community said he was crazy," remembered Elizabeth Abell.

The fact that Lincoln broke down after Rutledge's death, of course, doesn't necessarily mean that her death produced his breakdown. This is an important point, because from the very earliest writings on Lincoln, his relationship with Ann Rutledge has been controversial. Questions about whether he loved her and whether they were engaged have been debated fiercely, and still are. The myths and countermyths about this young woman played a big role in the early historiography of Lincoln — and, amazingly, played a large role in pushing Lincoln's melancholy to the margins of history. More on this in the Afterword, but for now the essential point is that leading scholars have long said that what we think about Lincoln's first breakdown must hinge on what we think about his relationship with Ann Rutledge. If his love for her is a myth, this thinking goes, then the breakdown must be a myth, too.

In fact, in the eyes of the New Salem villagers, questions of a love affair followed hard and irrefutable knowledge of an emotional collapse. As the original accounts make clear, his breakdown was impossible to miss. Nearly everyone in the community who gave testimony spoke of it, remembering its contours even decades later. Lincoln, after all, had become immensely popular, loved by young ruffians and old families alike. Now, all of a sudden he was openly moping and threatening to kill himself. Why? people asked. What accounted for the great change?

It was in an attempt to answer this question that people turned to his relationship with Rutledge. He had obviously been upset by her illness. And after her funeral he had fallen off an emotional cliff. "The effect upon Mr Lincoln's mind was terrible," said Ann's brother, Robert Rutledge. "He became plunged in despair, and many of his friends feared that reason would desert her throne. His extraordinary emotions were regarded as strong evidence of the existence of the tenderest relations between himself and the deceased." Notice the careful progression from fact (Lincoln's breakdown after Ann's death) to inference (they must have been tenderly involved). James Short, who was the Rutledges' neighbor, came to a similar conclusion. "I did not know of any engagement or tender passages between Mr L and Miss R at the time," Short said. "But after her death . . . he seemed to be so much affected and grieved so hardly that I then supposed there must have been something of the kind." Because Lincoln "grieved so hardly" and became "plunged in despair," it seemed reasonable to his friends that there must have been some proximate cause.

In fact, major depression, in people who are vulnerable to it, can be set off by all manner of circumstances. What would appear to a non-depressed person to be an ordinary or insignificant stimulus can through a depressive's eyes look rather profound. "It's not the large things that send a man to the madhouse," Charles Bukowski has written. "No, it's the continuing series of small tragedies . . . a shoelace that snaps, with no time left." In this light, it is worth noting that, according to reminiscences, the pivotal moment for Lincoln wasn't Rutledge's death but the dismal weather that followed. After the death, wrote John Hill, the son of Lincoln's friend Samuel Hill, "Lincoln bore up under it very well until some days afterwards a heavy rain fell, which unnerved him and — (the balance you know)." The intonation here suggests an understanding among Lincoln's friends that there was something precarious about him, and that — like Bukowski's shoelace — a factor as ordinary as poor weather could send him reeling. As we will see, cold temperatures would contribute to Lincoln's second breakdown. Lincoln himself would write that "exposure to bad weather" had proved by his experience "to be verry severe on defective nerves."

For whatever reason, or combination of reasons, in the late summer of 1835 Lincoln's depression was pushed out into the open. After several weeks of worrisome behavior — talking about suicide, wandering alone in the woods with his gun — an older couple in the area took him into their home. Bowling Green, a large, merry man who was the justice of the peace — and who became, other villagers said, a kind of second father to Lincoln — and his wife, Nancy, took care of Lincoln for one or two weeks. When he had improved somewhat, they let him go, but he was, Mrs. Green said, "quite melancholy for months."

Lincoln's behavior matches what the *Diagnostic and Statistical Manual of Mental Disorders,* the handbook of mental health professionals, labels a major depressive episode. Such an episode is characterized by depressed mood and/or a marked decrease in pleasure for at least two weeks. Other symptoms may include a change in appetite or weight, excessive or insufficient sleep, agitation or lethargy, fatigue or loss of energy, feelings of worthlessness or inappropriate guilt, indecisiveness or trouble thinking or concentrating, and thoughts of death and/or suicide. To be classified as major depression, at least five of these symptoms must be present, marking a definite change from usual functioning and with significant distress or impaired functioning. If the symptoms follow the death of a loved one by less than two months, it might be considered mourning unless, as in Lincoln's case, there is "suicidal ideation" — to ideate is to form an idea about something — or other equally severe symptoms. "What helps make the case for the diagnosis of depression," says Kay Redfield Jamison, a professor of psychiatry at Johns Hopkins University, "is Lincoln's suicidal behavior and the fact that it provoked a 'suicide watch.' Today people are much more sophisticated about suicide, but it's pretty unusual to do that. It speaks to the seriousness of what was happening with Lincoln."

Lincoln's breakdown also fits with the typical age for a first episode of major depression. Most serious psychiatric illnesses emerge at a particular time in life. For example, in males, schizophrenia usually surfaces in the late teenage years; manic depression in the late teens to early twenties.

Unipolar depression, which Lincoln would struggle with his whole life, typically breaks into the open in the mid- to late twenties. Lincoln was twenty-six.

Many people wonder if Marfan syndrome contributed to Lincoln's depression. Marfan is an inherited genetic disorder that diminishes the strength of connective tissue — the material that gives substance and support to bodily structures, from tendons to heart valves. People with the syndrome tend to be tall and thin, with elongated limbs out of proportion to their bodies. In other words, they look like Lincoln, which is one reason some researchers suspect he may have had the disorder. "Most of the Marfanologists think that it's a fifty-fifty chance that he did have it," says Victor A. McKusick, a professor of medical genetics at Johns Hopkins. "He might just by chance have been tall and gangly. The physiognomy is a good clue, but you can't make the diagnosis on that basis alone." Does Marfan syndrome cause depression? At least one study has suggested a higher presence of depression in people with the syndrome. But McKusick says, "From the massive numbers of patients I have seen, there is no characteristic personality of Marfan patients. I would think that Lincoln's depression was quite unrelated."

Another common question about Lincoln is whether he had manic depression, which is also known as bipolar disorder. This diagnosis is given to people who alternate between episodes of depression and mania — long periods of intensely heightened energy, often marked by euphoria, racing thoughts, disinhibition, and risk-taking. No evidence exists of mania in Lincoln. He didn't indicate trouble with *swings* in mood so much as with the low moods of depression. Nor did his contemporaries describe anything that sounds like mania. It is possible that he had what psychiatrists call hypomania — below full-scale mania, but still characterized by heightened energy. Often people with serious depression alternate between depressed moods and hypomanic ones. But here, too, there is no clear evidence of anything clinically significant.

On the other hand, it's plain that Lincoln had major depressive episodes. Even after he had brought himself under control, he still grappled with desperate thoughts. Robert L. Wilson, who joined Lincoln as a candidate for the state legislature in 1836, found him amiable and fun-loving. But one day Lincoln took Wilson aside and told him something surprising. As Wilson recalled, Lincoln told him "that although he appeared to enjoy life rapturously, Still he was the victim of terrible melancholly

He Sought company, and indulged in fun and hilarity without restraint, or Stint as to time Still when by himself, he told me that he was so overcome with mental depression, that he never dare carry a knife in his pocket. And as long as I was intimately acquainted with him, previous to his commencement of the practice of the law, he never carried a pocket knife."

Of those who've had a single episode of major depression, more than half will have a second. Lincoln's second breakdown, in the winter of 1840–1841, bore a remarkable similarity to the first. It came after a long period of intense work, when Lincoln pushed himself hard in pursuit of an ambitious goal. Then, under profound personal stress — and in a stretch of bleak weather — he collapsed. Once again, he spoke openly about his misery, hopelessness, and thoughts of suicide. He was unable to work. His friends feared that he might kill himself, and that if he lived, he might go insane. Lincoln himself despaired that he would never recover. This will be explored in depth in Chapter 3.

For now, it suffices to say that the breakdown was a second episode of major depression. According to the criteria in the *Diagnostic and Statistical Manual,* this qualifies Lincoln for the diagnosis of "major depressive disorder, recurrent." Strictly speaking, the illness is characterized by two or more major depressive episodes, separated by at least a month. More broadly, it suggests an underlying problem that can be expected to surface in various ways throughout a person's life. Consider: Someone with two episodes of major depression has a seventy percent chance of experiencing a third. And someone with three episodes has a ninety percent chance of having a fourth. (The phrase "clinical depression" can be applied to any incident of major depression or to people who experience major depressive disorder.)

What the statistics suggest, the course of Lincoln's life confirms: by the time he was in his early thirties, he faced a lifetime of depression. Still, the quality and character of his illness would change through the years. The acute fits of his young manhood gave way to less histrionic, but more pervasive, spells of deep gloom. Dramatic public avowals of his misery gave way to a private but persistent effort to endure and transcend his suffering. Yet the suffering did not go away. As we will see, in his middle years Lincoln demonstrated signs of chronic depression. And even when he began to do the work for which he is remembered — and took evident satisfaction in finding a great cause to which to apply his considerable talent — he continued to suffer.

Modern diagnoses can help initiate a discussion of Lincoln's troubles. With many physiological conditions, disease names are merely pointers. They stand in for the "real thing," which can be directly observed. But with psychological phenomena, language doesn't just name a reality; it creates a reality. This is crucial, given that the pain of depression is compounded, for sufferers, by the fact that it is hidden and often suspected of not being genuine. "In virtually any other serious sickness," writes William Styron in his memoir of depression, *Darkness Visible,* "a patient who felt similar devastation would be lying flat in bed, possibly sedated and hooked up to the tubes and wires of life support systems . . . His invalidism would be necessary, unquestioned, and honorably attained. However, the sufferer of depression has no such option." By identifying Lincoln's trouble directly and clearly, we acknowledge it as a basic fact, just as he did.

Yet all too often medical diagnosis is used to end, rather than begin, a conversation. To say, as recent scholars have, that Florence Nightingale suffered from bipolar disorder or that the Salem witch trials were driven by "epidemic hysteria, with conversion symptoms" is no substitute for knowing how the individual figures, and the communities they lived in, understood themselves. Such retrospective diagnoses often leave the impression that modern psychiatric categories are infallible, when in fact they are only one way to account for the complex reality of human trouble.

In their book *The Perspectives of Psychiatry,* Paul R. McHugh and Phillip R. Slavney identify four approaches to a suffering person. The first approach seeks to identify disease, or what the person *has.* The second seeks to identify a person's dimension, or who he or she *is.* The third focuses on behavior, or what the patient *does.* Each of these approaches has some value for a study of Lincoln's life, but none so much as the "life story" perspective, which seeks a holistic understanding of what patients *want* and what they can become.

Diagnosis, we must remember, exists primarily to facilitate treatment in a clinical setting. It is a snapshot at a moment in time. But here we want to make sense of a whole life. As the writer and physician Oliver Sacks has noted, "To restore the human subject at the centre — the suffering, afflicted, fighting, human subject — we must deepen a case history to a narrative or tale; only then do we have a 'who' as well as a 'what,' a real person, a patient, in relation to disease." This distinction between case history and narrative is right on point. The former tries to eliminate questions with facts, whereas the latter draws on facts to articulate the essential questions of a person's life.

Can we say that Lincoln was "mentally ill"? Without question, he meets the U.S. surgeon general's definition of mental illness, since he experienced "alterations in thinking, mood, or behavior" that were associated with "distress and/or impaired functioning." Yet Lincoln also meets the surgeon general's criteria for mental health: "the successful performance of mental function, resulting in productive activities, fulfilling relationships with other people, and the ability to adapt to change and to cope with adversity." By this standard, few historical figures led such a healthy life.

CHAPTER 2

A Fearful Gift

IN LINCOLN'S LATE TWENTIES, his friends and colleagues came to regard him as "melancholy." The word would be used to describe him for the rest of his life. What did it mean?

In a modern dictionary, the noun "melancholy" has two definitions. First, it means "thoughtful or gentle sadness." This comes through when, for example, Stanley Crouch writes of his "melancholy resentment" about the neglected history of African Americans or when Andrew Delbanco alludes to the "melancholy suspicion that we live in a world without meaning." Melancholy often qualifies ideas or feelings that are anguishing but familiar, and somehow connected to what William Faulkner called "the agony and sweat of the human spirit." Thus is melancholy the province of lovers, poets, philosophers — anyone who reflects on the true experience of sentient beings.

The second definition of melancholy is "the gloomy character of somebody said to have an excess of black bile (archaic)." This refers to an ancient theory of biology called humoral theory, which originated 2,500 years ago and hung on, in some form, until well after Lincoln's death. Humoral theory held that one's temperament, or bodily and psychological makeup, gave rise to one's character — that is, distinctive qualities, especially of mind and feeling. A person with a preponderance of black bile would have a melancholy temperament, and probably a melancholy character as well. The melancholy character fascinated Aristotle, who asked, in a famous passage, "Why is it that all men who have become outstanding in philosophy, statesmanship, poetry or the arts are melancholic, and some to such an extent that they are infected by the diseases arising from black bile?" Citing Plato and Socrates and "many other heroes" as examples, he continued, "Many such men have suffered from diseases which arise from this mixture in the body . . . In any case, they are all, as has been said, naturally of this character."

That passage is often cited for its reflections on the relationship between melancholy and creative achievement, a topic for Chapter 9. The point here is that Aristotle assumed that people of a certain character were also vulnerable to a certain disease. The sorrowful, existentially anxious, querulous, and insightful experience of *melancholy* was strongly tied to the raging, disabling illness of *melancholia*. (The suffix "ia" signifies disease.) In the early twentieth century, "depression" replaced melancholia as the preferred medical term for the serious disease. Modern descriptions of major depression have enough in common with age-old accounts of melancholia that, for the sake of this discussion, we can say that they are essentially the same thing.

The big difference is that today we often hear that the disease of depression is entirely distinct from the ordinary experience of being sad or in the dumps. But in the nineteenth-century conception of melancholy, these were part of the same overall picture. A person with a melancholy temperament had been fated with both an awful burden and what Byron called "a fearful gift." The burden was a sadness and despair that could tip into a state of disease. But the gift was a capacity for depth, wisdom — even genius.

In the spring of 1837, Lincoln left New Salem for Springfield, Illinois. He was twenty-eight years old. He had a law license and an invitation to join the practice of John Todd Stuart, one of the state's eminent attorneys. Lincoln's reputation preceded him; in the previous session of the legislature, he had emerged as a wunderkind leader of both the Whig party and Sangamon County.

Compared to New Salem, a one-road village cut from the forest, Springfield might have seemed like a teeming metropolis. It had broad streets laid out in a grid and sturdy brick buildings. There were taverns, hotels, and two newspapers, one run by the Democrats, the other (the *Sangamo Journal*) by Lincoln's Whigs. Shops sold all kinds of goods, from luxurious imports like Cuban cigars to staples like hardtack and sperm oil. On the west side of the town square, near the corner of Fifth and Washington streets, stood a general store co-owned by Joshua Fry Speed. A half block from Lincoln's law office, the store sold dry goods, groceries, hardware, books, medicines, bedclothes, and mattresses —

"every thing," Speed noted, "that the country needed." When Lincoln came into the store, he held the saddlebags that had been carried by his horse on the ride from New Salem. The bags contained all he owned. He set them down as he approached the counter. He told Speed that he needed to know the price of the "furniture" for a single bed — that is, a mattress, blankets, sheets, and a pillow.

Lincoln stood nearly six feet four inches tall, though his height was less commanding than awkward, as his shoulders stooped and his arms and legs were drastically long. His hands were large and bony. He had green eyes so light they looked almost gray. Speed was twenty-two years old, a handsome man with deep brown eyes and straight brown hair that curled slightly over his ears. He made the calculations with chalk on a piece of slate and told Lincoln the items would cost seventeen dollars. Lincoln answered that it seemed like a good price, but that he couldn't afford it. He said that he could go on credit, but even then he'd be able to pay only "if my experiment here as a lawyer is a success." But Lincoln added, "If I fail in this, I do not know that I can ever pay you." Speed listened to Lincoln with his eyes still on the slate, and noticed a sad tone in his voice. Then he looked up at his customer. "I thought then," he wrote years later, "as I think now, that I never saw so gloomy, and melancholy a face."

The appearance of melancholy on Lincoln's countenance was remarked upon by many people who met him around this time. "He was a sad looking man — gloomy — and melancholic," said William Herndon, who was a clerk in Speed's store in the late 1830s and later became Lincoln's law partner and biographer. O. H. Browning, another politician and lawyer, observed that Lincoln had a "constitutional melancholy" and was subject to "fits of despondency." James Lemen, Jr., still another member of the Illinois bar, said that Lincoln had "a settled form of melancholy, sometimes very marked, and sometimes very mild, but always sufficient to tinge his countenance with a shade of sadness, unless a smile should dispel it, which frequently happened." Like Browning, Lemen thought the melancholy a "constitutional trait, or characteristic."

These men did not consider Lincoln's melancholy a mere liability, nor did they distance themselves from Lincoln because of it. To the contrary, consider the reaction of Joshua Speed to the customer who came into his store and gloomily said he couldn't afford the cost of bedding. "The contraction of such a small debt, seems to affect you so deeply," Speed said. "I think I can suggest a plan by which you can attain your end, without incurring any debt. I have a very large room, and a very large double-bed in it; which you are perfectly welcome to share with me if you choose."

"Where is your room?" Lincoln asked.

"Upstairs," Speed said, pointing to the winding stairs at the back of the store.

Lincoln took his two bags, went up the stairs, and set them on the floor. When he came down again, he was beaming. "Well Speed," he said, "I'm moved." The two men lived together for the next four years.

This oft-told story captures several essential points about Lincoln's melancholy after he arrived in Springfield. First, he seemed to give wide rein to sadness, tenderness, and worry. One time, in 1839, he was riding from Christianburg, Illinois, to Springfield with a large group. They were riding two by two, with Lincoln alongside John J. Hardin. The group paused in a thicket of plum and crabapple trees to water their horses. After a while, Hardin came up. The others asked him where Lincoln was. "Oh," Hardin said, "when I saw him last, he had caught two little birds in his hand, which the wind had blown from their nest, and he was hunting for the nest." When Lincoln finally joined the group, some of the men laughed at him. "I could not have slept tonight," he told them earnestly, "if I had not given those two little birds to their mother." There were other stories like this and, as the laughing men showed, not everyone thought they reflected well on Lincoln. "In many things," remembered Mary Owens, a woman Lincoln courted, "he was sensitive almost to a fault."

Still, Lincoln's sensitivity worked for him. Speed's gesture of assistance in the face of his melancholy was not uncommon. "Men at once, at first blush, everywhere saw that Lincoln was a sad, gloomy man, a man of sorrow," recalled Herndon. "I have often and often heard men say: 'That man is a man of sorrow, and I really feel for him, I sympathize with him.' This sadness on the part of Mr. Lincoln and sympathy on the part of the observer were a heart's magnetic tie between the two."

Indeed, when Lincoln was in distress, he could count on receiving aid as surely as he gave it to stray animals. A few months before the encounter in Speed's store, for example, Lincoln was in session at the Illinois General Assembly, working to pass a bill that would make Springfield the state capital, replacing Vandalia. For a young politician seeking to bring the pork home to his constituents, it was a big opportunity. But four other cities were vying to be the capital. Vandalia wanted to keep its status. And one powerful cabal sought to build a new capital ("Illiopolis") on land its members owned. "The contest on this Bill was long and severe," recalled Robert Wilson, one of Lincoln's colleagues. After Springfield's opponents tabled the bill until the next session — a blow that was almost impossible to recover from — Lincoln went to the tavern room of his colleague Jesse K. Dubois. "He told me that he was whipped," Dubois recalled, "that his career was ended." "I can't go home without passing that bill," Lincoln said. "My folks expect that of me, and that I can't do and I am finished forever." Dubois suggested a parliamentary maneuver to resuscitate the bill. More important, he pledged his support — giving Lincoln a crucial vote that he hadn't been able to count on before. "We gave the vote to Lincoln because we liked him," Dubois explained, "and because we wanted to oblige our friend, and because we recognized his authority as our leader."

Lincoln's friends didn't merely help him. According to Herndon, they "vied with each other for the pleasure or the honor of assisting him." Such enthusiasm can be seen in an exchange that took place after the Assembly adjourned. Stopped for the night on the way home, Lincoln tossed and turned so much that he woke one of his traveling companions, William Butler. Butler asked what was the matter. "Well, I will tell you," Lincoln answered. "All the rest of you have something to look forward to, and all are glad to get home, and will have something to do when you get there. But it isn't so with me." Lincoln complained that he was poor and in debt, with no way to get out. "I am going home, Butler, without a thing in the world." Butler said that he first tried to cheer Lincoln up. Finding that he couldn't, he went and paid some of Lincoln's debts, took the young man's clothes home so his wife could wash them, and insisted that Lincoln come live with him.

To some extent these men acted out of sympathy. But they also apparently found Lincoln's melancholy character alluring. Gloom, in the early nineteenth century, was not seen as an absence of cheer. It was, for better and for worse, a unique experience with its own correlates. According to the *Encyclopaedia Americana* — which Lincoln owned and used — the "melancholic temperament" was characterized by not only gloominess, asceticism, and misanthropy, but also deep reflection, perseverance, and great energy of action. The encyclopedia noted, of all the temperaments, "Each has its advantages and pleasures, with some corresponding drawback." Aware of the drawbacks, people around Lincoln were also well attuned to melancholy's advantages. To be grave and sensitive — to feel acutely the agony and sweat of the human spirit — was admired, even glorified. "A fitful stain of melancholy," wrote Edgar Allan Poe, himself no stranger to the experience, "will ever be found inseparable from the perfection of the beautiful." In the same way that young men today tone their pectoral muscles to better resemble professional athletes, many young men of Lincoln's day thrust out their emotions so as to resemble the heroes of romantic poetry. Lord Byron was all the rage, not just in London and New York but also on the American frontier. His verse play *Manfred* began with a soliloquy that instructed:

> Sorrow is Knowledge: they who know the most
> Must mourn the deepest o'er the fatal truth.

In Byron's poem "The Dream," a favorite of Lincoln's, melancholy is described as "a fearful gift":

> What is it but the telescope of truth?
> Which strips the distance of its fantasies,
> And brings life near in utter nakedness,
> Making cold reality too real!

Speaking of what he called the "age of Introversion," Ralph Waldo Emerson wrote in 1837, "We are embarrassed with second thoughts; we cannot enjoy any thing for hankering to know whereof the pleasure consists . . . The time is infected with Hamlet's unhappiness, — 'Sicklied o'er with the pale cast of thought.'" But Emerson urged that this was only a symptom of a profound opportunity. "I look upon the discontent of the literary class, as a mere announcement of the fact, that they find themselves not in the state of mind of their fathers, and regret the coming state as untried; as a boy dreads the water before he has learned that he can swim."

In Lincoln's time, the word "melancholy" was used far more often to describe men than women — unlike today, when nearly twice as many women as men are diagnosed with major depression. In both cases, melancholy highlights distinctive aspects of a culture's prevailing view of masculinity. This point is worth some attention, because our conception of masculinity today is so problematic. Men often resist articulating their problems directly, weighed down by a vision of maleness that precludes such confession. "Men are not supposed to be vulnerable," writes the psychologist Terrence Real, an authority on depression in men. "Pain is something we are to rise above. He who has been brought down by it will most likely see himself as shameful." Yet, far from eliminating trouble, such reticence seems to contribute to it. While only half as many men as women are diagnosed with depression, men kill themselves at four times the rate of women. Psychologists connect the often muted depression of men with all manner of destructive behavior. Women, meanwhile, hardly benefit from having exclusive domain over sensitive feelings. Both sexes, as Real says, must "halve themselves." Both are kept from being whole.

The modern understanding of depression, which segregates its manifestation as a disease and its manifestation as a thoughtful, reflective sadness, is certainly connected to these overly narrow gender roles. In the late nineteenth century, Jennifer Radden explains, the "human, redeeming, ambiguous (and masculine)" aspects of melancholy became separated from "aberrant, barren, mute (and feminine) depression." But through Lincoln, we can glimpse a time in which these two aspects of melancholy could be integrated in a man's life. Along with his overt feeling, Lincoln impressed people with his physical strength and athletic prowess. Nor did he shy from getting aggressive. One time, Lincoln told an irascible crowd at a political rally to let his colleague speak, and vowed to whip anyone who tried to take him down. No one doubted that Lincoln meant it.

In Lincoln's day, melancholy could be a valuable aspect of a man's life. In a letter in the spring of 1837, Lincoln referred to the prospect of some old friends leaving the area. "That gives me the hypo," he wrote, "whenever I think of it." The word he used was an abbreviation of hypochondriasis, a disease akin to melancholia. But "the hypo" — also "the hyp" or simply "hypos" — used as Lincoln did in this letter, had its own flavor. It signified an existential unrest, a gloomy or morbid state that lurked in the background of one's life, but also a connection to insight and a drive for heroic action. The opening passage of Herman Melville's *Moby-Dick* contains a famous use of "hypos" that helps us understand not only a forgotten phrase but a forgotten character type. "Whenever I find myself growing grim about the mouth," Ishmael declares, "whenever it is a damp, drizzly November in my soul; whenever I find myself involuntarily pausing before coffin warehouses, and bringing up the rear of every funeral I meet; and especially whenever my hypos get such an upper hand of me, that it requires a strong moral principle to prevent me from deliberately stepping into the street and methodically knocking people's hats off — then, I account it high time to get to the sea as soon as I can." Ishmael's dour moods led to adventure. And when he found the *Pequod*, he reflected explicitly on the relationship between sadness and grandeur. "Take my word for it," Ishmael said upon seeing Ahab's ship, "you never saw such a rare old craft as this same rare old Pequod . . . A noble craft, but somehow a most melancholy! All noble things are touched with that."

The modern idea that depression is unmanly also had some resonance in Lincoln's age. In the midst of a hard time, Joshua Speed once wrote, "I have suffered so much of late from sick head ache and hypo that I am almost un-manned." Lincoln later used the same phrase in the same way. The verb "un-man" is defined in a nineteenth-century dictionary as "to break or subdue the manly spirit in; to cause to despond; to dishearten; to make womanish." In other words, there was a sense that truly going off the deep end — being unable to work or function, as happens in the disease of depression — ran contrary to true masculinity. The important point is that, then as now, moods were often tied to gender roles.

Lincoln's melancholy emerged at a time when both his feelings and his identity as a man were in flux. Young men like him and Speed were expected to undertake a journey from boyhood to manhood, which also involved a journey from the feminine realm of passion and emotion (extolled by romanticism) to the masculine realm of judgment and reason (the ideals of the Enlightenment). In other words, it may be that Lincoln began to express his melancholy at a time when he had especially wide cultural latitude to do so.

In order to understand Lincoln's melancholy, we need to understand the common features of such a transition. In a society where contact with women was limited, it was common for young men, after leaving home but before marriage, to pair off and form a special bond. As Anthony Rotundo explains in *American Manhood*, these friends helped each other weather the storms of their age. They gossiped, philosophized, and fretted to one another. One such pair of special male friends, Daniel Webster and James Harvey Bingham, addressed each other as "Lovely Boy" and "Dearly Beloved." "My heart is now so full of matters and things impatient to be whispered into the ear of a trusty friend," Webster wrote to Bingham, "that I think I could pour them into yours till it ran over." Compare this with Lincoln's message to Joshua Speed: "You know my desire to befriend you is everlasting — that I will never cease, while I know how to do any thing." The two were bedmates, allies, and confidants. Many people who knew Lincoln said it was a relationship that had no par in his life. Speed himself said, "No two men were ever more intimate."

Temperamental similarities probably deepened their tie. Both young men were melancholy, and drawn to the reflections of poetry and philosophy. Both were ambitious and had what Lincoln pronounced "the peculiar misfortune . . . to dream dreams of Elysium far exceeding all that any thing earthly can realize." An expansive Speed once described himself "like the rich fruit of the tropicks that bursts its vine because of its richness and luxurance — or like a tea kettle that is lifting its top and losing its contents by the constant boiling and evaporation within. — or like a china pitcher filled with ice water and oozing through the glass." Lincoln noted how, in his friend, "excessive pleasure" was sometimes accompanied "with a painful counterpart at times." They took turns consoling each other when the bottom fell out.

Because Lincoln and Speed were so intimate, and shared a bed, people sometimes assume they were homosexual. The conversation has been amplified in recent years. In 1999, the playwright Larry Kramer declared that Lincoln and Speed were lovers, quoting newly found Speed documents to prove it. News spread around the world of what the *Independent* of London called Lincoln's "outing." But Kramer has since quietly gone on record admitting that he invented the documents for a work of fiction. More recently, the late sex researcher C. A. Tripp concluded, in *The Intimate World of Abraham Lincoln,* that Lincoln measured a "5" on the Kinsey scale, where "1" is entirely heterosexual and "6" is entirely homosexual. That assertion, too, has more bluster than substance. Tripp's evidence adds up to the fact that Lincoln spent a good deal of time with men, sometimes sharing beds with them and often expressing fondness for them. On this basis, precious few men in the early nineteenth century would *not* be called gay.

The question, as it has recently been framed, of whether Lincoln was homosexual would make a good topic for a high school debating competition, because it will admit of no proof in either direction. We might as well undertake to answer definitively whether Macbeth was gay. The text of the play does not negate the possibility — and indeed, once considered, it has a certain salacious appeal. Sure he was married, but so are many gay men. And didn't he say to a male player in act 3, "I to your assistance do make love"? Clearly the man had a deep conflict. Perhaps he had a deep secret, too. But with characters in plays, as with people in history, our understanding is limited by available texts. Intuition and common sense can help, but only if they're leavened by an awareness that the world we see "onstage" is different from the world we live in.

This, of course, applies to Lincoln's melancholy as much as to his sex life. For instance, Lincoln often referred, in various letters, to being "anxious." And he frequently began letters by deprecating what would follow. But neither of these points illustrates his melancholy, for the simple reason that they were both so ordinary. The same is true with men sharing beds. In tight living quarters — Lincoln grew up in a one-room cabin, and even a wealthy family like the Speeds had only two bedrooms for nine children — many bodies shared the same covers. And before the invention of the coil spring mattress in 1865, a decent mattress was a real luxury. (A nice one had straw, horsehair, and feather stuffing, with cotton or linen ticking, carefully stitched and buttoned.) Not only families but strangers at inns and soldiers in the field often slept snugly against each other. Bed-sharing, in other words, was about as common as, and indeed was very similar to, the way that people today share apartments. Do some flatmates have sex with each other? Of course. Does the fact that two people share an apartment tell us anything about whether they are having a sexual relationship? Of course not.

Given how many homosexuals remain in the closet, it might sound like homophobia, or a refusal to deal with plain realities, to insist that it's not possible to know whether Lincoln and Speed were lovers. On the contrary, a frank avowal of our ignorance is the first step in honestly dealing with Lincoln's sexuality. Jonathan Ned Katz has studied male eroticism as it existed before "homosexuality" — a word coined in 1892 which, Katz argues, became associated with a discrete identity only in the early twentieth century. As Katz makes clear, the subject forces us to strip away modern assumptions. "I do start with a present interest in men's erotic and affectional relationships with men," Katz writes. "I also assume that such relationships existed in some form in this past era" — that is, 1820 to 1892. "But I assume, as well, that I do not know the particular historical character of these relationships *as they existed and functioned within the sexual and gender systems of the nineteenth-century United States*. Back then, they may have been socially organized, named, and perceived in ways quite foreign to us."

Lincoln's society had different baselines about how to name, and how to conceive of, same-sex relationships. We don't know what Lincoln and

Speed did in their bed together. But if, say, they snuggled or held hands, they wouldn't have had to decide on this basis about being different from other men. "In the early nineteenth century," explains Anthony Rotundo, "there wasn't a line in the sand between those who were affectionate with other men and those who weren't." While sharing a bed, Speed and Lincoln were occupied with finding wives. Speed also slept with prostitutes and at one point "kept" a pretty girl as an employee, from whom he received sexual favors. Indeed, Lincoln's good friend was known as an "old rat" in his predilection for professional women. Lincoln may well have slept with prostitutes, too.

Lincoln and Speed had an intimate friendship, buoyed by an emotional and intellectual connection. When we look at the friendship from *their* point of view, we see that the labels "homosexual" and "heterosexual" obscure more than they reveal. "The twentieth-century tendency," writes Carroll Smith-Rosenberg, is "to view human love and sexuality within a dichotomized universe of deviance and normality, genital and platonic love." But this, she argues, "is alien to the emotions and attitudes of the nineteenth century." In her study of female relationships of the period, she found women who clearly loved each other whose "eminently respectable and socially conservative families" acknowledged the love and found it compatible with heterosexual marriage. "Emotionally and cognitively," Smith-Rosenberg writes, "their heterosocial and homosocial worlds were complementary."

While the tensions of his sexual interests remain largely hidden from us, the tensions of Lincoln's emotional life are in plain view. He embodied all the potential and all the danger of a melancholy man. Speed, who introduced Lincoln to the poetry of Byron, said his friend seemed "artless," like the title character of *Childe Harold's Pilgrimage,* Byron's famous epic poem. "If I was asked what it was that threw such a charm around him," Speed wrote, "I would say that it was his perfect naturalness. He could act no part but his own." Speed noted how Lincoln's sadness coexisted with tremendous talent. "I was fresh from Kentucky then and I had heard most of the great orators," he later recalled. But after seeing Lincoln speak, "it struck me then, as it seems to me now, that I never heard a more effective speaker . . . The large crowd, seemed to be swayed by him, as he pleased."

In his late twenties, Lincoln was an up-and-comer, giving form to his own heroic ideal. He became a lawyer and developed his practice. He rose in the legislature to the point of leading his party. And he thundered on the vital causes that stirred him. "If ever I feel the soul within me elevate and expand to those dimensions not wholly unworthy of its Almighty Architect," he said in a speech on the national bank, "it is when I contemplate the cause of my country, deserted by all the world beside, and I standing up boldly and alone and hurling defiance at her victorious oppressors."

A palpable sensitivity underlay such bravado. At a debate in 1840, Lincoln faced Stephen Douglass, a young star for the Democrats. (He later dropped the second *s* from his last name.) Both sides thought that Lincoln did poorly. The Democratic newspaper said he "left the stump literally whipped off of it." One of Lincoln's allies, Joseph Gillespie, said, "Lincoln did not come up to the requirements of the occasion." Gillespie knew Lincoln to be "very sensitive" on these matters, and in this instance found him "conscious of his failure." "I never saw any man so much distressed," Gillespie said. Lincoln begged for another chance to speak, and his allies gave it to him. Surveying the thin crowd — it was the day after Christmas — Lincoln said that he found the low turnout "peculiarly embarassing," and he wondered aloud if people had come merely to "spare me of mortification." "This circumstance," he said, "casts a damp upon my spirits, which I am sure I shall be unable to overcome during the evening." Yet his speech, Gillespie said, "transcended our highest expectations." Afterward, Lincoln wrote to his law partner in Washington, "Well, I made a big speech, which is in progress of printing in pamphlet form. To enlighten you and the rest of the world, I shall send you a copy when it is finished."

It is striking how quickly Lincoln's dim pessimism could give way to supreme confidence. This, too, was consistent with the melancholy character, which gave a person access to the deep channels of the soul — the waters of sadness, the bedrock of constancy, the gold of mirth. Because he felt deeper and thought harder than others, Lincoln could be expected to alternate among states more quickly, returning, more often than not, to sadness, disquiet, perturbation, and gloom. After his first few years in Springfield, Lincoln told Herndon that he felt destined to be a great man. At the same time, he said that he feared he would come to ruin.

A hot topic in the literature on depression is whether — quite aside from what happens to people after they recover — the incidents of disease themselves have any use. One theory of evolutionary psychology holds that depression may serve as a response to need. Its premise is that while we use our brains and bodies to think and behave in the modern world, they developed in what's known as the Environment of Evolutionary Adaptedness. This "environment" wasn't a particular place or time, but the thousands of years during which the human species evolved. According to the theory of natural selection, qualities that help people survive and reproduce tend to spread in the species. Qualities that get in the way of survival and reproduction tend to die out. In the Environment of Evolutionary Adaptedness, depression might have helped people get things they wanted or needed when other strategies, such as aggression and persuasion, were less effective. It might also have quashed ineffective behaviors and forced useful change.

This isn't to suggest that our ancestors "faked" depression. To the contrary, the painful, debilitating — and real — nature of the condition is precisely what would have spurred others to help or the depressed person to change. Evolutionary psychologists suggest that the adaptive aspect of depression can still be seen in the modern world. Lincoln's case could be considered an illustration. His melancholy emerged at a time of profound need, and it seems to have helped him thrive. Feeling bad was part of what helped him do well, as his moods consistently provoked empathy, assistance, and admiration.

Many dispute this evolutionary perspective, claiming that for every conceivable advantage depression might convey, there are countless undeniable drawbacks. And for whatever reason it arises, depression can quickly take on a life of its own. Whether we look for an explanation to neuroplasticity (the ability of neurons to "reorganize" themselves) or the psychology of habit, it is plain that thoughts, feelings, and behavior beget like thoughts, feelings, and behavior. And unlike, say, the pain of a broken leg — which is linked to a specific stimulus and recedes in proportion to the recession of that stimulus — melancholy, by its nature, is free-floating, vague, and uncertain. Part of the appeal of melancholy in the early nineteenth century is that it was associated with a kind of reserved power that could take spectacular outward expression. Yet there was also ample awareness of the damage that could come from that power when, rather than moving outward to help a person meet some need, it ricocheted around inside — to use an anachronistic metaphor — like a mortar shell in a tank.

Suicide was on Lincoln's mind in his late twenties. He spoke of it frequently during his first breakdown, and the "suicide watch" shows that his friends took him seriously. As we have seen, he confessed to his friend and colleague Robert Wilson that he thought so often of suicide — and so seriously — that he didn't carry a knife in his pocket for fear of what he might do with it. In a famous passage of a speech in January 1838, Lincoln addressed the possibility of self-destruction on a national scale. Arguing that the United States could never be vanquished by foes from abroad, he urged, "If destruction be our lot, we must ourselves be its author and finisher. As a nation of freemen, we must live through all time, or die by suicide."

According to Joshua Speed, Lincoln addressed the subject of suicide in another literary work, a piece not on national destruction but on self-destruction. Speaking to a biographer after Lincoln's death, Speed said he was certain that Lincoln had written a poem on suicide and published it in the *Sangamo Journal*. But Speed said that he wasn't sure about the date. It might have been 1840 or 1841 or, Speed said finally, 1838.

For 139 years the poem remained undiscovered. One reason is that an influential early biography assigned it an incorrect date. Another reason is that for many decades Lincoln scholars were busy throwing out evidence relating to his melancholy, rather than seeking new material. But recently an independent scholar in Missouri named Richard Lawrence Miller noticed the poem and brought it to light.

On August 25, 1838, the *Sangamo Journal* carried its usual mix of ads, news, and editorials. Wallace and Diller's Drug and Chemical Store, at 4 Hoffman's Row, had just received a fresh supply of sperm oil, fishing rods, and French cologne. L. Higby, the town collector, gave notice that all must pay their street tax or face "trouble." And atop the news page, in the sixth column, between a report from the Schuyler County Presbytery and the Sangamon County Agricultural Society, the paper carried an unsigned poem titled "The Suicide's Soliloquy."

The lines are preceded by a note that explains that they were found "near the bones" of an apparent suicide in a deep forest by the Sangamon River. The conceit, in other words, is that this is a recovered suicide note. We learn from the poem that the woebegone narrator came to the riverbank to leap from the metaphorical brink between anguished thought and oblivion. As the poem begins, he announces his intention:

> Here, where the lonely hooting owl
>   Sends forth his midnight moans,
> Fierce wolves shall o'er my carcase growl,
>   Or buzzards pick my bones.

No fellow-man shall learn my fate,
  Or where my ashes lie;
Unless by beasts drawn round their bait,
  Or by the ravens' cry.

Yes! I've resolved the deed to do,
  And this the place to do it:
This heart I'll rush a dagger through
  Though I in hell should rue it!

Often understood as an emotional condition, depression is, to those who experience it, largely characterized by its thoughts. William Styron says his depression was like a storm in his brain, punctuated by a thunder of self-critical, fearful, despairing thoughts — one clap following another in an endless night. Oppressed by these thoughts, people often become hopeless. Hopelessness, in an extreme form, leads people to think that only one thing can break the cycle, and that is suicide. In what psychologists call "cognitive restriction," all the world's possibilities become narrowed to just two: whether to live or to die. "The single most dangerous word in all of suicidology," writes Edwin Shneidman, who founded the field of suicide studies, "is the four-letter word *only*," as in "only one thing to do . . . only way to get away from it . . . jump off something good and high."

Lincoln clearly knew the peculiar thought habits that are characteristic of depression. In 1842, called upon to comfort a friend in the midst of a severe depression, Lincoln wrote of "that *intensity* of thought, which will some times wear the sweetest idea thread-bare and turn it to the bitterness of death." "The Suicide's Soliloquy" is an eloquent illustration of such a torturous cycle of thoughts.

To ease me of *this* power *to think*,
  That through my bosom raves,
I'll headlong leap from hell's high brink
  And wallow in its waves.

The narrator of the poem makes a formal argument. He's willing to trade life on earth for life in hell. Many authors today would use "hell" as a metaphor for a hard place. In Lincoln's world, most people considered hell an actual place where one's soul would be subject to unending anguish and torture — conditions worse than a human being could conceive. Knowing how he strays from the path to heaven, the narrator fully expects an "endless night" of "frightful screams, and piercing pains," with devils burning and whipping him. But he cannot be dissuaded. "Think not with tales of hell to fright / Me, who am damn'd on earth!" the poem insists, before resolving in orgiastic imagery of the self-murder:

> Sweet steel! Come forth from out of your sheath,
>   And glist'ning, speak your powers;
> Rip up the organs of my breath,
>   And draw my blood in showers!
>
> I strike! It quivers in that heart
>   Which drives me to this end;
> I draw and kiss the bloody dart,
>   My last — my only friend!

Without an original manuscript or a letter in which ownership is claimed, no unsigned piece can be attributed definitively to an author. But the context points strongly to Lincoln. The reasons are, first, that it fits Joshua Speed's date; second, that its syntax, tone, reasoning, and references are characteristic of Lincoln; and third, that the poem has the same meter as Lincoln's other published verse. A number of scholars who have closely studied Lincoln in this period say that the poem rings true.

What strengthens the case is that the poem is illustrative of several paradoxical features of Lincoln's melancholy in his late twenties, which in turn illustrate the paradox of melancholy more generally. He often evinced both the pain of a sufferer from depression and the curiosity of an observer. He articulated a sense of himself as degraded and humiliated, but also, somehow, special and grand. And though the character of this poem chooses death by the dagger, the author of the poem — using his tool, the pen — gave voice to the impulse toward life. While the poem authentically portrays the suicidal mind in many respects, in one respect it falls short. Most suicidal people don't have a sense of what will come next. In particular, writes Edwin Shneidman, "The idea of Hell does not ordinarily enter into suicide . . . The destination (or concern) is not to *go* anywhere, except *away*. The goal is to stop the flow of intolerable consciousness; not to continue in an afterlife or an eternity. 'Escape' does not mean to escape from one torture chamber to enter another. In suicide the goal is to achieve a peace of mindlessness."

It might seem that writing a poem on suicide would be a sign of danger. In fact, Lincoln's poem both expressed his connection with such a morbid state of mind and, to some extent, announced a mastery over it. This is consistent with a pattern often observed by clinicians after a first severe episode of depression: people who struggle to recover take some pride in their ability to have overcome such a dismal time. If a second severe episode hits, it can be much worse. "Depression is the most difficult when people get better and then get sick again," says the psychiatrist Nassir Ghaemi. "They experience getting well. They hope that they'll stay well. And the next depression is all the harder. They just can't bear it."

CHAPTER 3

I Am Now the Most Miserable
Man Living

THE EVENTS SURROUNDING January 1, 1841, are among the most often mentioned, and the most frequently misunderstood, episodes in Lincoln's life. Countless works aver that, on that day, he split up with his fiancée, Mary Todd, then fell into an intense but short-lived depression, during which he missed work, made a spectacle of himself around town, and wrote a letter declaring, "I am now the most miserable man living."

In fact, it's unclear what happened on the day that Lincoln later referred to as "that fatal first of Jany. '41." Rather than a clear reference to a known event, Lincoln's phrase is better understood as the suggestive headline over a tumultuous, transformative period in his life — a time when a series of interwoven personal and professional crises stripped from him nearly every layer of his fragile identity and threw him into a profound, long-lasting depression. At a time when he had drawn closer than ever to suicide, Lincoln submitted himself to the care of a medical doctor, only to emerge from the "treatment" worse than when he went in.

It is essential to get to the truth of this story — and to acknowledge where the truth is elusive — because the episode is so essential to Lincoln's life. The crisis, or series of crises, proved to be a turning point. It marked the end of Lincoln's youth, with its dramatic fits of public melancholy, and the beginning of his manhood, with a quiet, weary suffering that many witnessed but few could understand. It marked the end of his startling rise as a provincial politician and the beginning of a long, slow trudge to find a voice in the affairs of the nation. Far from a simple period of sickness and recovery, it was a profound testing for Lincoln. In this period, he asked in stark terms whether he must die. And he arrived at a hard-fought clarity about the reason he would live.

During Lincoln's rise as a state politician in the late 1830s, the country's economy was booming, and nowhere more than in Illinois. In just ten years the state's population tripled, as immigrants from the eastern states and Europe spilled into the prairies. Stoking the fires of optimism, the Illinois General Assembly passed, and the governor signed, a bill to create an extensive system of rails, roads, and canals. The law authorized $11 million in bonds (more than $200 million in modern dollars) to finance it all. The fever for such projects — known as "internal improvements" — had spread from the East, where the Erie Canal, which opened in 1825, put New York City on the path to become the world's great commercial center. The canal's champion, DeWitt Clinton, a ten-time mayor of the city and three-time governor of the state, became a national hero. Lincoln showed his ambition, and his bravado, when he told a colleague that he wanted to be the DeWitt Clinton of Illinois.

While many politicians backed internal improvements for political or pecuniary gain, Lincoln was a true believer. At first, this redounded to his advantage. But in 1837, the United States fell into one of the worst financial depressions of its young history. Across the country, scores of banks failed. Unemployment and ruined fortunes led to food riots. In Illinois, which had been propped up by land speculation and massive state spending, the debt exploded from $400,000 in 1836 to $6.5 million in 1838 — compared with a puny $150,000 in annual revenue.

Early in the crisis, erstwhile backers abandoned the internal improvements program. But Lincoln fought to expand it. When the canals and roads were finished, he argued, the state would reap the rewards, so it ought to endure the short-term pain. Thus Lincoln tied his reputation even more closely to a disastrous policy. By the fall of 1839, with the debt continuing to rise and with mounting evidence of corruption among private builders, the projects were shut down — "without benefit of clergy," Lincoln noted sardonically. By the end of 1840, the state was a wreck. Bank-issued currency was worthless. The state debt now exceeded $13.6 million. The mere interest on those loans exceeded the state's annual revenue.

Lincoln's career suffered with the program he had strongly advocated. In August 1840, he was reelected to the legislature — but narrowly, with the fewest votes of any successful candidate. His colleagues frankly acknowledged that he, with the other partisans for internal improvements, would not be a viable candidate for higher office. That same season, Lincoln lost the biggest political fight of his young career when William Henry Harrison, the Whig candidate for president, lost Illinois, despite Lincoln's ferocious politicking. (Harrison did win the White House.) Before Lincoln returned to Springfield, he spent most of the year traveling, going over hard roads, eating lousy food, giving political speeches to mostly hostile crowds, and scrounging up legal work to pay his bills. "In short," writes Douglas Wilson, "arriving in Springfield in November 1840, Abraham Lincoln must have been physically and emotionally exhausted."

But he got no relief. Along with a stiff workload in the courts — in December, he had nine cases before the state supreme court alone — Lincoln had to serve as Whig floor leader for a special session of the legislature, which convened on November 23 to address the debt crisis. Lincoln put forth a bill — "with great diffidence," he said — to borrow more money and raise new taxes in order to deal with the stupefying state debt. While he worked to put out one political fire, a new one erupted. During the economic boom, the state bank had issued paper currency that, in theory, could be exchanged at any time for "specie" — actual silver or gold. With the economic collapse, however, the bank had put out far more paper money than it could support. The Assembly had granted a reprieve — a suspension of specie payments — that kept the bank alive. By law, specie payments would resume when the legislature adjourned. Everyone assumed that would be the following year, when the regular session ended. But in a maneuver to crush the bank — a pillar of the Whig program — the Democrats moved to formally adjourn the special session, forcing the bank to come to account months earlier than previously expected.

With the vote set for Saturday, December 5, the final day of the special session, the Whigs knew they would lose. In a gambit to prevent a quorum, they left the building, with Lincoln and Joseph Gillespie remaining inside to manage things. According to the Democratic newspaper, the *Illinois State Register,* Lincoln "appeared to enjoy the embarrassment of the House" when it seemed that the vote would be hijacked. Then the sergeant at arms, who had police powers, went out and rounded up the absent members. A new count, including Lincoln and Gillespie, showed exactly sixty-one people in the room — just the number to achieve a quorum. Lincoln, said the *Register,* "suddenly looked very grave . . . The conspiracy having failed, Mr. Lincoln came under great excitement, and having attempted and failed to get out at the door, very unceremoniously raised the window and jumped out." Mocking him, the *Register* joked that Lincoln was probably not hurt, "as it was noticed that his legs reached nearly from the window to the ground!"

Lincoln not only lost a key fight but made a fool of himself in the process. And the political pressure did not let up. During the regular session, which convened on December 7, the Democrats put forth a plan to pack the state courts and won. Lincoln tried to unseat the Democratic public printer and lost. In the latter campaign, Lincoln learned that one of his Whig colleagues, Andrew McCormack, planned to go against him. Departing sharply from his usual cool, determined tone, Lincoln declared his "utter astonishment" at McCormack's plans. "It *can not* be, that one so true, firm, and unwavering as you have ever been, can for a moment think of such a thing . . . All our friends are ready to cut our throats about it." Lincoln's composure had begun to unwind — no surprise, given that this career crisis coincided with an equally grave, confusing, and stressful period in his personal life.

After Ann Rutledge's death, Lincoln had drawn close to marriage once, with disastrous results. He courted a bright, witty, wealthy young woman named Mary Owens, but quickly lost interest and found himself in a painful dilemma. On the one hand, he thought he'd committed to the marriage and, he wrote, "I made a point of honor and conscience in all things, to stick to my word." On the other hand, he didn't want to marry the girl. "Through life I have been in no bondage, either real or imaginary from the thraldom of which I so much desired to be free," he wrote. Finally, he proposed, and Mary Owens refused him. This made him think that maybe he loved her after all.

Lincoln said at the end of the affair that he'd never marry, because "I can never be satisfied with any one who would be block-head enough to have me." Practical complications compounded these psychological ones. Compared with a rural outpost like New Salem, Springfield was a hive of social activity, but the cast of characters in a town of only a few thousand was still sharply limited. It was not unlike scenes in many Victorian novels in which the entrance of an eligible figure puts everyone in a dither.

Though awkward with women, Lincoln gamely continued to try to find a mate. Joshua Speed, the scion of a wealthy Kentucky family, helped usher Lincoln into one locus of courtship in Springfield: the hilltop home of Ninian Edwards, the son of Illinois's former territorial governor, and his wife, Elizabeth Edwards, the daughter of the prominent Kentucky banker Robert Todd. "Mr. Lincoln and Mr. Speed were frequently at our house," Mrs. Edwards recalled, and they "seemed to enjoy themselves in their conversation beneath the dense shade of our forest trees." Late in 1839, Elizabeth Edwards's younger sister, Mary Todd, came from Lexington to stay on indefinitely. Twenty years old, with light brown hair, blue eyes, and long lashes, she immediately made her presence known. She was witty, daring, politically astute — and a terrific flirt. Her younger cousin, Presley Judson Edwards, remembered that "if there were several gentlemen in the room with her, each one seemed to think he had received a special notice from Miss Todd." Her brother-in-law Ninian Edwards said bluntly, "She could make a bishop forget his prayers."

Mary Todd was an ambitious woman at a time when courtship was one of the few outlets where women could exercise power. The power was not of the vote, but of the veto. What made Mary Todd ambitious — a dubious compliment for a Victorian female — was how hard she worked to solicit proposals that she could then accept or reject. At some point, she lit on Lincoln, and he on her. Precious little detail exists of their early contact, but they probably met soon after she arrived in town. According to Mrs. Edwards, Lincoln found her sister beguiling and sat silently while Mary led the conversation. She would have had much to talk about that interested him — stories of Henry Clay, for instance, a friend of the Todd family and Lincoln's political hero. Ninian and Elizabeth Edwards at first favored the match. After all, Lincoln and Todd shared political interests and literary tastes. Abe Lincoln wanted to achieve high political office. Mary Todd often said she was destined to marry a president.

Often awkward, courtship in the early nineteenth century was awkward in its own special way. For Lincoln's parents' generation, families were understood to serve a largely practical purpose. If men and women loved each other, it was an outgrowth of shared responsibility and familiarity — and a matter of luck. With limited choices and no chance of divorce, people had to take a stab at a good match and live with it. But as Lincoln came of age, marriage increasingly became seen as an emotional and spiritual union. Young men and women were being instructed that they should find "true love." Yet if anyone knew what that meant, there were few good ways to find it. Courtship was fraught with tension, for the moment a man began to "come see" a woman, the prospect of marriage sat in the room with them like an elephant. And there were few opportunities for young couples — at least those who followed the rules — to spend time together alone.

Meanwhile, declaring an interest in marriage could trigger a massive responsibility. "In nineteenth-century America," writes Jean Baker, in *Mary Todd Lincoln: A Biography*, "a matrimonial pledge was as legally binding a contract as any commercial agreement, and the right of the rejected to seek damages was a familiar litigation." Lincoln himself had successfully represented a plaintiff in a "breach of promise" suit. And, of course, once married, there was no turning back. "Love might not be eternal," Baker writes, "but marriage, with divorce not yet an established civil procedure, was . . . The choice of a bad mate was an irrevocable error."

In this environment, letters were one good way for couples to get to know each other. According to Joshua Speed, that's how Todd and Lincoln began their tortured affair, exchanging notes in the late summer and early fall of 1840. In September and October, when Lincoln was down in "Egypt," the southern part of Illinois, campaigning for William Henry Harrison, he sent letters back to Springfield. "She darted after him — wrote him," Speed recalled. "She had taken a fancy to Mr. Lincoln," said his friend O. H. Browning, "and I always thought she did most of the courting until they became engaged." Apparently Lincoln expressed enough interest that, by the time he returned to Springfield in November, they were considered an item.

But he quickly decided he had made a mistake. According to a variety of observers, the proximate cause of Lincoln's change of heart was a new arrival in town. In the middle of November, Matilda Edwards, a wry, self-assured, pretty eighteen-year-old, came to Springfield for the winter, accompanying her father, a member of the General Assembly. She turned heads with her willowy figure and her blond hair that hung in curls, "like the wind at play with sunbeams," said one admirer. Like Mary Todd, Matilda Edwards stayed in the Edwards home on the hill — in fact, the two young women probably shared a bed. Mary took note of the new arrival: "a most interesting young lady," she wrote, "her fascinations, have drawn a concourse of beaux & company round us."

Lincoln was among the "concourse of beaux." "Mr. Lincoln," said Browning, "became very much attached to her, (Miss Matilda Edwards) and finally fell desperately in love with her." Yet he judged that, as a matter of honor, he couldn't approach Edwards — or any other girl — until he secured a "release" from Todd. He may have thought that she, too, desired a release from their engagement. For Mary Todd was still encouraging a number of men in their affections — not just Lincoln, but the Democratic buck Stephen Douglas, a Whig widower named Edwin Webb, and Lincoln's good friend Joseph Gillespie. "Miss Todd is flourishing largely," one socialite reported in January. "She has a great many Beaus."

Maybe Mary Todd had decided she wanted Lincoln and used the other men to tease out his interest. Maybe she hadn't yet decided and wanted to keep an open field. Maybe she had committed to Lincoln but strayed herself. "Lincoln's & Mary's engagement &c were broken off by her flirtations with [Stephen] Douglas," offered her sister and brother-in-law in a joint interview. An intriguing remark by Mary herself — and one of very few she made about the troubled courtship — suggested a sense of wrongdoing. "My beloved husband," she wrote in 1865, "had so entirely devoted himself to me, for two years before my marriage, that I doubtless trespassed, many times & oft, upon his great tenderness & amiability of character."

According to Speed, what pained the tender Lincoln was that he wanted out of the relationship, but he didn't know how to get out. He had a strict sense of rectitude — "especially when it comes to women," he wrote — and knew that his reputation would suffer if he behaved dishonorably. Mary Todd's relations, prominent and wealthy Whigs in Kentucky and Illinois, were not people to cross. Finally deciding he had to act, Lincoln wrote her a letter, took it to Speed, and asked him to deliver it to her. When he said no, Lincoln rejoined, "Speed, I always knew you were an obstinate man. If you won't deliver it I will get someone else to do it." But Speed wouldn't give the letter back. "Words are forgotten," he said, "misunderstood — passed by — not noticed in a private conversation — but once put your words in writing and they stand as a living and eternal monument against you. If you think you have *will* and manhood enough to go and see her and speak to her what you say in that letter, you may do that."

Lincoln did as his friend suggested, but — maybe this is why he wanted to write — he bungled the job. Here is how Speed (the only good source for this exchange) told the story, in an interview, as recorded by Lincoln's law partner William Herndon: "Went to see 'Mary' — told her that he did not love her — She rose — and Said 'The deciever shall be decieved wo is me.'; alluding to a young man She fooled — Lincoln drew her down on his Knee — Kissed her & parted — He going one way & She an other."

Some of the details here are unclear: Which young man did she "fool"? Who told Speed about it, Lincoln or Todd? Regardless, the gist of the exchange was plain enough. Intending to break things off, Lincoln had told Todd that he didn't love her. But when she got upset, he drew her to him and kissed her. When Lincoln reported the exchange to Speed, he said, "The last thing is a bad lick but it cannot now be helped." In other words, with his gesture of affection, Lincoln made matters more ambiguous than before.

Here is how Speed reported the next step of this affair, as recorded by Herndon: "Lincoln did Love Miss Edwards — 'Mary' Saw it — told Lincoln the reason of his Change of mind — heart & soul — released him." In other words, though Lincoln didn't have the nerve to say it, Todd saw that he fancied Matilda Edwards. She came to him and told him that she knew what was going on and that he could consider himself freed from any obligations to her. Then, according to both her sister and brother-in-law, she made another point, which proved to be the kicker. "Miss Todd released Lincoln from his Contract," Ninian Edwards told Herndon, "leaving Lincoln the privilege of renewing it if he wished." Elizabeth Todd Edwards described the same exchange and added flavor to her sister's motivation. "The world had it that Mr L backed out. And this placed Mary in a peculiar Situation & to set herself right and to free Mr Lincoln's mind She wrote a letter to Mr L Stating that She would release him from his Engagements . . . yet She Said that She would hold the question an open one — that is that She had not Changed her mind, but felt as always."

The message may sound innocuous, or even kindly. But for Lincoln there was a scolding subtext. He had extended himself to a woman, who still loved him, yet he was dallying with others. "His conscience troubled him dreadfully," said Browning, "for the supposed injustice he had done, and the supposed violation of his word which he had committed." Desiring a woman he was not free to approach, bound to a woman he had decided he didn't love — facing all the while the crack-up of his political career — Lincoln now faced a direct challenge to the one asset that mattered to him above all others, his reputation. He fell apart. "Lincoln went Crazy," Speed said, "— had to remove razors from his room — take away all Knives and other such dangerous things — &c — it was terrible —

was during the Special session of the Ills legislature in 1840." "Lincoln," said Ninian Edwards, "went Crazy as a *Loon*."

From here, we need to leap ahead fifteen months. In the interim, Lincoln had helped Joshua Speed through his own emotionally tumultuous engagement. Finally Speed had married, and he wrote to Lincoln that he was "far happier" than he ever expected to be. Lincoln replied, in a letter of March 27, 1842, "I am not going beyond the truth, when I tell you, that the short space it took me to read your last letter, gave me more pleasure, than the total sum of all I have enjoyed since that fatal first of Jany. '41. Since then, it seems to me, I should have been entirely happy, but for the never-absent idea that there is *one* still unhappy whom I have contributed to make so. That still kills my soul. I can not but reproach myself, for even wishing to be happy while she is otherwise."

There is no question that Mary Todd was the "*one* still unhappy," nor that Lincoln associated her, somehow, with the events surrounding "that fatal first." An early biographer seized on this connection and assumed that the breakup between Abraham and Mary had taken place on January 1, 1841, sending him into a depression. From the publication of that book, in the early 1870s, until very recently, scholars have made the same assumption.

When we look at the actual letter, however, questions arise. Lincoln said that the news of *Speed's* happiness brought him more pleasure than anything since "that fatal first." In a long exchange that preceded that remark, Lincoln had been deeply occupied with Speed's trouble, and he'd repeatedly professed his own sympathetic misery. It bears asking: Might "that fatal first" have referred to something in Speed's life? Might it allude to something that affected both friends? Might Lincoln's breakup with Mary Todd have been part of a much larger story?

With these questions in mind, we return to the available evidence about the winter of 1840–1841 in Springfield. Nothing else suggests that Lincoln and Mary Todd split on January 1, and three pieces of evidence suggest that, at the very least, we should consider the case unsettled.

First, we have Joshua Speed's testimony. Speed told Herndon that Lincoln got his fraught release from Mary, then went crazy during the special session of the legislature in 1840. It may be that Speed meant to refer to the whole session, which ran from late November 1840 to early March 1841. More precisely, though, the *special* session was over on December 5. The fact that Democrats used the session's endpoint as a pretext to try to kill the state bank — which led to Lincoln's inglorious window jump — would have made this date memorable.

Second, we have a letter from Mary Todd, written in December 1840, and its cryptic mention of Lincoln. Referring to changes that had taken place in her world, Todd wrote, "*Lincoln's, lincoln green,* have gone to dust." What on earth did she mean by this? It helps to know that Lincoln green was a style of dyed wool — famously worn by Robin Hood — that originated in Lincoln, England. The phrase "Lincoln green" appears in a passage of Sir Walter Scott's epic poem *Rokeby.* It is intriguing to consider that Todd, who loved Scott's work, was alluding in her letter to this poem, which is the story of a maiden named Matilda, who married a commoner rather than the nobleman to whom she had been promised. In Springfield, Lincoln's status as the son of a poor farmer — as opposed to the many young burghers about town — was often remarked upon. Using clever shorthand, Todd may have been saying that a connection between her and Lincoln had dissolved and that the commoner was now tied to Matilda Edwards. Or perhaps "gone to dust" signified a mental breakdown, in which a person's outward character (metaphorically his suit of clothes) vanishes, showing something naked and shocking underneath.

Third, a recently discovered letter indicates that Lincoln and Todd may have been sixty miles from each other on January 1, 1841. On Christmas Eve day, a party that included Todd and Matilda Edwards traveled from Springfield to Jacksonville, Illinois. A few days later, Matilda's father, Cyrus Edwards, wrote a letter from Springfield in which he said that the young women "will return on Monday." This letter was postmarked Tuesday, December 29, 1840. If we assume he didn't mean Monday, December 28 (which had already passed when the letter was mailed), this puts Mary Todd in Jacksonville until January 4.

For well over a century, students of Lincoln's life have accepted the pat story of a breakup on the fatal first and called it the cause of the depression that followed. But in acknowledging that we don't know *when* this breakup happened, we soon see that we don't know *why,* either. Lincoln's exchange with Mary Todd, far from being the single precipitant of his trouble, was just one factor among others in the emotional and existential equivalent of a perfect storm.

This, it bears mentioning, is characteristic of nervous breakdowns generally, including those that end in suicide. However urgently we try to find clear narrative lines — x stress led to y reaction — the picture is never that clear. In the midst of a depressive crisis, the question "What's wrong?" can be infuriating, because the answer, in the depressive's mind, is "Everything!" Even the assumption that stresses lead to reactions is problematic, because very often the case is reversed: We might feel bad because something has gotten screwed up. We might screw things up because we feel so bad. Or both.

When we consider the winter of 1840–1841 with fresh eyes, and mindful of the realities of depression, it is astonishing how much has been left out of traditional accounts. For example, the terrific stress in Lincoln's political life has, until recently, been considered separately from his emotional turmoil, when it has been considered at all. But the legislative session of 1840–1841 represented an amazing and, we can imagine, devastating turn of events in Lincoln's career. In the mid-1830s, he had been a rising star, making deals, passing big bills, and coming to lead his party. However, he had gone far out on a limb to advocate and defend the internal improvements scheme, which had manifestly destroyed the state economy. Even a sanguine man in Lincoln's situation could easily have feared that his career would be over. But as Lincoln wrote in 1840, "You know I am never sanguine."

The courtship, too, was more than a minor matter of individual relationships. Any serious romance, even a pleasant one, would have produced great stress. Marriage today is a serious matter for many people, but it's nothing compared with the early nineteenth century. The fact that it was a lifetime, irreversible commitment was just the start. When a man placed a ring on a woman's finger, he accepted the burden of supporting a family, both financially and emotionally. This decision brought many young men to question who they were, what they were capable of, and what kinds of lives they were going to lead. Sensitive as he was, Lincoln felt the full weight of these questions.

Lincoln had a companion on this journey. His intimacy with Joshua Speed was fueled by the momentous questions both faced as they moved toward marriage. This raises yet another issue that made the winter of 1840–1841 such hell, and of all the long-overlooked aspects of this period, it may be the most vital. Even in the best circumstances, there would have been tension between Lincoln and Speed. A friendship like theirs thrived on a transition from boyhood to manhood, and as Anthony Rotundo has shown, the pattern is that once the first of the two friends got married, the friendship fell apart. It's as if a ship designed to carry two people over rough waters had to be destroyed at the end of the voyage. That's fine if you care only about reaching the destination, but it's awfully hard if you've grown attached to the vessel.

Speed had his own drama. His father had died in March 1840. Around that time, Farmington, his family's plantation outside Louisville, was hurt badly in the financial downturn. With the price of hemp, its core crop, cut by more than half, Farmington was a "tottering concern," Speed wrote. His family urged him to come home and help prop it up. But he wasn't sure what to do. He had lived in Springfield for five years. "I have many friends here," he wrote to his sister at Farmington, "and while I have not done anything to rank me among the first men here, either for mind or money — I feel confident that I have credit for as much talent as I deserve and I *think* have made as much money as I could have expected for one with as little age, experience, credit, or capital as I had to start upon." How much money he'd made wasn't just an index of his overall success, but a factor to consider as he weighed his future. Part of the job of managing the plantation, as Speed put it, would be "to govern the negroes" — fifty-plus slaves. In Springfield, Speed had a very different life, working as a merchant in a free state. His family's pressure notwithstanding, he didn't relish "the life of a farmer," which, he said, "has always seemed tasteless to me." Though still undecided, Speed sold his stock in the store and would soon choose "to go or stay, as I think best."

Here's where it gets interesting. In the middle of the letter, beginning a new paragraph, Speed wrote, "Two clear blue eyes, a brow as fair as Palmyra marble touched by the chisel of Praxalites — Lips so fresh, fair, and lovely that I am jealous even of the minds that kiss them — a form as perfect as that of the Venus de Medicis — a Mind clear as a bell a voice bewitchingly soft and sonorous and a smile so sweet lovely and playful and countenance and soul shining through it . . . All these charms combined in one young lady if nothing else interposed would be enough to keep me here — Would they not!"

The "young lady" Speed so desired was almost certainly Matilda Edwards. His interest in her was known around Springfield. In December 1840, Mary Todd noted that "*Mr Speed's* ever changing heart I suspect is offering *its young* affections on her shrine, with some others." Ninian Edwards noticed Speed's crush, too, and he encouraged it, believing that Speed would be a good, pragmatic match for "policy reasons."

It is hard to imagine a more painful situation for Abraham Lincoln. All at once, he faced the prospect that his political career was sunk; that he might be inextricably bound to a woman he didn't love; that his best friend was going to either move to Kentucky or stay in Illinois and marry the woman whom Lincoln really wanted.

On top of everything else, in late December 1840 the weather turned bitterly cold. On the prairie of central Illinois, where no hills or valleys break the landscape, dark winters made one feel as though the world were covered in a shroud. "I am sure I have seen colder weather in Connecticut," wrote one newcomer to Illinois in 1837. "But I have never seen a place where cold is to be dreaded so much . . . Imagine yourself in the middle of a large prairie where you might look East, West, North or South and where the eye could rest upon nothing above but clouds curtaining down to the earth on every side and the earth covered with snow." That, plus the "keen piercing wind," he added, created "a dread of cold which words cannot express." After a respite in mid-December, temperatures dropped below zero by New Year's. Freezing temperatures and snow would continue through January. It was colder in Illinois, said Lincoln's friend David Davis, than anyone could remember.

Thus we arrive at the first of January 1841 — "that fatal first." What happened on that day remains a mystery. In addition to the traditional story, that the phrase referred simply to a breakup between Lincoln and Mary Todd, we should now consider three other possibilities.

For one, January 1 was the day that Speed's partnership in his store officially dissolved, ending his business ties with Springfield and allowing him to depart. Speed certainly knew about this in advance, and it is possible that "fatal first" was a phrase used between the friends to signify the end of an era. Speed lived above the store as its co-owner and, whether or not he stayed in Springfield, he — and Lincoln — would have to move out.

Second, January 1 was also the deadline on which the state of Illinois owed $175,000 in debt interest. This was the immediate reason why the legislature had been called into special session. If the state didn't make its payments, it would go into receivership. Given how Lincoln's political fate had become tied to the debt debacle, and given the practical necessity of securing the funds to pay the debt, this deadline would have been an actual source of stress and also a symbol of a political nightmare.

Third, as anyone who has nursed a hangover on New Year's Day can attest, the first of the year is a time to dwell on the painful, embarrassing, and regretful occurrences of the night before. In Victorian America, New Year's Eve held an even more prominent place in the social calendar than it does today. And on the last night of the leap year of 1840, according to tradition, male suitors were supposed to declare their intentions for betrothal. It may have been that on New Year's Eve, or on "that fatal first" itself, Lincoln learned of Speed's intention to propose to Matilda Edwards.

Two more factors bear mention. One is a young woman named Sarah Rickard, the sixteen-year-old sister of Mrs. William Butler, at whose home Lincoln boarded. At some point in the winter of 1840–1841, Lincoln proposed to her, but she turned him down, saying that she was too young to marry. And for some reason Sarah Rickard was a mutual concern of Lincoln and Speed's. Lincoln wrote to his friend in March 1842, "One thing I can tell you which I know you will be glad to hear, and that is that I have seen Sarah — and scrutinized her feelings as well as I could, and am fully convinced she is far happier now than she has been for the last fifteen months past." Fifteen months before March 1842 was January 1841.

Another factor: some people believe that Lincoln's stress had to do with venereal disease. According to Herndon, Lincoln believed he might have contracted syphilis in 1835 or 1836. If he did have such a worry, it might have contributed to his anxiety about marriage. It was a common worry: as many as half of the men in Lincoln's day had some kind of sexually transmitted disease, and even more feared that they did. According to a leading physician of the time, fear of syphilis was a typical feature of hypochondriasis.

Though it would be satisfying to know for sure what Lincoln meant by "that fatal first," the lingering mystery of the phrase serves as a reminder that history is not what happened in the past, but the best story we can tell with the available material. When there are conflicting narratives, we sometimes must admit our ignorance and live with the frustration. But just as controversy over Lincoln's relationship with Ann Rutledge does not diminish the significance of his first breakdown, the uncertainties around the "fatal first" ought not distract us from the fact of his collapse. Whatever the reasons, in early January 1841, Abraham Lincoln was in very poor shape. He began to miss votes in the legislature. Several times on Saturday, January 2, the clerk called the roll and he didn't answer. He missed eight votes on Monday the fourth, and three on Tuesday the fifth. The next week, he missed many sessions. Then, beginning on Wednesday, January 13, he was absent for an entire week.

By this time, Lincoln's illness was the talk of the town. The *Register* poked fun at his "indisposition." And letters came from out of town inquiring about him. "We have been very much distressed on Mr. Lincoln's account," a woman in Jacksonville wrote to her brother in Springfield, "hearing that he had two Cat fits and a Duck fit . . . Is it true?" It was true. "Lincoln you know was desponding & melancholy when you left," wrote Edwin Webb to O. H. Browning on January 17. "He has grown much worse and is now confined to his bed sick in body & mind."

Lincoln was not only confined to his bed. He submitted himself to the care of a medical doctor. In the week that he was absent from the legislature, he spent several hours a day with Dr. Anson Henry. When he emerged, on January 20, he wrote that he had a disease called "hypochondriaism" and that he had "got an impression that Dr. Henry is necessary to my existence." A tall, fastidious thirty-six-year-old man, Anson Henry had grown up in New York and studied medicine at the Ohio Medical College in Cincinnati — though the full course comprised only two three-month semesters. Like Lincoln, Henry settled in central Illinois in the early 1830s. And like Lincoln, he was a politically ambitious Whig. The two were close allies. The political and social tie — not Henry's medical expertise — is the probable explanation for why Lincoln went to Henry during his crisis.

The traditional narrative of this period places Lincoln's treatment by Dr. Henry at the end of his troubles, suggesting that it set him on the course of recovery. But a close look at events shows that Lincoln hardly improved during his week of treatment. Before, he was depressed, agitated, and "crazy." After his treatment he looked beaten down, weak, almost inhuman. "Poor L!" wrote James Conkling, a young lawyer in town, on January 24, "how are the mighty fallen! He was confined about a week, but though he now appears again he is reduced and emaciated in appearance and seems scarcely to possess strength enough to speak above a whisper. His case at present is truly deplorable but what prospect there may be for ultimate relief I cannot pretend to say." "Poor fellow, he is in rather a bad way," a Springfield woman named Jane Bell wrote of Lincoln on January 27. "Just at present he is on the mend now as he was out on Monday for the first time for a month dying with love they say.

The Doctors say he came within an inch of being a perfect lunatic for life. He was perfectly crazy for some time, not able to attend to his business at all. They say he don't look like the same person."

Lincoln was "reduced and emaciated" and didn't "look like the same person" probably because he had spent a week being subjected to what a medical authority of the time called "the desolating tortures of officious medication."

Hypochondriasis was a form of melancholia, less severe than others, though still serious enough to demand medical attention, lest the patient succumb to insanity or suicide. Literally, the word refers to a disease of the organs below (*hypo*) the cartilage of the rib cage (*khondros*) — that is, the liver, gallbladder, spleen, stomach, and intestines. In practice, following the theory that black bile resided naturally in the gut, hypochondriasis became the term for melancholia that fell short of full-scale madness.

A treatment regimen was readily available to a physician like Dr. Henry, in the form of the first American textbook on mental diseases, written by Dr. Benjamin Rush, the preeminent physician of the early republic. Titled *Medical Inquiries and Observations upon the Diseases of the Mind,* the 367-page book — printed on thick linen paper and bound in leather — devoted its third chapter to hypochondriasis.

Rush favored "direct and drastic interferences" with patients' bodies and minds. Doctors at the time "literally assaulted their patients," writes the historian Robert C. Fuller, "in an effort to stimulate and reinvigorate their constitutions." Rush's main treatment strategy for hypochondriasis was to "plumb" patients' systems by, to start, bleeding them severely. "The quantity of blood drawn should be greater than in any organic disease," Rush wrote, noting a case of hypochondriasis in which he drew 200 ounces (12½ pints) in less than two months, and another case in which he drew 470 ounces (about 29 pints) in ten months. (Adult bodies have ten to twelve pints of blood.) The next step was to blister a patient, or "cup" him, by applying small heated glass cups at the temples, behind the ears, and at the nape of the neck. This brought blood to the surface of the skin. "Leeches may be used for the same purpose, and in the same places," Rush advised. The next step was to give the patient drugs that induced vomiting and diarrhea. While emptying the body of its contents, doctors were enjoined to keep their patients on strict diets — fasting for two or three days, Rush said, was efficacious, noting how elephant tamers made their beasts less ferocious by starving them. Once the body had been cleaned out, Rush prescribed stimulants: sherry or red wine; tea and coffee; ginger and black pepper in large doses; tar pills in water; garlic or peppermint tea; magnesia, limewater, and milk; and mustard rubs. Quinine, derived from a South American tree bark, was widely used. Rush also suggested a warm bath to induce sweats, followed by a cold bath. Rubbing the trunk of the body and the limbs was helpful, as was exercise, especially on horseback.

Most of these treatments were physically punishing. Mustard rubs produced terrific pain. Black pepper drinks were like a bomb in the stomach. Mercury, the principal substance used to purge the stomach and the bowels, poisoned the body. (Arsenic and strychnine were also used.) Doctors approved of the green stools that resulted, believing that black bile was being cleared out. Actually, we now know that mercury was killing the healthy intestinal bacteria that make stools brown. Since it binds to the central nervous system, mercury also produces quick effects on mood: depression, anxiety, irritability.

The torturous quality of these treatments did not diminish them in the eyes of physicians. To the contrary, the more a patient suffered, the more evidence that the body was being stirred up and cleaned out. Unless a doctor was imaginative enough to buck conventional wisdom, "treatment" was hell. Dr. Henry's record, left in medical opinions published in the *Sangamo Journal,* showed him to be an eager adherent of the aggressive mode of treatment advocated by Dr. Rush. All we know for sure of Henry's treatment is that he put Lincoln to bed and kept him isolated. But if Dr. Henry followed the standard course with Lincoln, he would have bled him, purged and puked him, starved him, dosed him with mercury and pepper, rubbed him with mustard, and plunged him in cold water.

It has long been a footnote in the study of Lincoln's life that, in the winter of 1840–1841, he wrote a lengthy letter to Dr. Daniel Drake, describing his case. Lincoln read the letter to Joshua Speed — except for one section, which he skipped over — and he showed his friend the reply, in which Drake suggested a personal interview. Speed later urged a biographer to find Lincoln's letter: "It would be worth much to you if you could procure the original . . . I would advise you to make some effort." Neither Lincoln's letter nor Drake's reply has been found, however, which is the main reason this exchange has remained a footnote. The other reason is that Lincoln scholars have not appreciated Drake's significance, and so have not appreciated the potential impact of even a brief contact between these two men.*

Drake was one of the top American doctors of his time, and no medical man was better known or regarded in the American West. The founder of six medical schools, the editor of journals, and the author of books, Drake was considered a leading public intellectual. One nineteenth-century historian called him "the Benjamin Franklin of the West." Lincoln's known contact with Drake naturally heightens our interest. What did the great medical man think about depression, and what did he suggest for its treatment? These questions become all the more interesting when we see how clearly he answered them.

Drake wrote widely on mind diseases, and he bemoaned "the long and frightful train of distempers, known under the names of dyspepsia, hypochondriaism, hysteria, palpitation of the heart, and weakness of the nerves." These diseases, he noted, did more to detract from the happiness of society than any others, "infusing poison into every cup of enjoyment, and rearing spectres in all our paths; — transforming courage into cowardice, — and that period of our lives, which on the plan of nature should be most gay and enterprising, into a state of debility and gloom." He knew mind diseases better than most, for he had cared for many patients with such "frightful diseases" — among them, himself.

About twelve years before Lincoln wrote to him, a fire broke out in Daniel Drake's house. He was forty-three years old and recently widowed. His late wife's sister, a twenty-year-old woman named Caroline Sisson, who was living in the house, was sleeping in her bedroom when her mosquito netting caught on fire. The flames leaped to her calico bedcovers and then her nightgown. Hearing her screams, Dr. Drake rushed into the room, pulled the woman from the bed, and pressed his bare hands against her clothes to put out the fire. Severely burned — she had been in the flames for as long as half a minute — Sisson soon fell into a coma. Drake, too, was badly hurt. The skin on his hands had been seared off, and the layer beneath had turned black. He plunged his hands first into a bowl of whiskey, then into a mixture of flaxseed oil and

---

* It has also been overlooked that Lincoln may have had the meeting that Drake suggested. During Lincoln's five weeks at the Speed home in Farmington (see below), he rode most days into downtown Louisville, where he visited with James Speed, Joshua's older brother, at his law office. Dr. Drake was, at the time, in residence at the Louisville Medical Institute. He saw patients in his office on the south side of Chestnut, between Eighth and Ninth streets, just a few blocks from James Speed's office, on Seventh Street between Grayson (now Cedar) and Walnut (now Muhammad Ali). (G. Collins, *The Louisville Directory for the Year 1841* [Louisville, 1841]).

limewater. Then he wrapped them in rags, which he'd treated with oil and white lead. For several hours the pain was excruciating, despite the use of laudanum (opium and alcohol).

The cause of Drake's injury — an attempt to save the life of his sister-in-law — proved in vain. She died eight hours after the fire had started. In the wake of her death, suffering from the pain in his hands and unable to work, Drake fell into a deep depression. He found his own case intriguing enough that, when he had recovered several years later, he wrote about it in a journal he edited.

For years, Drake had experienced milder depressions — afternoon attacks of what he called "cerebral oppression," accompanied by drowsiness and a sinking feeling in his gut. But after the fire he sank into despondency. "None of the ordinary stimuli of life, either moral or physical, produced their characteristic effects . . . In short every sensation both of mind and body, was unpleasant if not painful."

At first, he treated himself aggressively. He bled himself and gave himself "pukes," which he knew often "revives and regulates the sensibilities of the system." He swallowed various tonics, including large doses of quinine sulfate. He also used sulfuric ether, ammoniated alcohol, piperine (a crystal extracted from black pepper), opium, and morphine. None of this helped his "nervous depression and perversion." He felt "a sense of muscular debility and a consciousness of mental imbecility, extreme restlessness, and morbid vigilance . . . In short every sensation both of mind and body, was unpleasant if not painful; and this continued to be the case for at least five weeks." Drake concluded that his aggressive self-treatment not only failed to help; it added to his problems. It took several years for the depression to fully lift, and when it did, he owed his recovery not to any of the medicines but to fresh air and exercise. So long as the body hasn't been permanently damaged, he concluded, such movement will bring benefits and eventually a restoration of health.

Drake had one other positive recommendation, which was that victims of depression, when in the worst of their pain, should use opium, long considered "the medicine of the mind." Drake himself used opiates for about five weeks, and while they didn't fix the problem, they greatly helped him to endure it. And he urged that virtually all other treatments not be used. States of chronic nervous irritation, he concluded, "are not uncommon; may spring from various causes, afflict persons of both sexes and of different ages; subject the unfortunate patient to the derision of his acquaintances, and too often bring upon his constitution the desolating tortures of officious medication. I have seen many persons in this sad and pitiless state of physical and moral imbecility."

Apparently, when he emerged from "treatment" in late January 1841, Lincoln was one of those persons. He seemed as desperate as ever — and it wasn't just his observers who thought so. On January 20, right around the time that Lincoln got out of bed and "appear[ed] again," he wrote to his law partner John Stuart in Washington, D.C., "I have, within the last few days, been making a most discreditable exhibition of myself in the way of hypochondriaism . . . Pardon me for not writing more; I have not sufficient composure to write a long letter."

On January 22, Lincoln went to a political meeting and heard some news that concerned Stuart's prospects for reelection. He wrote him again on January 23, but he began with an apology: "From the deplorable state of my mind at this time, I fear I shall give you but little satisfaction." Lincoln delivered the political news. Then he stopped writing for a time. When he started again, his handwriting was smaller and he pressed harder on the page. "For not giving you a general summary of news," he wrote, "you *must* pardon me, it is not in my power to do so. I am now the most miserable man living. If what I feel were equally distributed to the whole human family, there would not be one cheerful face on the earth. Whether I shall ever be better I can not tell; I awfully forebode I shall not. To remain as I am is impossible; I must die or be better, it appears to me."

Assigning undue credit to Lincoln's medical treatment imposes an unjustified endpoint on his crisis of the winter of 1840–1841. It is true that, at the end of January 1841, as the worst of the cold weather lifted, he got hold of himself enough to get back to work. He made a morbid joke of it. "Dear Stuart," he wrote to his law partner on February 3. "You see by this, that I am neither dead nor quite crazy yet." The stress on Lincoln had not abated, however. He still had to resolve what a friend called his "embrigglement" with Mary Todd. In March 1841, a friend remembered seeing Lincoln "hanging about — moody — silent & &c. The question in his mind was Have 'I incurred any obligation to marry that woman.'" Speed, too, was depressed, complaining of his "sick head ache and hypo" and pining away for Matilda Edwards, who rebuffed him. In early March, he acknowledged the game was up. "All feeling is dead and dust," he wrote. In a deep funk, he wrote home about the "treachery of false friends," which he connected to his rejection. In April, Speed left for Kentucky and had another attack of the hypo aboard the boat.

Politically, Lincoln may have been relieved when the legislative session drew to an end in early March. But he could not have been encouraged by his prospects in the wake of a ruined economy and a Democratic stranglehold on state offices. In fact, it would be another six years before Lincoln again took public office. In Washington, John Stuart set about trying to get him a posting overseas, as chargé d'affaires in New Granada (now Colombia). Lincoln told him to go ahead, "as I fear I shall be unable to attend to any bussiness here, and a change of scene might help me."

Though Lincoln's public histrionics did not last, his melancholy did. In June 1841, Mary Todd wrote that Lincoln had been avoiding "the gay world" for months. She wished that he would "once more resume his Station in Society," and, in a reference to the brooding king-poet of Shakespeare's *Richard II*, "that 'Richard' should be himself again." In July, Speed wrote to his friend William Butler in Springfield, "Say to Mrs. Butler I'm glad to hear Lincoln is on the mend" — indicating that, last he heard, his friend still had some serious mending to do. In a move that observers described as a kind of convalescence, Lincoln traveled to Louisville in July and August, to spend five weeks on the Speed estate outside town. Throughout Lincoln's visit, he was "moody & hypochondriac . . . at times very melancholy," Speed said. Speed's mother, no stranger to melancholy, noticed it and tried to comfort Lincoln. Indeed, the empathy Lincoln received from the Speed family was probably unlike anything he had experienced before. He knew the kindness of friends and strangers, but never from quite such a warm, bright, well-read, and close-knit group.

Farmington was less like a farm than a private village. Approaching it from Bardstown Road, one traveled down a long drive lined with locust and walnut trees. On the grounds, slaves planted and picked hemp, made rope and bags, and cooked meals for the family in a kitchen house next to Mrs. Speed's formal garden. At the center of the property was a red-brick home built in the Federal style; its rooms had fourteen-foot ceilings and smooth poplar floors. Lincoln had seen such luxury before, but always from the outside. Here he was made to feel one of the family. The Speeds provided him with a horse and assigned a slave to be his valet. At their mahogany dining table, they served him saddle of mutton and peaches and cream.

When he left Farmington, Lincoln saw something dramatically at odds with the luxury he had just known. He and Speed took the steamboat

Lebanon down the Ohio River to St. Louis. They shared passage with a slave trader, who had a dozen "negroes," as Lincoln called them, in chains. After Lincoln got home, he wrote a letter to Mary Speed, Joshua's sister, and discussed these slaves. This letter is the earliest extended statement by Lincoln on enslaved African Americans, thirteen years before he made the future of slavery a major part of his public life, and twenty years before he became president.

While this letter is often quoted, it has rarely been placed in the context of Lincoln's philosophical journey in the midst of his melancholy. Indeed, Lincoln brings up the slaves to illustrate an idea. "By the way," he began, "a fine example was presented on board the boat for contemplating the effect of *condition* upon human happiness." The condition of these slaves could hardly have been worse. Chained together "like so many fish upon a trot-line," they had been torn away from their homes and families, to be taken to "where the lash of the master is proverbially more ruthless and unrelenting than any other where." Yet despite this, Lincoln wrote, "They were the most cheerful and apparently happy creatures on board. One, whose offence for which he had been sold was an over-fondness for his wife, played the fiddle almost continually; and the others danced, sung, cracked jokes, and played various games with cards from day to day. How true it is that 'God tempers the wind to the shorn lamb,' or in other words, that He renders the worst of human conditions tolerable, while He permits the best, to be nothing better than tolerable."

Lincoln's description did not go deeper than what was apparent to him, not presuming to account for the inner state of the slaves. And he was moved by the contrast with his own condition. A free man, relatively prosperous, just ending five weeks in luxury's lap, and he was quite unhappy. The slaves, treated abominably, at least showed cheer — the appearance of happiness. Later, he would refer again to the slaves he encountered on the boat, profess that the sight was a "torment" to him, and justify his political position in part on that emotional connection. But at the time, Lincoln articulated no political point of view. His mind was elsewhere, trying to construct, from the throes of difficulty and uncertainty, a way of understanding the world and his place in it. In these early musings, Lincoln was still searching to understand who he was, where he was going in the world, and, indeed, whether he could survive. Yet this self-centered concern with his own suffering led him, slowly, to see and grapple with the suffering around him.

Previously, Lincoln had responded to his troubles by seeking help from others, either explicitly or implicitly. Now he spent an increasing amount of time alone. "Today, the fact that isolation can be therapeutic is seldom mentioned in textbooks of psychiatry," writes Anthony Storr, in *Solitude: A Return to the Self.* Yet, Storr points out, the capacity to be alone, sometimes for long periods, can be profoundly important, as people come to terms with loss, sort out their ideas, or go through serious change. "That solitude promotes insight as well as change," Storr continues, "has been recognized by the great religious leaders" — including the Buddha, Jesus, and Mohammed — "who have usually retreated from the world before returning to it to share what has been revealed to them."

Lincoln, in his early thirties, was decades away from attaining the sort of wisdom that would justify comparison with such figures. But like them, he turned from his suffering to the great questions of existence. In his seminal book, *Man's Search for Meaning,* the psychiatrist Victor Frankl described the essence of what has come to be known as an existential approach to the human condition with this metaphor: "If architects want to strengthen a decrepit arch," he wrote, "they *increase* the load which is laid upon it, for thereby the parts are joined more firmly together." It is similarly true, he said, that therapy aimed at fostering mental health often should lay increased weight on a patient, creating what he described as "a sound amount of tension through a reorientation toward the meaning of one's own life."

Lincoln certainly followed the spirit of this advice — looking, in his time of hurt, not to lighten his load so much as to increase it. Having flirted with a desire to die, he asked himself what he needed to live for, and he found an answer that would stay with him throughout his adult life. In the nadir of his friend's depression, Speed told Lincoln that he would die unless he rallied. Lincoln said that he *could* kill himself, that he was not afraid to die. Yet, he said, he had an "irrepressible desire" to accomplish something while he lived. He wanted to connect his name with the great events of his generation, and "so impress himself upon them as to link his name with something that would redound to the interest of his fellow man." This was no mere wish, Lincoln said, but what he "desired to live for."

More than two decades later, the two men would meet again, this time in the midst of a civil war, and Lincoln would remind Speed of the conversation.

PART TWO

CHAPTER 4

A Self-Made Man

FOR SOME PEOPLE, psychological health is a birthright. For many others, like Abraham Lincoln, it is the realization of great labor. In the early 1840s — his early thirties — Lincoln began that labor in earnest. An exchange with his law partner in those years, Stephen T. Logan, is perhaps illustrative. Lincoln told Logan one day that he despaired of ever competing effectively against a certain lawyer who had great advantages in education. "It does not depend on the start a man gets," Logan answered him. "It depends on how he keeps up his labors and efforts until middle life."

Lincoln liked that advice, and he came to fulfill it, not only in his intellectual and material labors, but in his philosophical and emotional ones as well. But before we can see the work he did to attain psychological health, we have to understand what tools he had to draw on and what, truly, he was up against. While his breakdowns dramatically illustrated his emotional trouble, Lincoln faced a more fundamental challenge, one rooted in the culture he lived in. The same ideas that governed his life — giving him structure and guidance — also spelled out what could easily have been a path of doom.

It was an ironic coincidence that, on January 1, 1841 — a day at the center of Lincoln's second breakdown — the *Quincy (Illinois) Whig* described him as a "self-made man." But the irony is worth seizing on. No label better spoke to the complex psychological culture through which Lincoln would have to find his way, so it is fitting that it attached to him at the symbolic nadir of his emotional life. Today, "self-made" has rather narrow, even cartoonish connotations, applying mainly to people who make fabulous amounts of money in some idiosyncratic enterprise. In

Lincoln's time, the word had just been coined (its first use is credited to Henry Clay in 1832), and it had a much stronger charge. The change in its meaning can be compared with the way that "hippie" went from an explosive term to a tired relic in a few short decades. Like those shaggy-haired creatures of the sixties, self-made men in the early nineteenth century were widely understood to be a wedge undercutting tradition.

For most of history, people had been "made," primarily, by the circumstances of their birth. Children of farmers had grown up to work the land. Children of the elite had assumed their parents' mantle. But in the early-nineteenth-century United States, the political and religious freedoms of the new republic, combined with a new economic reality, allowed young people to construct lives of their own. What had been a dream just a generation before — democracy in government, liberty in speech and religion — became a matter of daily life. The dream still eluded women, Native Americans, and African Americans; many minority ethnic groups had to struggle for their own. Such shortcomings, though, must not obscure the boldness of the country's basic proposition. To say that "all men are created equal" — even when the phrase, in practice, applied only to white men — and that they could do what they wished, unfettered by church or crown, was to go further than any nation had gone before.

Over this landscape blew the winds of economic change. In the late eighteenth century, Thomas Jefferson had imagined a nation of independent farms. But by the 1820s, various forces were combining to create what historians call the market revolution, driven by the exchange of cash for goods and services. Like the industrial revolution, to which it was intricately connected, the market revolution was not any one event but many broad changes over time in the way people worked and what they worked for. Today we take for granted that most people earn a wage or salary, which they use to buy what they need, and that the basic economic unit is the mobile working person, subject to individual opportunities and risks. In the early nineteenth century, such a system was in its infancy. The word "market" still referred not to a whole area of economic activity, with buyers and sellers subject to supply and demand, but to a place where people gathered, often at great effort, to sell or trade things. As late as 1820, families made three quarters of all goods — food, clothing, tools — for their own use.

With the advent of the market revolution, more workers earned wages and more farmers sold crops for cash. Shops and factories multiplied.

Villages grew into towns. Towns grew into cities. Advances in transportation made new kinds of markets possible. Before the early 1800s, human beings had never traveled faster than an animal or the wind could carry them. A trip from Louisville to New Orleans and back took about a month — floating downstream and trudging back by horse or foot. Then came steam travel for both sea and land. Robert Fulton launched the first commercially viable steamship on the Hudson River in 1807. And the railroad, the "iron horse," began puffing in the United States in the 1820s. By the 1840s, that same trip between Louisville and New Orleans could be done in a few days.

Technology not only spurred the new economy but also raised basic questions about what was physically possible. Electricity could travel like lightning over long distances. This promised to make a great practical difference in people's lives, but had just as much power as a symbol. In 1844, Samuel Morse inaugurated the first major U.S. telegraph line, using his newly devised code to translate words into electric blips. Morse's first message was "What hath God wrought."

Indeed, nothing less than the understanding of God's earth was in flux. For centuries, the church had censored scientific ideas that were contrary to Christian doctrine. When censorship ended, new questions flourished. For example, biblical scholars had long said with confidence that the world was about six thousand years old — that it had been created in six days, beginning at 9 A.M. on October 23, 4004 B.C. Then geologists showed that the world had been created over the course of eons. This in turn led to theories of evolution, to which Charles Darwin, in 1859, would add his theory of natural selection. Imagine living at a time of such discovery. Lincoln became a proponent of evolution.

The pragmatic innovations that swept through the first half of the nineteenth century were accompanied by a series of religious revivals known as the Second Great Awakening. The historian William G. McLoughlin explains that the word "awakening" broadly applies to the period around the 1830s — just as it does, for instance, to the 1960s. Both are examples of times, writes Robert C. Fuller, "in which a people reshapes its identity, transforms its patterns of thought and action, and redefines the means for sustaining a healthy relationship with the wider powers upon which its well-being is dependent." Naturally, the Awakening of the 1830s spread to new ideas about mental health and healing.

The fact that we still find Lincoln relevant shows how much of human life remains constant through history. Yet a period's character does affect individual character. Psychology, the study of what happens in our minds, is tightly interwoven with culture, the name we give to our beliefs, practices, and social behaviors. The scholar Andrew Delbanco goes so far as to define culture as a collective psychological notion. "Human beings need to organize the inchoate sensations amid which we pass our days — pain, desire, pleasure, fear — into a story," Delbanco writes. "When that story leads somewhere and thereby helps us navigate through life to its inevitable terminus in death, it gives us hope. And if such a sustaining narrative establishes itself over time in the minds of a substantial number of people, we call it culture."

In the early nineteenth century, a new culture — a new idea about what to hope for — emerged for many Americans, centered around the independent self, under nation and God. It had long been the case — in the receding world of subsistence agriculture, with a settled state and an established, unyielding church — that the *person* mattered much less than the family or tribe, its land, and its consuming, collective mission to advance and survive. Individuals mattered little compared to rulers or priests. Slowly but powerfully, the new culture tugged at the threads of this tapestry. It gave rise to something new, which even needed a new word. "Individualism" first appeared in the United States in 1835, in the translation of Alexis de Tocqueville's *Democracy in America*. Tocqueville, a Frenchman, had traveled around the country in 1831 — the same year Lincoln settled at New Salem — and found himself intrigued by its distinctive qualities. "*Individualism*," he wrote, "is a novel expression, to which a novel idea has given birth." The novel idea was that every person can "sever himself from the mass of his fellows" and draw apart into his own circle. This was a strange frontier, where "inner" values could take the place of those rooted in land, kin, and tradition.

Today, many people not only take the self for granted but struggle mightily to connect it to anything larger. In Lincoln's time, the idea of the self had the power — tinged with uncertainty, even with danger — of something emerging and ascending. A barrage of literature instructed people about the possibility of an inner life and a personal ambition. What's more, this literature insisted on the necessity, the moral value, of such a life. "A new culture of achievement demanded a regimen of self-culture or 'self-help,'" writes the historian Kenneth Winkle. "A veritable cult of self-improvement emerged to encourage young men to nurture a host of inner qualities that readily became the values of the new society."

Where did Lincoln encounter this culture? The better question would be: Where did he *not* encounter it? He needn't have done more than read the Whig newspaper in Springfield, the *Sangamo Journal,* later renamed the *Illinois State Journal.* One piece on "how to succeed" is worth quoting at length.

> Push along. Push hard. Push earnestly . . . You can't do without it. The world is so made — society is so constructed that it's a law of necessity that you must push. That is if you would be something and somebody.
>
> Who succeeds? Who makes money, honor, and reputation? He who heartily, sincerely, manfully *pushed* and *he only.* Be what you may at the top or bottom of the scale, you have got to *push* in it to command success. It's so with every man. Do you point to what is called the man of *genius?* And you think he doesn't *push?* Why, he's your companion pusher — he pushes all the time. It's the very philosophy of his height and power . . .
>
> If things look dark, push harder. — Sunshine and blue sky are just beyond. If you are entangled, push — if your heart grows feeble, push, push. You'll come out glorious, never fear. You are on the right track, and working with the right materials. So push along, keep pushing.

Such motivational squibs were addressed to a generation of young men whose fathers had been farmers or tradesmen and who had seemed plenty content if the day had work enough, the night had food enough, and no dread sickness besieged family or livestock. Tom Lincoln, later portrayed as a shiftless ne'er-do-well, was in fact a perfectly respectable man at a time when it was perfectly respectable to have modest aims. He was said to have been satisfied with his life. In his son's world, this kind of satisfaction was somehow suspect, if it kept you from pushing.

In many respects, Lincoln embraced this new culture wholeheartedly. As a boy, he had disliked physical work, the mainstay of a subsistence economy, preferring the mental labor that the market economy would make abundant. He also saw wages as a kind of liberation. When he was a teenager, Lincoln kept a skiff on the Ohio River, a thoroughfare of the American market. One day two men hired him to row them out to a larger boat. Lincoln expected "a few bits" in payment, but as the men climbed out, they threw back two silver half-dollars. "I could scarcely believe my eyes," Lincoln recalled when he was president. "Gentlemen, you may think it was a very little thing . . . but it was a most important incident in my life. I could scarcely credit that I, a poor boy, had earned a dollar in less than a day . . . The world seemed wider and fairer before me." The world was wider because he could find his fortune outside the rural areas in which he had grown up. He could visit New Orleans (which he did twice as a young man) and settle in a village or town. It was fairer because he could pursue his own interests rather than do manual labor without individual reward.

Lincoln's choice of both political party and profession signaled his interests. His kin had been Democrats, the party of cheap land and western expansion. Under Andrew Jackson, president from 1829 to 1837, the Democrats fought to keep government small and the economy decentralized, opposing the burgeoning system of banks, paper currency, and public spending on roads and canals. The Whigs — named, during Jackson's rule, after the antimonarchist party in Britain — were the party of upward mobility, of merchants and urban elites. They favored an aggressive government plan to build a national economy with internal improvements, central banks, and a tariff to protect domestic manufacturers. Meanwhile, both politics and the law played key roles in the development of the market economy. Legislators wrote laws to govern economic exchange. Lawyers made it so the laws would be enforced.

Lincoln cut the strings of tradition. He clambered into the ranks of educated, upwardly mobile Whiggery. He did his best to make himself the model lawyer-citizen, nurturing the qualities that would be essential for this new world, with an intense devotion to matters of honor, insisting, "I want in all cases to do right." "Honest Abe" was an early nickname. Lincoln had many assets in this new world — "physical assets and strength of character that permitted him to tell things as he saw them," Douglas Wilson has observed, "and not as he was expected or pressured to by his peers." He was unusually bright and hardworking. He built a network of allies who cared for him like family.

Yet Lincoln encountered trouble along with the opportunity. He was not even five years out of his father's house when he had his first breakdown. He began to wonder aloud whether he could do anything with his life, or whether he ought to "let the whole thing go by the board." He saw plainly that with the chance of rising high came the risk of falling fast and hard.

At the same time that "self-made" entered the nation's lexicon, so did the notion of abject failure. Once reserved to describe a discrete financial episode — "I made a failure," a merchant would say after losing his shop — "failure" in antebellum America became a matter of identity, describing not an event but a person. As the historian Scott Sandage explains in

Born Losers: A History of Failure in America, the phrase "I feel like a failure" comes to us so naturally today "that we forget it is a figure of speech: the language of business applied to the soul." It became conventional wisdom in the early nineteenth century, Sandage explains, that people who failed had a problem native to their constitution. They weren't just losers; they were "born losers."

The failure identity was a stopgap for the shortcomings of a new system, a way of blaming its inevitable dark side on the very people who were bearing the brunt of it anyway. "We never knew a man in the world, who was a light smart pusher, who finally did not become rich, respectable, wise, and useful," instructed Lincoln's newspaper, the *Journal.* If this was true, as so many new experts on the human condition professed, how to account for those who were pushing in a field of mud and sinking? And what was such a sinking man to think about himself? Had the middle ground between triumph and failure disappeared? When Henry David Thoreau wrote, in 1854, that "the mass of men lead lives of quiet desperation," he was quarreling with an emerging culture that scorned a man who did odd jobs, lived on a pond, and wrote poetry for no money. At Thoreau's funeral, his mentor Ralph Waldo Emerson conceded, "I cannot help counting it a fault in him that he had no ambition."

The painful irony of Lincoln's situation in his late twenties and early thirties is that the very successes that could prop him up also exerted an equally powerful force that could tear him down. Failure — which he stared in the face as he went deep into debt at New Salem — was hardly the worst of it. As we have seen, when Lincoln was having his dark episodes, first in 1835 and again in the winter of 1840–1841, people didn't just call him "depressed" or "melancholy"; they worried that he was going, or had already gone, insane. "Many of his friends feared that reason would desert her throne," remembered Robert Rutledge, of Lincoln's turmoil after his sister's death. Six years later, Lincoln was diagnosed with hypochondriasis, a form of partial insanity that doctors said often led to the full-blown condition. According to Jane Bell, a Springfield woman who described Lincoln's case in a January 1841 letter, "The Doctors say he came within an inch of being a perfect lunatic for life." One 1841 textbook on insanity explained that "more persons are attacked between the ages of 30 and 40 years, than during any other interval of ten years in life." As Lincoln reeled in the aftermath of his second breakdown, he was thirty-two.

It was more than age and temperament that made Lincoln seem in danger. For it was an article of faith that the newly mobile culture made people vulnerable to insanity, and that "self-made" men like Lincoln were prime candidates for such a miserable fate. This outrageous claim had a strong basis in contemporary biological thought. Mendelian genetic theory, that parents pass on to their children the raw material of life, became well known long after Lincoln's death. The dominant thinking on inheritance in his time, following Jean Baptiste Lamarck's influential theory of evolution, was that parents transmitted the sum of what they had learned, experienced, and suffered. According to this theory, at the moment of conception, writes the medical historian Charles Rosenberg, "the particular biological identities of both parents" — that is, the cumulative interaction of all their habits, debilities, and knowledge, plus their original constitutional endowments — were passed on to the child. The theory held that emotion and temperament flowed from the mother, intellect from the father. So a man who spent most of his life drawing a plow across a field and calculating lengths of wood for a proper cabinet (Tom Lincoln) would produce a child well equipped for farm work and carpentry, but rather poorly equipped for, say, jurisprudence or political philosophy.

Medical authorities asserted that this biological reality caused no difficulty as long as people gauged their expectations to their capacities. Isaac Ray, from 1845 to 1866 the superintendent of the Maine State Hospital for the Insane, wrote that in the "old world" it was "agreeable enough to people . . . to follow on the same path their father trod before them, turning neither to the right hand, nor to the left, and perfectly content with a steady and sure, though it may be slow progress." The United States, physicians warned, may have gone too far in casting off rigid tradition. Now the sons of poor, uneducated men sought wealth and education, participated in elections, and even found places in government. The new culture, noted the physician William Sweetser in a layman's guide to mental hygiene, beckoned "each citizen, however subordinate may be his station, to join in the pursuit of whatever distinctions our forms of society can bestow." "Every one sees bright visions in the future," Sweetser wrote. But the reality, he cautioned, was not nearly so luminous. People expected too much, pushed themselves too hard, and therefore brought strains upon their minds that they were constitutionally incapable of withstanding. "Mental powers," explained the popular medical writer Edward Jarvis, "are strained to their utmost tension . . . Minds stagger under the disproportionate burden." The result was an insanity that did not creep up slowly but struck frightfully and suddenly. Any person, at any time, could go mad and commit horrific violence or sink into permanent idiocy.

For proof, the doctors turned to the favorite plaything of the early-nineteenth-century intellectual classes, statistics. They published charts that showed the United States near or at the top of international rankings of insanity per capita. In March 1844, for example, the *Southern Literary Messenger* published a short article, "On the Distribution of Insanity in the United States" by C. B. Hayden. On the whole, the article observed, rates of insanity were higher in the new republic than in the nations of Europe. "We might at first refuse to admit the existence in our country of any peculiar causes, calculated to produce insanity," wrote Hayden, "accustomed, as we are, to congratulate ourselves upon the very diffusion among all classes of those blessings of existence, which contribute to mental and physical health and happiness." But it turned out, Hayden argued, that the very conditions that so pleased Americans — religious freedom, economic opportunity, political equality — promoted mental imbalance. "Life in our republic," Hayden explained, "has all the excitement of an olympic contest. A wide arena is thrown open, and all fearlessly join in the maddening rush for the laurel wreath, or golden chaplet." The resulting rancor, excitement, and anxiety produced "sickness of hope deferred, ambition maddened by defeat, avarice rendered desperate by failure."

Whether or not Lincoln read this article (he subscribed to the *Southern Literary Messenger*), he couldn't have avoided such a widespread and commonly accepted argument. Fears of insanity were incessant, creating what the historian David J. Rothman calls "a heightened, almost hysterical sense of peril." Before 1810, the United States had only a few asylums for the insane, and only one received public funding. By 1860, twenty-eight of thirty-three states had a public institution for the insane, and many had several. At a time when government provided neither education for children nor pensions for the aged, legislators across the country — responding to horror stories of sudden, violent insanity — voted to levy special taxes to build these institutions. Lincoln's Illinois was among them. After an 1846 visit from Dorothea Dix, the leading advocate of asylums, the Illinois General Assembly voted to fund, with new taxes, a State

Hospital for the Insane at Jacksonville, not far from Lincoln's home at Springfield. This is the hospital where his cousin's daughter, Mary Jane Lincoln, was later committed.

The existence of an ostensible cure for insanity may have led to greater alarm. Seeking to extend and strengthen their field, asylum superintendents lectured widely on the dangers of insanity. The superintendents virtually created modern psychiatry. (The Association of Medical Superintendents of American Institutions for the Insane later became the American Psychiatric Association.) The big leather-bound books they used to classify the patients entering their institutions would lead to systematic diagnoses seen in the modern *Diagnostic and Statistical Manual of Mental Disorders.* Yet for many people, to be entered into one of those books was not the beginning of treatment but the end of an independent life: many who went to the asylum never came home. Mary Jane Lincoln died at Jacksonville after twenty-one years there.

A creeping fear of madness often accompanies depression. Sufferers wonder if their black moods will ever lift, or if their feelings of alienation from the healthy world will deepen and widen. "These fears are at least fifty percent of what it is to be melancholy," says Lauren Slater, a clinical psychologist who has written about her struggles with mental illness. "If you were to be really, really depressed but know that it was going to end in five days, it wouldn't be depression. The terror is in what the future holds." The psychologist William James famously wrote about this "panic fear . . . the worst form of melancholy" in *The Varieties of Religious Experience.* He told of being in a state of "philosophic pessimism and general depression of spirits about my prospects" one night, when suddenly an image descended on him of a madman he'd seen in an asylum. "This image and my fear entered into a species of combination with each other," James wrote. "THAT SHAPE AM I, I felt, potentially."

Did such fears occupy Abraham Lincoln? He was doubtless well acquainted with the way a person could become, as he put it, "locked . . . in a mental night." In the mid-1840s, Lincoln wrote a poem about a madman whom he had known intimately in Indiana. Matthew Gentry was one of Lincoln's peers, "rather a bright lad," he recalled, and the scion of the wealthiest family in the Little Pigeon Creek area. When Lincoln was sixteen and Gentry nineteen, "he unaccountably became furiously mad," Lincoln said, and Gentry never recovered, only settling gradually into a "harmless insanity." On a return trip to the area, Lincoln had seen him "lingering in this wretched condition." He said later, "I could not forget the impression his case made upon me."

The poem Lincoln wrote, published as "The Maniac," gives three perspectives of madness. It describes a violent breakdown, with Gentry maiming himself, fighting with his father, and trying to kill his mother before he was physically restrained, howling and shrieking. This sensational picture is followed by a more subtle and compassionate view, describing Gentry's "mournful song" rising on a still night, to which the narrator "stole away" before dawn to listen.

> Air held his breath; trees, with the spell,
> Seemed sorrowing angels round,
> Whose swelling tears in dew-drops fell
> Upon the listening ground.

The poem concludes with a kind of clinical view of madness, as a state in which the higher soul of humanity has left the body, leaving nothing more than a "brute," in a condition worse than death.

The crucial mental health question in Lincoln's time was whether a person was sane or not. On the right side of that line, one had considerable latitude for expressions of distress. On the wrong side, one could be cast off from civilized society.

It bears mentioning, in this context, that madness struck Lincoln's family. His first cousin Mordecai Lincoln, who lived in Hancock County, Illinois, was a bright and energetic man, a cobbler, carpenter, and violinist. A florid man, he was prone to dramatic gestures, like appearing in the door of the schoolhouse and rolling apples to the children and the teacher. But something went awry with Mordecai Lincoln as he grew older. Raised a Catholic, he grew embittered toward the church and especially Jesuit priests. His eccentricities, once charming, gave way to something darker. Eventually he became paranoid, observing plots to ruin him and writing detailed accounts of these conspiracies. He stopped working for pay and lived like a hermit with hundreds of pigeons — he built elaborate houses for them — and a dog named Grampus. He sometimes visited his kin and, without saying a word, would pick up a violin and walk the floor weeping while he played. In the 1850s, Abraham Lincoln visited his cousin Mordecai and inquired about him, giving one man in Hancock County the impression that he was "quite attached." This doesn't mean that Lincoln identified with his cousin's mental difficulties. But it would not be surprising if he did, or if he ruminated on the family history that led a jury in the county to decide, when committing Mary Jane Lincoln to the asylum, "The disease is with her hereditary."

The irony is that by seeking what he wanted in life, Lincoln put himself in a position where he might lose everything. He might be consigned to misery, failure, perhaps madness. But what matters here is not just that prospect but Lincoln's response to it. Despite the fears, or perhaps in part because of them, he worked all the harder in his thirties and forties to "make himself," emotionally as well as materially, and go on to do the special work he longed for. Perseverance and forbearance became core aspects of Lincoln's character, and he would one day give the same advice his law partner Stephen Logan gave him, that what matters is whether a person "keeps up his labors and efforts until middle life."

In 1860, when Lincoln was the Republican nominee for president, a schoolmate of his son Bob's was denied admission by Harvard College. Lincoln wrote the boy that "I have scarcely felt greater pain in my life" than on learning the news. "And yet," he added, "there is very little in it, if you will allow no feeling of discouragement to seize, and prey upon you." He told him to go see Harvard's president and learn what obstacles he had to overcome, and how to overcome them. "In your temporary failure," he wrote, "there is no evidence that you may not yet be a better scholar, and a more successful man in the great struggle of life, than many others, who have entered college more easily." Lincoln said he knew this was true from his own "severe experience." Indeed, many people of this era sought success in the "great struggle of life," but there were few who felt the struggle more acutely.

CHAPTER 5

A Misfortune, Not a Fault

ONE OF THE REASONS that depression is so problematic — and deadly, leading to many of the forty thousand suicides in the United States each year — is that people are often loath to admit they are suffering, let alone explore it in detail. Given the dangers Lincoln faced, it is exceptional that he energetically investigated his own condition, and the experience of other suffering people, both in practical and existential terms. It is all the more unusual when we see the tradition that Lincoln came from, which viewed the more pronounced forms of melancholy as aberrant, even sinful — a kind of infestation of the body or soul by external, malevolent forces that needed to be cast out or violently suppressed. Rejecting this tradition, Lincoln struck out into his own intellectual territory, slashing through thickets of medical theory, philosophy, and theology. He arrived tentatively at his own idea, that melancholy arose from natural, sometimes beneficent forces. Talking about it in plain human terms was his first step toward claiming his own ground as a person who, through no fault of his own, needed help.

Lincoln was raised in the thick of Old School Calvinism. In Kentucky and Indiana, his parents belonged to a fire-breathing sect called Separate Baptism, in which congregants heard — in the tradition of Jonathan Edwards's famous sermon "Sinners in the Hands of an Angry God" — that they were bound for eternal hellfire, and nothing they could do or say or think would change their fate. Preachers did allow that a chosen few were ordained for grace and would be saved, but these fortunate ones had been selected by God before time began. As one Baptist preacher in Lincoln's Kentucky explained it, "Long before the morning stars sang together . . . the Almighty looked down upon the ages yet unborn, as it were, in review before him, and selected one here and another there to enjoy eternal life and left the rest to the blackness of darkness forever." Such Baptist ministers were so intense that it has been said that they "out-Calvined Calvin."

Doctrine affected conceptions of health and psychology. Inspired by Jesus himself, Christian ministers from the earliest days cast themselves as healers, especially of ailments that sprang from unseen causes. In the fourth century, John Cassian described a condition among his fellow monks that he called "acedia": a "weariness or distress of heart . . . akin to dejection" that took "possession" of unhappy souls and left them lazy, sluggish, restless, and solitary. Later, acedia became widely translated as sloth, one of the seven deadly sins, and blended with melancholy in the popular mind. Both required, at the very least, confession and penitence. More stubborn cases called for exorcism to cast out evil spirits.

This view of melancholy as aberrant strongly influenced both the clergy and the physicians of North America. The English Calvinists, or Puritans, who colonized Massachusetts in the early seventeenth century, believed that melancholy, in many forms, came from demonic posses-sion. "Some Devil is often very Busy with the poor Melancholicks," wrote Cotton Mather. "Yea, there is often a Degree of Diabolical Possession in the Melancholy." Though it may be hard to take such talk seriously as psychology, the historian David Harley observes that the Calvinist sys-tem had hierarchies of disorders, consistent diagnostic criteria, and wide popular acceptance. The system's message boiled down to this: "For the godly," Harley writes, "the correct response to any affliction was to search for God's purpose and to repent, before seeking removal of the affliction through the use of the appropriate means."

As decisively as Lincoln left the rural life, he left the Baptist church as well. In New Salem he became widely known as an infidel. He rejected eternal damnation, innate sin, the divinity of Jesus, and the infallibility of the Bible. For a time it seemed that there was nothing sacred that Lincoln *didn't* reject. He recited the poetry of Robert Burns, the notorious Scot-tish freethinker. He carried around a Bible, reading passages and arguing against them. It reached a point where it hurt Lincoln politically, with people loudly refusing to vote for a man with such "shocking" views. When Lincoln put his ideas about the Bible and Christ on paper, even one of his fellow skeptics thought he'd gone too far, and threw the manu-script into the fire.

Lincoln never joined a church, but this didn't mean he was indifferent to moral and existential matters. To the contrary, his mind was on fire with ideas and beliefs and concerns. And as energetically as he flung aside some influences, he eagerly cultivated others. Indeed, in the early days of the nation, having a roving, doubting mind was itself a kind of august tradition. A number of the Founders — including Benjamin Franklin, George Washington, and Thomas Jefferson — were freethinkers. "Often defined as a total absence of faith in God," writes Susan Jacoby, in *Freethinkers: A History of American Secularism,* "freethought can better be understood as a phenomenon running the gamut from the truly antireligious — those who regarded all religion as a form of superstition and wished to reduce its influence in every aspect of society — to those who adhered to a private, unconventional faith." Turning away from orthodox religion, many freethinkers constructed a faith in their own minds, working with evidence from the natural world.

The American tradition of separation of church and state grew directly from the freethinking of the Founders. After political independence, they considered independence of thought and belief a logical next step. In 1779, Jefferson proposed, for his state of Virginia, a guarantee of equality for citizens of all beliefs, and nonbeliefs — "meant to comprehend, within the mantle of its protection," Jefferson wrote, "the Jew and the Gentile, the Christian and Mahometan, the Hindoo, and infidel of every denomination." This act inspired the secular spirit of the U.S. Constitution. Legal barriers to equality still remained — Connecticut, for example, withheld equal rights from Jews until 1843 — but guided by Thomas Paine's plea for freedom of conscience, *The Age of Reason,* Americans moved in the direction of religious liberty.

As the nineteenth century dawned, a strong reaction set in against this secular heritage. A series of religious revivals, the Second Great Awakening, swept the country. Dozens of new Christian sects sprang up, including the Methodists and the Mormons. Between 1776 and 1845, the number of preachers in the United States, per capita, tripled. Many of these new Christians saw the liberty of the Revolution as the liberty to decide which kind of Christianity to practice. Paine became castigated as a Judas, a reptile, and a louse, and the attacks only intensified after he died, in 1809. In the 1820s and 1830s, "Paine's memory," Jacoby writes, "was kept alive only by small, marginalized groups of freethinkers" — among them a young Illinoisan named Abraham Lincoln.

The swirl of ideas in the first half of the nineteenth century can make it hard to find Lincoln's place, but the challenge is proportionate to the reward. The multiplicity of traditions he drew from — and the original way he synthesized them, and also held on to contrasting ideas — is what makes Lincoln so fascinating. In some ways, he was rejecting an old tradition, the religious dogma of his youth, for the new faith of the nation, individualism and liberty. But given that Paine's deism had become hotly controversial, in another sense Lincoln was defending an American tradition against the onslaught of the new.

These intellectual currents connected to a vital struggle going on in Lincoln's mind. Figuring out what he thought about the big questions of existence was not an abstract or academic matter. The rumblings of his mind and the ocean of ideas he swam in can be seen in a series of letters he wrote to his friend Joshua Speed in early 1842.

Speed, remember, had left Springfield in the spring of 1841, disconsolate, in part owing to romantic disappointment. Over the summer, he met and courted Fanny Henning, a religious young woman with what Lincoln called "heavenly black eyes." When he finally proposed marriage, and she said yes, he began to have a nervous breakdown. On hand at Farmington when the young couple courted, and with Speed at Springfield in the fall of 1841, Lincoln watched his friend slide into misery. Speed noted the parallels: "In the winter of 40 & 41, he was very unhappy about his engagement . . . How much he suffered then on that account none Know so well as myself — He disclosed his whole heart to me — In the summer of 1841. I became engaged . . . and strange to say something of the same feeling which I regarded as so foolish in him — took possession of me."

Around the first of the year, 1842, Speed set out from Springfield to Louisville, where he intended to make Miss Henning his bride. Lincoln gave his friend a letter before his departure, full of counsel and succor. "Feeling, as you know I do, the deepest solicitude for the success of the enterprize you are engaged in," he began, "I adopt this as the last method I can invent to aid you, in case (which God forbid) you shall need any aid. I do not place what I am going to say on paper, because I can say it any better in that way than I could by word of mouth; but because, were I to say it orrally, before we part, most likely you would forget it at the verry time when it might do you some good."

It is a signal feature of depression that, in times of trouble, sensible ideas, memories of good times, and optimism for the future all recede into blackness. Lincoln had good reason to expect that Speed would "forget" his words just when they were most important. And he intended his

letters to be of practical use. "As I think it reasonable that you will feel
verry badly some time between this and the final consummation of your
purpose," he wrote, "it is intended that you shall read this just at such a
time." He continued: "Why I say it is reasonable that you will feel verry
badly yet, is because of *three special causes,* added to the *general one which
I shall mention.* The general cause is, that you are *naturally of nervous
temperament;* and this I say from what I have seen of you personally, and
what you have told me concerning your mother at various times and
concerning your brother William at the time his wife died." Speed's
mother had a tendency to melancholy, and his older brother William,
when his wife died in the spring of 1841, was thought by relatives "almost
crazy." There was plenty more emotional difficulty in the Speed family,
but it is telling that Lincoln cited only two family members. If he considered this sufficient evidence, Lincoln — the son of a mother whom he
described as sensitive and sad, and a father who sometimes had spells of
the blues — probably judged that melancholy ran in his family, too.

But this was just a step on the way to Lincoln's main idea: however
Speed's trouble came down to him, it was inherent in his makeup, or
temperament, and thus a basis of his character. There was no more use
protesting this fact than protesting one's height. In Lincoln's thinking,
this "nervous temperament," the "general cause" of trouble, had been exacerbated by three "special causes":

> The first special cause is *your exposure to bad weather* on your jour-
> ney, which my experience clearly proves to be verry severe on defective
> nerves.
> The second is, *the absence of all business and conversation of friends,*
> which might divert your mind, and give it occasional rest from that
> *intensity* of thought, which will some times wear the sweetest idea
> thread-bare and turn it to the bitterness of death.
> The third is, *the rapid and near approach of that crisis on which all
> your thoughts and feelings concentrate.*

Lincoln made it clear that he spoke about Speed's case from experience. Bad weather, he said, had been hard on his own "defective nerves."
He knew both the intense, grinding thought cycles of melancholy and
how, with the approach of a crisis, vague fears could concentrate into
sharp, crippling pains. Though these letters are addressed to Speed and
are written mainly in the second person, Lincoln refers explicitly to himself several times: "my experience clearly proves . . ." and "let me, who

have some reason to speak with judgement on such a subject, beseech you . . ." In substance, the voice is first-person plural. As Lincoln saw it, most people could handle the stress of courtship and marriage, endure poor weather, and separate from their friends without collapsing. But for others — like himself and Speed — these "special causes" of woe were like a shove off a cliff. "*The particular causes*," he wrote, "to a greater or lesser extent, perhaps do apply in all cases; but the *general one*, nervous debility, which is the key and conductor of all the particular ones, and without which *they* would be utterly harmless, though it *does* pertain to you, *does not* pertain to one in a thousand. It is out of this, that the painful difference between you and the mass of the world springs."

Many people, faced with a suffering friend, would just tell him to go see a doctor. Perhaps because Lincoln had experienced medical treatment himself, and come out the worse for it, he put no stock in conventional therapy. He took Speed's condition as an opportunity to tear the problem of suffering down to its foundations: What was its origin? What caused it to manifest itself? What could be done about it?

It's apparent that he'd given the matter some thought and that he was influenced by contemporary science. Notice that he called "nervous debility" the "key and conductor" of the exacerbating causes. A key, of course, is a device that opens, closes, or switches circuits, and a conductor is a medium through which current passes. Notice, too, how he used the word "nervous" rather than "melancholy." These terms suggest Lincoln's awareness of the scientific evidence for the existence in the human body of discrete systems, including a nervous system responsible for bodily and mental sensations. With this innovation, which became widely accepted in the early nineteenth century, diseases that had been attributed to black bile or the influence of demons now were believed to arise from an injury or "debility" of the nervous system. The idea was that, for some, the body's circuits and wires improperly processed sensations of the outside world. Thus, people with nervous illnesses could feel worse than they really were. In other contexts, Lincoln had used "melancholy" and "hypochondriasis," but he avoided them here, probably because they had different connotations. "Melancholic" suggested an ancient malady, the affliction of Aristotle, Martin Luther, Saint Augustine, and Robert Burton. "Nervous" was a modern term, and Lincoln used it in the modern sense.

This is not to say that Lincoln was poring over books on medicine or science, only that he was alive and curious about his world. It's like a person in the early 1990s using the word "neurotransmitter." It would signal familiarity with a concept that was seeping into popular thinking but not yet universally held.

The substance of Lincoln's message to Speed also reflected new influences. One of the basic ideas of the evangelical movement in the early nineteenth century was that people could help themselves. Rather than wonder and fear the fate God decreed for them, they could actively change their lives by renouncing sin and accepting Christ. From this same pool of thought rose a wave of healers who claimed that disease wasn't a product of inscrutable humors that needed to be poisoned or purged from the body, but natural phenomena that could be studied and understood. This idea blended Enlightenment rationalism with evangelical optimism.

H. L. Mencken joked that Puritanism was "the haunting fear that someone, somewhere, may be happy." There was something in this of the old doctors, too, forever torturing their already suffering patients. But the new healers said that happiness was intended by divine and natural law. In the early nineteenth century, new healing systems sprouted like weeds, forerunners of today's natural or "alternative" medicine. Grahamism — the child of preacher-turned-hygienist Sylvester Graham — proposed that good health came from a natural diet, including bread from unbolted wheat flour (hence the "graham cracker"). Hydropaths proposed to cure all disorders by internal and external application of water. And homeopaths offered the startling idea that the best medicine was administered in infinitesimal doses, as little as a millionth of a gram.

Lincoln had some contact with and some interest in the progressive and fundamentally optimistic approaches to health and healing. In late-eighteenth-century Vienna, a physician named Franz Anton Mesmer proposed that, just as Newton had shown an invisible physical force called gravity, he could demonstrate the existence of a potent invisible force called "animal magnetism." Illness, Mesmer argued, was caused by a disconnection from this great force, and talented healers could bring people back into salutary contact with it. In 1836, a Frenchman named Charles Poyen came to the United States and began lecturing on mesmerism. Packed halls greeted him, and by the early 1840s, Boston alone had several hundred practitioners of mesmerism, claiming to cure everything from heart disease to melancholia.

As in the rest of the country, Springfield, Illinois, saw "a profound stir . . . on the subject of mesmerism, animal magnetism, and so forth," remembered Sophie Bledsoe Herrick. "My father was found to have uncommon power in this line." Herrick's father, Albert Taylor Bledsoe, a former Episcopalian minister, practiced law alongside Lincoln and, for a time, lived in the same boarding house. Lincoln watched with interest as Bledsoe performed his experiments. For example, there was a "Mrs. B," who suffered from a painful nervous tic. Bledsoe moved his hands over her body — using the "classic passes" of mesmerism, his daughter said — to great success. Once when Lincoln and Bledsoe were discussing mesmerism in the Globe Tavern, they could hear the sounds of Mrs. B's piano playing from a room in an adjoining building. Bledsoe said he believed he could make her stop playing without going near her. Try it, Lincoln said. As Bledsoe's daughter told the story, the next moment, the playing ceased. Bledsoe and Lincoln went to the other building and knocked on Mrs. B's door. When she answered, Lincoln exhorted her to continue playing. She said that she didn't know what was the matter. She had never felt this way before, but however hard she tried, she just couldn't go on playing.

At bottom, mesmerism was an accessible scheme for self-improvement. It proposed a semi-scientific language with which to discuss fundamentally spiritual, moral, and psychological concerns. And it offered to meet people just where they were and help them get to a better place. It probably owed its effectiveness to the placebo effect. But the idea that the plain acts of one person could beneficially affect the mind of another person was a breath of fresh air after centuries of scolding, punishing treatments. Hypnotism came out of mesmerists' practice, and it led, eventually, to Freudian psychoanalysis.

Another innovation with great appeal came in the field of temperance. In 1830, per capita consumption of distilled spirits — whiskey, gin, rum, and the like — had reached four gallons, the highest in U.S. history. In reaction, a massive temperance movement emerged, centering on religious and moral denunciations of drink. In 1840, a group of reformed drunkards in Baltimore began to meet and offer each other support and fellowship. They decided to take their message to other drunkards, and chapters sprang up around the country. They called themselves the Washington Temperance Union. Soon a chapter formed in Springfield. On the occasion of George Washington's birthday in 1842, the members invited Lincoln to speak to them.

He took the opportunity to explain why "old-school" temperance efforts had failed and why the Washingtonians had so much success. To denounce drinkers "in the thundering tones of anathema and denunciation," Lincoln argued, was not only unjust but impolitic. It simply worked better to reason with, coax, and convince people, he said. Quitting drink was a good thing, he continued, because people could work and support their families better sober than drunk. The Washingtonians got reformed drunkards to speak about these advantages and to encourage others by the force of their example. In contrast, Lincoln said, harsh condemnation could no more pierce a man's heart than a rye straw could penetrate the hard shell of a tortoise.

His references to "Old School" Calvinism and "Hard Shell" Baptism were subtle, but Lincoln was not subtle about his critique of the old theology. Calvinism saw human beings subjected to a harsh and wrathful God; Lincoln proposed that people could shape their own lives by the exercise of will. Of the Washingtonians, he said admiringly, "They teach hope to all — despair to none. Denying the doctrine of unpardonable sin, they teach, 'While the lamp holds out to burn / The vilest sinner may return.'" Drunkards, Lincoln said, should be "pitied and compassionated, just as are the heirs of consumption and other hereditary diseases." Their failings ought to be treated as a "*misfortune,* and not as a *crime,* or even as a *disgrace.*"

He made the same point about melancholy. After he spent time with Joshua Speed's fiancée, Fanny Henning, Lincoln wrote, "There is but one thing about her, so far as I could perceive that I would have otherwise than as it is. That is something of a tendency to melancholly. This, let it be observed, is a misfortune not a fault." The distinction is essential. Fault implies a failure or weakness for which a person should be held to account, if not outright blamed. Misfortune is an unhappy circumstance, something bad that has happened to a blameless good person.

In his letters to Speed, Lincoln showed that he had a keen eye for the misfortune that he and his friend shared — a nervous temperament. This led him to think pragmatically about how to live with such a condition. In particular, he named three kinds of troubles that could beset a person with a nervous temperament: poor weather, isolation or idleness, and stressful events. In the winter of 1841–1842, Speed faced all three. That is why Lincoln predicted a rough season. "If from all these causes," he wrote, "you shall escape and go through triumphantly, without another 'twinge of the soul,' I shall be most happily, but most egregiously deceived." Lincoln advised his friend to adjust his expectations to the unavoidable reality. Don't expect to marry with feelings of delight, he said.

Rather, aim to get "through the ceremony *calmly*, or even with sufficient composure not to excite alarm in any present." In that case, Lincoln said, "you are safe, beyond question, and in two or three months, will be the happiest of men." For the future, Lincoln predicted, "I incline to think it probable, that your nerves will fail you occasionally for a while; but once you get them fairly graded now, that trouble is over forever." In other words, just as it would take a good amount of work to level a tall hill in order to build a road there, Speed could, with effort, "grade" his nerves and achieve happiness. If, however, he did feel agonized or distressed in the future, Lincoln begged his friend to ascribe it to natural causes and "not to some false and ruinous suggestion of the Devil." Suffering was not a punishment from beyond or a malevolent infestation of the soul. Like the earth turning on its axis or energy passing through a conductor, it was a part of the natural world, to be studied, understood, and, when possible, managed.

Yet even as Lincoln argued for science, reason, and progress, he brought forward a quite different but equally vital point of view. Determined in his belief in the power of human beings to improve their lives, Lincoln was also determined to accept things the way they were. He subscribed to a school of thought known as fatalism, which said that events on earth were preordained and humans powerless to change them. For example, when Speed expressed worries about his fiancée's health — she had taken ill with consumption and traveled to New Orleans on the advice of doctors — Lincoln sympathized with him, but urged that he see the big picture. "The death scenes of those we love," he wrote, "are surely painful enough; but these we are prepared to, and expect to see. They happen to all, and all know they must happen." Lincoln knew that Speed, like himself, was a skeptic, an infidel. And he knew that his fiancée was a devout Methodist. In this instance, he said, it was her faith, and not his disbelief, that would bring the truest comfort. "Should she, as you fear, be destined to an early grave, it is indeed, a great consolation to know that she is so well prepared to meet it."

"Destined," in that sentence, was no metaphor. Lincoln believed that individuals had destinies that had been laid out for them in advance, and which they had little, if any, power to affect. Indeed, in this same passage Lincoln went on to suggest that Fanny Henning's illness itself might be part of a divine plan, to assuage Speed's doubts about his love for her.

Lincoln thought that Speed's "present anxiety and distress about *her* health and *her* life, must and will forever banish those horid doubts, which I know you sometimes felt, as to the truth of your affection for her." He continued, "If they can be once and forever removed, (and I almost feel a presentiment that the Almighty has sent your present affliction expressly for that object) surely, nothing can come in their stead, to fill their immeasurable measure of misery."

Far from a passing fancy, Lincoln's fatalism was one of his bedrock beliefs. He would quote Shakespeare: "There's a divinity that shapes our ends / Rough-hew them how we will." Brutus, he argued, by way of example, had been drawn inexorably by laws and conditions to kill Caesar. Neither could have escaped that fate. Though it may seem that we choose a particular action, he suggested, we are in fact like billiard balls: struck from behind, we move according to fixed laws and strike what is in our path. "His idea," recalled his law partner William Herndon, "was that all human actions were caused by motives" — motive, in this sense, being the power or energy behind something. In discussions with Lincoln, Herndon took the opposite view, arguing for something akin to free will. "I once contended," Herndon recalled, "that man was free and could act without a motive." Lincoln smiled at him and replied that it was impossible, "because the motive was born before the man." Far from being free, Lincoln argued, man was a mere tool, a cog in the wheel of a great machine that, in Herndon's words, "strikes and cuts, grinds and mashes, all things, including man, that resist it."

As the scholar Allen Guelzo has shown, Lincoln was a serious philosophical thinker who kept abreast of the leading ideas of his time. He said, in 1846, that he followed "what I understand is called the 'Doctrine of Necessity' — that is, that the human mind is impelled to action, or held in rest by some power, over which the mind itself has no control." John Stuart Mill, who used the phrase "philosophical necessity," said that it boiled down to the proposition that people's actions and thoughts are subject to laws, as clearly as are physical events. In one sense, this brand of determinism was anticlerical, substituting a kind of scientific or philosophical perspective for a spiritual one. "Virtually all of the major deistic or 'infidel' literature published in America in the late eighteenth and early nineteenth century," Guelzo explains, "incorporated some form of determinism, largely as a way of accounting for order in the universe without invoking a personal God to create and provide for it." The classic image was of a "watchmaker God," who set the universe in motion as though winding a clock, then took no active role in human affairs. Yet when people began to describe how such a clock worked, they quickly moved to a cosmology that transcended empirical method. Lincoln, in particular, occupied an ambiguous middle ground. In some conversations he spoke of "motives" and "laws." In others he spoke about "God" and "destiny." It seems he was talking about the same thing.

Religious language helped Lincoln cover over the liability of being associated with unorthodox thought. It was one thing for a cloistered intellectual like John Stuart Mill to argue for "necessity," and quite another for a politician to do so. For Lincoln to say that "laws" governed the mind flew in the face of one of the basic assumptions of evangelical Christianity, that a living God (or "Providence") governed the world, watching out for his flock, guiding and correcting them, rewarding them for correct behavior. Lincoln in the early 1840s was not ready to acknowledge the existence of Providence. In his temperance speech he seemed to compare such a belief to one of the weird quirks of humankind, like a thirst for alcohol, that needed to be respected only because it was so common. "The universal sense of mankind on any subject is an argument, or at least an influence, not easily overcome," he said. "The success of the argument in favor of the existence of an overruling Providence mainly depends upon that sense."

Yet, whether he identified laws or Providence as the guiding force of the world, Lincoln's philosophy led him to an idea of self akin to the Calvinist one — as a speck of dust in an infinite scheme, a humble witness to the grand mystery of life. When Speed thanked him for his help, Lincoln answered, "The truth is, I am not sure there was any merit, with me, in the part I took in your difficulty; I was drawn to it as by fate; if I would, I could not have done less than I did. I always was superstitious; and as part of my superstition, I believe God made me one of the instruments of bringing your Fanny and you together, which union, I have no doubt He had fore-ordained. Whatever he designs, he will do for *me* yet. 'Stand *still* and see the salvation of the Lord' is my text just now." This didn't mean that Lincoln thought God would take care of him. It meant that whatever God had planned, good or bad, he would find out soon enough.

"Superstition" perfectly describes Lincoln's self-consciousness about his spirituality. He believed in something he knew to be irrational, yet he did not push away the superstition. He seemed to draw closer to it. It was around 1841, Lincoln later said, that he left off making public arguments in favor of the "Doctrine of Necessity," which public shift seems to have coincided with a private one. When he was at Farmington with the Speed family that summer, the family matriarch, Lucy Gilmer Speed, noticed and felt pained for Lincoln's suffering. One morning when they were alone, Mrs. Speed approached him and pressed into his hand an Oxford edition of the Bible. She told him to read it, adopt its precepts, and pray for its promises. If he wanted help, she said, he would find it there. "It made a deep impression on him," Joshua Speed said of the exchange. "I often heard him allude to it — even after he was President."

Why would this moment make such an impression? For one thing, Mrs. Speed was not the Bible-thumping sort who provoked Lincoln to refer to the Illinois countryside as "priest ridden." Her family was theologically liberal, attending the church of a famous Unitarian minister named James Freeman Clarke, who was based in Louisville in the 1830s. Such an affinity with Lincoln, on top of her own experience with melancholy, may have made her an effective messenger. "If you would win a man to your cause," Lincoln advised in his temperance address, "*first* convince him that you are his sincere friend. Therein is a drop of honey that catches his heart, which, say what he will, is the great highroad to his reason."

If the encounter with Mrs. Speed marked a turning point, it wasn't because it ended a struggle for Lincoln but commenced a new phase, one in which he brought his search for his own beliefs to the fore. "Tell your mother," he wrote to Mary Speed, "I have not got her 'present' with me; but that I intend to read it regularly when I return home. I doubt not that it is really, as she says, the best cure for the 'Blues' could one but take it according to the truth." That phrase — "could one but take it according to the truth" — speaks directly to Lincoln's predicament. Human beings can exercise their will over the conditions for faith, but faith itself, by definition, is a matter beyond the self. In *The Varieties of Religious Experience*, William James notes how diverse traditions — from Christian monks to Christian Scientists — all describe profound spiritual experiences as a lapse of will, where one is decisively overtaken by a powerful, unknowable force. James professed himself unable, despite great interest, to be so taken. In the early 1840s, Lincoln was apparently in a similar predicament. "He always seemed to deplore his want of faith as a very great infelicity," said Albert Taylor Bledsoe, "from which he would be glad to be delivered." Yet deliverance eluded him. Belief coexisted with doubt. He would have to find his way through this muddled terrain.

Joshua Speed and Fanny Henning were wed on February 15, 1842. Lincoln eagerly waited for news of the ceremony. When Speed's letter arrived, Lincoln opened it with what he called "intense anxiety and trepidation." He was so worked up, he said, that ten hours later "I have hardly yet . . . become calm." He felt chastened since, true to his character, he had given way to fear rather than resting in hope: "I tell you, Speed," he wrote, "our forebodings, for which you and I are rather peculiar, are all the worst sort of nonsense . . . You had so obviously improved, at the verry time I so much feared, you would have grown worse."

Once Speed got married, and reported to Lincoln that he was indeed feeling better, the tone of Lincoln's letters changed dramatically. For months he had countered his friend's gloom, assuring him that he would be all right and that the future would treat him kindly. Now, though, the vigilant, relentlessly consoling persona washed away. Hearing that Speed had decided to take up the plantation life on land that he had inherited outside Louisville, Lincoln bemoaned, "How miserably things seem to be arranged in this world. If we have no friends, we have no pleasure; and if we have them, we are sure to lose them, and be doubly pained by the loss . . . I feel somwhat jealous of both of you now; you will be so exclusively concerned for one another, that I shall be forgotten entirely." Having gamely stepped up to play caretaker, Lincoln fell back to the role of a friend in need of care.

Again Lincoln faced the unnerving prospect of marriage to Mary Todd and the turmoil of his own indecision. For a time, it may have appeared to Lincoln that fate would settle the question, whisking away his might-be bride in the arms of another suitor. Yet one by one Todd's other suitors dropped away. After several seasons with no interaction, the two were reintroduced at a gathering of friends sometime in the summer of 1842. One of the agents of the reunion was Dr. Anson Henry, who probably thought — this was one of Benjamin Rush's prescriptions for hypochondriasis in the case of bachelors — that marriage would be good medicine.

Shortly after the first break in their courtship, Lincoln concluded that he would not be happy with Todd, going so far as to tell a confidant that marrying her "would just kill me." But in addition to the vexing question of his honor — had he made a pledge to this woman? would he be a knave to forsake her? — Lincoln faced the questions that so often afflict depressives: Could he trust his own judgment? When he made a decision, could he act on it, or would he be hobbled by the divisions within him? "Before I resolve to do the one thing or the other," he wrote to Speed on July 4, 1842, "I must regain my confidence in my own ability to keep my resolves when they are made. In that ability you know, I once prided myself as the only, or at least the chief, gem of my character; that gem I lost — how, and when, you too well know. I have not yet regained it; and until I do, I can not trust myself in any matter of much importance."

Though Lincoln had clearly professed his agony at the prospect of marriage to Mary Todd, he now seemed to be wondering whether those emotions were simply the product of his "nervous debility." With Speed, he'd believed strongly that his friend had found a good woman and that he needed to stiffen his resolve and marry her. "I believe now," he wrote Speed, "that, had you understood my case at the time" — that is, the winter of 1840–1841 — "as well as I understood yours afterwards, by the aid you would have given me, I should have sailed through clear; but that does not now afford me sufficient confidence, to begin that, or the like of that again." In October, he wrote to Speed again. Eight months into his marriage, Lincoln knew that Speed must be happier, "for without, you would not be living." Still, he wanted to know: "'Are you now, in *feeling* as well as *judgment*, glad you are married as you are?' From any body but me, this would be an impudent question not to be tolerated; but I know you will pardon it in me. Please answer it quickly as I feel impatient to know."

As hard as Lincoln had worked to dissect the nature of suffering and mental health, he found himself in much the same place he'd been around that "fatal first of Jany. '41." Beset by the big questions about his future, the travails of ordinary life came hard upon him. Bowling Green, his friend and mentor from New Salem, died in 1842, and Green's Masonic lodge held a funeral in early September. Lincoln came to deliver a eulogy, but soon after he stood up and began to speak, he "commenced choaking & sobbing," said one observer. He told the mourners that he was "un-manned" and could not proceed. Other scenes made Lincoln's friends look on him with alarm. James Matheny, who worked across the hall from Lincoln, often saw him alone in his law office, deep in thought, and with a tortured look on his face — the word Matheny used was "glooming." He worried that Lincoln would kill himself.

It was the first election-year fall in ten years in which Lincoln had no campaign to run, no stump speeches to give, no constituents to court. He had plenty of time to think, which may have done him more harm than good. "I think if I were you," he had written Speed, "in case my mind were not exactly right, I would avoid being *idle*; I would immediately engage in some business, or go to making preparation for it, which would be the same thing." This age-old prescription for melancholy has been often repeated. The idea is to try to set the mind on a concrete project, something outside oneself. Otherwise, the morbid, self-accusing, hopeless thoughts can take on a life of their own, creating a frenetic powerlessness, the mental equivalent of an insect trying to work its way out of a spider's web.

Trapped by temperament and circumstance, Lincoln chose a way out, not with relief but with resignation. In early November, he went to his friend James Matheny and said to him, "Jim, I shall have to marry that girl." Other incidents round out the picture of Lincoln's attitude toward his matrimony. A boy who saw Lincoln dressing for his wedding asked him where he was going. Lincoln answered, "To Hell, I suppose." According to Matheny, who was his best man, "Lincoln looked and acted as if he was going to the Slaughter." Nevertheless, as he had advised Speed earlier in the year, he got through the ceremony calmly, at least calmly enough not to excite alarm in any present. At Ninian and Elizabeth Edwards's mansion on the hill — where, three years before, Lincoln had first come to know Mary Todd — they stood as bride and groom. Charles Dresser, an Episcopalian minister, presided. Lincoln offered up a ring engraved "A. L. to Mary, Nov 4. 1842, Love is Eternal."

CHAPTER 6

The Reign of Reason

A CCORDING TO A POPULAR psychological theory of Lincoln's day, the human mind had three powers, called "faculties." In good health, they fell into line in a strict hierarchy. The highest faculty, called reason, regulated both the "mechanical faculties," including reflexes and instincts, and the "animal faculties," including desires and emotions. The catchall term for everything that needed subduing was "passions." A good life demanded cultivating the virtues of reason and keeping unruly passions in check, with the aim of constructing a balanced character.

As a young man, Lincoln loudly declared his allegiance to the powers of reason, which were especially valued in the moral and political program of the American Whigs. In a speech delivered in 1838, "The Perpetuation of Our Political Institutions," Lincoln considered the benefits brought by the American Revolution, in which people had let out much deep-rooted hate and a wish for revenge, channeling these passions into a fight against the British for civil and religious liberty. Heirs to the Revolution, Lincoln said, must see that passion could help them no more. "It will in future be our enemy. Reason, cold, calculating, unimpassioned reason, must furnish all the materials for our future support and defence."

In 1842, Lincoln returned to the theme, this time in a discussion of intemperance. With kind words for those in the grip of their passions, he urged that the "most powerful moral effort" be summoned to counteract them. Instructing drunkards to subdue their "fixed habits, or burning appetites" and others to aid them by taking the temperance pledge, Lincoln said that such concerted action could lead to a "moral freedom" surpassing the political freedom gained by the Revolution. With judicious self-control, he said, "every son of earth shall drink in rich fruition the sorrow-quenching draughts of perfect liberty." "Happy day," he concluded his speech, "when — all appetites controlled, all poisons subdued, all matter subjected — *mind*, all conquering *mind*, shall live and move, the monarch of the world. Glorious consummation! Hail, fall of Fury! Reign of Reason, all hail!"

But as he spoke these encomiums to reason, his own passions were running wild. During his first breakdown, said Robert B. Rutledge, "many of his friends feared that reason would desert her throne," using a common image for insanity. In his courtships with Mary Owens and Mary Todd, Lincoln bemoaned his inability to control himself. He often gave way to physical and emotional impulses. In 1840, he once mocked an opponent so mercilessly that the man left the scene crying, an episode Lincoln sorely regretted. Another pang of regret came when he heaped such disdain on a political opponent that the man challenged him to a duel. His reign of reason had not yet begun.

His decision to marry was a big turning point. And the miserable reserve Lincoln exhibited at the ceremony itself was the very picture of the manly self-denial he would come to embody. James Matheny observed that as a young man Lincoln showed "fancy, emotion, and imagination," but as he got older he grew more abstracted and contemplative. This development was tied to a change in the nature of his melancholy. In Lincoln's middle years, a loud insistence on his own woe evolved into a quiet, disciplined yearning. He yoked his feelings to a style of severe self-control, articulating a melancholy that was, more than anything, philosophical. He saw the world as a sad, difficult place from which he expected considerable suffering. "There was a strong tinge of sadness in Mr Lincolns composition," said his friend Joseph Gillespie. "He felt very strongly that there was more of discomfort than real happiness in human existence under the most favorable circumstances and the general current of his reflections was in that channel." In the late 1850s, a girl named Rosa Haggard, the daughter of a hotel proprietor in Winchester, Illinois, asked Lincoln to sign her autograph album. Lincoln took the book and wrote:

> To Rosa —
> You are young, and I am older;
>   You are hopeful, I am not —
> Enjoy life, ere it grows colder —
>   Pluck the roses ere they rot.

From the perspective of modern clinicians, the persistence and quality of Lincoln's symptoms call for a new diagnostic framework. Major depressive disorder, which applies to Lincoln's earlier years, best describes a series of discrete episodes, even if they go on for many months at a time. But when a condition lasts for more than two years, even with some breaks in symptoms, it is considered to be a chronic depression. Episodic and chronic depressions have much in common, but the distinction matters. Imagine a person who begins to travel abroad as a tourist. The first few trips are memorable — when they started, how long they lasted. But if the trips grow in frequency and duration, at some point the tourist would become known as an expatriate. The destination need not have changed, but the nature of the journey would call for a qualitative, not just a quantitative, distinction.

As it turns out, the "land" of chronic depression is one for which few guidebooks have been written. The psychologist James P. McCullough, Jr., one authority on the condition, describes it as "grossly misdiagnosed, understudied, and undertreated." This poses both a challenge and an opportunity in the study of Lincoln. The existing literature can't definitively contextualize his experience. But his life, supplemented with the shards of knowledge on chronic depression, can offer a new and valuable context. In particular, it shows how depression, for good and for ill, can blend slowly, subtly, but surely with a person as he works to bring himself into balance.

One crucial distinction between major depression and chronic depression is that, in the latter, one largely ceases to howl in protest that the world is hard or painful. Rather, one becomes accustomed to it, expecting such hardship and greeting it with, at best, a stoic determination. As the influential psychiatrist Emil Kraepelin wrote in 1921, people with a depressive temperament see life as "a burden which they habitually bear with dutiful self-denial without being compensated by the pleasure(s) of existence."

This phrase captures a quality that began to show up increasingly in Lincoln in the years following his marriage. It was no coincidence. For many men in the early nineteenth century, as we have seen, marriage brought a sharply new material environment (the man had to lead and provide for his family) and a new emotional environment. Before marriage, young men had a fair amount of latitude when it came to expressing the "feminine" qualities of tenderness, vulnerability, and emotional volatility. After marriage, though, the reins of expectation tightened. According to the 1828 *Webster's*, females were the "humane, tender" sex, while the male was "master of his mental powers." A married man had to act like a man.

Abraham and Mary Lincoln took these sex-specific cultural roles almost to the point of caricature. As a single young woman, Mary Todd had been known as bright, studious, and ambitious. Insistently and playfully, she defied society's rigid expectations for a southern belle. She openly participated in politics, though she admitted it to be "rather an unladylike profession." She flirted with men she liked, regardless of their background. (Many women of her class would have seen Lincoln as unsuitable.) Once she caused twitters in Springfield when, unable to walk the muddy streets, she hitched a ride in the back of a horse-drawn cart, allowing herself to be delivered home like a bale of hay. Such avenues for self-assertion and idiosyncrasy were closed to her after marriage. By law, she became an extension of her husband. By tradition, she became the steward of their household. They moved into a small room in the Globe Tavern, a boarding house that served communal meals for a weekly fee. Mary Lincoln — historians always call her Mary Todd Lincoln, though she never again used her maiden name — quickly became pregnant, perhaps as soon as her wedding night. This considerably augmented the major change in her circumstances. A woman with child was not supposed to be seen in public. For this twenty-four-year-old so used to gallivanting about, it may have been a shock. Even her private life had always been social: dining at her father's table, going to fancy schools in Lexington, attending parties at her sister's home in Springfield. Now she had only one steady companion, her husband, and he was gone for many weeks of the year on business.

The Lincolns had their first child in August 1843, a boy they named Robert Todd Lincoln, known as Bob. In 1844, they bought a cottage at Eighth and Jackson streets in Springfield. It had three rooms on the ground floor and two rooms in a half loft upstairs. The house was painted light brown with dark green shutters. The back yard had a small stable and a privy. A white picket fence ran around the property. In 1846, they had a second son, Edward Baker Lincoln, whom they called Eddie. As the family grew, Lincoln's time at home shrank. Twice a year, he traveled the eighth judicial circuit, an 830-mile journey through fourteen counties, with a group of lawyers and judges who held court sessions in town after town. "Riding the circuit" was no small project. In the year

Eddie was born, he was gone all of April, most of May, a week in June, a week in July, three weeks in October, and a week each in November and December. In 1850, records place him in Springfield for only 100 days, while he was away for at least 175 days. In a rare but touching acknowledgment of the distance between them, Mary Lincoln once said that if her husband had spent more time at home, she could "love him better."

Even those who know next to nothing about Lincoln do know that he had a troubled wife who was eventually committed to an asylum. Upon hearing of Lincoln's melancholy, many people ask whether his marriage caused it. Clearly not. As we have seen, his melancholy emerged before he met his future wife. But as in any long-standing relationship, the partners influenced each other. The influence he had on her, and the intricacies of Mary Lincoln's psychological life, deserve their own study. Considering her influence on him, we should not take for granted its prosaic and salutary aspects. She presided over a well-run home, taking care of chores, supervising a servant (they usually kept one), and raising the boys. This was hard work that, when done best, got little attention. She also was widely regarded to have been a spur to her husband's career, prompting him to keep at his youthful ambitions. We know from William Herndon that Lincoln's ambition was a "little engine that knew no rest," but we also know from Herndon that the engine was continually retooled at home, for his wife was "in fact endowed with a more restless ambition than he."

The same qualities that drew the couple together in the first place — a shared love of poetry, for instance — animated their lives. Both cared deeply for their boys. The few letters from him to her that survive — an unknown number were burned — show glimpses of affection, albeit couched in paternalistic endearments. Once while away from home, Lincoln heard that his wife wished to join him. He wrote to her, "Will you be a good girl in all things, if I consent? Then come along, and that as soon as possible. Having got the idea in my head, I shall be impatient till I see you . . . Come on just as soon as you can. I want to see you, and our dear — *dear* boys very much." When he was president, she was often away, and he once sent a similar message: "I really wish to see you." As Michael Burlingame has pointed out, these are mere spoonfuls compared to the ladles of romance doled out by many of Lincoln's colleagues to their wives.

And the Lincolns' marriage had barrels of difficulties, exacerbated by her volatility and his withdrawal. She had long teetered between emotional extremes. "She was very highly strung, nervous, impulsive, excitable," said her cousin Margaret Stuart, who grew up with her, "having an emotional temperament much like an April day, sunning all over with laughter one moment, the next crying as though her heart would break." In Springfield, she became known for these mood swings. "As we used familiarly to state it," said O. H. Browning, "she was always 'either in the garret or cellar.'" After her marriage, she seemed to have a kind of tripwire surrounding her. Easily triggered, it set off tantrums of sadness, fear, and anger veering toward rage. She often shouted at her servants and at her husband, and even struck him for, say, bringing home a poor cut of meat or ignoring her call to tend the fire. She had a "very violent temper," said her cousin John Stuart.

Lincoln's main strategy was to ignore her. Sometimes, when she had what he called "one of her nervous spells," he would stay away for days at a time. He kept a couch in his office that was long enough for him to sleep on. "If she became excited or troublesome," explained their neighbor James Gourley, ". . . he would apparently pay no attention to her. Frequently, he would laugh at her, which is a risky thing to do in the face of an infuriated wife; but generally, if her impatience continued, he would pick up one of the children and deliberately leave home as if to take a walk." The withdrawal seems to have provoked his wife further — as Gourley understood, the last thing an angry person wants is to be scoffed at or ignored.

But Lincoln put his stock in enduring domestic trouble without complaint. Once Mary Lincoln slapped a servant girl whose work dissatisfied her. The girl went home and complained to her father, a man named Jacob Taggart, who came to investigate. Soon enough, he, too, provoked Mrs. Lincoln's wrath, and she struck him with a broom. Taggart stormed out and went looking for Lincoln, to whom he angrily recounted what had happened. Hearing the story, Lincoln hung his head and said something to the effect of, "Can't you endure this one wrong done you while I have had to bear it without complaint for lo these many years?" Sympathetic, Taggart immediately dropped the matter.

Lincoln did little to cultivate intimacy with his wife, or with any other person. His colleagues on the circuit, though they liked and admired him, also felt an impassable distance from him. The one relationship that had obviously transcended business, with Joshua Speed, was by the late 1840s clearly a thing of the past. Physical separation ruled out the kind of day-to-day intimacy that they had once enjoyed. And their letters grew increasingly infrequent. Lincoln identified a reason in an 1846 letter to Speed: "You, no doubt, assign the suspension of our correspondence to the true philosophical cause." Speed had become a Kentucky planter and a slave owner, which created the conditions for all kinds of ideological divides from an Illinois Whig. Without more details on this "philosophical cause," though, the significance of the letter is the dissipation of their bond. Lincoln wrote to Speed: "It must be confessed, by both of us, that this is rather a cold reason for allowing a friendship, such as ours, to die by degrees." By then the friendship seemed mostly dead.

The key feature of Lincoln's life in the 1840s and early 1850s was his hard work at politics and the law. Though major depression is often associated with lethargy to the point of being frozen, many people with chronic depression not only work well but devote more energy to their vocation than to any other endeavor. The psychologist Hagop S. Akiskal, who has written widely on the condition, notes that chronic depressives "seem to derive personal gratification from over-dedication to professions that require greater service and suffering on behalf of other people." Many chronic depressives say that they feel empty in every realm *except* their work. Akiskal proposes that two factors might lead to such a "mono-categorical existence." Depressives might withdraw from social pursuits until work is all that's left, or work might be a compensatory response — an asset that is conscientiously developed and protected.

Both factors apply to Lincoln. His social network, such as it was, largely radiated around his work. "Friend," in Lincoln's letters, is used to refer to political allies and contacts. When he modified the term, as in "personal friend," "particular friends," "most highly valued friends," or "partial friends," it was to emphasize the depth of ties and loyalty. "The better part of one's life consists of his friendships," Lincoln wrote in the midst of a dispute with a man whom he judged "one of the most cherished." The man was no intimate of Lincoln's, but a partner of long standing. Political work also provided an outlet for Lincoln's talent. "Every man is proud of what he does *well*," Lincoln said, "and no man is proud of what he does *not* do well. With the former, his heart is in his work; and he will do twice as much of it with less fatigue. The latter performs a little imperfectly, looks at it in disgust, turns from it, and imagines himself exceedingly tired." For insight into the melancholy of day-to-day life, Byron and Poe had nothing on Lincoln.

In February 1843, a few days after his thirty-fourth birthday, Lincoln wrote an ally a letter that nicely captured the frankness of his ambition. "Now if you should hear any one say that Lincoln don't want to go to Congress, I wish you as a personal friend of mine, would tell him you have reason to believe he is mistaken. The truth is, I would like to go very much." His campaign never got off the ground. He was rebuffed by his own county delegation, which sent the name of Lincoln's colleague Edward Baker to the district-wide convention. There, another candidate, John Hardin, prevailed. The results meant that Lincoln would have to wait for both men to serve in Congress before he had his own clear shot at the seat. "The people of Sangamon," Lincoln wrote, "have cast me off."

Three years later, after great effort, Lincoln did become the Whig nominee for the House of Representatives. (Baker stepped aside to make way for him, and shortly afterward, Lincoln named his son after this special friend.) In the general election, he won with fifty-six percent of the vote. He was thirty-seven years old and headed to Washington, where he would take a seat in the same Congress with such dearly respected elders as John Quincy Adams, Henry Clay, and Daniel Webster. Yet Lincoln's only extant personal reaction to the victory came in a letter to Joshua Speed. "Being elected to Congress," he wrote — in the same letter that noted the death by degrees of their friendship — "though I am very grateful to our friends, for having done it, has not pleased me as much as I expected."

Why would he be less pleased than he expected? Lincoln had, some years before, noted to Speed that they both had the "peculiar misfortune" of dreaming dreams of Elysium "far exceeding all that any thing earthly can realize." In other words, they wanted things not only beyond what was realistic but beyond what was humanly possible. In itself, such an unquenchable thirst is an old quality, the stuff of countless myths and tragedies. The reverse of a constant desire for more and better is an ennui that comes with achievement. In a famous example, Lincoln's contemporary John Stuart Mill realized, at age twenty, that if he accomplished all his goals, he would still feel no great joy or happiness. "At this," he wrote in his autobiography, "my heart sank within me. The end had ceased to charm, and how could there ever again be any interest in the means?" He fell into a deep depression that lasted most of a year.

While many people feel a letdown after a success or an achievement, research on chronic depression shows that for dysthymics, the letdowns can be more severe. What looks to the world like a triumph, many depressed people see as merely another step on an unending ladder. In extreme cases, a dramatic achievement can create as strong a sense of dislo-cation and loneliness as would a dramatic setback, and may lead to suicide.

The period around Lincoln's election — that is, just after he could rea-sonably expect to win the seat in Congress — was marked by more than the usual introspection. Just days after he sewed up the nomination, he began to produce poetry concerned with the inevitability of suffering and the elusiveness of emotional peace. All told, one is left with the sense that, rather than the first step toward an illustrious future, Lincoln took his election as another indication that the earthly world had no real plea-sure in store for him. Remember, according to his friend Joseph Gillespie, he didn't merely maintain that the world was full of discomfort and dif-ficulty; he said that such was the case even "under the most favorable cir-cumstances." The paradox, then, is that a strong step forward could in fact serve to powerfully illustrate the inability of accomplishments to sat-isfy him.

Lincoln's experience in Washington tended to underscore rather than dissipate his innate dissatisfaction. The major issue of his first session was the war against Mexico, which the Democratic president, James K. Polk, launched in 1846. Whigs were suspicious of Polk's motives and questioned his justification for the war — that Mexico had fired on U.S. troops on American soil. Lincoln made himself a visible element of the Whig opposition, giving a speech that accused Polk of lying and war-mongering. Opposing a war is rarely good politics. Lincoln's timing proved to be especially unfortunate. Two weeks after a speech in which he demanded to know precisely where the war had started — by way of challenging Polk's justification — a courier arrived in Washington with a peace treaty that announced it had ended, with outstanding terms for the United States, which gained a vast swath of new territory.

Lincoln soon heard that his position on the war was hurting him in Illinois. He pronounced some other disappointing political news as "heart-sickening." Indeed, his work seemed to bring little pleasure. He gave a speech on internal improvements "which," he wrote, "I shall send home as soon as I can get it written out and printed and which I suppose nobody will read." The one clearly personal letter of his first term showed a broader sense of displeasure. Though his wife and two boys at first ac-companied him to Washington, they decamped after a few months to Lexington, Kentucky, where she had family. In April 1848, Lincoln wrote her a letter that began: "In this troublesome world, we are never quite satisfied. When you were here I thought you hindered me some in attending to business; but now, having nothing but business — no variety — it has grown exceedingly tasteless to me. I hate to sit down and direct documents, and I hate to stay in this old room by myself."

Even a hot presidential race was strangely depressing. At their convention in the summer of 1848, the Whigs had a chance to nominate two party heroes who were personal favorites of Lincoln's: Daniel Webster and Henry Clay. However, they passed over these men, choosing instead Zachary Taylor, a general and slave owner whose reputation rested solely on his association with President Polk's war. On a plank that contained no statement of party principles or policies, the Whigs ran a candidate who had no political record. Knowing that he was the most electable, Lincoln backed Taylor.

When Congress met again in 1849, Lincoln made a move to secure a lasting achievement. He authored a bill that would gradually free slaves in the District of Columbia while providing compensation to their owners. But his support fell away — he was "abandoned," Lincoln said — even before he introduced the bill. Lincoln went home from Congress with no great standing among voters. He had previously committed himself to serve only one term. Had he run again, he probably would have lost. He told Herndon that he had committed "political suicide." Most scholars see Lincoln's stint in Congress as a respectable first term. From his own point of view, though, Lincoln found himself in a political hole.

Even the one piece of good political news quickly turned sour. President Taylor, whom Lincoln had backed enthusiastically, won the election in November 1848 and took office in March 1849. Lincoln earnestly sought a position, for himself or one of his allies, as head of the General Land Office. When he learned that a Whig who had opposed Taylor was being considered for the position, he objected strenuously. "It will now mortify me deeply," he wrote, "if Gen. Taylor's administration shall trample all my wishes in the dust." His wishes were trampled in the dust. As a consolation, he was offered the governorship of the newly organized Oregon Territory. His wife opposed the move, and Lincoln turned the job down. He said later that, at this moment, he was "disgusted" with politics and that he'd made up his mind to "retire" and practice law. This was an astonishing claim. For nearly two decades, politics had not been merely an avocation for Lincoln but the center of his existence, the arena where he focused both his day-to-day attention and his long-term hopes to contribute to a lasting good for which he would be re-membered. Outside politics, Lincoln had little prospect for achieving that goal.

If Lincoln thought he had hit bottom with his poor showing in Congress, he soon experienced a sharper, personal loss. On February 1, 1850, three-year-old Eddie Lincoln died after a long illness. Given Lincoln's history, we might expect that the death would have thrown him profoundly off balance. After all, the death of Ann Rutledge, along with other factors, had precipitated his first breakdown fifteen years before. Yet in William Herndon's voluminous oral histories, in which Rutledge's death is men-tioned scores of times, Eddie's death comes up not once. This does not mean that Lincoln didn't express any grief, but it does suggest that he said or did little that registered with his contemporaries. In his writings, there are only two mentions of his son's death — the second when he left Springfield for Washington, D.C., in 1861, and the first in a brief note to his stepbrother John Johnston. "As you make no mention of it," Lincoln wrote on February 23, 1850, "I suppose you had not learned that we lost our little boy. He was sick fifty two days & died the morning of the first day of this month. It was not our *first,* but our second child. We miss him very much."

Two years later, Lincoln learned that his father was sick and dying. Three letters came to Springfield imploring Lincoln to visit. He finally wrote to his stepbrother that he hadn't replied "because it appeared to me I could write nothing which could do any good." He could not visit because he was too busy with his work, but said to give his father this message: "Say to him that if we could meet now, it is doubtful whether it would not be more painful than pleasant; but that if it be his lot to go now, he will soon have a joyous meeting with many loved ones gone be-fore; and where the rest of us, through the help of God, hope ere-long to join them." Tom Lincoln died five days later. His son did not attend his funeral or mark his grave.

To some extent, Lincoln's muted reaction can be accounted for by cul-tural norms. Death, in the mid-nineteenth century, was much more likely than today to be accepted as a decree of God, to be suffered quietly. Yet even by the standards of his contemporaries, Lincoln became known, as he grew older, as a man of profound emotional reserve. At New Salem in the mid-1830s, he had been seen as frank and "open souled." In Springfield, a decade later, he appeared — in Herndon's oft-cited phrase

— to be "the most secretive — reticent — shut-mouthed man that ever existed." Joseph Gillespie, who found his friend to be temperamentally gloomy, said, "If he had griefs he never spoke of them in general conversation," and "He was tender-hearted without much shew of sensibility."

Mary Lincoln put her finger on the crucial dynamic. With all of her husband's "deep feeling," she said, "he was *not*, a demonstrative man, when he felt most deeply, he expressed, the least." Lincoln developed this tendency — or perhaps we should say this tendency developed him — in concert with a range of related qualities. By a combination of idea, effort, and force of experience, he began sometime in his mid- to late thirties actually to live under the "reign of reason" that he had so dramatically called for as a young man. "His reason and his logic," said his friend James Matheny, "swallowed up all his being." This captured a dominant visual image of Lincoln by people who knew him well in his middle years, which was perhaps the most profound and frequent indication of his melancholy.

From 1845 to 1847, a young man named Gibson Harris worked with Lincoln and his law partner, William Herndon, as a clerk. Spending his days in the firm's cluttered second-floor room above the post office on Springfield's center square, Harris soon noticed that Lincoln would regularly slip away from conversation and fall into what Harris called one of his "blue spells." His face, Harris wrote, "wore a sad, or more correctly a far-away, expression, that made one long to wake him up, as it were, and bring him back to his accustomed geniality and winning smile." Harris didn't consider the spells to be very serious. "It took me no great time," he said, "to learn that a very slight thing would break up his brooding."

That brooding — the silent, penetrating mood of melancholy and the look that came with it — became more intense as time went on. "Soberness of thought Commenced Growing on Mr Lincoln I think When he was Elected to Congress," said his friend Abner Ellis. When Lincoln returned from Washington, Ellis said, he brought back with him "That Star gazing thinking Look, as if Looking at vacancy." Around the same time, Mary Lincoln's nephew Presley Edwards observed that one of Lincoln's chief features was "a far-away, absent minded look, scarcely to be classed as sad, yet falling little short of it." Three years later, in 1851, Edwards saw Lincoln again and thought the look had intensified.

By the mid-1850s — Lincoln's mid-forties — the cast of his face and body when in repose suggested deep, abiding gloom to nearly all who crossed his path. The young lawyer Henry C. Whitney first met Lincoln around this time. In his memoirs, Whitney recounted an afternoon in the spring of 1855 at court in Bloomington, Illinois. He had recently arrived in Illinois and was getting to know the characters at the bar. "I was sitting with John T. Stuart" — Lincoln's first law partner — "while a case was being tried," Whitney recalled, "and our conversation was, at the moment, about Lincoln, when Stuart remarked that he was a hopeless victim of melancholy. I expressed surprise, to which Stuart replied; 'Look at him, now.'" Whitney turned and saw Lincoln sitting by himself in a corner of the room, "wrapped in abstraction and gloom." Whitney watched him for a while. "It appeared," he wrote, "as if he was pursuing in his mind some specific, sad subject, regularly and systematically through various sinuosities, and his sad face would assume, at times, deeper phases of grief: but no relief came from dark and despairing melancholy, till he was roused by the breaking up of court, when he emerged from his cave of gloom and came back, like one awakened from sleep, to the world in which he lived, again."

Another time, Whitney shared a bed with Lincoln at a Danville, Illinois, inn on a cold night. Whitney remembered, "One morning, I was awakened early — before daylight — by my companion sitting up in bed, his figure dimly visible by the ghostly firelight, and talking the wildest and most incoherent nonsense all to himself. A stranger to Lincoln would have supposed he had suddenly gone insane. Of course, I knew Lincoln and his idiosyncrasies, and felt no alarm." Five minutes later, Lincoln jumped out of bed, washed himself, and put on his clothes. Then he laid some wood on the fire and sat beside it, "moodily, dejectedly, in a most somber and gloomy spell," Whitney observed, "till the breakfast bell rang, when he started, as if from sleep, and went with us to breakfast."

Descriptions of these moods are a staple of reminiscences of Lincoln. A journalist named Jesse Weik, who interviewed dozens of Lincoln's close associates, concluded, "The most marked and prominent feature in Lincoln's organization was his predisposition to melancholy or at least the appearance thereof as indicated by his facial expression when sitting alone and thus shut off from conversation with other people. It was a characteristic peculiar as it was pronounced. Almost every man in Illinois I met . . . reminded me of it . . . My inquiry on this subject among Lincoln's close friends convinced me that men who never saw him could scarcely realize this tendency to melancholy, not only as reflected in his facial expression, but as it affected his spirits and well being."

Accounts of Lincoln's spells have several points in common. First, they portray Lincoln in the company of other people and appearing oblivious to their presence. Jonathan Birch, who knew Lincoln, said that he could often be seen surrounded by a group of men, listening in rapt attention to one of his inimitable stories. His eyes would be lit up with laughter. Just an hour later, Birch recounted, "he might be seen in the same place or in some law office near by, but, alas, how different! His chair, no longer in the center of the room, would be leaning back against the wall; his feet drawn up and resting on the front rounds so that his knees and chair were about on a level; his hat tipped slightly forward as if to shield his face; his eyes no longer sparkling with fun or merriment, but sad and downcast and his hands clasped around his knees. There, drawn up within himself as it were, he would sit, the very picture of dejection and gloom. Thus absorbed have I seen him sit for hours at a time."

A second common feature of these accounts is that even those close to Lincoln did not approach or interrupt him, but rather left him, as one said, "severely alone." "No one ever thought of breaking the spell by speech," said Birch, "for by his moody silence and abstraction he had thrown about him a barrier so dense and impenetrable no one dared to break through." His colleagues were deeply respectful of his moods, none more so than William Herndon. "I could always realize when he was in distress, without being told," Herndon recalled. "He was not exactly an early riser, that is, he never appeared at the office till about nine o'clock in the morning. I usually preceded him an hour. Sometimes, however, he would come down as early as seven o'clock — in fact, on one occasion I remember he came down before daylight . . . He would either be lying on the lounge looking skyward, or doubled up in a chair with his feet resting on the sill of a back window. He would not look up on my entering, and only answered my 'Good morning' with a grunt." Herndon would go about his business, "but the evidence of his melancholy and distress was so plain, and his silence so significant, that I would grow restless myself, and finding some excuse to go to the courthouse or elsewhere, would leave the room."

The door of their office had a window, with a calico curtain hung on brass rings. Leaving, Herndon drew the curtain across the glass, leaving Lincoln "alone in his gloom." He continued, "I would stay away — say an hour, and then I would go into the office on one pretense or another and if Lincoln did not then speak I did as before — go away &c. In the course of another hour I would go back and if Lincoln spoke I knew it was all over." Thus did Lincoln move through middle age, evincing a melancholy that, as Henry Whitney said, "was part of his nature and could no more be shaken off than he could part with his brains."

In all the accounts of Lincoln's gloomy spells, there exists not a single instance in which one of his friends or colleagues asked him what he was *thinking* about. If the true experience of his melancholy is a canvas, the details of what people saw are but dabs of color surrounded by a gaping white space. The feelings that emanated from him, which set off such strong feelings in others, undeniably show that he was suffering — but from what? We could theorize, but it would be like taking a brush to a grand, haunting work by an old master. Better to stand back and observe.

As we do so, it's worth pointing out that his "blue spells," while in one sense an indication of melancholy, may also have represented a response to it. Paradoxically, such obvious suffering may actually have been the visible side of Lincoln's effort to contain his dark feelings and thoughts — to wrestle privately with his moods until they passed or lightened. "With depression," writes the psychologist David B. Cohen, "recovery may be a matter of shifting from protest to more effective ways of mastering helplessness." Lincoln was indeed extremely effective. He worked consistently and well in his law practice, representing a range of clients from railroads to needy old friends. Though not the kind of work that generally gets into the history books, it did bring the prosaic satisfactions of everyday contact and at times the stirring sense of justice done. Lincoln also worked assiduously to develop his mind, carrying with him around the circuit, in the early 1850s, the first six books of Euclid's *Elements,* which move from definitions to postulates to axioms to proofs. In Lincoln's time, this text represented the apex of logical rigor. Studying such topics as the side-angle-side proof of triangle congruency, the Pythagorean theorem and its converse, and the properties of circles, he came to master them, a quiet triumph of reason in an unreasonable world.

CHAPTER 7

The Vents of My Moods and Gloom

A T A TIME WHEN newspapers were stuffed with ads for substances to cure all manner of ailments, it wouldn't have been unusual for Lincoln to seek help at the pharmacy. In at least one case he did, taking a pill known as the "blue mass," a ubiquitous treatment prescribed for everything from tuberculosis to hypochondriasis. These small round pills, about the size of a peppercorn, were made of pure ground mercury with a bit of rosewater and honey added for flavor. The blue mass was supposed to ameliorate melancholy by clearing black bile out of the body — laxative and antidepressant all at once.

Lincoln may have tried other medicines for his melancholy over the years. He didn't drink alcohol for pleasure, but he did drink occasionally for medicinal reasons. In the vernacular of his time, he "drank his dram." At least once in Washington, he drank a glass of champagne for his nerves, at a doctor's recommendation. Lincoln also had a charge account at the Corneau and Diller drugstore, at 122 South Sixth Street in Springfield, where he bought a number of substances, including opiates, camphor, sarsaparilla, and, on one occasion, fifty cents' worth of cocaine. In 1899, when Merck & Company published its first *Manual of the Materia Medica*, these substances were all listed as treatments for melancholia. It would have been unexceptional for Lincoln to have taken such medicines for ongoing pain in body and mind. Opium in particular was considered indispensable, in small doses, for chronic mental conditions. And all medicines were what we now consider to be "over the counter," since the federal government didn't regulate food or drugs until 1906. Still, while the charge account is suggestive, no record exists of Lincoln's actually using these substances. He may have bought them for his wife or children.

To whatever extent Lincoln used medicines, his essential view of melancholy discounted the possibility of transformation by an external agent. He believed that his suffering proceeded inexorably from his constitution, that it was his lot to bear. "You flaxen men with broad faces are born with cheer, and don't know a cloud from a star," he once said to a visitor at the White House. "I am of another temperament." The main therapies Lincoln employed reflected this understanding. He told stories and jokes, studiously gathering new material from talented peers and printed sources. And he gave voice to his melancholy, reading, reciting, and composing poetry that dwelled on themes of death, despair, and human futility. These strategies offered him relief, sustenance, and a movement toward wisdom.

Still, he neither cured his underlying problem nor eliminated his symptoms. Somewhat in the way that insulin allows diabetics to maintain their lives without eliminating the underlying problem, humor and poetry gave Lincoln succor without taking away his need for it. Rather than quash his conflicts, his therapies may actually have heightened them, for these were not medical strategies but moral and existential ones. Faced with questions about the meaning of his life, Lincoln chose responses that engaged many of the same questions. Thus did "therapy" and "malady" come together in Lincoln's journey toward wholeness.

The idea of humor as a therapy has deep roots. "A merry heart doeth good like a medicine," instructs Proverbs. In *The Taming of the Shrew*, Shakespeare wrote, "And frame your mind to mirth and merriment, which bars a thousand harms." The mid-nineteenth-century *Manual of Psychological Medicine* refers to the case of a French actor who, despairing and melancholy, seeks help from a physician. The doctor recommends that his patient see a comic play for relief — preferably something with the infectious humor of an actor named Carlini. "Your distemper must be rooted indeed," the doctor says, "if the acting of the lively Carlini does not remove it." This oft-told anecdote identifies humor as an essential weapon against distress, which has been borne out by modern research. Yet the Carlini story also captured how, when applied to melancholy, the medicine shared something essential with the disease. In the story, the patient replies to the doctor, "I am the *very* Carlini whom you recommend me to see; and, while I am capable of filling Paris with mirth and laughter, I am myself the dejected victim of melancholy and chagrin!"

Though we associate humor with pleasure — and for good reason — it's not necessarily a sign of joy to laugh, or to provoke laughter in others. The fact that people laugh when they're sad and cry when they're happy points to a physiological relationship between mirth and sadness. Both are social phenomena. The neuroscientist Robert Provine has shown, for example, that laughter practically disappears in isolation — no matter how happy someone is, she's not likely to laugh alone. And it flowers in groups, though laughing people aren't necessarily in a good mood. Similarly, professional comics, whose job it is to find humor in life, are not typically happy people. "The core of all humor," says Robert Mankoff, the cartoon editor of The New Yorker, "the reason for it all, is unhappiness." Many comic legends — including Buster Keaton, Rodney Dangerfield, and John Belushi — had regular and severe depressions. In a study of professional clowns and comedians, the psychologists Rhoda and Seymour Fisher found these performers often deeply unhappy and alienated, even compared with a control group of noncomic actors. Nor does professional success make the pain go away. Profoundly alienated, comics often described themselves to the Fishers as set apart from life, as though watching it on a movie screen. They channeled this perspective into their work.

Being funny is more than telling jokes. Comics achieve their effect largely by the way they present themselves — the way they see the world, the way they speak and act. A good "bit" is not necessarily a joke. Words that bring on howls of laughter when told by a talented comic might draw awkward silence if told by anyone else. While the style of self-presentation can be cultivated, the basic drive to be funny, for many comics, begins at a young age. This was the case for Lincoln. When he was a teenager, neighbors remembered him commanding crowds with his humor. Once he was at a house-raising and he determined that it was time for work to stop. He started cracking jokes and telling stories, and soon enough the men had all stopped to listen, laughing so hard they cried.

Lincoln learned the art of storytelling in Kentucky and Indiana, by watching his father, the Hanks boys, and his stepbrothers — or perhaps simply by absorbing from the soil what they had absorbed before him. The best stories, he said, came from rural areas and the "country boys" there. A country boy himself, he brought the voice, rhythm, and manner of that place wherever he went. His images were rooted in the realities of rural life. As president, when he heard complaints that masters couldn't make a living without their slaves, Lincoln was reminded of an old Illinois farmer who had the bright idea to turn his hogs into the potato patch, saving the labor of both feeding the hogs and digging up the potatoes. A neighbor asked him what the hogs would do when the ground froze. "Well," the farmer said, "it may come pretty hard on their snouts, but I guess it will be 'root, hog, or die!'" It's poignant to consider that Lincoln, estranged from his father, so often practiced an art he learned, in part, from the old man — "Thomas Lincoln . . . could beat his son telling a story, cracking a joke," said Lincoln's cousin Dennis Hanks — and that a man who traveled so far and suffered so much found his simplest comfort by going home in the landscape of his imagination.

At New Salem, Lincoln quickly established himself as a premier humorist, even in a region known for conspicuous talent. His well of stories never ran dry because he was always refilling it. He gathered material from other people and from books. Though he was saturated in the ethos of the backcountry, the laconic Yankee style also influenced his humor. Once he told a story about an extremely ugly man walking on a narrow road. A woman came by and examined him closely. "You," she said, "are the ugliest man I ever saw." Sadly, the man answered, "Perhaps so, but I can't help that." "No," the woman allowed, "but you might stay at home."

Though many of them were retold, and collected into books during Lincoln's lifetime, the heart of his stories eludes reproduction. You could get down every word, period, and comma, said the lawyer Henry Whitney, "but the real humor perished with Lincoln." The humor came from his voice — he could mimic any accent or vernacular — his timing, his ludicrous facial expressions, his body movements, and his masterly use of the English language. The other reason the stories perished is that so many of them were, as one friend of Lincoln's said, "dirty and smutty," their charge coming from brushing up against taboos. These, of course, were not written down.

He had a great sense of the ludicrous. One time, a fellow lawyer split his pants, and his colleagues, to rib him, began passing around a sheet of paper soliciting donations to buy the "poor but worthy young man" a new pair of trousers. A few people put down their names and pledges before the paper reached Lincoln. He glanced at it, then wrote after his name, "I can contribute nothing to the end in view." In a storytelling session where one witticism led to another, he might have told the one about the man at the theater who put his hat on the adjoining seat, open side up. Becoming engrossed in the play, he failed to note the approach of a well-dressed, heavyset woman. Before he knew it, she had plumped down on his hat. Gazing ruefully at her, he said, "Madam, I could have told you the hat wouldn't fit before you tried it on." A hint of the other kind of jokes he told came in a letter to Lincoln from a colleague in the Thirtieth Congress. "Do you remember the story of the old Virginian stropping his razor on a certain *member* of a young negro's body which you told and connected it with my mission to Brazil . . ." Asking for help getting a job, the man went on, "I want this application to be like your story of the old womans *fish* — get *larger*, the more it is handled."

Lincoln's jokes often played on racial and ethnic stereotypes, a sobering fact today, when such jokes make us wince rather than laugh. "It was the wit he was after," said his lawyer friend Leonard Swett, "the pure jewel, and he would pick it up out of the mud or dirt just as readily as he would from a parlor table."

After his melancholy emerged in his mid-twenties, and took a deeper hold in his thirties, Lincoln turned to humor for help. "Fun and gravity," said his friend Abner Ellis, "grew on him alike." "The ground work of his social nature was Sad," added the lawyer John M. Scott. "But from the fact that he studiously cultivated the humorous it would have been very sad indeed." The phrase "coping mechanism" comes from the function served by a coping, the top of a wall that protects against the elements. Humor gave Lincoln some protection from his mental storms. It distracted him and gave him relief and pleasure. A good story, he said, "has the same effect on me that I think a good square drink of whisky has to the old roper. It puts new life into me . . . good for both the mental and physical digestion." And he often said, "If it were not for these stories — jokes — jests I should die; they give vent — are the vents of my moods & gloom."

Humor also gave Lincoln a way to connect with people. Withdrawal is an essential feature of depression, and once withdrawn a person can grow steadily more awkward in company. Many chronic depressives find simple small talk to be a Herculean challenge. By his late thirties and early forties, Lincoln frequently withdrew into spells of gloom, but he had a sure-fire method to socialize when he wanted to. Herndon, who poignantly described how Lincoln fell into depressions at the law office, said that these spells often ended with him gathering himself up, saying something or other, and then continuing, "Billy, that reminds me of a story." "He would tell it," Herndon remembered, "walk up and down the room laughing the while and now the dark clouds would pass off his withered and wrinkled face."

In repose, Lincoln's face had a cold, chiseled look. When he began a story, however, his eyes lit up and his face twisted and molded itself to capture the character of the tale. He would often be sitting on a dry goods box, and he'd have his legs planted on the floor. But as he went on, he'd draw up his right leg. At the climax or punch line, he would throw his head back, lift his right leg over his left, and let out an unrestrained laugh — "in which," said Robert Wilson, "every one present willing or unwilling were compelled to take part." This picture of a mirthful, story-telling Lincoln played a role in making his melancholy so shocking. No one could truly appreciate the gloom, said the lawyer Orlando B. Ficklin, without seeing the awful contrast between his face in pleasure and in agony. Using shorthand, people often said that Lincoln had two distinct moods. But those who knew him well saw, as Ficklin did, that he "was naturally despondent and sad." It's not that his moods turned in a cycle, as day gives way to night, but that he lived in the night and made a strong effort to bring the sun in. "Gloom and sadness were his predominant state," said Herndon. Another colleague, Ward Lamon, explained that Lincoln would "in special times become cheerful with chums." Then, when they left him, Lamon said, "he would relapse."

Lincoln always laughed at his own jokes. Many comics maintain a strict distance from their own humor, noticing its effect but not really experiencing it. Lincoln ate the meals he made. Actually, it's not clear how much he cared about making other people laugh, but he couldn't do it alone. We associate groups of laughing people with intimacy, but David Davis, Lincoln's longtime colleague, hastened to point out that he remained essentially a solitary man. Noting that Lincoln swapped jokes with all kinds of people, Davis insisted, "It was wit & joke meeting & loving wit & Jokes — not the man for the men. Lincoln used these men merely to whistle off sadness — gloom & unhappiness . . . He used such men as a tool — a thing to satisfy him — to feed his desires, &c."

However naturally humor came to Lincoln, he worked to use it. One time, his sister-in-law Frances Wallace came to the house on Eighth and Jackson and found Lincoln in his rocking chair, abstracted and blue. After twenty minutes or so, Wallace recalled, he "all at once burst out in a joke — though his thoughts were not on a joke." "His mirth to me," said John M. Scott, "always seemed to be put on and did not properly belong there. Like a plant produced in the hot-bed it had an unnatural and luxuriant growth." In other words, the humor wasn't always a complete covering for Lincoln's gloom — keeping it entirely out of view. But it did keep him active. That's why his image of a "vent" is so apt, for his humor served largely to let what was within him circulate, keeping his system in a kind of equilibrium with the environment.

The psychologist George Vaillant, a student of adaptations, or strategies used to combat depression and anxiety, identifies humor as the most effective of all, even among a handful of other "mature strategies." The reason, he explains, is that one can be lively without pushing from one's mind what's painful and real. Indeed, the best jokes often draw on the worst conceivable scenarios. Lincoln once told the tale of a traveler on the frontier who found himself in rough terrain one night. A terrific thunderstorm broke out. His horse refused to go on, and so the man had to proceed on foot in the dark. The peals of thunder were frightful, and only the lightning afforded him clues to find his way. One bolt, which seemed to shatter the earth beneath him, brought the man to his knees. He wasn't a praying man, but he issued a short and clear petition: "O Lord, if it is all the same to you, give us a little more light and a little less noise."

Comics sometimes seem to be like nihilists who will do anything for a laugh. But Rhoda and Seymour Fisher found that they are, in fact, usually obsessed by moral and ethical dilemmas. "A central theme in the comedian's life," the Fishers write, "is whether he is good or evil." Comics also often describe themselves as healers. Jackie Mason's first career was as a rabbi. At a congregation in North Carolina, he started to introduce humor into his sermons — "to lighten the burden," he explained, of "all the misery."

There is meaning to Lincoln's humor as well. He wasn't just melancholy and funny. He used his humor to respond to his melancholy, and drew on his melancholy to fashion a worldview rooted largely in humor. Lincoln frequently joked about people at the mercy of great forces. In court once, Lincoln told a story of an Irish sailor who had been overtaken at sea by a heavy storm. The sailor thought he ought to pray, but didn't know how. So he fell to his knees and said, "Oh Lord! You know as well as meself that it's seldom I bodder ye, but if ye will only hear me and save me this time, bedad it will be a long time before I bodder ye again." The point of these stories was to get a laugh, and a break. They were his "medicine," Lincoln said, and he insisted that other people needed them as much as he did. But even in his diversions Lincoln often revealed his tendency to search for beauty and meaning. As president, he explained why he would pardon soldiers who deserted for cowardice: "It would frighten the poor devils to death to shoot them." Humor brought Lincoln relief while it brought him closer to the nub of life. "For a sense of humor," writes the Lincoln biographer Benjamin Thomas, "connotes an intimate acquaintance with human nature and life, a sense of proportion, and thus of disproportion, a realization of the petty conceits, the affectations, the foibles and weaknesses of men."

Lincoln's other principal therapy grew from the same instincts. On the circuit, after spending much of his day telling stories, Lincoln often turned to poetry at night. He would go to his room, strip off his coat, lie down on the bed, and read by the light of a candle. In the early 1840s, shortly after its publication, Lincoln read Poe's "The Raven." He loved it, recalled John Stuart. He carried a copy around on the circuit and "repeated it over and over." "He never read poetry as a thing of pleasure, except Shakespeare," Stuart said. "He read Poe because it was gloomy." Even with Shakespeare, Lincoln preferred the tragedies. "Some of Shakespeare's plays I have never read," he noted, "while others I have gone over perhaps as frequently as any unprofessional reader. Among the latter are Lear, Richard Third, Henry Eighth, Hamlet, and especially Macbeth. I think nothing equals Macbeth. It is wonderful."

Nearly everyone who spent substantial time with Lincoln after 1845 knew his favorite piece of verse. One powerful story of him reciting the poem comes from Lois Newhall, a member of the Newhall Family troupe of singers. In the fall of 1849, they were on tour in central Illinois, doing "'one night stands' in thriving towns." Lois was one of three sisters in the group, which also featured their father, mother, and brother. A week into the tour, just as the family arrived at a hotel, they saw three men approach on horseback. They were politicians, in town for an event of their own. "As we were in a way public characters," Lois said, "we introduced all around, and that evening — these gentlemen having held their political meeting in the afternoon, attended our concert in one of the local churches." For the next eight days, Lincoln, his colleagues, and the Newhall Family followed the same path, down the same roads and through the same small towns. They came to hear him speak, and he went to hear them sing. After their eighth and final day together, the crowd retired to a tavern. They sat up late in the parlor, singing songs and telling stories. The family sang every song they knew, with Lois playing a melodeon.

"Now Abe," one of Lincoln's colleagues called to him, "you have been listening to these young women for more than a week, and I think it only fair that you should sing them some of your songs."

Lincoln demurred, saying that he never sung a note in his life. But both of his companions stayed on him. "Why over on the Sangamon," one said, "Abe has a great reputation as a singer. It is quite a common thing over there to invite him to farm auctions and have him start off the sale of stock with a good song."

"Naturally," recalled Lois, "we became very eager to have Mr. Lincoln sing." Lincoln looked embarrassed. He stood to leave. "You fellows are trying to make a fool of me," he said, "and I am going to bed." As he walked out, he passed by Lois and she pointed to the melodeon. "Mr. Lincoln," she said, "if you have any song that you can sing I know that I can play the accompaniment for it so as to aid you. If you will just tell me what it is, I can follow you even if I am not familiar with it."

"Why, Miss Newhall," Lincoln answered, "if it was to save my soul from hell, I couldn't imitate a note that you would touch on that. I never sung in my life and never was able to. Those fellows are simply liars."

The room grew quiet. Lincoln was near the door that led to the stairwell, but he didn't leave. "I'll tell you what I'll do for you," he said after a pause. "You girls have been so kind singing for us. I'll repeat to you my favorite poem." Leaning against the doorjamb, which looked small behind his lanky frame, and with his eyes half closed, Lincoln recited a poem from memory.

> O[h] why should the spirit of mortal be proud!
> Like a swift, fleeting meteor — a fast-flying cloud —
> A flash of the lightning — a break of the wave —
> He passeth from life to his rest in the grave.
>
> The leaves of the oak and the willow shall fade,
> Be scattered around, and together be laid;
> And the young and the old, and the low and the high
> Shall molder to dust and together shall lie.

Lincoln first came across the poem — titled after its first line, "Oh why should the spirit of mortal be proud!" — in the early 1830s. Then, in 1845, he saw it in a newspaper, cut it out, and quickly committed it to memory. He didn't know who wrote it, as it had been published without attribution. He repeated the lines so often that people suspected they were his own. "Beyond all question, I am not the author," he wrote. "I would give all I am worth, and go in debt, to be able to write so fine a piece as I think that is." When he was president, Lincoln learned that the poem had been written by William Knox, a Scotsman who died in 1825. Knox self-consciously imitated Ecclesiastes, perhaps the most artful lamentation in the Bible. Compare Ecclesiastes 1:9 —

> The thing that hath been, it is that which shall be;
> And that which is done is that which shall be done;
> And there is no new thing under the sun.

— to Knox's ninth stanza:

> For we are the same thing that our fathers have been
> We see the same sights that our fathers have seen
> We drink the same stream, and we feel the same sun,
> And we run the same course our fathers have run.

The last two verses of the poem were Lincoln's favorites:

> Yea! Hope and despondency, pleasure and pain,
> Are mingled together in sun-shine and rain;
> And the smile and the tear, and the song and the dirge,
> Still follow each other, like surge upon surge.

> 'Tis the wink of an eye, 'tis the draught of a breath,
> From the blossoms of health, to the paleness of death.
> From the gilded saloon, to the bier and the shroud
> Oh, why should the spirit of mortal be proud!

When Lincoln finished, the room was still. "I know that for myself," recalled Lois Newhall, "I was so impressed with the poem that I felt more like crying than talking." She asked, "Mr. Lincoln, who wrote that?" He told her he didn't know, but that if she'd like, he would write out a copy of the poem for her. She was eating pancakes the next morning when she felt something behind her. A great big hand came around her left side and covered hers. Then, with his other hand, Lincoln laid a long piece of blue paper beside her.

Suffering and futility were pervasive themes in American literature of the early nineteenth century. Edgar Allan Poe, Herman Melville, and Nathaniel Hawthorne emerged in this period, as well as many lesser artists, whose work tended toward the lachrymose and maudlin. Melancholy, then, can be considered a cultural, not just an individual, "condition." Still, even among people whose tastes ran to the dark, Lincoln stood out. Knox's poem, one colleague observed, was "a reflex in poetic form of the deep melancholy of his soul." "The music of Lincoln's thought," another colleague noted, "was always in the minor key." Other artists who influenced Lincoln included Thomas Gray, Lord Byron, William Wordsworth, and Oliver Wendell Holmes, Sr., one of whose verses, in the poem "The Last Leaf," Lincoln often recited:

> The mossy marbles rest
> On the lips that he has pressed
>   In their bloom;
> And the names he loved to hear
> Have been carved for many a year
>   On the tomb.

"For pure pathos," Lincoln said, "in my judgment, there is nothing finer than those six lines in the English language." From him, this was a grand compliment.

Lincoln also tried his hand at writing poetry. He may have written a great deal of it, and even published some of it — as shown by the recent discovery of the anonymously published "Suicide's Soliloquy." The one sustained effort we know of grew out of a trip Lincoln took to southern Indiana in October 1844. The Whigs had nominated Henry Clay to run for president. "Thinking I might aid some to carry the State for Mr. Clay," Lincoln wrote, "I went into the neighborhood in that State in which I was raised . . . where my mother and only sister were buried, and from which I had been absent about fifteen years." Lincoln gave a speech in Rockport, an Ohio River town about ten miles from the Lincoln farm. He also visited Gentryville, the town nearest to Little Pigeon Creek. He saw old neighbors, including Nathaniel Grigsby, whose brother had married Lincoln's sister, and the Gentry family, after whom the town had been named.

The trip stuck with Lincoln. On the one hand, he found the area where he had spent his teenage years entirely uninspiring. "That part of the country," he wrote, "is, within itself, as unpoetical as any spot of the earth." Yet the landscape stirred something in him. "Seeing it," he said, "and its objects and inhabitants aroused feelings in me which were certainly poetry; though whether my expression of those feelings is poetry is quite another question."

Perhaps Lincoln's distinction between "feelings in me" and "expression of those feelings" was polite self-deprecation. Or perhaps he intended to signal that his true feelings were ineffable. It is powerful that he described those feelings as "poetry." His contemporary Emily Dickinson defined the word this way: "If I read a book [and] it makes my whole body so cold no fire ever can warm me, I know *that* is poetry. If I feel physically as if the top of my head were taken off, I know *that* is poetry. These are the only way I know it. Is there any other way."

Lincoln said he wasn't sure he had constructed the poem properly. Indeed, that longing for something elusive, and grappling with the knowledge that it will forever remain so, was the subject of his poem, which began:

> My childhood's home I see again,
> And gladden with the view;
> And still, as memory crowds my brain,
> There's sadness in it too.
>
> O Memory! thou midway world
> 'Twixt earth and paradise,
> Where things decayed and loved ones lost
> In dreamy shadows rise.

Lincoln worked from a common form, recalling an early home, the distant images of childhood, and the deaths of loved ones. Yet the typical course of amateur poetry was to strain for a sentimental cheer or piety. Lincoln went the other way, emphasizing how his experience in his home village brought him into contact with the idea of death.

> I hear the loved survivors tell
> How nought from death could save,
> Till every sound appears a knell,
> And every spot a grave.
>
> I range the fields with pensive tread,
> And pace the hollow rooms,
> And feel (companion of the dead)
> I'm living in the tombs.

The next set of stanzas turned to Matthew Gentry, the young man Lincoln grew up with and watched go insane. We have already examined this poem for the light it sheds on Lincoln's ideas of madness. But it should also be mentioned in the context of the larger piece.

> But here's an object more of dread
> Than ought the grave contains —
> A human form with reason fled,
> While wretched life remains.

Just as the narrator trod the land of his childhood home and drew closer to death until he felt as though he were living in a tomb, this part of the poem circles around the mind of a madman, drawing closer and closer. As strong as was Lincoln's attachment to reason, these lines show a lingering taste for the expression of the passions, albeit hewed to the form of art. Lincoln wondered, said his friend Joseph Gillespie, whether "the perceptions were sometimes more unerring than reason and outstripped it." It is a sign of the tension between passion and reason that the section on Gentry contained two endings. The first emphasized the narrator's own relationship to the madman:

> And now away to seek some scene
> Less painful than the last —
> With less of horror mingled in
> The present and the past
>
> The very spot where grew the bread
> That formed my bones, I see
> How strange, old field, on thee to tread
> And feel I'm part of thee.

These stanzas tied together Matthew Gentry with his childhood home. The narrator was a part of all this death, all this madness, all this history, all this unknowable, untouchable material that sits on the emotional or spiritual surface of a landscape in southern Indiana. In a second draft, Lincoln deleted those two stanzas, with their sense of intense, morbid intimacy, and he wrote:

> O death! Thou awe-inspiring prince,
> That keepst the world in fear;
> Why dost thou tear more blest ones hence,
> And leave him ling'ring here?

This revised ending cuts the tension by distancing the narrator from it. It goes to sympathy (sorrow or pity for another person) rather than empathy (affinity with a person's sorrow or difficulty), yet it still begs essential questions. Would the narrator be an observer of this kind of pathetic woe, or the subject of it? Was he going to leave that childhood home for some special destiny? Or would he, too, end up mute and inglorious? Matthew Gentry had been "fortune favored" — and look what had happened to him. Lincoln seemed haunted by fears that his destiny was an awful one. Herndon said that Lincoln had told him more than a dozen times, "I fear I shall meet with some terrible end."

What is striking about Lincoln's therapies is that they did not dampen, but rather highlighted, the essential tension of his life. Had he chosen to take high doses of opium, he might have found relief from his pain, but at the expense of a great loss of energy. Had he devoted himself to a guru or medical practitioner — spending months each year taking the water cure or attaching himself to a talented mesmerist — he may have found comfort in someone else's prescription for him, at the cost of a vision that he'd already come to understand — that is, his desire to do something meaningful for which he would be remembered. In the late 1840s and early 1850s, the odds that he would accomplish anything worthy of remembrance looked increasingly small. Lincoln held on to his dreams along with his fears: "Hope and despondency, pleasure and pain, / Are mingled together in sun-shine and rain."

PART THREE

CHAPTER 8

Its Precise Shape and Color

IN HIS MID-FORTIES, the dark soil of his melancholy began to bear fruit. When Lincoln threw himself into the fight against the extension of slavery, the same qualities that had long brought him so much trouble played a role in his great work. The questions that beset him about how he could make his own life meaningful took on a new significance and vitality when applied to the public sphere. The suffering he had endured lent him clarity, discipline, and faith in hard times — perhaps especially in hard times.

It was not what we would call a recovery, and certainly not what we would call a cure. Lincoln's story confounds those who see depression as a collection of symptoms to be eliminated. But it resonates with those who see suffering as a potential catalyst of emotional growth. "What man actually needs," the psychiatrist Victor Frankl argued, "is not a tension-less state but rather the striving and struggling for a worthwhile goal." Many believe that psychological health comes with the relief of distress. But Frankl proposed that all people — and particularly those under some emotional weight — need a purpose that will both draw on their talents and transcend their lives. For Lincoln, this sense of purpose was indeed the key that unlocked the gates of a mental prison. This doesn't mean his suffering went away. In fact, as his life became richer and more satisfying, his melancholy exerted a stronger pull. He now responded to that pull by tying it to his newly defined sense of purpose. From a place of trouble, he looked for meaning. He looked at imperfection and sought redemption.

The keenness with which Lincoln understood the world around him and his place in it had long been a source of pain. In the early 1850s,

William Herndon remembered a day when "Lincoln was speculating with me about the deadness and despair of things and deeply regretting that his human strength and power were limited by his nature to rouse and stir up the world. He said gloomily, despairing, sadly: 'How hard, oh, how hard it is to die and leave one's country no better than if one had never lived for it.'" In retrospect, this moment stands out as a fulcrum in Lincoln's life in which he was able to articulate both his pain and his potential. He was desperate because, after more than four decades, he still had no apparent prospect to contribute anything significant to the world around him. Yet it was a kind of strength that he could look the reality straight in the eye. Humbled as he had been by years of obscurity, Lincoln held on to his hope to "stir up the world." It's no wonder that the dream brought him pain. Perhaps the wonder is that he tolerated the pain long enough and well enough that he could keep his hope alive and stay ready.

In 1854, the debate over American slavery, long dominated by the extremes on both sides, moved squarely to the political center. Lincoln had previously said little on the subject, but he quickly came forward with a vigorous argument that slavery must be restricted as a moral, social, and political wrong. In his rhetoric, he tore the subject down to its foundations, exposing his core beliefs. "Slavery," he said, "is founded in the selfishness of man's nature — opposition to it, is his love of justice. These principles are an eternal antagonism; and when brought into collision so fiercely, as slavery extension brings them, shocks, and throes, and convulsions must ceaselessly follow." More than a statement of mere policy, Lincoln laid before audiences a narrative that explained where the country had come from, where it stood, and where it might go. This narrative resonated with the story of his own life. The ethic that he proposed for his country — continued struggle to realize an ideal, knowing that it could never be perfectly attained — was the same ethic he had used to govern himself.

The first enslaved Africans in North America were purchased in 1619 from a Dutch ship that had wandered off course and found its way to Jamestown, Virginia. By the end of the seventeenth century, slave labor was a staple of southern tobacco plantations. It had a marked presence in the North as well. On July 4, 1776, the day the Continental Congress issued the Declaration of Independence, slavery was legal throughout the thirteen colonies. But even before independence was realized, a legal schism had emerged in the colonies when Vermont enacted gradual emancipation. The other northern colonies — states after the Constitution took effect in 1789 — soon followed. In contrast, southern states not only retained slavery but built an entire economy and culture around it.

A fault line now ran through the country, which would be aggravated by economic change and westward expansion. The market and industrial revolutions that so affected the psychological landscape of Lincoln's America also played a major role in heightening sectional differences. Northern states developed an economy best served by wage labor. The South grew rich from cotton, which was planted, picked, and processed by slaves. Strangely, the very interdependence of the regions fueled their conflict. In the North, mills made products from southern cotton and sold them to a voracious consumer market. This helped create a wealthy elite and a class of free workers, both of whom began to see slavery as a threat. In the South, meanwhile, cotton wealth drove the culture in the opposite direction. Aided by the cotton gin and the mechanical reaper, U.S. cotton production rose at an astonishing rate — from two million pounds in 1791 to a billion pounds in 1860. The southern press and clergy, which had once tolerated slavery as a necessary evil, now declared it a positive good.

Westward expansion forced sectional differences to the foreground. At independence, the country extended only to the Mississippi River. The Louisiana Purchase in 1803 took it west to the Rocky Mountains. With the annexation of Texas in 1845, a treaty with Great Britain over Oregon in 1846, and war cessions from Mexico in 1848, the United States elbowed its way west to the Pacific Ocean, south to the Rio Grande, and north to the 49th parallel.

How would slavery be regulated in the new land? Would it be slave or free? Who would decide? The stress of these questions — and the underlying differences they exposed — would crack the Union. The first sign of trouble came in 1819, when Missouri — a territory gained with the Louisiana Purchase — asked to come into the Union as a slave state. Northern senators refused, provoking outrage among their southern counterparts. What business, they asked, had Congress with the domestic institutions of a (soon-to-be) state? Crisis was averted only with the acrobatic diplomacy of a young senator from Kentucky named Henry Clay. With the Missouri Compromise he drew a line to the western edge of the Louisiana Territory. Slavery could exist south of it, but not north, excepting Missouri itself, which was admitted as a slave state.

The Missouri Compromise held fast even in the midst of contentious arguments over the gains from Mexico, which came to a head in 1850. By then, relations between North and South were so strained that talk of war was already in the air. South Carolina's John C. Calhoun told the Senate that northern "acts of aggression and encroachment" justified southerners to take "all means necessary" in self-defense. Once again Clay attempted a compromise. The old lion, now in his eighth decade, authored a measure that included admission of California as a free state, abolition of the slave trade in the District of Columbia, and a strong Fugitive Slave Law that commissioned federal marshals to act as slave catchers in free states.

The law did nothing but exacerbate the conflict. In the North, it brought the violence of slavery into the direct view of people for whom it had previously been an abstraction. This prompted Harriet Beecher Stowe to write an antislavery parable that, after serial publication, was issued as a book: *Uncle Tom's Cabin, or, Life Among the Lowly*. Released in 1852, it sold 20,000 copies in three weeks. In a year, it sold 300,000 copies in the United States and ten times that internationally. When, in Boston, a captured fugitive slave named Anthony Burns was escorted by federal troops to a Virginia-bound ship, a textile magnate named Amos A. Lawrence said, "We went to bed one night old fashioned, conservative, Compromise Union Whigs & waked up stark mad Abolitionists."

Still, centrists regarded bellicose words from both sections as the ideological extremes. President Millard Fillmore said the slavery problem had, with the 1850 compromise, reached its "final settlement" — which phrase, James M. McPherson observes, in *Battle Cry of Freedom,* "became the hallmark of political orthodoxy." Indeed, the major outstanding questions of slavery's reach had been settled. With the exception of some scraggly desert in the Southwest, where local voters would decide on slavery for themselves, every piece of the United States had been declared slave or free.

Aside from a handful of statements and one attempt at legislation while in Congress, Lincoln had sat out the fight over slavery. He called it "both injustice and bad policy" in 1837, an "evil" in 1845, and in 1850 he saw that slavery presented "the one *great* question of the day." But he hadn't done much to press his point of view. Why not? Put plainly, Lincoln was a politician, building a public life on points that could be sustained by popular opinion — or, in extreme cases, sustained despite popular opinion.

Doing good depended on winning elections. Not incidentally, his work as a lawyer nurtured this perspective, bringing him before panels that decided guilt and innocence, truth and falsehood. Lincoln had to constantly keep in mind the predilections and prejudices of ordinary people in Illinois — especially central Illinois, a region thick with hostility to antislavery agitation.

But in 1854, the politics of slavery changed dramatically. On January 4, Stephen Douglas introduced in the Senate a bill to organize governments in the Nebraska Territory. This huge swath of land, including most of present-day Kansas, Nebraska, North Dakota, South Dakota, Oklahoma, Montana, Wyoming, and Colorado, was covered by the Missouri Compromise, which would have banned slavery in the entire territory. Douglas's bill would repeal the Missouri Compromise. Douglas knew it would "raise a hell of a storm," but he built in a clever political shelter. He divided the territory into two prospective states, Kansas and Nebraska. Rather than dictate from Congress where slavery should go, voters in the territories themselves would decide. He called his plan "popular sovereignty" and said it put the power where it belonged, with the people. In May 1854, the bill became law.

There has been nothing quite like the Kansas-Nebraska Act in modern times. It killed one major political party, the Whigs; permanently split another, the Democrats; and led in short order to actual violence. The law (often referred to as "Nebraska") was a transformative event, on par with the September 11 attacks or the stock market crash that signaled the Great Depression. In all three cases, long-standing trends led to the seismic moment. But that didn't make them any less shocking at the time. "[Douglas] took us by surprise — astounded us — by this measure," Lincoln said. "We were thunderstruck and stunned; and we reeled and fell in utter confusion. But we rose each fighting, grasping whatever he could first reach — a scythe — a pitchfork — a chopping axe, or a butcher's cleaver. We struck in the direction of the sound; and we are rapidly closing in upon him." Lincoln would come to articulate precisely where the disparate groups could be most strongly joined. And he would help hold the center of a new coalition until, amazingly, it came to national rule, with Lincoln as its leader.

In retrospect, all opposition to slavery tends to be remembered as "abolitionism," but that name, in the mid-nineteenth century, referred to a radical minority who not only opposed slavery but questioned the legitimacy of a government that would allow it. A more moderate group of antislavery opponents sought to work within the system to restrict it. Both groups hated the Kansas-Nebraska Act, but a huge number of opponents of the act were not, strictly speaking, antislavery at all. They simply opposed the extension of slavery into the West.

To moderate northerners, remember, the West had tremendous practical and symbolic significance. When the *New York Tribune* editor Horace Greeley advised, in 1854, "Go West, young man, and grow up with the country," he invoked the basic promise that every American could improve his prospects with hard work. Hemmed in by low wages or scarce work? Go west. The region was a "safety valve," Greeley said, for anyone fallen on hard times or captivated by new ambition. In part because of the gold rush in California, the early 1850s saw great numbers of people push west, past Iowa and Missouri into the Nebraska Territory. Since 1820, it had been guaranteed free, which meant that labor would be king. But Douglas's bill changed that. Now slave plantations threatened to edge out industrial projects and family farms. Self-interested northerners took notice. Oliver Morton, the future Indiana governor, put it succinctly: "If we do not exclude slavery from the Territories, it will exclude us."

It is tempting to imagine that northerners harbored both a deep animosity toward slavery and a deep sympathy for the enslaved. In fact, the "free labor" ideology was strongly tied to a staunch racism that sought the exclusion not just of slavery but of anyone with dark skin. Lincoln's own Illinois adopted a constitution in 1847 that forbade free black people from entering the state. Those who did live there could not vote, serve on juries, or testify in court. The state's "black laws," said an Illinois Negro leader named H. Ford Douglass, "would disgrace any Barbary state, or any uncivilized people in the far-off islands at sea."

The selfish interest of whites in blocking slavery's extension, along with a moral opposition to slavery itself, created a political opportunity in 1854. Even fierce rivals can join to fight a common enemy. Senator Stephen Douglas presented just such an enemy. On his train ride home from Washington to Illinois, he saw his figure burning in effigy. When he rose to speak in Chicago, crowds hollered insults and threw things at him. But Douglas was no man to be shouted down. Only forty-one years old, the "Little Giant" had recently won his second Senate term and was widely hailed as a future president. No crowd of rabble-rousers could stifle him. To rally his supporters and subdue his opponents, Douglas went on a tour of the state, which eventually brought him to Springfield in early October. The town was in the midst of a state agricultural fair, with competitions for prize crops and livestock, horse races, and booths displaying new breeds and machines. "It is estimated that over 15,000 persons were on the Fair Grounds today," reported the *Illinois Daily Journal* — this in a town of about seven thousand. Many had come to see Douglas, who spoke before a packed Hall of Representatives on Wednesday afternoon, October 3.

In addition to Lincoln, a number of other prominent politicians in Springfield that week would respond to Douglas, including Lyman Trumbull, Sidney Breese, and John Calhoun. As an opposition coalition, they had a steep uphill climb. Douglas had one of the best-organized political operations in history; his opponents had no experience working together. The Whigs and Democrats who opposed the Nebraska bill had long clashed on other issues. Two new organizations, meanwhile, were going in sharply different directions. The American party, or Know-Nothings, had grown out of anti-immigrant, anti-Catholic secret societies into a serious political force. It sought to limit slavery, along with the rights of anyone who wasn't a white, native-born Protestant. A second new organization, the Republican party, centered on abolitionists and antislavery politicians, devoted itself to ending slavery throughout the country.

Among all the talented people rising to challenge Douglas, how did Abraham Lincoln become the one we remember? It was by no means inevitable. When Lincoln stood at the podium on October 4, 1854, wearing just a short-sleeved shirt on that unseasonably warm day, he seemed an uncharismatic challenger. Horace White, a reporter for the *Chicago Tribune,* observed Lincoln closely before he began to speak. "It was a marked face," White said, "but so overspread with sadness that I thought that Shakespeare's melancholy Jacques had been translated from the forest of Arden to the capital of Illinois." White saw soon enough that the man's gloom came from a depth of character. "His speaking went to the heart," White said, "because it came from the heart." Whereas other orators could hit all the right notes and spark thunderous applause, few had Lincoln's ability to change people's minds. "Mr. Lincoln's eloquence was of the higher type," he explained, "which produced conviction in others because of the conviction of the speaker himself. His listeners felt that he believed every word he said, and that, like Martin Luther, he would go to the stake rather than abate one jot or tittle of it."

White's comparison of Lincoln with Martin Luther captures something about how Lincoln appeared to those who saw him in person and how an individual temperament infused a public identity. Lincoln didn't need to explain in detail how his personal experience related to the ideas he expressed in public. Today we often expect aspiring politicians to make known their deepest and most private motives. Lincoln was reserved in personal details but quite open in showing his true emotional self, including the suffering that sometimes overtook him. Reporters, allies, and ordinary citizens who watched Lincoln rarely came away thinking they knew his secrets, but they often came away thinking they'd seen the man. And they were right. He brought into the public realm, and into the argument about public questions, a vision that had been nurtured in him over many years, and to which he still turned in his own hour of need. Lincoln saw the world as a deeply flawed, even tragic, place where imperfect people had to make the best of poor materials. At his worst, the burdens of this vision pressed him into ruts and troughs. At his best, it fueled a passion for redemption.

Lincoln's reputation for looking on the dark side of things politically ran through his career. "You know I am never sanguine," he wrote in 1840. In 1864, he complained, "The most trying thing in all of this war is that the people are too sanguine; they expect too much at once." The tendency to see the darkness was ingrained in him, a political instinct that his friends connected to his personal temperament. Some people, Lincoln's partner William Herndon observed, see the world "ornamented with beauty, life, and action." Lincoln, on the other hand, "crushed the unreal, the inexact, the hollow, and the sham . . . Everything came to him in its precise shape and color." Herndon continued, "His fault, if any, was that he saw things less than they really were; less beautiful and more frigid." Notice that at first Herndon praises Lincoln for cutting through ornament, but then he acknowledges that there was some fault in his perception. In other words, in some situations Lincoln was like the sourpuss at a picnic, seeing only ants and grass stains amid baskets full of bread and wine. We call such a person a pessimist — usually pejoratively. But looking on the dark side, in some scenarios, is valuable. In the midst of a disaster, the man who loudly proclaims the coming trouble will surely be more valuable than the optimist who sits dreamily admiring the daisies.

It is common sense that some situations call for pessimism, but as a culture Americans have strangely decided to endow optimism with unqualified favor. Politicians today compete to be the most optimistic, and accuse their opponents of pessimism, as if it were a defect. This trend is visible in psychology as well. Whereas "melancholy" in Lincoln's time was understood to be a multifaceted phenemenon that conferred potential advantages along with grave dangers, today we tend to discount its complexities. Psychiatrists see only a biological brain disease. Psychologists see only errors in thinking. That is, if you don't like yourself, or you feel hopeless, or you see life as fundamentally dissatisfying, you've fallen victim to what researchers call "learned helplessness." By some blend of bad genes and bad experience, you have come to see the world in dark hues. Therapy and medication can help you see the world the way healthy optimists do.

In fact, a wide range of research has painted a much richer portrait of depression. None of this research discounts the real trouble that depression can bring. It can be a serious, and sometimes fatal, disease. At the same time, depression often springs from fundamentally accurate perceptions that, in some situations, can be an advantage. This understanding of "depressive realism" emerged in a landmark laboratory experiment by Lyn Abramson and Lauren Alloy in 1979. Abramson and Alloy wanted to know whether depressed subjects perceived reality differently from nondepressed subjects. So they set up a simple game-show-like experiment in their lab: Individual subjects were placed in front of a panel with a green light, a yellow light, and a spring-loaded button and were instructed to try to make the green light flash as often as possible. In one segment, they would win money every time the green light went on. In another, they would lose money when it didn't. A screen in the room showed their score. Afterward, the subjects were asked how much control they had. Their answers differed according to several variables. Among the "normal," nondepressed subjects, it depended on whether they were losing money or making money. When they were winning money, they thought they had considerable control, between 60 and 65 on a scale where 0 indicates no control and 100 indicates total control. When they were losing money, they thought they had virtually no control. In other words, these subjects took credit for good scores and dished off blame when scores were poor.

The depressed subjects saw things differently. Whether they were winning or losing money, they tended to believe that they had no control. And they were correct. Abramson and Alloy were carefully limiting the extent of real control. The "game" was a fiction. "The results of these now classic, 1979, experiments constitute some of the most controversial, and fascinating, findings in depression research from the past few decades," writes the science journalist Kyla Dunn. "Previously, depressed people were believed to be drawing conclusions about themselves and their experiences that were unrealistically distorted towards the negative. Yet as this research suggests, one cognitive symptom of depression may be the loss of optimistic, self-enhancing biases that normally protect healthy people against assaults to their self-esteem. In many instances, depressives may simply be judging themselves and the world much more accurately than non-depressed people, and finding it not a pretty place."

Abramson and Alloy termed the benefit that depressed people showed in the experiment the "Depressive Realism" or the "Sadder but Wiser" effect. Since then, these phrases have come to represent a perspective on depression that raises a whole host of unsettling questions. For example, one standard definition of mental health is the ability to maintain close and accurate contact with reality. "The perception of reality is called mentally healthy," one textbook declares, "when what the individual sees corresponds to what is actually there." But research shows that, by this definition, happiness itself could be considered a mental disorder. "We have a tendency to regard people in their ordinary moods as rational information processors, relatively free of systematic bias and distorted judgments," Alloy writes. In fact, "much research suggests that when they are not depressed, people are highly vulnerable to illusions, including unrealistic optimism, overestimation of themselves, and an exaggerated sense of their capacity to control events. The same research indicates that depressed people's perceptions and judgments are often less biased." The psychologist Richard Bentall has taken this research to its extreme conclusion, humorously proposing to classify happiness as a psychiatric disorder — "major affective disorder (pleasant type)."

In Lincoln's time, people understood the obvious point that this research bears out: every cognitive style has assets and defects, which change according to circumstances. This seems surprising today because, by some quirk of culture, some cognitive styles are held to be superior and others inferior; one emotion (joy) is "positive" and all others (sadness, fear, anger, and shame) are "negative." If we value accurate perception, however, we must qualify our worship of joy and happiness. People actively seek to filter out painful stimuli, and while this may help them limit distress, it can also sharply distort their actual environment. "If most of us remain ignorant of ourselves," wrote Aldous Huxley, "it is because self-knowledge is painful and we prefer the pleasures of illusion."

Certain people — Lincoln was one of them — break through illusion and experience that painful self-knowledge. This helps explain the widely acknowledged but poorly understood phenomenon of melancholic success. "Throughout history," writes the psychiatrist Peter Kramer, "it has been known that melancholics, though they have little energy, use their energy well; they tend to work hard in a focused area, do great things, and derive little pleasure from their accomplishments. Much of the insight and creative achievement of the human race is due to the discontent, guilt, and critical eye of dysthymics." Note the word "insight." In many cases, insight is precisely what depressed people lack: they fail to see the clearly good things about their lives. But the same forces that hold comfort at bay can lead, in the right circumstances, to valuable perspectives on the world.

People who have experienced depression often note the way that episodes give way to insight. Herman Melville, Lincoln's contemporary and fellow melancholic, wrote, "The intensest light of reason and revelation combined can not shed such blazonings upon the deeper truths in man, as will sometimes proceed from his own profoundest gloom. Utter darkness is then his light, and cat-like he distinctly sees all objects through a medium which is mere blindness to common vision." Of course, such "cat-like" vision is not always appreciated in its time. Melville died in obscurity, his works languishing while sunnier artists thrived. But his writings received their acclaim when later generations came to value the way he pierced the bubbles of American life and character, telling bleak and truthful tales of mad one-legged captains and stubborn introverted clerks and mutinous slaves on a ship. Similarly, where the optimists of his time would fail, Lincoln would succeed, by articulating a durable idea of free society and exposing the fallacies in which many of his contemporaries tried to find comfort.

It is no coincidence that Lincoln found his power at a time when the skies turned dark in the United States. His power came in part because he quickly saw the approaching storm. In his opponent Lincoln faced a preternatural optimist. Popular sovereignty, Stephen Douglas believed, solved the slavery problem. The United States could now expand from the Arctic Ocean to the tip of South America. Some regions would be free, some would be slave; all would be part of a perfect Union.

The physical contrast between the two men underlined their political differences. Douglas stood five feet four inches tall, a foot shorter than Lincoln, and seemed packed in every inch with charisma. He had penetrating blue eyes and dark hair that he styled in a pompadour. He dressed like a dandy, drank the finest liquor, and smoked the best cigars. He could afford these luxuries, because he owned large chunks of Chicago and a 2,500-acre Mississippi plantation to boot — left to him by his father-in-law, along with more than one hundred slaves. Lincoln, on the other hand, was not just tall and gaunt but a truly odd physical specimen, with cartoonishly long arms and legs that made him look as if he wore stilts under his trousers. He never seemed to have a decent-fitting suit. He spoke with a kind of high-piping voice, but at the pace of a Kentucky drawl. He was deeply sad and often had a faraway, dreamy look in his eye.

Speaking on that hot afternoon at the Hall of Representatives in Springfield, in a "thin, high-pitched falsetto," Lincoln explained that the United States had been founded with a great idea and a grave imperfection. The idea — liberty was the natural right of all people. The flaw — the "cancer" in the nation's body — was the gross violation of liberty by human slavery. The Founders recognized the evil, Lincoln said, and made accommodation to restrict it, believing that the very experiment in liberty could be spoiled if they acted to end it too quickly. "Thus, the thing is hid away, in the constitution," Lincoln explained, "just as an afflicted man hides away a wen or a cancer, which he dares not cut out at once, lest he bleed to death; with the promise, nevertheless, that the cutting may begin at the end of a given time." Indeed, the Constitution made several provisions that were clearly understood to refer to slavery but used the phrase "persons held to service or labor," thus preserving the text for a day when slavery would be abolished. In the nation's first decades, leaders banned the foreign slave trade, then made violation of the ban punishable by death; and they prohibited slavery in large swaths of territory. To Lincoln, these were but patches in an overall principle. "We see the plain unmistakable spirit of that age, towards slavery," he said, "was hostility to the PRINCIPLE, and toleration, ONLY BY NECESSITY."

Lincoln found the clearest statement of that spirit in the Declaration of Independence, with its claim for the self-evident truth that "all men are created equal." Lincoln's interpretation of the phrase became the centerpiece of his narrative about the nation. The Founders, Lincoln said, in adopting the Declaration, did not declare that all people were at that time living in a state of equality. To say so would have been absurd, given not only the widespread bondage of black people but the restricted suffrage of many whites and the legal inequality of women. Nor did the Founders declare that they intended to secure complete equality in their lifetimes. The spirit of the Declaration, Lincoln said, was meant to be realized — to the greatest extent possible — by each succeeding generation. The Founders cast off despotism and created the framework for a free republic, invoking, as they did, not arguments of mere self-interest but the ideal of natural, universal, God-given rights. "They meant to set up a standard maxim for free society," Lincoln said, "which should be familiar to all, and revered by all; constantly looked to, constantly labored for . . . even though never perfectly attained."

The idea expressed here shows up at many points in Lincoln's life. He often argued that one needed to work hard, trusting that rewards would come in due time. To succeed in "the great struggle of life," he said, one had to endure failures and plod on. The wisdom of what he called his own "severe experience" taught him so. We need not dally over such impossible questions as cause and effect. "Which comes first, personal temperament or the political philosophy?" is much like the question of the chicken and the egg. But there was a plain relationship between the private thoughts and the public ideas. Just as his own life had been a struggle, with pain that he recognized and had to tolerate and contain, Lincoln viewed all of American history as a struggle — one that the Founders foresaw and made contingencies for. "The assertion that 'all men are created equal' was of no practical use in effecting our separation from Great Britain," Lincoln explained, "and it was placed in the Declaration, not for that, but for future use. Its authors meant it to be, thank God, it is now proving itself, a stumbling block to those who in after times might seek to turn a free people back into the hateful paths of despotism. They knew the proneness of prosperity to breed tyrants, and they meant when such should re-appear in this fair land and commence their vocation they should find left for them at least one hard nut to crack." Slavery, Lincoln argued, presented just such a temptation, "now when we have grown fat, and have lost all dread of being slaves ourselves." He argued that the South, in its advocacy of slavery, and the

Douglas Democrats, in their apology for it, followed the same logic as that of kings and despots throughout the world who said that one group should work and another should benefit from it.

While he called slavery a "moral, social, and political evil," Lincoln did not propose its eradication. To the contrary, he said it had to be left alone where it existed. The core question of the United States, he thought, was whether it could steadily advance the liberty of its white citizens while moving slowly toward emancipation. Slavery must be set on a path to "eventual extinction," he said. A peaceful, lawful end to it, he said at one point, might take one hundred years. Also, while favoring legal freedom for blacks, Lincoln did not support social and political rights — the full range of what we call civil rights. After legal freedom, he proposed, dreamily, that black people would migrate to Africa or other foreign lands.

This was a widely shared white fantasy, adopted by Henry Clay, among others. A founder of the American Colonization Society, whose voyages to Africa led to the establishment of Liberia, Clay wrote, "There is a moral fitness in the idea of returning to Africa her children, whose ancestors have been torn from her by the ruthless hand of fraud and violence." In an 1852 eulogy for Clay, Lincoln enthusiastically endorsed his vision, saluting his "deep devotion to the cause of human liberty — a strong sympathy with the oppressed every where, and an ardent wish for their elevation."

The primary mechanism with which to lift the "oppressed," Lincoln believed, was to maintain and protect the American experiment. To some extent, the success of that experiment hinders our appreciation of its role in Lincoln's imagination. Francis Fukuyama's 1992 book, *The End of History and the Last Man,* argued that an age-old struggle over the proper forms of government was giving way to a global consensus on American-style "liberal democracy" as a superior system. Though the thesis remains controversial, it nevertheless articulated a widespread idea that a form of governance considered revolutionary at the end of the eighteenth century had triumphed at the end of the twentieth. In the world Lincoln saw, by contrast, monarchy remained the default setting throughout Europe and Asia. The British were moving slowly toward representative government, but with most power retained by the aristocracy. The Greeks proclaimed their independence in 1829 — and promptly set up a monarchy. Probably the most influential lesson in the minds of American politicians was that of France. The French Revolution in 1789 went much further than its American counterpart in 1776, declaring itself for universal liberty, brotherhood, and equality. Yet it quickly dissolved into violent factional rivalries. By 1799, Napoleon had established his imperium.

Lincoln had long insisted that the gravest threat for the United States lay at home. He did not expect a foreign nation to conquer it. "If destruction be our lot," he wrote in 1838, "we must ourselves be its author and finisher. As a nation of freemen we must live through all time, or die by suicide." For a good part of his career, he saw a real threat in abolitionism. These opponents of slavery spoke of tearing apart the Union to create an all-free nation unsullied by the abomination of bondage. Lincoln answered that the evil could not be cast off so easily. It had to be continually restricted, not by force of guns but by the peaceful measures of democracy. The United States could not instantly realize universal freedom. For the time being, it had to bear the burden of preventing the erosion of freedom.

But nothing the abolitionists had done could be compared to the threat of the Kansas-Nebraska Act. This, to Lincoln, was nothing less than a knife held to the nation's throat. Previous compromises on slavery had allowed it some new land in return for restrictions. From Lincoln's perspective, they maintained the principle of slavery's wrong. Douglas, though, professed not to care about slavery one way or the other — a sure path, Lincoln thought, to domination by those who cared dearly about it. Douglas argued that he'd come to his views by his own commitment to democracy. But what Lincoln suspected, history has borne out. The Kansas-Nebraska Act followed a "deal you can't refuse" offer to Douglas from a key bloc of southern senators. He wanted to organize the territory, to build a railroad through it. They told him that he'd never get their support without repealing the Missouri Compromise. He agreed to their demand.

As Lincoln understood, the political power of slavery was disproportionate, for the wealthiest interests had the most invested in the institution. What troubled him more than such brazen power plays, though, was that Douglas acquiesced to them. Grant this extension to the Nebraska Territory, Lincoln said, and what would keep the slave power from insisting that northern free laws were another abrogation of their rights? "Popular sovereignty" was no more than a fancy phrase for surrender to slavery. Without clearly banning it from the start, nothing would stop slave owners from moving to a territory. And once slavery took root in a place, it could not be easily dug out.

For a short time, Lincoln had good reason to believe that he would be rewarded for his work with the job he prized above all others: United States senator from Illinois. "At that time it was the height of his ambition to get into the U.S. Senate," said one of his colleagues. Even years later he said he'd prefer a full term in the Senate to one as president, no surprise in an age when the great orator-statesmen — Henry Clay, Daniel Webster, and John Calhoun — had served in the upper house of Congress. Senators at the time were not directly elected but sent to Washington by the state legislatures. To win the seat, then, Lincoln first had to assemble a like-minded majority — and he did. When the Illinois General Assembly convened in January 1855, it had a majority of anti-Nebraska members, many of whom owed their election to Lincoln's work in the fall campaign. The term of James Shields, a Democrat, was up, and he was expected to get the boot. "It was agreed that . . . Mr. Lincoln would succeed General Shields," remembered Elihu Washburne, a congressman from Illinois. "I know that he himself expected it." Lincoln lobbied hard for the post. "I have really got it into my head to try to be United States Senator," he wrote to Joseph Gillespie, "and if I could have your support my chances would be reasonably good."

Few votes would be as clear-cut as Gillespie's, though. The breakdown of party loyalties had resulted in a thicket of shifting rivalries and many loci of power. Lincoln sized up allegiances, sought support, made lists of members and their preferences — and, near the end, tried to head off the "double game" of a candidate who was running without having declared so. The actual voting took months even to start. Lincoln led on the early ballots. At various times, forty-seven members went for him, only three short of the majority needed. But he fell shy of a winning margin. It quickly emerged that five key votes were in the hands of Independents who wouldn't go for him. Lincoln saw that he couldn't get those votes — and worse, that if he stayed in the fight, the seat might go to the scheming Democratic governor Joel Matteson. To his supporters' dismay, he told them to fall in behind an anti-Nebraska Democrat named Lyman Trumbull.

After the election, Lincoln was "cut and mortified," said Joseph Gillespie, who went home with him after Trumbull's victory. "I never saw him so dejected," said Gillespie, who'd known Lincoln since the late 1830s.

"He said the fates seemed to be against him and he thought he would never strive for office again He could bear defeat inflicted by his enemies with pretty good grace, but it was hard to be wounded in the house of his friends." This episode showed Lincoln's continuing emotional and cognitive vulnerability. Notice how, as is common with depression, he extrapolated grandly from a single negative stimulus, finding in his defeat evidence that nothing less than fate conspired against him.

Yet we can also see in Lincoln's reaction the discipline that he had come to after so many years. "There is no event in Mr. Lincoln's entire political career," Washburne said, "that brought him so much disappointment and chagrin as his defeat for United States Senator in 1855, but he accepted the situation uncomplainingly." While he expressed his disappointment to a close circle of intimates, in public he was the picture of reserve. At a reception for Trumbull, someone asked if he was upset. "Not too upset to congratulate my friend Trumbull," Lincoln said, extending his hand to the senator-elect.

At first glance, the discrepancy in these reactions might seem to be the simple difference between private moments and public display. But a closer look shows a dynamic exchange between Lincoln's disappointment and his renewed dedication to a cause (of which his friend Trumbull was now a chief representative). Lincoln never renounced his belief that "the fates seemed to be against" his winning a good office. To the contrary, as his career grew hotter, he turned all the more to a deeply embedded belief that his life was controlled by a force beyond him. Nor did he discount the real effect that the loss had on him emotionally. In a letter to Washburne, he called it an "agony." The key question was what he would do with that agony, and how he would direct the energy he had, knowing that the outcome was not in his control. He also said to Washburne, "I regret my defeat moderately, but I am not nervous about it." "Nervous" here is probably a reference to a disease state. Rather than turn inward and stew in his own regret — missing work, making a "discreditable exhibition" of himself as he had a decade before — Lincoln would draw on his feelings to strengthen his commitment to a cause.

Indeed, his explanations for why he had dropped out of the race expressly articulated his own subservient role in an important project. "I could not . . . let the whole political result go to ruin," he wrote, "on a point merely personal to myself." Elsewhere, he said, "I think the cause in this case is to be preferred to men." These are things that many politicians *say* but that Lincoln believed and acted upon. In the many disappointments of the coming years, he would turn to deepen and strengthen his own commitment. Another way to see this is that, when he tumbled momentarily backward, he rubbed his eyes and saw more clearly than before just how fantastic a peak he had engaged to climb. With that, every step forward was imbued with a new significance, for every bit of honest energy he contributed would be drawn upon by others. The altitude he himself reached seemed increasingly insignificant.

According to Herndon, Lincoln's loss in 1855 was a crucial moment in the initiation of this dynamic. His ambition had been profoundly awakened by the chance to become senator. "This frustration of Lincoln's ambition," he wrote, "had a marked effect on his political views . . . With the strengthening of his faith in a just cause so long held in abeyance he became more defiant each day. But in the very nature of things he dared not be as bold and out spoken as I. With him every word and sentence had to be weighed and its effects calculated, before being uttered."

Indeed, the combination of defiance and discipline went far to define Lincoln's work in the mid-1850s. One rare peek at how his private thoughts rumbled beneath his public work came in an August 1855 letter he wrote to his old friend Joshua Speed. Speed and Lincoln illustrated the divergent paths available to industrious young men in central Illinois. For a time in his young manhood Speed considered making Springfield his permanent home. Instead he returned to Kentucky, married a girl there, and took up life as a planter. He had owned slaves since his father's death in 1840, and he never again was without them until 1865. His brother James Speed (later Lincoln's attorney general) had taken up lawyering in Louisville and had freed his few slaves entirely by 1846. But Joshua, even after moving into town and working in business, continued not only to own slaves but to make money in their traffic. His firm acted as a broker in the renting of slaves by their owners.

In politics, Speed had been a Whig, but by the late 1850s, he had fallen in behind Stephen Douglas. When he wrote to Lincoln in 1855, Speed asked where his old friend stood, told him he expected they differed, and said that while he could admit the abstract wrong of slavery, he denied that any northerner should meddle in something that was exclusively the interest of slave owners. Lincoln's response cut straight to a personal point. "It is hardly fair for you to assume," Lincoln objected, "that I have no interest in a thing which has, and continually exercises, the power of making me miserable. You ought rather to appreciate how much the great body of the Northern people do crucify their feelings, in order to maintain their loyalty to the constitution and the Union."

In his public utterances, Lincoln spoke first about the immorality of slavery. He spoke only rarely and at the margins about his personal objection to it, let alone an objection that began with an emotional reaction. The reason is not hard to fathom. A public man needs to find universal justifications, even in our own age, in which the cult of personal stories has come to reign. Furthermore, as Lincoln made clear throughout, he believed that the cause required discipline. To effectively oppose slavery's extension, other differences had to be set aside. Likewise, the cause of the Union, as he said to Speed, required that he and others who object to slavery "crucify their feelings" with respect to its existence in the states.

While Lincoln stifled his feelings in public, his letter to Speed shows that they lay just beneath the surface, and that at the right moment he could express them sharply. Nearly fifteen years before, after five weeks together at Speed's Farmington, the two men traveled down the Ohio River on their way back to Springfield. Now Lincoln reminded Speed of that trip, and of the fact that they saw about a dozen slaves shackled together in irons. "That sight was a continual torment to me," Lincoln wrote, "and I see something like it every time I touch the Ohio, or any other slave-border." "I confess," he wrote, "I hate to see the poor creatures hunted down, and caught, and carried back to their stripes, and unrewarded toils; but I bite my lip and keep quiet."

It has often been suggested that, between 1841 and 1855, Lincoln changed his mind about the scene he had witnessed that day on the Ohio River. In an 1841 letter describing the scene, he said nothing about being miserable. But it is no contradiction to make a new point about an old experience. The letter, to Mary Speed, was a polite, decidedly nonpolitical note to a young lady in a slaveholding family, in which Lincoln concentrated on a philosophical idea about the conditions of human happiness. Lincoln's 1855 letter to Mary Speed's brother, on the other hand, was a careful and candid political argument. And it raised the issue of his feelings not only to make the point that he *had* those feelings, but also to demonstrate how powerfully he worked to subdue them, out of loyalty to the Union. In other words, to allege inconsistency is not only wrong; it obscures something essential that this letter helps reveal. It was central to

Lincoln's view that his personal feelings had always to be put into context and subjugated to his judgment about his responsibilities. The imagery — "bite my lip," "crucify their feelings" — showed that it was no easy task, but that he was committed inexorably to it.

With Speed Lincoln opened the vent more than usual. In public, he had been urging people to maintain allegiance to the laws, including the Nebraska bill. To Speed, he called the Nebraska bill not a law but "*violence* from the beginning. It was conceived in violence, passed in violence, and is maintained in violence." He seethed about the actions of the proslavery men in Kansas, who had passed a constitution that made it a hanging offense to aid an escaping slave, or even to talk about the rights of black people. This, to Lincoln, recalled the story of Haman, in the Book of Esther, a wicked figure who built gallows intending to kill all the Jews, but ended up, when he was discovered, being hanged himself. "If, like Haman, they should hang upon the gallows of their own building, I shall not be among the mourners for their fate."

While Speed's old friendship meant that Lincoln could trust him to keep the letter private, Speed also stood on ground that inspired Lincoln's venom. Professing faith in the Union, Speed clung to his slaves, which he said was a right he would never give up, even if the Union had to be dissolved. Speed also said that he would support democracy and a free Kansas if that's where the votes went. Lincoln practically snarled at his friend. "All decent slave-holders *talk* that way," he wrote. "But they never *vote* that way . . . The slave-breeders and slave-traders are an odious and detested class, among you; and yet in politics, they dictate the course of all of you, and are as completely your masters, as you are the masters of your own negroes."

Speed had asked Lincoln where he stood, and Lincoln said he didn't know, that he still considered himself a Whig, although he understood that the Whig party was dying. He did not believe that his opposition to the extension of slavery placed him outside the Whig mainstream. He continued, "I am not a Know-Nothing. That is certain. How could I be? How can any one who abhors the oppression of negroes, be in favor of degrading classes of white people? Our progress in degeneracy appears to me to be pretty rapid. As a nation, we began by declaring that '*all men are created equal.*' We now practically read it, 'all men are created equal, *except negroes.*' When the Know-Nothings get control, it will read, 'all men are created equal, except negroes, *and foreigners, and catholics.*' When it comes to this I should prefer emigrating to some country where they make no pretence of loving liberty — to Russia, for instance, where despotism can be taken pure, and without the base alloy of hypocracy."

In public, though, Lincoln bit his lip. He said nothing critical of the Know-Nothings, who by the end of 1855 had elected more than one hundred members of Congress, eight governors, and mayors of several major cities. Most of Lincoln's old Whig allies in Springfield were at least sympathetic to, if not full-fledged members of, the Know-Nothing group. "Until we can get the elements of this organization," Lincoln wrote, "there is not sufficient materials to successfully combat the Nebraska democracy with. We can not get them so long as they cling to a hope of success under their own organization; and I fear an open push by us now, may offend them, and tend to prevent our ever getting them."

Lincoln had a knack for involving himself in fights where the odds were against him. His campaign against the Mexican War had nearly killed his career in the late 1840s. His irrevocable commitment to emancipation would come near to costing him reelection in 1864. Now, in the mid-1850s, when he began to campaign against slavery's extension, he had no base and no political home. The Whig party was fading fast. The antislavery Republicans wanted to draft him, but Lincoln could not risk association with a group perceived as radical in central and southern Illinois. In fact, when a Republican group held a meeting following his reply to Douglas on October 4, 1854, they found that Lincoln had quickly left town.

While he continued to speak against the expansion of slavery and for the restoration of the Missouri Compromise, Lincoln found himself stuck politically. He had no office to run for, no party to run with. His prospects looked exceedingly dim. It was clear that the slave power held the upper hand. The reason was simple. On the slavery question, he wrote that "the people of the South have an immediate palpable and immensely great pecuniary interest; while, with the people of the North, it is merely an abstract question of moral right, with only slight, and remote pecuniary interest added." He elaborated, "The slaves of the South, at a moderate estimate, are worth a thousand millions of dollars. Let it be permanently settled that this property may extend to new territory, without restraint, and it greatly enhances, perhaps quite doubles, its value at once. This immense, palpable pecuniary interest, on the question of extending slavery, unites the Southern people, as one man. But it can not be demonstrated that the North will gain a dollar by restricting it. Moral principle is all, or nearly all, that unites us of the North. Pity 'tis, it is so, but this is a looser bond, than pecuniary interest. Right here is the plain cause of their perfect union and our want of it."

In his public work, Lincoln rarely departed from the formal, restrained tone of this note. "Pity 'tis, it is so" could have been an anthem of Lincoln's political life, so well does the phrase capture not only his basic stance but the spirit of calm resignation he evinced in the face of hardship. Not only did he rarely let on about any vexation or disappointment, but in the exchanges between him and his colleagues, he is often the one bucking *them* up, trying to lift *their* spirits, encouraging *them* that their efforts would have their eventual reward. In this we see that Lincoln was not just a depressive realist. He was what the psychiatrist Victor Frankl calls a "tragic optimist." Rooted as his ideas were in the imperfection of the past and the danger of the future, he repeatedly invoked a promise as well. The country was capable of improvement because potential lay in the "abundance of man's heart." "Our republican robe is soiled, and trailed in the dust," he said. "Let us repurify it. Let us turn and wash it white, in the spirit, if not the blood, of the Revolution . . . Let north and south — let all Americans — let all lovers of liberty everywhere — join in the great and good work. If we do this, we shall not only have saved the Union; but we shall have so saved it, as to make, and to keep it, forever worthy of the saving. We shall have so saved it, that the succeeding millions of free happy people, the world over, shall rise up, and call us blessed, to the latest generations."

Lincoln's greatness owes considerably to his internal growth. But what primarily accounted for his increasing success — and his vital relevance — was not his own growth to a place where he could speak to the country's needs, but the country's regression to the place where Lincoln was needed. What deflated the Know-Nothing balloon, and allowed Lincoln to "fuse" with the Republicans on ground that suited him, was an emerging violence and fractiousness that had no peer in the nation's history. Kansas — one of two states that Douglas's bill had created out of the Nebraska Territory — became a battleground between proslavery and antislavery forces in 1854 and 1855, as settlers funded by northeastern money poured into the territory and were met by southerners who had come for the same purpose: to organize, win elections, and control the state. Each side set up its own government in its own capital, the slave-friendly minority at Lecompton and the antislavery majority at Lawrence. Violence soon followed. In the spring of 1855, a mob sacked Lawrence, looting buildings and destroying printing presses. In response, a group led by an abolitionist named John Brown murdered five men associated with the proslavery groups.

A reaction to Kansas in Washington, D.C., showed how quickly the violence could spread. In May 1856, Charles Sumner, a senator from Massachusetts, gave an outraged speech about the "crimes of Kansas" in which he charged Andrew Butler of South Carolina with taking "a mistress . . . the harlot, Slavery." Three days later, Butler's nephew, Preston Brooks, a member of the House of Representatives, came up to Sumner's desk in the Senate chamber. While a fellow congressman warded off other members of the Senate with a pistol, Brooks beat Sumner to a bloody pulp with his metal-tipped cane until he was unconscious. Sumner became a northern martyr. Brooks became a southern hero.

In Illinois, the Republican party held sway as the center of opposition to the slave power. As animus to that power increased, its political capital grew. The Know-Nothings had reached their peak in 1856. Now the Republicans were gaining strength. In May of that year, the state party officially formed with a rousing convention in Bloomington. Lincoln joined them, giving his most famous speech that has never been read. The traditional story of the "lost" speech of Bloomington is that people were so moved by what Lincoln said that reporters dropped their pens in their rapture. In fact, the reporters who dropped their pens were Lincoln's allies. And even if they were moved by the occasion to do so, they had a practical reason, too: the party was still considerably to the left of dominant public sentiment, especially in the center and south of the state. The words Lincoln spoke to animate the party faithful were probably best kept out of the public eye. The hard struggle ahead was clear when the party held a rally in Springfield. Aside from Lincoln and his law partner Herndon, there was one man in the room. "While all seems dead," Lincoln assured his audience of two, "the age itself is not. It liveth as sure as our Maker liveth. Under all this seeming want of life and motion, the world does move nevertheless. Be hopeful, and now let us adjourn and appeal to the people."

The first widespread Republican appeal to the people failed. In 1856, the first Republican candidate for president, John C. Frémont, lost to the Democrat James Buchanan. The Democrats had a strong hand: their base in the South was solid, and their presence in the North — largely courtesy of Stephen Douglas — still formidable. Had Frémont prevailed, Lincoln would have been rewarded for his toil with a choice of offices. His prominence in the national party could be seen when, at the first national Republican convention, more than one hundred delegates identified him as their top choice for vice president. But after the election, he was again without a place in government. His old nemesis, Stephen Douglas, meanwhile, had free access to the White House. "With *me*," Lincoln wrote in 1856, "the race of ambition has been a failure — a flat failure; with *him* it has been one of splendid success. His name fills the nation; and is not unknown, even, in foreign lands."

This bald statement of his own lack of success led to an equally bald statement of his fundamental desires. "I affect no contempt for the high eminence he has reached. So reached, that the oppressed of my species, might have shared with me in the elevation, I would rather stand on that eminence, than wear the richest crown that ever pressed a monarch's brow." With slavery, Lincoln had urged, people had to take the long view. They had to fight for its eventual extinction and set themselves to making it happen — not expect too much too quickly, and not give up the fight until right eventually prevailed. And as he developed his gospel of the imperfect, he pressed it to himself in private. Faced with the prospect of defeat, he responded by clarifying his sense of personal mission. Lincoln's mental instincts and the events of his life were in a dynamic exchange. Much the way a healthy ecosystem integrates decay and death with growth and life, Lincoln was able to integrate his difficulty into his overall purpose.

In March of 1857, the stakes of the fight became even clearer. Just after President Buchanan took the oath of office, the Supreme Court handed down its decision in *Dred Scott v. Sandford*. A slave who had lived for a time in a federal installation in Illinois, Scott sued for his freedom on the grounds that he had been living in free territory. The Court was divided on the case. The majority opinion, written by Chief Justice Roger Taney, a slaveholder and staunch supporter of the institution, held that Scott had no standing to sue in federal court because no Negro, free or slave, had that right. Not only that, but Scott could not have achieved freedom by going into free territory, the Court ruled, because Congress had no power to prohibit slavery in the territories. What had just a few years before been only an outrageous specter seemed a realistic prospect: that northern laws against slavery would be ruled unconstitutional. What's more, in the fall of 1857, President Buchanan said he would accept Kansas into the Union with a constitution written in Lecompton by a proslavery minority — an illustration of slavery's vise grip on the Democratic party.

Stephen Douglas had endorsed the Dred Scott decision, but the Lecompton constitution proved too much for him. He broke with his party over it and fought to keep a slave Kansas out of the Union. Suddenly the Republicans' archenemy looked like a new ally. Party leaders like Horace Greeley, the powerful editor of the *New York Tribune*, began to look on Douglas with great interest. Lincoln, who had his eye on a race against the Little Giant for the Senate in 1858, was aghast. "What does the New-York Tribune mean by it's constant eulogising, and admiring, and magnifying Douglas?" he wrote to Lyman Trumbull in December 1857. "Does it, in this, speak the sentiments of the republicans at Washington? Have they concluded that the republican cause, generally, can be best promoted by sacraficing us here in Illinois? If so we would like to know it soon; it will save us a great deal of labor to surrender at once." The truth was that Greeley did speak for many powerful Republicans. "The Republican standard is too high," Greeley told Herndon, who went to see him on Lincoln's behalf. "We want something more practical."

This sentiment was Lincoln's most vexing obstacle yet. For three years he had labored faithfully against Douglas, creating in Illinois one of the bedrocks of the nationally ascendant Republican party. Now the party's leaders threatened to cut him off — and, more severely, cut off the principle that he had devoted himself to. Privately, Lincoln was in a funk that Greeley would support Douglas, "a veritable dodger," over himself, a "true Republican . . . tried already in the hottest part of the anti-slavery fight." He said to Herndon, on a day of profound gloom, "Greeley is not doing me right." What was worse, to go with Douglas was to adopt his argument that slavery had no standing as a moral concern, that it mattered not whether it was voted up or down. In other words, as Lincoln put it, if a man decided to make a slave of another, no third man should object.

Lincoln regarded Douglas as a political con man with no sense of right and wrong, who took whatever position best suited his immediate aim. He never failed, because when cornered he altered himself, or his cause, in order to win. He was attended, Lincoln said, by an "evil genius." "What will Douglas do now?" Lincoln wrote to himself at one point. "He does not quite know himself. Like a skillful gambler he will play for all the chances . . . He never lets the logic of principle, displace the logic of success."

In self-conscious opposition to his nemesis, Lincoln approached a brink, and the way he crossed it shows the man he had become. He wanted to be the next senator from Illinois, but he wanted more to strike a blow for a cause he believed in. "I have never professed an indifference to the honors of official station," he wrote in the summer of 1858, in another revealing private note, "and were I to do so now, I should only make myself ridiculous. Yet I have never failed — do not now fail — to remember that in the republican cause there is a higher aim than that of mere office." In the struggle over slavery in Great Britain, Lincoln noted, the proslavery forces dominated for generations. Two of the main antislavery advocates, Granville Sharp and William Wilberforce, did not live to see the abolition bill become law. Nevertheless, Lincoln wrote, even schoolboys knew of Sharp and Wilberforce. And who could name one of their opponents? "Though they blazed, like tallow-candles for a century, at last they flickered in the socket, died out, stank in the dark for a brief season, and were remembered no more, even by the smell." "Remembering these things," Lincoln concluded, "I can not but regard it as possible that the higher object of this contest may not be completely attained within the term of my natural life." This was a logical extension of his idea. If one expected to move a cause only a bit forward — or, in harder times, to lean one's weight against it and keep it from sliding too far back — one could not expect to see, personally, much in return. "Whoever heard of a reformer reaping the reward of his labors in his lifetime?" he asked. Lincoln not only articulated this principle but, in the heat of a great political campaign, acted on it, too.

In the summer of 1858, the state Republicans met at Springfield and endorsed Lincoln as their sole choice for the Senate. Lincoln drafted a speech for the occasion and showed it to his colleagues for their comment. They said it would lose him the Senate and maybe end his career. Lincoln confidently replied that it would prove to be the most valuable thing he'd ever said. But he didn't tell his friends that they were wrong. He explained that he wanted to "strike home to the minds of men in order to raise them up to the peril of the times," and that if "it is decreed that I should go down because of this speech, then let me go down linked to the truth."

The speech began, "If we could first know *where* we are, and *whither* we are tending, we could better judge *what* to do, and *how* to do it." The Kansas-Nebraska Act, Lincoln noted, had promised to put an end to "slavery agitation." In fact, though, that agitation has not only, *not ceased*, but has *constantly augmented*. In *my* opinion, it *will* not cease, until a *crisis* shall have been reached, and passed.

"A house divided against itself cannot stand."

I believe this government cannot endure, permanently half *slave* and half *free*.

I do not expect the Union to be *dissolved* — I do not expect the house to *fall* — but I *do* expect it will cease to be divided.

It will become *all* one thing, or *all* the other. Either the *opponents* of slavery, will arrest the further spread of it, and place it where the public mind shall rest in the belief that it is in course of ultimate extinction; or its *advocates* will push it forward, till it shall become alike lawful in *all* the States, *old* as well as *new* — *North* as well as *South*.

With this opening salvo, Lincoln defined his campaign against Douglas, which would be amplified in seven head-to-head debates in August, September, and October. It would be a campaign on the fundamental question of the future of slavery — whether it was right or wrong, whether it should spread or be restricted. Douglas came into the campaign wanting to argue that no choice needed to be made, that a middle ground existed and its name was "popular sovereignty." Lincoln denied the possibility of papering over such a question — and helped precipitate the very crisis that he said would have to be reached, and passed.

It was one thing for Lincoln to privately reconcile himself to the possibility that he would not live to see the fruits of his work. It was quite another for him to strategically diminish his own chances at high office in exchange for striking a blow for his cause. Yet this is precisely what he did, not only with the "House Divided" speech but with another highlight of the 1858 campaign, the question that elicited Douglas's Freeport Doctrine. As we have seen, Douglas had endorsed the Dred Scott decision, which held that the Constitution guaranteed the right of slaves as property in the territories. At their second debate, in Freeport, Lincoln demanded that he explain whether it was possible, then, for a territory to legally proscribe slavery. He knew that Douglas would say, as he had previously, that yes, a territory could proscribe slavery simply by withholding the legislation necessary to protect it. It didn't serve Lincoln's immediate interests for Douglas to highlight this point, which endeared him to Illinois voters. Indeed, Lincoln's allies berated him for giving Douglas the opening, telling him he'd lose the race for senator. "I am after larger game," Lincoln answered. "The battle of 1860 is worth a hundred of this." Lincoln reckoned that he could help drive a wedge into the crack between Douglas and the slave power and ensure their split for the election of 1860.

We need to remember that Lincoln had no idea that *he* would be a part of the presidential race in 1860. He didn't plan to take a fall in order to win a larger office in two years. So far as he knew, this was his last, best chance to win an office, to receive some personal reward in honor and in salary. The "larger game" was not his career but the cause of liberty. Indeed, throughout the campaign Lincoln continually placed the struggle of the moment in the context of the past and the vast future, "when these poor tongues of Judge Douglas and myself shall be silent." "Think nothing of me," Lincoln said at Lewistown on August 17; "take no thought for the political fate of any man whomsoever, but come back to the truths that are in the Declaration of Independence. You may do anything with me you choose, if you will but heed these sacred principles. You may not only defeat me for the Senate, but you may take me and put me to death."

Douglas replied that the "Black Republicans" wanted only to elevate Negroes to superiority and force black men on white women. To illustrate this point, he told of how the abolitionist Frederick Douglass, a black man, was being driven around Illinois in the back of a carriage with a white woman while her husband drove the team. Having been hammered by Douglas on these points, Lincoln began the fourth debate with a response. "I am not," he said, "nor ever have been in favor of bringing about in any way the social and political equality of the white and black races." It is sobering, to say the least, to see Lincoln articulating white supremacy, as it was to hear him tell racist jokes and propose colonization. A growing number of critics insist on accounting for his racism.

The harshest critics of Lincoln often fail to see just how ugly were his opponents' ideas and tactics. While Lincoln frankly dismissed the possibility of black equality, then turned again to his argument against slavery, Stephen Douglas constantly stoked racist fears. At the same time, defenders of Lincoln often fail to fully acknowledge the whole truth of his limitations. But both can find common ground in Lincoln's spirit of progress. If anyone was prepared to admit his imperfections — the ones he could see and the ones he could not — it was the man himself. To pretend that all traces of racism must be scrubbed out of his life in order for him to have been a champion of progress is to create a claim that any but a perfect person must fail.

This point of view, applied to Lincoln, misses one of the essential aspects of his life, in his belief and in his biography. In both the man was imperfect, and in both the man embraced the reality of his imperfection. In his belief, Lincoln argued that Negroes were embraced by the founding principle of the Declaration of Independence, that "all men are created equal." This document, in his view, did not speak to the immediate necessity of legislating equal rights, but rather to the long-term promise of a nation that would be forever trying to improve itself, to move toward perfection. As Lincoln said, "There is no reason in the world why the negro is not entitled to all the natural rights enumerated in the Declaration of Independence, the right to life, liberty, and the pursuit of happiness. I hold that he is as much entitled to these as the white man."

The principle of equality that Lincoln sought to sustain the Union was one of equality of opportunity. Every person had the ability and the right, he thought, to work in order to better his condition. Occasionally Lincoln made it explicit that he was an example of how that right could bear fruit. "I happen temporarily to occupy this big White House," he told a group of soldiers as president. "I am a living witness that any one of your children may look to come here as my father's child has."

Lincoln had educated himself; he had worked hard in a country where he had the right and privilege to do so. It is a step in interpretation, but a justifiable one, to say that Lincoln's own sense of improvement probably came, in some measure, from what he had gained emotionally, too. Indeed, Lincoln conceived improvement — and the slavery that could prevent it — as more than merely material. There was a time, he said, when men "were utterly unconscious, that their *conditions,* or their *minds* were capable of improvement. They not only looked upon the educated few as superior beings; but they supposed themselves to be naturally incapable of rising to equality . . . It is difficult for us, *now* and *here* to conceive how strong this slavery of the mind was; and how long it did, of necessity, take, to break it's shackles, and to get a habit of freedom of thought, established." He not only supported material freedom but also declared it a "great task" to "immancipate the mind from this false and under estimate of itself."

Throughout this period, Lincoln struggled to maintain his own "freedom of thought" and feeling. We recall how, beginning in the mid-1840s,

Lincoln began to stand apart from crowds, exhibiting a sense, to all who saw him, that he was caught in the throes of melancholy. Reports of these spells increase after the fall of 1854. This may be partly due to the fact that Lincoln was more in the public eye, so people who crossed his path were more inclined to take notice of him. Even so, the intensity of the spells seems to have increased. What had looked like a sad, faraway look now seemed an intense and morbid preoccupation, which could last for hours at a time.

By the late 1850s, Lincoln regularly sat for photographs, a new and popular art form. Lincoln's portraits, showing his sunken cheeks, his unruly hair, his thick lips pressed solemnly together, have inspired wonder in many generations, and they communicate — even to those who know not a whit of the evidence of his melancholy — a feeling of it. In fact, according to those who witnessed his spells firsthand, the photographs do represent them, but not fully. Because Lincoln had to hold his expression for several minutes for the camera's long exposure, his countenance in the images did reflect his gloom. But his contemporaries said that no one could truly appreciate the gloom without seeing the awful contrast between his face when at ease and when in agony. "The pictures we see of him only half represent him," said the lawyer Orlando B. Ficklin. Observing him in the motion of storytelling, and then falling back into misery, made the latter state all the more dramatic.

A young man who first saw Lincoln in 1859 showed what that looked like in real time. John Widmer was in Ottawa, Illinois, when he heard that "Abe Lincoln is up from Springfield" to argue a case before the Illinois Supreme Court. He walked over to the courtroom and saw a man with a "lank, gaunt figure" sitting near a table and "thoughtfully studying the floor." "I did not take my eyes off of him during the short time I was in the room," Widmer recalled. "I noticed that he had a very pale, long face, big hands and feet, but the thing that impressed me most of all in regard to Abraham Lincoln was the extreme sadness of his eyes. Lincoln had the saddest eyes of any human being that I have ever seen." After a few minutes, "his melancholy expression had so impressed me that I should not have felt more solemn if I had been at a funeral." Soon Lincoln stood and addressed the court, and when he began to tell a funny story, his eyes brightened and a "faint smile spread over his features." When he sat down, Widmer said, "it was but a few minutes until that old, sorrowful look came over him."

Widmer knew he was watching, as he said, "an able man," a solid and dependable man, a man capable of great work. The young men of Illinois now chattered about Lincoln, and those who had seen him would always remember the moment. Hardly any of them who left a reminiscence failed to mention his melancholy, and hardly any thought it strange, or inconsistent, or contradictory. They saw him as he was, a full man whose griefs and solaces and talents ran together. They had the feeling that we are still capable of having, though it is rare for ordinary citizens to feel this way about the people in public life, the feeling of recognizing someone full, someone real, someone who has lived and suffered as we have and who has come out stronger for it — willing and able to wield his strength in service.

Many popular philosophies propose that suffering can be beaten simply, quickly, and clearly. Popular biography often expresses the same view. Many writers, faced with the unhappiness of a heroic figure, make sure to find some crucible in which that bad feeling melted into something new. "Biographies tend conventionally to be structured as crisis-and-recovery narratives," writes Louis Menand, "in which the subject undergoes a period of disillusionment or adversity, and then has a 'breakthrough' or arrives at a 'turning point' before going on to achieve whatever sort of greatness obtains." Lincoln's melancholy doesn't lend itself to such a narrative. No point exists after which the melancholy dissolved — not January 1841, not during his "reign of reason" in middle age, and not at his political resurgence beginning in 1854. Some scholars aver that Lincoln's melancholy abated in the war years, as he was too busy with his work to give space to his own gloom. We'll see evidence to the contrary. Whatever greatness Lincoln achieved cannot be explained as a triumph over personal suffering. Rather, it must be accounted for as an outgrowth of the same system that produced that suffering. This is not a story of transformation but one of integration. Lincoln didn't do great work because he solved the problem of his melancholy. The problem of his melancholy was all the more fuel for the fire of his great work.

In his campaign against Douglas, Lincoln did his best to win, consistent with his principles. He made lists of key legislators to sway, dispatched lieutenants to key districts, and heeded the response of crowds. In the November 1858 election, Illinois Republicans did win the popular vote. But owing to favorable apportionment, the Democrats elected more members to the Assembly, who in turn elected Douglas U.S. senator. According to the lawyer Henry Whitney, Lincoln on that day said his life had been a failure. "I never saw any man so radically and thoroughly depressed," Whitney wrote, "so completely steeped in the bitter waters of hopeless despair." Lincoln wrote, "The emotions of defeat . . . are fresh upon me."

Nevertheless, his main message was defiance. "The fight must go on," he wrote to an ally. "The cause of civil liberty must not be surrendered at the end of *one*, or even, one *hundred* defeats." His own defeat scarcely mattered. "Though I now sink out of view and shall be forgotten," he wrote to his old friend Anson Henry, "I believe I have made some marks which will tell for the cause of civil liberty long after I am gone." Lincoln again reminded his allies of the long view. "I hope and believe seed has been sown that will yet produce fruit," he wrote to one colleague. To another he wrote, "You are feeling badly. '*And this too shall pass away.*' Never fear."

Lincoln explained the origin of that phrase in a speech he gave in 1859. At a state fair in Wisconsin, he spoke to the crowd just before farm prizes were to be handed out. "Some of you," Lincoln said, "will be successful, and such will need but little philosophy to take them home in cheerful spirits; others will be disappointed, and will be in a less happy mood." To those who did need a philosophy — most of the crowd, since prizes went only to a few — Lincoln offered, "To such, let it be said, 'Lay it not too much to heart.' Let them adopt the maxim, 'Better luck next time,' and then, by renewed exertion, make that better luck for themselves." Lincoln then articulated the philosophy that he thought could help those with less than cheerful spirits. This same philosophy, he said, ought be heeded by those who were successful. "Let it be remembered," he said, "that while occasions like the present, bring their sober and durable benefits, the exultations and mortifications of them, are but temporary; that the victor shall soon be the vanquished, if he relax in his exertion; and that the vanquished this year, may be the victor the next, in spite of all competition." The point of exertion was not to win a contest and then relax. Work, Lincoln suggested, was its own end, for when one worked for a proper end, neither victory nor defeat could remain; rather, both led to the need for continued effort and diligence. He concluded his speech by citing an old parable, of an Eastern monarch who charged his wise men to invent a sentence that would apply to all times and in all situations. The wise men returned with "And this too shall pass away."

Lincoln lingered over the line. "How much it expresses!" he exclaimed. "How chastening in the hour of pride! — how consoling in the depths of affliction! And this, too, shall pass away." Still, to the wisdom of these wise men from the East he had something to add. "And yet," he said, "let us hope it is not *quite* true. Let us hope, rather, that by the best cultivation of the physical world, beneath and around us; and the intellectual and moral world within us, we shall secure an individual, social, and political prosperity and happiness, whose course shall be onward and upward, and which, while the earth endures, shall not pass away." In the face of present disappointments, Lincoln first articulated acknowledgment, then serene resignation, and finally the sad, sweet hope that better times would someday come.

CHAPTER 9

The Fiery Trial Through Which We Pass

O BSERVERS HAVE LONG noticed how Lincoln combined sets of opposite qualities. Harriet Beecher Stowe wrote that he was unsteady but strong, like a wire cable that shakes in storms but tenaciously moves toward its end. Carl Sandburg described Lincoln as "steel and velvet . . . hard as rock and soft as drifting fog." As these metaphors indicate, Lincoln not only embraced contrasts — self-doubt and confidence, hope and despair — but somehow reconciled them to produce something new and valuable. In this lies the key to his creative work as president — and an enduring lesson.

Living a good life often requires integrating a bundle of contrasts into a durable whole. The psychiatrist Leston Havens explains, in his book *Learning to Be Human*, that mental health depends on both freedom and compliance, radical independence and persistent loyalty. "My model will be Lincoln," Havens writes, "who seemed as hard as granite and as soft as a cloud. I will learn to be as strong and as weak as I need to be." We began this study of Lincoln by drawing on psychology. Now we find psychology drawing on Lincoln — seeing that his life teaches something that no mere prescription can about how to live a successful life in the face of suffering.

Lincoln's rise to the White House was swift and largely unexpected. As late as April 1859, he actively discouraged local admirers who spoke of him as a candidate for the White House. "I must, in candor, say I do not think myself fit for the Presidency," he wrote. "I certainly am flattered, and gratified, that some partial friends think of me in that connection;

but I really think it best for our cause that no concerted effort, such as you suggest, should be made." His modesty was justified, as he was still largely unknown on the national scene. In the fall of 1859, when his son Robert applied to Harvard College, Lincoln supposedly asked Stephen Douglas to write a recommendation. The administration at Harvard might not have known Abraham Lincoln's name.

Then, in October 1859, another man-made earthquake shook the nation. At Harpers Ferry, Virginia, a picturesque town on a bend in the Potomac River, the abolitionist John Brown stormed a federal arsenal with a small corps of armed men. Brown had hoped to initiate a slave revolt. Instead, he was quickly caught, tried, and sentenced to be hanged. The significance of this raid came in the reaction to it — that is, the reaction in the South to the reaction in the North. Brown played the martyr perfectly. On his way to the gallows he offered a final statement: "I, John Brown, am now quite *certain* that the crimes of this *guilty land* will never be purged away — but with *blood*."

On the day of his hanging, northern church bells tolled and preachers eulogized him as a crusader for liberty. "The death of no man in America has ever produced so profound a sensation," wrote the editor of the *Lawrence (Kansas) Republican,* noting the "deep and sorrowful indignation" at Brown's hanging. Such words drove southerners to rage. Can we "live under a government, the majority of whose subjects regard John Brown as a martyr and a Christian hero?" asked the influential *De Bow's Review.* Of course the answer was no. "Thousands of men," a joint editorial of two rival Richmond, Virginia, newspapers declared, "who, a month ago, scoffed at the idea of a dissolution of the Union . . . now hold the opinion that its days are numbered." Thus did the nation enter the election year, 1860, so shaken that anything was politically conceivable, even that an obscure, quasi-successful politician might emerge as a national leader.

On Saturday, February 25, 1860, Lincoln stepped off a train in Jersey City, New Jersey. After a journey of 1,200 miles, from Springfield, Illinois, in lurching rail cars that made frequent stops and demanded relentless transfers, he had reached the end of the line. He claimed his trunk and made his way to a crowded pier on the west side of the Hudson River. There he faced Manhattan Island, where two days later, on the strength of a single speech, he would send himself hurtling toward the center of the nation's mounting crisis.

Eastern Republicans knew Lincoln for having gamely challenged Stephen Douglas in 1858. However, few outside the prairie states had *seen* Lincoln or considered him in his own right. That would change on Monday night, when Lincoln was slated to appear at the Great Hall at the Cooper Institute, the largest venue in Manhattan. He would speak as part of a series devoted to western Republicans, sponsored by a group of party insiders who wanted to find someone to challenge William Seward for the presidential nomination. The stakes could not have been higher.

At Exchange Street in Jersey City, Lincoln caught the Paulus Street Ferry, a service of the Pennsylvania Railroad, which carried its eastbound passengers into New York. (The great city in 1860 had neither bridges nor tunnels.) The ferry docked at Cortlandt Street, only a few blocks from Lincoln's hotel, the famous Astor House on Broadway — itself around the corner from his first stop in the city: the offices of the antislavery *New York Independent.* Calling on the editor, Henry C. Bowen, Lincoln sprawled out on the sofa, his long legs dangling over the edge, his clothes rumpled from the long trip, his face, Bowen observed, wearing a "woebegone look." Bowen invited Lincoln to stay at his house. Lincoln said no, that he would stay at his hotel and continue working on his speech. He said that he feared he'd made a mistake in coming to New York. He'd have to give his whole time before Monday night to the text; "otherwise he was sure he would make a failure."

True to his word, Lincoln threw himself at the work. Before he left Springfield, he had laid the foundation for the speech, consulting texts and organizing his ideas into an argument. He had neither speechwriters nor research assistants, unless Herndon, as he sometimes did, found a relevant passage for him or lent him a book. While Lincoln often spoke extemporaneously over the course of his career, most of the great works of his mature years were composed on the page. Going through many drafts, he worked out his thoughts by writing and rewriting.

For the Cooper Institute speech, Lincoln may have felt a special urgency to revise, since he had originally planned to speak at Henry Ward Beecher's church in Brooklyn and found out about the move to Manhattan only when he arrived in the city. Lincoln several times articulated his central motivation: he was determined not to fail. On Sunday, February 26, Bowen prevailed upon Lincoln to attend services at Beecher's church in Brooklyn Heights, but afterward the Illinoisan turned down an invitation to lunch. "Now, look here, Mr. Bowen," he said, "I am not going to make a failure at the Cooper Institute to-morrow night, if I can help it." The work, he said, "is on my mind all the time . . . Please excuse me and let me go to my room at the hotel, lock the door, and there think about my lecture."

On Monday night, February 27, 1860, a crowd of more than 1,500 people filed into the Great Hall, paying the twenty-five-cent admission and taking seats in the long, rectangular theater, which ran the length of a city block. Lincoln mounted the podium wearing a new suit, but it didn't fit well. One young Republican called it as "unbecoming" as it could be. "I had a feeling of pity for so ungainly a man," said a member of the audience. "I said to myself, 'Old fellow, you won't do; it's all very well for the wild West, but this will never go down in New York.'"

Well aware of the "wild West" stereotype, Lincoln had prepared a speech that drew its core strength not from colorful anecdotes but from solid research. For years, the country had been roiled by the question of whether the federal government could constitutionally regulate slavery in the territories. The Democrats argued that it could not. Although the Dred Scott decision had cited Fifth Amendment protections of property, Stephen Douglas, Lincoln's ideological sparring partner, cited the Tenth Amendment, which reserved all powers not explicitly delegated to the federal government "to the States respectively, and to the people." "Our fathers, who framed the Government under which we live," Douglas said, "understood this question just as well, and even better, than we do now." Lincoln agreed. But, he asked, what did those fathers think about regulating slavery? The subject hadn't been raised at the Constitutional Convention in Philadelphia. So Lincoln spent the first portion of his speech examining the opinions on record for each of the thirty-nine signers.

Lincoln opened with a good idea — a new way into an old question — and did the hard work to draw it out. Had it been easy to discover how all the individuals who signed the Constitution stood on slavery regulation, someone would have done it long before. He began in 1784, when Congress, meeting under the Articles of Confederation, prohibited slavery in the Northwest Territory and three of the thirty-nine signers voted for the ban. He continued through the votes for the Missouri Compromise in 1819, when one signer, present in the Congress, voted steadily for the prohibition of slavery in the territories. In total, Lincoln found that of twenty-three signers who voted on the question, twenty-one supported a federal power to regulate slavery in the federal territories. Of the other sixteen, many had expressed opposition to slavery. The case was devastating, all the more so because, in Lincoln's presentation, it was not opinion but fact. After this speech, to say that the Founders had opposed the regulation of territorial slavery would be like saying the Constitution created six houses of Congress.

On this foundation, Lincoln built a stirring appeal that tied Republican ideals to the Founders' vision. Addressing the people of the South, he said, "You say you are conservative — eminently conservative — while we are revolutionary, destructive, or something of the sort. What is conservatism? Is it not adherence to the old and tried, against the new and untried? We stick to, contend for, the identical old policy on the point in controversy which was adopted by 'our fathers who framed the Government under which we live'; while you with one accord reject, and scout, and spit upon that old policy, and insist upon substituting something new." Slavery's extension must be opposed, he insisted, on the principle of slavery being wrong, even while the institution as it existed was tolerated out of devotion to the Union and its laws.

As Lincoln drew to the end, the hall was so quiet that when he paused, one could hear the sizzle of the gas burners. "Let us stand by our duty fearlessly and effectively," he said. "Let us be diverted by none of those sophistical contrivances wherewith we are so industriously plied and belabored — contrivances such as groping for some middle ground between the right and the wrong: vain as the search for a man who should be neither a living man nor a dead man; such as a policy of 'don't care' on a question about which all true men do care; such as Union appeals beseeching true Union men to yield to Disunionists, reversing the divine rule, and calling, not the sinners, but the righteous, to repentance . . . Neither let us be slandered from our duty by false accusations against us, nor frightened from it by menaces of destruction to the government, nor of dungeons to ourselves. LET US HAVE FAITH THAT RIGHT MAKES MIGHT, AND IN THAT FAITH LET US TO THE END DARE TO DO OUR DUTY AS WE UNDERSTAND IT."

The crowd whooped, whistled, and stamped their feet. There was little doubt that Abraham Lincoln had made a stunning New York debut. Four city newspapers would carry the full speech. Perhaps the most influential Republican voice in the nation, the *New York Tribune,* said that Lincoln's speech "was one of the happiest and most convincing political arguments ever made in this city . . . No man ever before made such an impression on his first appeal to a New York audience."

The contrasts on display in New York City help us see Lincoln's character on the eve of his political ascension. Few orators stood down the slave power more fearlessly than he. Few framed the contest so nakedly — right versus wrong, liberty versus slavery, patriotism versus greed. Yet the man throwing these verbal daggers onstage seemed, before he went on and after he stepped off, diffident, doubtful, and sad. Whisked off to a celebratory dinner at the Athenaeum Club, on Fifth Avenue and Sixteenth Street, Lincoln seemed strangely impervious to the praise ringing in his ears. "No man in all New York," remembered Charles Nott, "appeared more simple, more unassuming, more modest, more unpretentious, more conscious of his own defects." After dinner, Nott rode the streetcar downtown with Lincoln. After he got off at his stop, he regretted that he hadn't accompanied Lincoln to his hotel — "not because he was a distinguished stranger," Nott said, but because he "seemed a sad and lonely man." The next morning, when another admirer rushed to congratulate him, Lincoln's face brightened for a moment at the praise. Then, with a diffident tone, he said, "I am not sure that I made a success." A few days later he allowed, in a letter home, that the Cooper Institute address "went off passably well," but said his subsequent speeches were giving him trouble. "I have been unable to escape this toil," he wrote. "If I had foreseen it, I think I would not have come East at all."

Given how much it bears on his case, it may seem surprising that the relationship between creativity and suffering has never been applied to Lincoln. That's largely due to a blinkered view of creativity that considers it the exclusive province of cloistered artists. Politics, many people believe, is for glad-handing and persuasion, a realm where elegance of thought can be a hindrance and gains come only by pile-driving force. But a precise definition of creativity can help us see how it bears on Lincoln.

In a study on "the psychology of discovery and invention," drawing on analysis of high achievers in fields from science to diplomacy to the arts, the psychologist Mihaly Csikszentmihalyi defines creativity as the making of something genuinely new that is valued enough to be added to the culture. "Creativity doesn't happen in people's heads," writes Csikszentmihalyi, "but in the interaction between a person's thoughts and a sociocultural context. It is a systemic rather than an individual phenomenon." Also, being creative isn't the same as being socially interesting or stimulating. "Some of the people who have had the greatest impact on history," Csikszentmihalyi writes, "did not show any originality or brilliance in their behavior except for the accomplishments they left behind — neither Leonardo da Vinci nor Isaac Newton nor Thomas Edison would have been assets at a party."

What, then, distinguishes creative people? Csikszentmihalyi explains that one word best sums up what he has learned about them: complexity. "I mean," he writes, "that they show tendencies of thought and action that in most people are segregated." The prestigious creators he studied were both wild and subdued, rebellious and pragmatic, cooperative and aggressive. Crucially, Csikszentmihalyi observes, they found ways to use these extremes to their advantage — for instance, trusting their intuition to make novel connections in language or imagery, and then trusting others to edit and publish their work.

Research on the mental health of creative people shows another angle of this complexity. The idea of the tortured genius is simplistic, insofar as it suggests that being tortured, by itself, is worth anything. As the psychiatrist Kay Redfield Jamison writes, "There is a great deal of evidence to suggest that, compared to 'normal' individuals, artists, writers, and creative people in general are both psychologically 'sicker' — that is, they score higher on a wide variety of measures of psychopathology — and psychologically healthier (for example, they show quite elevated scores on measures of self-confidence and ego strength)."

To elaborate on "sicker": numerous studies have shown that rates of mood disorders are far higher among artists than the overall population. One in-depth study of 113 German artists found rates of "abnormality" much higher than in the general public — fifty percent of the poets in the group had clinically significant mental trouble. Another well-known study, led by Nancy Andreasen, used structured interviews and matched control groups to examine thirty writers at the prestigious University of Iowa Writers' Workshop. Eighty percent of the writers met formal criteria for a major mood disorder, compared with thirty percent of controls matched for age, education, and sex.

Lincoln, of course, is not the only nineteenth-century figure in whom intense suffering coexisted with great achievement. Modern researchers have identified one or more major mood disorders in John Quincy Adams, Charles Darwin, Emily Dickinson, Benjamin Disraeli, William James, William Tecumseh Sherman, Robert Schumann, Leo Tolstoy, Queen Victoria, and many others. We may accurately call these luminaries "mentally ill," a label that has some use — as did our early diagnosis of Lincoln — insofar as it indicates the depth, severity, and quality of their trouble. However, if we get stuck on the label, we may miss the core fascination, which is how illness can coexist with marvelous well-being.

In fact, the popular use of medical diagnoses — a mark of progress in many respects — has often hindered a proper understanding of prominent people who suffer so much. Perhaps the best example is the short-lived vice presidential candidacy of Thomas Eagleton in 1972. Tapped by the Democratic nominee, George McGovern, to join his ticket, Eagleton told campaign staffers that on three occasions he had received in-patient psychiatric treatment for depression. Twice he had been treated with electroconvulsive therapy — "electroshock."

McGovern's staff was split over what to do. "This had never happened before," said Gary Hart, the campaign manager. "No one knew the rules." McGovern, after reviewing the facts, met with Eagleton and decided that he should stay on the ticket, but a barrage of negative press and nervous donors changed his mind. From that point on, "Eagleton" became synonymous with the toxic political effects of mental health treatment. When Congress was considering President Nixon's appointment of Gerald Ford to replace Spiro Agnew as vice president in 1973, rumors surfaced that Ford had seen a psychotherapist. He denied it, as did the physician in question. "Consulting a psychiatrist or psychotherapist," the *New York Times* noted, "is still an unforgivable sin for an American politician."

The *Times* got it right. The problem that dogged both Eagleton and Ford wasn't mental trouble per se but the treatment for that trouble — and the language and imagery created by that treatment. When Eagleton first, sheepishly, told McGovern aides about his history, he said that he'd suffered from depression and fatigue. But as Hart has recounted, this raised fears that Eagleton's medical records would contain "technical terms that unfriendly experts can twist and turn." Indeed, the psychiatric term "psychosis," which could refer to profound illogical thinking, a characteristic of depression, came to haunt Eagleton. The fact that he'd had electroshock therapy may have been what sank him.

Over the past few decades, a stigma in politics against mental health treatment has extended to any display of unscripted emotion. In the primaries leading up to the 2004 campaign, a front-page story in *USA Today* noted that Vermont governor Howard Dean, a candidate for the Democratic nomination, "is continuing to feed the perception . . . that he is angry, edgy, and — a cardinal sin in politics — not cheerful." It's telling that *USA Today*, like the *Times* in 1973, used the word "sin." Somehow, anything short of constant cheer has come to be perceived as a violation of the American religion. Even as we practically drown in information about politicians' predilections — from snack foods to underwear — a kind of supposition of infallibility keeps us from a real discussion of character, because the real things human beings actually experience are considered taboo. We all know that our presidents, as Bob Dylan sang, "sometimes must have to stand naked." Yet anyone who dared to be nakedly emotional would face death by a thousand cuts.

With that in mind, it's interesting to see how the power brokers and pundits of 1860 reacted to Lincoln's depressions. Many people didn't seem to care. The *Chester County (Pennsylvania) Times*, in the first extended profile of Lincoln published outside Illinois, noted with a shrug that he had mood swings — "passing easily from grave to gay, and from gay to grave." Even political rivals who knew the worst of it didn't see the melancholy as a knock on Lincoln. After his election, a Democratic newspaper told the story of Lincoln's first breakdown, noting how his friends "placed him under guard for fear of his committing suicide." The author of the piece, an Illinois Democrat named John Hill, raised the history of depression not to question Lincoln's fitness for office but to celebrate his triumph over difficulty. The piece enjoined young people that they, too, could become great if they "await the occasions which shall rule their destinies."

If Lincoln were alive today, his depression would be considered a "character issue" — that is, a political liability. But in his time, it may have helped more than it hurt. While many found his moods odd and curious, the most common reaction was positive interest. Even as he rose to great heights, people tended to feel sympathy for him. As the biographer David Herbert Donald has observed, "Many of Lincoln's advisors viewed him as a man who needed to be encouraged and protected." Nathan Knapp, an Illinois Republican, said of Lincoln, "He has not known his own power — uneducated in Youth, he has always been doubtful whether he was not pushing himself into positions to which he was unequal." Lincoln's close ally David Davis called him a "guileless man" who "has few of the qualities of a politician." Of course Davis knew how skillful and savvy Lincoln could be, but his point was that on a personal level, he seemed unvarnished and unaffected. This contributed to an intense loyalty in his circle of friends and colleagues, which played a large role in his astonishing rise.

There was a felicitous resonance between his emotional struggle and the material struggles that so impressed his Republican brethren. When Richard Oglesby came up with the "rail-splitter" label at the state party convention in Decatur, it so excited the crowd because it spoke to the dignity and strength of Lincoln's story — how he had raised himself up, both mentally and materially, and achieved tremendous personal power. At the same convention, you will recall, Lincoln made a strong impression on the delegates with his sad, diffident look onstage. After the convention closed, he sat with his head in his hands and said, pathetically, "I'm not very well." There was a mystery to this man, a secret pain in his heart. To some people, this made Lincoln all the more alluring. In any case, no one discussed it as a liability.

Illinois Republicans officially made Lincoln their candidate for president on May 10, 1860, in Decatur. After the state convention, tradition held that Lincoln should go home, while his friends went on to the national party convention in Chicago to win him the nomination. The odds against his success were stiff. The convention site had been chosen, five months before, because it seemed to be neutral ground — Illinois had no serious candidate. Many thought that Seward was a shoo-in; before the proceedings commenced in Chicago, he had locked up more than 150 delegates — two thirds of what he needed to win. But if Seward had the power of a strong reputation, Lincoln had the benefit of his ferociously energetic and skillful advocates. David Davis, as Lincoln's manager on the scene, led one of the great political operations in history, presenting the man from Illinois as the embodiment of Republican heroism, a living example of upward mobility through free labor. This, combined with round-the-clock cajoling and dealmaking, helped boost Lincoln as a serious contender. A stream of telegrams came to Lincoln at Springfield:

> "Things are working; Keep a good nerve . . . We have got Seward in the attitude of the representative Republican of the East — *you* of the West . . . Be not too expectant, but rely on our discretion. Again I say, brace your nerves for any result." — N. M. Knapp, May 14, 1860

> "We are quiet but moving heaven & Earth . . . the heart of the delegates are with us." — David Davis and Jesse Dubois, May 15, 1860

> "Dont be frightend Keep cool Things is working."
> — Norman Judd, May 16, 1860

It turned out that electoral realities were in Lincoln's favor. To prevail in November, Republicans needed to capture four states they'd lost in 1856: Illinois, Indiana, Pennsylvania, and New Jersey. The right candidate would have solid credentials in the fight against slavery expansion, without having alienated nativists (who were strong in Illinois) or tariff advocates (who were strong in Pennsylvania). Lincoln, who had done enough to be recognized but not enough to be disliked, fit the bill. Though the first ballot brought Seward just sixty-one votes shy of victory, his support had topped out. Lincoln made big gains on the second tally and prevailed on the third. Charles Zane, a young lawyer who spent the day with Lincoln, said that he showed "no nervousness or excitement" upon hearing the news, but that he did seem "graver and at times sadder than usual . . . I attributed this to an anticipation of the great responsibility that would await him if elected."

Indeed, his chances were good, for as the new, untested Republican party settled on Lincoln, the old, great Democratic party fell to ruins. Its convention in Charleston, South Carolina, collapsed when southern delegates, who insisted on a federal slave code for the territories, clashed with northerners, who fought that plank. Six weeks later, a second convention, in Baltimore, nominated the slave-code opponent Stephen Douglas, but southerners stormed out, convened again in Richmond, and sent up their own candidate, John C. Breckinridge of Kentucky. To make matters worse for the Democrats, the old Know-Nothing organization joined with southern Whigs to form yet another party, which promised to drain votes from the Democratic upper South. In a four-way race — Lincoln for the Republicans, Douglas for the northern Democrats, Breckinridge for the southern Democrats, and John Bell for the Constitutional Unionists — the "rail-splitter" had the upper hand. "I think the chances were more than equal that we could have beaten the Democracy *united*," Lincoln wrote on July 4, 1860. "Divided, as it is, it's chance appears indeed very slim." On November 6, Lincoln and his running mate, Maine senator Hannibal Hamlin, won every free state — except for New Jersey, which the ticket split with Douglas — assembling an electoral majority with just forty percent of the popular vote. Abraham Lincoln, the son of a mostly illiterate farmer, would be the sixteenth president of the United States.

Overnight, the same divisions that had thrust Lincoln to victory became his burden. Repulsed by the ascension of an antislavery party, the cotton states of the lower South quickly seceded — first South Carolina, followed by Mississippi, Florida, Alabama, Georgia, Louisiana, and Texas. Officials from these states withdrew from Washington and resigned their military commissions. On February 18, 1861, the Confederate States of America inaugurated Jefferson Davis as their provisional president.

Northern eyes turned expectantly to the man in Springfield. Newspapermen who came to see Lincoln noticed the same contrasts that had intrigued his friends for decades. Describing the president-elect's "careworn" appearance, the *New York Herald*'s Henry Villard reported, "The vigor of his mind and the steadiness of his humorous disposition are obviously unimpaired." Samuel R. Weed, a reporter from St. Louis, found Lincoln "in good spirits," greeting his supporters "with sincere pleasure." "There was a sort of sadness in his face," Weed wrote, "which was remarked by more than one of those present. But he kept it under." These glimpses of Lincoln — haggard, vigorous, and funny; seeming sad but "keeping it under" — hinted at the man's complexity. Lincoln himself offered a telling introduction with a line he used on allies who had campaigned for him. "He repeated this remark a half-dozen times in two hours," reported Weed, "and I have no doubt it came direct from his heart": "Well, boys," Lincoln said, "your troubles are over, but mine have just begun."

Politics aside, the real question about Lincoln's melancholy in his public life is how it affected his judgment and outlook. After a lifetime of inner turmoil, Lincoln had the experience and judgment to look trouble straight in the eye. Many old political hands were rattled by secession. Some northerners brashly said good riddance to the South, claiming that the country would be better off split. Others rushed to find something, anything, that would pacify the aggrieved states and bring them back into the Union. Watching these negotiations, Lincoln said plainly that he wouldn't budge on the bottom line. "Let there be no compromise on the question of *extending* slavery," he wrote. "Stand firm. The tug has to come, & better now, than any time hereafter."

That phrase reflected a judgment informed by old instincts. Having felt the tug come many times, Lincoln knew that putting it off would do no good. As Frederick Douglass said, "If there is no struggle, there is no progress." A dramatic concession might have prevented a conflict, only to intensify it on another day. And as Lincoln repeatedly explained, compromise on the essential issue of the election would set a fatal example. If the losers at the ballot forced the victors to yield on the central point, the result could hardly be called democracy. "We must settle this question now," Lincoln said, "whether in a free government the minority have the right to break up the government whenever they choose."

Good leaders can navigate skillfully between a steady set of principles and the exigencies of the moment. From the start, Lincoln made clear his commitment to a Union dedicated to the spread of liberty under the rule of law. At the same time, he took clear stock of the threat. As the scholar Matthew Pinsker has observed, "Mediocre presidents run from bad news. Great presidents face it." A history of mental struggle is surely no prerequisite for facing bad news, but for Lincoln, a tendency to depressive realism — a temperamental inclination to see and prepare for the worst — gave him an advantage. Having seen that his troubles began after his election, Lincoln also watched, with unclouded vision, as his troubles deepened.

While the Confederacy mobilized its militias and seized federal forts, mints, and customhouses, President Buchanan dithered in his response. Calling secession illegal, he said he could do nothing to stop it and found fault chiefly with northern agitators who had given slaves "notions of freedom," leaving their masters no choice but to act in self-preservation. Lincoln was aghast. "The present administration does nothing to check the tendency toward dissolution," he told his friend Joseph Gillespie. "I, who have been called to meet this awful responsibility, am compelled to remain here, doing nothing to avert it or lessen its force when it comes to me." Referring to the place where Jesus awaited execution and begged that the cup of bitterness be taken from his mouth, Lincoln said, "I am in the Garden of Gethsemane now, and my cup of bitterness is full and overflowing."

As this dramatic language suggests, the border between Lincoln's public responsibilities and his private burdens was porous. Perhaps the best, early illustration of this came at the scene of his departure from Springfield for Washington, D.C. On February 11, 1861, Lincoln arrived at the Great Western Railway sometime after 7 A.M. and entered the red-brick depot. "His face was pale," observed the *New York Herald*'s Villard, "and quivered with emotion so deep as to render him almost unable to utter a single word." At five minutes to eight, Lincoln left the depot building and made his way to the tracks, where he boarded the last of three cars hitched to a wood-fired locomotive. He climbed the rear steps of the car and, on reaching its platform, turned to face the crowd that had gathered despite a cold rain. When Lincoln took off his hat, men in the crowd followed suit. As he prepared to speak, he paused for a few seconds — "till he could control his emotions," noted a reporter.

"My friends," he began. "No one, not in my situation, can appreciate my feelings of sadness at this parting. To this place, and to the kindness of these people, I owe every thing. Here I have lived for a quarter of a century, and have passed from a young to an old man. Here my children have been born and one lies buried. I now leave, not knowing when, or whether ever, I may return, with a task before me greater than that which rested upon Washington." His farewell was the essence of emotional clarity. Frankly acknowledging his sadness, Lincoln neither lingered on maudlin details nor withdrew into sentimentality but stood anchored in his history, grasping the awful work of his future.

Never had the conditions for a president-elect been so severe, and never had one seemed, by his credentials, so poorly prepared. Lincoln's fifteen predecessors had included war hero generals, vice presidents, secretaries of state, and veterans of Congress. His own résumé listed, as he put it, "one term in the lower house of Congress." He'd had barely a year of formal education; he had few connections in the capital and no executive experience. Before coming to Washington, he had been east of the Alleghenies just a handful of times and still bore the stamp of a man raised on the frontier. Surveying the start of Lincoln's term, Harriet Beecher Stowe compared the nation to a ship on a perilous passage, at its helm "a plain working man of the people, with no more culture, instruction, or education than any such working man may obtain." She continued, "The eyes of princes, nobles, aristocrats, of dukes, earls, scholars, statesmen, warriors, all turned on the plain backwoodsman . . . watched him with a fearful curiosity, simply asking, '*Will* that awkward old backwoodsman really get that ship through?'" Edward Everett, the former senator and Harvard president who would share the dais with Lincoln at Gettysburg, offered his blunt assessment in a diary entry on February 15. "The President-elect is making a zigzag progress to Washington," he wrote, "called out to make short speeches at every important point. These speeches thus far have been of the most ordinary kind, destitute of everything, not merely of felicity and grace, but of common pertinence. He is evidently a person of very inferior cast of character, wholly unequal to the crisis."

On the morning of March 4, Lincoln appeared on a platform before the Capitol to take the oath of office. "He was tall and ungainly," recalled an Associated Press reporter, "wearing a black suit, a black tie beneath a turn-down collar, and a black silk hat. He carried a gold- or silver-headed walking-cane. As we came out into the open . . . he drew from his breast pocket the manuscript I had seen him reading at the hotel, laid it before him, placing the cane upon it as a paper-weight." As Lincoln took off his hat, Senator Stephen Douglas, his lifelong rival, stepped forward and offered to hold it. Putting on a pair of steel-framed spectacles, Lincoln began to read, his voice, the reporter said, "high pitched, but resonant."

Lincoln declared his intention to maintain the Union under the law, simultaneously assuring aggrieved southerners that he harbored no hostile intent and insisting that he would not countenance secession. In a long, careful speech, what stands out is an uncannily mature assessment of the nature of struggle. No one could deny the divisions over slavery, Lincoln said. Eventually these divisions would have to be faced head-on. "A husband and wife may be divorced," he observed, "and go out of the presence, and beyond the reach of each other; but the different parts of our country cannot do this. They cannot but remain face to face; and intercourse, either amicable or hostile, must continue between them." From this domestic metaphor emerged a central strain of Lincoln's thought. To remain face to face, whether in the midst of hostile differences or amicable agreement, is the human burden. In Springfield, Lincoln once noted how people needed to learn to live with their neighbors' irritations. If they moved, he said, they would merely trade old annoyances for new ones. In the realm of national affairs this melancholy principle remained. Best to face trouble directly, and in peace. He would not invade the South unless provoked, nor would he withhold lawful protection of slavery as it existed. He would "hold, occupy, and possess" federal property throughout the nation. But, he insisted, "in doing this there needs to be no bloodshed or violence; and there shall be none, unless it be forced upon the national authority."

In his original draft, Lincoln closed by emphasizing his hard line: "In *your* hands, my dissatisfied fellow countrymen, and not in *mine,* is the momentous issue of civil war . . . With *you,* and not with *me,* is the solemn question of 'Shall it be peace, or a sword?'" William Seward, his secretary of state designate, had written out his suggestion for a softer ending:

I close. We are not we must not be aliens or enemies but fellow countrymen and brethren. Although passion has strained our bonds of affection too hardly they must not I am sure they will not be broken. The mystic chords of memory which proceeding from so many battle fields and so many patriot graves pass through all the hearts and all the hearths in this broad continent of ours will yet again harmonize in their ancient music when breathed upon by the guardian angel of the nation.

Lincoln edited Seward's passage, and the result gives us a rare glimpse of Lincoln's literary mind in action. Insertions are shown in italics, deletions in strike-through type:

> I *am loth to* close. We are not ~~we must not be aliens or~~ enemies, but ~~fellow countrymen and brethren~~ *friends. We must not be enemies.* ~~Al-~~ *Though* passion *may have* ~~has~~ strained, *it must not break* our bonds of affection ~~too hardly they must not, I am sure they will not be broken.~~ The mystic chords *of memory, stretching* ~~which proceeding~~ from *every* ~~so many~~ battle-fields, and ~~so many~~ patriot graves, *to every living* ~~pass through all the~~ hearts and ~~all the~~ hearth*stone, all over*~~in~~ this broad land, ~~conti-nent of ours~~ will yet ~~again~~ *swell the chorus of the Union,* ~~harmonize in their ancient music~~ when *again touched* ~~breathed upon~~, *as surely they will be,* by the ~~guardian angel of the nation.~~ *better angels of our nature.*

Lincoln's choices show his keen rhetorical skills. From Seward's "I close," he wrote, "I am loth to close," reprising a wish to be in open intercourse with his friends and enemies both. From the clunky "We are not we must not be aliens or enemies but fellow countrymen and brethren," Lincoln wrote simply, "We must not be enemies but friends." The rhythm in Lincoln's paragraph better serves the message. Three short, punchy sentences create a tension that mounts through the tight clauses of the final sentence and delivers a breathless listener to the ultimate phrase.

Lincoln's most interesting alteration was substantial, not merely rhetorical. Seward had invoked "the guardian angel of the nation." Lincoln wrote, "the better angels of our nature." These phrases have much in common: both describe a holy force bringing an end to conflict. But whereas Seward's words called on some vague deity, a separate and external power, Lincoln's beckons something within. "Surely," Lincoln wrote, "the better angels of our nature" will touch us again. He does not suggest that the worse angels will be hounded away or killed. On the contrary, the image contains within it a sense of perpetual complexity, of lasting tension. Individuals and nations are multifaceted, capable of better and prone to worse, ever locked in struggle. "Better angels of our nature," as with many of Lincoln's phrases, reaches deep into the psyche, because it reflects an experience that every human being knows intuitively, one of division and conflict, brokenness and harmony, suffering and reward, a journey and its challenges. These were ideas that Lincoln lived and grappled with much of his life.

Upon taking office, as Lincoln faced the prospect of war, the weight lay hard upon him. He said the troubles he felt "were so great that, could I have anticipated them, I would not have believed it possible to survive." He couldn't sleep. He said he was in "the dumps." On March 30, according to a contemporary letter, he "keeled over with sick headache." Much of the early stress centered on Fort Sumter. An unfinished garrison in the harbor of Charleston, South Carolina, Sumter had become the symbolic center of the secession crisis. On Lincoln's first day in office, he learned that the federal garrison couldn't hold for more than six weeks without relief. To resupply the fort might provoke the South Carolina militia that huddled on the shore. To abandon it, Lincoln thought, would send a signal of capitulation. After agonizing over the question, he chose to alert the state's governor that he would ship in food but no arms. This turned out to be provocation enough. The first Confederate blasts rang out at 4:30 A.M. on April 12, 1861. Two days later, the American flag went down in surrender. Lincoln said that, with regret, he "found the duty of employing the war power" and called for 75,000 volunteers from the state militias. It would take four years for the flag to be raised again at Sumter. Before then, 3 million soldiers would fall into ranks. More than 620,000 of them would die.

For Lincoln, the plain physical realities of war rang in his ears and marched in front of his eyes and registered painfully in his melancholy mind. Consider the geography of his position. Washington, D.C., was itself a slave city with a southern culture, a nest for Confederate sympathizers. To the north and east lay Maryland, a slave state that for a time seemed poised to secede. To the south and west lay Virginia, which seceded after Sumter — along with Tennessee, North Carolina, and Arkansas. Active belligerents were posted just across the Potomac River. With a spyglass Lincoln could see an early Confederate flag flying over an Alexandria hotel. When the Confederate States of America moved its capital to Richmond, Jefferson Davis took up residence with his government about a hundred miles away from Lincoln and his.

As if to underscore the personal toll the war would take on him, the first celebrated death of the conflict was one of Lincoln's close friends. A slight young man with black hair and hazel eyes, Elmer Ellsworth had clerked for Lincoln in the late 1850s and traveled with him to Washington on the presidential train. In peacetime, Ellsworth had made a great reputation by leading a disciplined, colorful local militia. With the defection of so many talented southern officers, he gave people hope for the Union. Assembling a militia from among New York City firefighters, he paraded them through Washington, lending solace to a beleaguered city. On May 24, 1861, Ellsworth led a raid into Alexandria, Virginia. First seizing the railroad depot, he went on to secure the telegraph office, passing on the way the Marshall Hotel, a three-story brick building, which flew the Rebel flag Lincoln could see from the Executive Mansion. With four men Ellsworth charged up the hotel stairs to a top window, where he leaned out and grabbed the flag. On the way down, the innkeeper, James W. Jackson, shot and killed the young militiaman with a double-barreled shotgun.

A navy captain, Gustavus V. Fox, delivered the news to President Lincoln in the White House library, an oval room in the center of the mansion's second floor. Just after Fox left, Senator Henry Wilson of Massachusetts came in with a reporter for the *New York Herald.* They found Lincoln looking out the window over the Potomac. When they drew closer, Lincoln spun around, took a step toward them, and extended his hand. "Excuse me," he said, his voice breaking, "but I cannot talk." The men were about to ask what was the matter, but before they could say anything, Lincoln began to cry. He put a handkerchief over his face. Then he walked about the room in silence. The surprised guests stepped aside — "not a little moved," the reporter wrote, "at such an unusual spectacle, in such a man and in such a place." After a while, Lincoln sat down and invited the men to join him. "I will make no apology, gentlemen, for my weakness," he said, as reported by the *Herald,* "but I knew poor Ellsworth well, and held him in great regard. Just as you entered the room, Captain Fox left me, after giving me the painful details of his unfortunate death. The event was so unexpected, and the recital so touching, that it quite unmanned me." At this the president made what the reporter described as a "violent attempt to restrain his emotion."

In one sense, as president, Lincoln regressed emotionally. As a young man, he had often wept in public, loudly proclaimed his despair, and feared that he would break under the weight of his misery. He was, as a friend from New Salem said, an "open souled" man. In his middle years, he ceased making such dramatic displays, seeming more remote and reserved. Now the outwardly emotional style returned, as if intense grief thawed something in him that had been in a deep freeze.

On July 21, the war's first major battle left hundreds dead on the fields of Manassas, Virginia, followed by a clash in Missouri that produced 2,600 combined casualties. These battles, both Union defeats, dashed hopes for a quick end to the conflict. Lincoln called for the enlistment of 500,000 men, which he doubled three days later. Among those who stepped up to serve was Edward D. Baker, Lincoln's old political ally from Illinois. Though a member of the Senate, Baker now took a commission as colonel. On October 21, 1861, he led 1,700 men across the Potomac River from Maryland to Virginia, where they scaled a hundred-foot, nearly perpendicular bank called Ball's Bluff. At the top waited four Confederate regiments, which opened fire as soon as the Union soldiers clambered onto even ground. "A kind of shiver ran through the huddled mass upon the brow of the cliff," said a Virginia private. Panicked soldiers rushed backward and fell off the cliff, some onto the bayonets of their comrades. More than half the force was killed, wounded, or captured. Colonel Baker was shot in the head and died immediately.

Lincoln learned the news by telegraph at the Army of the Potomac's headquarters. Shortly afterward, the journalist Charles Carlton Coffin saw the president leaving the office. His head was down, his chest was "heaving with emotion," and he was crying. "He almost fell as he stepped into the street," Coffin wrote, "and we sprang involuntarily from our seats to render assistance, but he did not fall." At a memorial service for Baker, Coffin said, "again the tears rolled down his cheeks." Lincoln later said that Baker's death smote him like a whirlwind from a desert.

Another whirlwind soon struck Lincoln's family. By winter, both sides had dug in for a long conflict. Wartime Washington bulged in population, from 60,000 to 200,000. The Potomac, which was the source of the White House's drinking water, became fouled with the refuse of army camp latrines and broken sewage mains. In January 1862, William and Thomas, the two Lincoln children at the White House — Robert was at Harvard — took sick from what doctors called bilious fever — probably typhoid, which comes from contaminated water. Before their illnesses, the boys had the run of the Executive Mansion, and playing with them seemed to give Lincoln precious relief. Willie in particular was a gem of a boy. Sensitive, bright, and gentle, he had a sparkle about him and an uncanny poise. Unlike "Tad," who had a fiery temper and a speech impediment that made him hard to understand, and Bob, who was cold and aloof, Willie seemed to have inherited his father's best qualities.

After an illness marked by stomach cramps and diarrhea, Willie fell into a coma on February 18, 1862, and he died two days later. He was eleven years old. Elizabeth Keckly, Mary Lincoln's dressmaker, was washing the boy's body when the president came into the room and saw his son dead for the first time. Lincoln walked over to the bed, lifted the cover from Willie's face, and gazed at it for a long time. He said that the boy was too good for this earth. "It is hard, hard to have him die," he said, his words choked with sobs. "He buried his head in his hands," Keckly said, "and his tall frame was convulsed with emotion. I stood at the foot of the bed, my eyes full of tears, looking at the man in silent, awe-stricken wonder. His grief unnerved him, and made him a weak, passive child."

In itself, a father's grief over his son's death is no evidence of peculiarity or extreme suffering. But Lincoln's observers immediately saw that his was no reactive or temporary sadness. "He had a Sad Nature," said one army officer who got to know Lincoln. Edward Dicey, an English journalist who visited Washington in the spring of 1862, noticed the "look of depression" in Lincoln, "which, I am told by those who see him daily, was habitual to him, even before the then recent death of his child, whose loss he felt acutely. You cannot look upon his worn, bilious, anxious countenance, and believe it to be that of a happy man."

Lincoln took a risk showing himself so openly. Modern observers tend to see him as a man of little experience but solid character who faced a crisis and rose to great heights of practical and moral power. But many of his contemporaries saw a decent but ill-equipped man who collapsed into incompetence in the face of overwhelming events. Dicey wrote that Lincoln had "sense enough to perceive his own deficiencies" and that he "unites a painful sense of responsibility to a still more painful sense, perhaps that his work is too great for him to grapple with." The president's sadness, in other words, could be perceived as weakness — and this when his administration was dangerously weak. After several months in Washington, Dicey wrote a dispatch that summed up the conventional wisdom at the time: "Abraham Lincoln," Dicey wrote, "was regarded as a failure. Why he, individually, was elected, or rather, selected, nobody, to this day, seems to know." Surely, had the secession been foretold, Dicey believed, "a very different man would have been chosen."

Yet Lincoln continued to utter profoundly dark thoughts with seeming equanimity. Early in the war, he wondered aloud why anyone would want to be president, complaining about the incessant demands made by office seekers. Gazing out at the south lawn of the White House, he told a friend that he sometimes thought his only escape would be to hang himself from a tree. Perhaps because our society is so influenced by advertising, which blurs the distinction between perception and reality, there is a sense today that people in positions of strength must never waver, never doubt themselves. God forbid they should speak thoughts of suicide. But Lincoln, by whatever combination of habit and choice, took his own path. He did not pretend to be anything other than he was.

Paradoxically, his expressions of pain also conveyed how much pain he could tolerate while continuing to function. We have seen how, at the tail end of his second breakdown as a young man — and this following years of severe melancholy — Lincoln came away with a new clarity about what he would live for and suffer for. This resolve underlay his every move as president. "I expect to maintain this contest until successful, or till I die, or am conquered, or my term expires, or Congress or the country forsakes me," he wrote in the early summer of 1862.

He needed every ounce of this resolve. Though the Union had made some potent military gains, especially with its navy, the battle of Shiloh in February 1862 left twenty thousand total killed and wounded and raised the specter of total war. General William T. Sherman described the shocking piles of "mangled bodies," limbs and heads ripped from bloody trunks. "The scenes on this field would have cured anybody of war," Sherman said, yet he thought that only ruthless destruction would bring a Confederate surrender.

General George B. McClellan was considerably more cautious. A compact, red-headed, wellborn man, McClellan had known only success in his career as a railroad executive and military officer. Shortly after the war broke out, McClellan, only thirty-four, won an important victory in western Virginia, and Lincoln called on him to command the Army of the Potomac in the fall of 1861. His troops, fond of his dashing style and prodigious organizational skills, called him "the Little Napoleon." Within months of his arrival in the East, McClellan had deposed the Union's chief general, the aged Winfield Scott, and took control of the whole war effort. But while he built a great army, he seemed reluctant to use it. After months of prodding, he began a movement to Richmond. Marshaling 400 boats, he took 112,000 men, 1,200 vehicles, and 15,000 horses by sea to a narrow peninsula between the York and James rivers in Virginia. From there, his armies crossed the muddy fields toward the Confederate capital. He dug in for a siege, then clashed with Robert E. Lee's Army of Northern Virginia in a miserable seven days of fighting. Finally McClellan withdrew. Lincoln said that when the campaign ended, "I was as nearly inconsolable as I could be and live." He wrote to his secretary of state that he would ask for more men "were it not that I fear a general panic and stampede would follow — so hard is it to have a thing understood as it really is."

Lincoln often observed, in a resigned tone, how people were too optimistic, expected too much. For some, perhaps, it was the burden of their own constitutions — "pathological optimism" as opposed to Lincoln's "depressive realism." Others, like McClellan, teetered between unfounded pessimism and hysterical grandiosity. The general constantly portrayed his position as weaker than it really was — once, for example, insisting that the enemy had 150,000 men when the real number was 45,000, a third of McClellan's force. In the face of his own failures, McClellan heaped scorn all around — the president was an "idiot" and a "baboon," Secretary of State Seward an "officious, incompetent little puppy," Secretary of the Navy Gideon Welles "a garrulous old woman" — while indulging in self-pity: "I am thwarted and deceived by these incapables at every turn." "Perhaps," observes James McPherson, "McClellan's career had been too successful. He had never known . . . the despair of defeat or the humiliation of failure. He had never learned the lessons of adversity and humility." Lincoln had clearly learned those lessons.

Yet his ability to see into the dark heart of the matter might have derailed him were it not for an uncanny resilience. If comparison with McClellan highlights Lincoln's realism, a vivid character closer to home highlights his capacity for self-control. Like her husband, Mary Lincoln faced grave challenges from the start. Suspicious of her Kentucky heritage — of her fourteen brothers and half-brothers, eight supported the Confederacy — the northern press was merciless with her. She worked hard to restore the White House and preside over the nation as its First Lady, a term coined to describe her. But she quickly showed signs of erratic judgment, once buying eighty-four pairs of kid gloves in less than a month. Her profligate spending and her dealings with dubious characters led to rumors of corruption. According to O. H. Browning, an old friend of the Lincolns who now served as senator from Illinois, the president said several times "that he was constantly under great apprehension lest his wife should do something which would bring him into disgrace."

After their boy Willie's death, Lincoln faced an even greater fear — that his wife would go insane. She spent three weeks in bed, and when she rose, she wore nothing but mourning clothes for a year. She regularly had what her biographer Ruth Painter Randall describes as "paroxysms of convulsive weeping." In the midst of one, the president led her by the arm to a window and pointed across the Anacostia River to the Government Hospital for the Insane. "Mother," he said to her, "do you see that large white building on the hill yonder? Try and control your grief, or it will drive you mad, and we may have to send you there."

To keep himself sane, Lincoln drew on familiar strategies. He turned first to poetry, often repeating his favorite, "Oh, why should the spirit of mortal be proud." The tragedies of Shakespeare were a constant companion. Once, in a spell of melancholy, he rang his bell and asked a secretary to bring him a book of poetry by Thomas Hood. "It was brought to him," said O. H. Browning, "and he read to me several of those sad pathetic pieces — I suppose because they were accurate pictures of his own experiences and feelings. I remained with [him] about an hour & a half, and left in high spirits, and a very genial mood but as he said a crowd was buzzing about the door like bees, ready to pounce upon him as soon as I should take my departure, and bring him back to a realization of the annoyances and harrassments of his position."

In the face of both annoyance and sadness, nothing comforted Lincoln more than his jokes and stories. He spent much of his leisure time reading humor, with favorite volumes at the ready on his desk or in his coat pocket. His favorites included Charles Farrar Browne (who wrote as "Artemus Ward"), David Locke ("Petroleum V. Nasby"), and Robert H. Newell ("Orpheus C. Kerr"). These were first-class literary artists in the tradition that produced Mark Twain, and they sometimes poked fun at "Linkin." More often, they took aim at the arrogance, hypocrisy, and pieties that always make good fodder for a sharp comic eye. Locke's Nasby, for example, was an indolent and confused "Dimekrat" — "No man hez drunk more whiskey than I hev for the party — none hez dun it moar willingly" — who was always applying for office. Using the character, Locke dissected everything from northern fears of racial equality to draft dodgers to secessionists. Lincoln not only enjoyed these stories for himself but often read them aloud to visitors. David Locke noted, "He offended many of the great men of the Republican party this way." Imagine a distinguished visitor encountering a chief executive today, in the aftermath of a disaster or in the midst of a crisis, cracking up at *The Daily*

Show or *The Onion.* "Grave and reverend Senators," said Locke, "who came charged to the brim with important business . . . took it ill that the president should postpone the consideration thereof while he read them a letter from 'Saint's Rest, wich is in the state uv Noo Jersey.'" Lincoln said repeatedly that he didn't care. An exchange with James Ashley was typical. When the Ohio Republican objected to one of Lincoln's yarns, the president said, "Ashley, I have great confidence in you and great respect for you, and I know how sincere you are. But if I couldn't tell these stories, I would die. Now you sit down."

The stories were not mere amusement or relief. He also used them to ease friction and make a point. Once Lincoln told a Kentucky delegation that he couldn't satisfy any of their demands. It reminded him of a story about a family that was constantly moving. The chickens got so used to being moved that when they saw the wagons being readied, they'd lie on their backs and cross their legs. "If I listen to every committee that comes in at that door," Lincoln said, "I had just as well cross my hands and let you tie me." The visitors left empty-handed, but in good humor.

Sometimes Lincoln, like a black belt in karate, used others' thrusts to disarm them. Urged to give an office in Hawaii to a man whose friends said he needed the good climate for his health, Lincoln answered, "Gentlemen, there are eight other applicants for that position and they are all sicker'n your man." Though Lincoln's melancholy didn't take hold in popular culture, his humor did. One joke had two old ladies talking about the war. One said, "I think Jefferson Davis will succeed because he is a praying man." The other replied, "But so is Lincoln." The first responded, "Yes, but when Abraham prays, the Lord will think he's joking." Lincoln said this was the best story about himself that he ever read in the newspapers.

The psychiatrist George Vaillant has shown that the bedrock of character comes not by good fortune but by how people deal with problems. Through longitudinal studies of generally healthy subjects, Vaillant has identified a series of discrete adaptations, or defenses, that people repeatedly turn to. "If we use defenses well," Vaillant writes, "we are deemed mentally healthy, conscientious, funny, creative, and altruistic. If we use them badly, the psychiatrist diagnoses us ill, our neighbors label us unpleasant, and society brands us immoral." What's striking is that all five of the "mature" defenses Vaillant identifies were present in Lincoln as he managed the country and himself. Humor, as we've seen, allows a person to fully engage with reality while enjoying its absurdities. Healthy people also practice suppression, which, quite unlike denial, is the selective, forceful act of pushing away oppressive stimuli; anticipation, which involves dealing with the moment in part by looking ahead to the good and the bad that lie in the future; altruism, or placing the welfare of others above oneself; and sublimation, which involves channeling passions into art.

Viewing Lincoln through the lens of his adaptations allows us to throw off the restrictive view of illness versus health. An attempt to label Lincoln is an exercise in frustration. Consider the scene that unfolded when, not long after McClellan's calamities at the Peninsula, O. H. Browning came to the White House. The president was in his library, writing, and had left instructions that he was not to be disturbed. Browning went in anyway and found the president looking terrible — "weary, care-worn, and troubled." Browning wrote in his diary, "I remarked that I felt concerned about him — regretted that troubles crowded so heavily upon him, and feared his health was suffering." Lincoln took his friend's hand and said, with a deep cadence of sadness, "Browning, I must die sometime." "He looked very sad," Browning wrote. "We parted I believe both of us with tears in our eyes." A clinician reading this passage could easily identify mental pathology in a man who looked haggard and distressed and volunteered morbid thoughts. However, one crucial detail upsets such a simple picture: Browning found Lincoln *writing* — doing the work that not only helped guide his nation through its immediate struggle but also became the guidepost for future generations. "The struggle of today, is not altogether for today," Lincoln wrote, "it is for a vast future also."

Like the compass of a sailor in a mounting storm, Lincoln's eye on the future became increasingly vital as the war dragged on and slavery — which, as Lincoln said, everyone knew to be the true cause of the war — became inextricably bound up with it. In the flush of the war's first months, many in the North desired a direct strike at the peculiar institution. General John C. Frémont, who commanded the Western Department of the military, took it upon himself to issue a general emancipation order in Missouri. But Frémont's decree sent loyal Kentuckians into spasms at a time when the Union was no stronger than its weak links to the border states. "I think to lose Kentucky is nearly the same as to lose the whole game," Lincoln wrote, explaining his decision to rescind Frémont's emancipation decree. "Kentucky gone, we can not hold Missouri, nor, as I think, Maryland. These all against us, and the job on our hands is too large for us. We would as well consent to separation at once, including the surrender of this capitol."

By the beginning of 1862, the slavery question created three distinct Republican camps. Radicals — a powerful bloc, especially in Congress — were with Frémont, wanting to confiscate slaves under martial law. Conservatives spoke of a long-term solution, with voluntary emancipation tied to a plan to send freed slaves abroad. Moderates sympathized with radicals as to the desired end — wanting freedom sooner rather than later — but leaned toward conservatives as to the means. Lincoln was a consummate moderate, trying to balance not only Republican factions but Democrats as well, who, combined with the slave border states, could turn him out of office, cripple resistance to secession, or both. Throughout his first year as president, Lincoln held to the line of his inaugural address that he wouldn't interfere with slavery where it existed. "I have been anxious and careful," he wrote in December 1861, "that the inevitable conflict for this purpose shall not degenerate into a violent and remorseless revolutionary struggle. I have, therefore, in every case, thought it proper to keep the integrity of the Union prominent as the primary object of the contest on our part, leaving all questions which are not of vital military importance to the more deliberate action of the legislature." Deferring *on* slavery and *to* Congress, he conveyed a dedication to restoring the Union to its condition before the breakup.

The events of the spring and summer of 1862 pulled Lincoln away from what had been a steady ideological course, not just as president but throughout his political career. Up to this point, he had ruled out emancipation by decree. But he came to allow that it could be done under military authority, if "it shall have become a necessity indispensable to the maintenance of the government." He preferred, however, to see loyal slave states emancipate slaves on their own, on a gradual schedule and in exchange for federal compensation. This middle-of-the-road position displeased almost everyone. Frederick Douglass said that Lincoln "is no more fit for the place he holds than was JAMES BUCHANNAN, and the latter was no more the miserable tool of traitors and rebels than the former is allowing himself to be." At the same time, Democrats began to coalesce around an anti-emancipation plank, including an increasing number of Copperheads, or Peace Democrats, who sought to end the war by negotiation, widely seen as a sop to secession.

On Sunday, July 13, 1862, riding in a carriage with Secretary of the Navy Gideon Welles and Secretary of State Seward on their way to a funeral, Lincoln said that unless the Rebels ceased the war — and he saw no evidence they would — he would take a drastic step. "He had given it much thought," Welles wrote, "and had about come to the conclusion that it was a *military necessity absolutely essential* for the salvation of the Union, that we must free the slaves or be ourselves subdued." Emancipation would help the Union strategically by draining a southern asset, the labor of its slaves, and turning it to work for the Union. "This is not a question of sentiment or taste," Lincoln wrote, "but one of physical force which may be measured and estimated as horse-power and Steam-power are measured and estimated." Scores of thousands of people currently enslaved were ready to fight for the Union. "Keep [that force] and you can save the Union," Lincoln wrote. "Throw it away, and the Union goes with it."

On July 22, Lincoln read his cabinet the first draft of the Emancipation Proclamation. On Seward's suggestion, he decided to hold the proclamation until after a Union victory, lest it seem a desperation move. The wait proved quite painful. After promoting, then demoting, then firing, then reinstating McClellan, Lincoln called on him to command the Army of the Potomac when southern troops threatened Washington, D.C. Five of his cabinet secretaries formally disapproved of the move. At a cabinet meeting, wrote Attorney General Edward Bates, "The Prest. was in deep distress . . . he seemed wrung by bitterest anguish — said he felt almost ready to hang himself." Bates went on, "He was manifestly alarmed for the safety of the City." Three weeks later, McClellan stopped a drive of southern forces at Antietam, Maryland. Hardly a triumph, it was the deadliest day in the history of the United States military. Twenty-six thousand men were killed or wounded or went missing. Still, it was victory enough, and on September 22, Lincoln issued his preliminary Emancipation Proclamation, to take effect on January 1, 1863.

Lincoln's decree of freedom, an object of reverence for succeeding generations, has lost some of its shine under the scrutiny of recent years. Critics notice the dry, technical language, the absence of any moral claim, and most of all the limited nature of the order itself. No one would be freed upon its issue, since it applied only to slaves in areas of Confederate control. But as Allen Guelzo has argued, these criticisms miss the point. The language is dry and technical because the proclamation was an act of law, which Lincoln expected to be tested in court. The same conditions made moral claims potentially dangerous to the moral cause. Reasonable critics have sought to correct excesses of the "Great Emancipator" myth

— insisting, for example, that hundreds of thousands of slaves freed themselves, running away from their masters and fighting for the Union. Still, few Americans were more aware, and more grateful, for the bravery and sacrifice of formerly enslaved African Americans than President Lincoln.

The creative force of the Emancipation Proclamation came not in the words on the page but in its conception. The measure untied a legal knot that had bound up many exacting minds, both adhering to the Constitution and effecting the aim of freedom. And the measure was immediately understood as the first step toward universal emancipation. From slaves in southern fields to mill workers in England to old-school northeastern abolitionists, the acclaim rang clear. "Sincere thanks for your Emancipation Proclamation," Vice President Hamlin wrote to Lincoln on September 25. "It will stand as the great act of the age." The commendations from around the world, Lincoln replied, were indeed "all that a vain man could wish."

Yet here, too, Lincoln saw the dark points at hand. "My expectations are not as sanguine as are those of some friends," he wrote Hamlin. Deserters were laying down their arms, and volunteers were not coming forward to replace them. "We have fewer troops in the field at the end of six days than we had at the beginning — the attrition among the old outnumbering the addition by the new. The North responds to the proclamation sufficiently in breath; but breath alone kills no rebels. I wish I could write more cheerfully." Indeed, the measure inflamed the opponents of black freedom in the North, not to mention the border slave states. Copperheads made big gains in the fall elections. They denounced the "wicked, inhuman and unholy" movement, as they said, to liberate Negroes and enslave white men.

The cold winter month of December 1862 powerfully illustrates the depths Lincoln could sink to and the heights he could rise to all the while. After a year and a half of war, with the Union armies bogged down in the East and the West, a federal assault on Fredericksburg, Virginia, produced twenty-six thousand casualties and not a whit of advantage. After the battle, Lincoln's face was "darkened with particular pain," his secretary said. He walked the floor of his office, moaning in anguish, asking over and over, "What has God put me in this place for?" In Washington, rumors swirled of a coup d'état — this on top of the threat that Confederate troops would overrun spotty defenses and storm the capital.

Visitors to the White House around this time often found Lincoln hopeless and distressed. He was awake at all hours of the night. His six-foot-four-inch frame seemed to stoop under the weight of his burdens, a reporter noticed, and his eyes looked "sunken" and "deathly." Lincoln's nominal allies in the Republican party — never a bedrock of support — heaped opprobrium on him, ascribing the nation's troubles to the "fourth-rate man" who served as chief executive.

On December 17, Republican senators met. "Many speeches were made," recorded Browning in his diary, "all expressive of want of confidence in the President and his cabinet. Some of them denouncing the President and expressing a willingness to vote for a resolution asking him to resign." The next evening, Browning came to the White House, brushed past the porter, and proceeded to Lincoln's second-floor office. "He soon came in," Browning wrote. "I saw in a moment that he was in distress — that more than usual trouble was pressing upon him." Lincoln told Browning that he felt worse than at any other time in his life: "We are now on the brink of destruction," he said. "It appears to me the Almighty is against us, and I can hardly see a ray of hope." "They wish to get rid of me," Lincoln said darkly of the Republican Senate caucus, "and I am sometimes half disposed to gratify them."

The next day, December 19, Lincoln held two separate meetings of his cabinet, sent dispatches to his general-in-chief, and heard an offer of resignation from his postmaster general. In the midst of this melee, his old colleague David Davis came around. Davis had recently been appointed by the president to the U.S. Supreme Court. Today he asked Lincoln for a personal favor. Would he write a letter of condolence to a young woman in Bloomington, Illinois? She was in the midst of a deep depression, nearly at the edge of her wits, and Davis thought a word from the president could do her good.

William McCullough, a one-armed, half-blind man, had died in a skirmish outside Coffeeville, Mississippi, on December 5. The forty-nine-year-old Union lieutenant colonel had been riding with his regiment, the 4th Illinois Cavalry, on a muddy road through a thicket of jack oak and brush on a pitch-black night when the 14th Mississippi Infantry, hidden in the woods, opened fire. Three days later, a telegram arrived in Bloomington, where McCullough had worked as a sheriff and clerk of courts and raised a family. From the clicks of the telegraph, an operator wrote out the message:

Oxford Miss.

Dec 8, 1862

Col McCullough killed in battle — buried by the enemy, flag of truce gone for the body

Leonard Swett was the first to hear of the death. An old friend of the colonel's and himself a veteran of the Mexican War, Swett said that he would have preferred to go to battle himself than tell this "evil" news to the McCullough family. He especially dreaded telling "Fanny." Mary Frances "Fanny" McCullough, the colonel's twenty-one-year-old daughter, was a witty young woman who could be both flirtatiously coy and endearingly earnest. Slight and pretty, she had chestnut hair and wide, dark eyes. She also had a "nervous condition," Swett said, and with all the griefs that attended the death of Colonel McCullough, Swett declared that anxiety for her "led us all to forget everything else." Indeed, when he delivered the news, Fanny quickly showed signs of what Swett called "nervous excitement." She wrung her hands and cried out, "Father's dead! Father's dead! Poor Father! Is it so? Why don't you tell me? Why don't you tell me?" "The doctor," Swett said, "was sent for." Fanny gradually became calmer. Then she went to her room, shut the door, and sank into a ghastly depression. For days, she refused to eat and would not sleep, but alternated, a friend said, between "pacing the floor in violent grief, or sitting in lethargic silence."

Lincoln knew the late colonel and his family. He had stayed at their house and once held young Fanny on his knee. He said he would write to her. Two days later Justice Davis came back to remind him. "The cares of this Government are very heavy on him now," Davis wrote, "and unless prompted the matter may pass out of his mind." On December 23, the day after Congress adjourned, giving Lincoln a brief respite from what he called the "extreme pressure" of his official duties, he took a piece of Executive Mansion stationery and wrote in brown ink, his script sloping slightly to the right:

Dear Fanny

It is with deep grief that I learn of the death of your kind and brave Father; and, especially, that it is affecting your young heart beyond what is common in such cases. In this sad world of ours, sorrow comes to all; and, to the young, it comes with bitterest agony, because it takes them unawares. The older have learned to ever expect it. I am anxious to afford some alleviation of your present distress. Perfect relief is not possible, except with time. You can not now realize that you will ever feel better. Is not this so? And yet it is a mistake. You are sure to be happy again. To know this, which is certainly true, will make you some less miserable now. I have had experience enough to know what I say; and you need only to believe it, to feel better at once. The memory of your dear Father, instead of an agony, will yet be a sad sweet feeling in your heart, of a purer, and holier sort than you have known before.

Please present my kind regards to your afflicted mother.

Your sincere friend
A. Lincoln

The issues at stake in the Civil War included the future of slavery, the nature of democracy, and the fate of the United States. Lincoln's letter to Fanny McCullough dealt explicitly with none of these things. But its plain words shine light on the heart of a man who saw suffering and sought to endure it and forge from it something meaningful. Like Fanny McCullough, Lincoln had long understood himself to be one whose heart was uncommonly affected by the pain of life. Like her, he had often found himself fearing the pain would never end. He had learned from severe experience that suffering had to be acknowledged and tolerated and that it might, with patience, lead to something "purer, and holier" than could be known without it. The same progression can be seen in his presidency. The qualities associated with his melancholy — his ability to see clearly and persist sanely in conditions that could have rattled even the strongest minds; his adaptations to suffering that helped him to be effective and creative; and his persistent and searching eye for the pure meaning of the nation's struggle — contributed mightily to his good work.

Lincoln himself had the connection between the personal and the political well in mind. Sometime in the cold winter months of 1862, Joshua Speed came to see his old friend, now the president of the United States. Speed had voted against Lincoln in 1860 but afterward dedicated himself to keeping Kentucky for the Union. The owner of eleven slaves, Speed opposed the Emancipation Proclamation, and he told Lincoln so. Knowing that Speed had opposed emancipation in the past, Lincoln was still surprised by his protest, because he expected Speed would see the benefits of the act. By way of illustrating how deeply he believed in its benefits, he reminded Speed of the winter of 1840–1841 when, around "that fatal first of Jany.," Lincoln had been so depressed that he came close to killing himself, and Speed, the concerned friend, had told him he must rally or die. Lincoln had said that he was ready to die, but that he "desired to live," to do something meaningful that would "redound to the interest of his fellow man." Now, speaking of the Emancipation Proclamation, Lincoln said, "I believe in this measure my fondest hopes will be realized." He had fulfilled his dream — "which," Speed reflected, "few men live to realize."

When he had articulated the goal more than two decades before, Lincoln had announced his deliberate decision to live despite the suffering that life would entail. Similarly, when he concluded that the goal had been reached, he saw that it would still entail considerable struggle to see it through. The final portion of Lincoln's message to Congress in December 1862 is widely quoted, but perhaps we can appreciate it anew. The bulk of the speech was an argument for voluntary, compensated emancipation. To those who feared the sword of the Emancipation Proclamation, this was the olive branch. Take it, Lincoln said, and there would be peace. No matter what happened now, he told his colleagues, the struggle had been joined. No one could turn back from it. "Fellow-citizens," he said, "*we* cannot escape history. We of this Congress and this administration, will be remembered in spite of ourselves. No personal significance, or insignificance, can spare one or another of us. The fiery trial through which we pass, will light us down, in honor or dishonor, to the latest generation." The test of this generation of Americans, Lincoln said, was whether they would "nobly save, or meanly lose, the last, best hope of earth."

CHAPTER 10

Comes Wisdom to Us

> And even in our sleep, pain that cannot forget falls drop by
> drop upon the heart until, against our will, comes wisdom
> to us by the awful grace of God above.
>
> — AESCHYLUS

IT IS A PECULIAR feature of Lincoln's story that, throughout his life,
his response to suffering led to still greater suffering. As a young man,
he stepped back from the brink of suicide, deciding he must live to do
some meaningful work. This sense of purpose sustained him but also led
him into a wilderness of doubt and dismay, as he asked, with vexation,
what work he would do and *how* he would do it. This pattern was repeated in the 1850s, when his work against the extension of slavery gave
him a sense of purpose but also fueled a nagging sense of failure. And as
president, he identified the Emancipation Proclamation as the culmination of his life's work. But his commitment to the measure led, over the
next year and a half, to the real prospect of his own personal defeat and,
more important, the defeat of the cause he valued more than life itself.

With hard work and good fortune, he met and triumphed over the
final challenge that lay before him. And then a man came up behind him
and put a bullet in his head because of what he had done and stood for.
Lincoln died as he had lived, a dramatic illustration of how suffering can
be bound up with greatness. His story endures in large part because he
sank so deeply into that suffering and came away with increased humility
and determination. The humility came from a sense that, whatever ship
carried him on life's rough waters, *he* was not the captain but merely a
subject of the divine force — call it fate or God or the "Almighty Architect" of existence. The determination came from a sense that, however

humble his station, Lincoln was no idle passenger but a sailor on deck with a job to do. In his strange mix of deference to divine authority and willful exercise of his own meager power, Lincoln achieved transcendent wisdom, the delicate fruit of a lifetime of pain.

Emancipation threw oil on the fire of Lincoln's northern opposition, the antiwar Democrats, or Copperheads, who began to actively oppose a war that they argued, with increasing success, was really about freeing Negroes and enslaving whites. In January 1863, Lincoln said that he feared this "fire in the rear" even more than the military struggle. Indeed, the two fires began to burn together. While the war's northern opponents seized on every piece of bad news — defeats in battle, high taxes, conscription — Confederate leaders saw that every blow they struck had a political as well as a military effect. In May, Robert E. Lee's Army of Northern Virginia bested a Union force twice its size at Chancellorsville. His confidence high, Lee then invaded southern Pennsylvania in early June, believing he could crush northern morale and perhaps secure diplomatic recognition from England and France.

Either way, Lee's invasion was bound to be a turning point, and Lincoln hoped that it could bring the war to an end. These hopes were buoyed when, over the first three days of July, around the small crossroads town of Gettysburg, Pennsylvania, the Union army under General George Meade prevailed in a huge, ugly battle that left 50,000 dead, wounded, or missing. Lee lost 28,000 men, a third of his army, and limped back to the Potomac River, only to find the river swollen by rain and his pontoon bridges wrecked. He was trapped. Meanwhile, on July 4, General Ulysses S. Grant captured Vicksburg, the Confederate fortress that for more than two years had held the Mississippi River. Hearing this, Lincoln was in a rare good mood — "very happy," wrote his secretary John Hay, "in the prospect of a brilliant success."

His hopes were dashed, though, when Meade failed to pursue Lee. With three days to build a new bridge, the Confederates scampered safely back to Virginia. Robert Todd Lincoln, in a visit with his father, noted that he was "grieved silently but deeply about the escape of Lee." Underscoring the troubles of war, on July 13 riots broke out in New York City, a culmination of months of unrest over a March draft law. The law made all men between the ages of twenty and forty-five eligible for military conscription, while exempting anyone who could pay $300. A combination of resentments — political, economic, racial — ignited groups of

Irish immigrants, who sacked homes and lit buildings on fire. Blacks in particular felt their wrath. The Colored Orphan Asylum was burned to the ground. In four days of rioting about 120 people died. On July 14, Lincoln was, in his own words, "oppressed" and in "deep distress." "My dear general," he wrote to Meade, "I do not believe you appreciate the magnitude of the misfortune involved in Lee's escape. He was within your easy grasp, and to have closed upon him would, in connection with our other late successes, have ended the war. As it is, the war will be prolonged indefinitely . . . I am distressed immeasurably because of it." But the damage was already done. Lincoln kept his letter, putting it in an envelope that he took care to mark "never sent."

Though there were practical reasons for Lincoln's restraint, it may also reflect a shift that people noticed in him around this time. John Hay wrote in early August that the president "is in fine whack. I have seldom seen him more serene & busy . . . There is no man in the country, so wise so gentle and so firm." Unhappy as he was, and as intense as the pressure continued to be, Lincoln found peace by acknowledging his own powerlessness over events. According to General James F. Rusling, Lincoln said that during the fighting at Gettysburg he turned to prayer, felt the whole thing to be in God's hands, and "somehow a sweet comfort crept into his soul."

It was also in the summer of 1863 that Elizabeth Keckly, Mary Lincoln's dressmaker, watched the president drag himself into the room where she was fitting the First Lady. "His step was slow and heavy, and his face sad," Keckly recalled. "Like a tired child he threw himself upon a sofa, and shaded his eyes with his hands. He was a complete picture of dejection." He had just returned from the War Department, he said, where the news was "dark, dark everywhere." Lincoln then took a small Bible from a stand near the sofa and began to read. "A quarter of an hour passed," Keckly remembered, "and on glancing at the sofa the face of the President seemed more cheerful. The dejected look was gone, and the countenance was lighted up with new resolution and hope." Wanting to see what he was reading, Keckly pretended she had dropped something and went behind where Lincoln was sitting so she could look over his shoulder. It was the Book of Job.

Throughout history, a glance to the divine has often been the first and last impulse for suffering people. "Man is born broken," the playwright Eugene O'Neill has written. "He lives by mending. The grace of God is glue!" Many conversion narratives include spates of melancholy — the dark night of the soul. And many secular stories of depression end with a spiritual awakening, as does Leo Tolstoy's memoir, *My Confession,* about how a crisis of spirit became a crisis of faith, which he resolved by turning to Christianity.

Today the connection between spiritual and psychological well-being is often passed over by psychologists and psychiatrists, who consider themselves a branch of secular medicine and science. For most of Lincoln's lifetime, scientists assumed there was some relationship between mental and spiritual life. In the 1830s, when Johannes Müller and other physiologists identified the function of nerves in human sensation and perception, they held that these observable phenomena owed their vitality to a mysterious "life force." Things began to change when, in the 1850s, Hermann Helmholtz showed that the workings of the nervous system could be empirically measured, and he rejected Müller's vitalism for a principle of mechanism. Helmholtz and his circle even composed and swore to an oath that began, "No other forces than the common physical-chemical ones are active within the organism." The groundwork was being laid for a major conceptual shift.

In 1860, Gustav Fechner published an experiment showing that the phenomenal world could be measured against the material, external world. In 1879, the first laboratory was established for the quantitative study of the senses. And in the late nineteenth and early twentieth centuries, Emil Kraepelin founded what we now call biological psychiatry, and Sigmund Freud developed psychoanalysis. Both Kraepelin and Freud sharply distinguished their endeavors from religion. But their contemporary William James, the great philosopher and psychologist, objected to the rigid separation of religion and psychology. Having written the standard psychology textbook, James turned to study how spirituality could benefit suffering people. In the masterpiece that resulted, *The Varieties of Religious Experience,* James defined religion broadly, giving equal value to such diverse systems as Christianity, Emersonian transcendentalism, Buddhist mysticism, and civic or personal ideals. The essence of religious experience, he wrote, is "the belief that there is an unseen order, and that our supreme good lies in harmoniously adjusting ourselves thereto."

James describes two basic spiritual paths. For optimistic people — James calls them "healthy-minded" — religion can affirm core beliefs about the goodness of the world and ward off doubt and dismay. For healthy minds, belief in God serves like a moat around a castle, providing order and protection. When difficulties arise — troubling thoughts, painful events — rituals of prayer and repentance can help set the world right again. But another group of people, dogged by doubt and discord, lack the sense that the world is right in the first place. James calls them "sick souls" and proposes that religion has frequently provided a way out of mental agony. Through what James describes as an awakening or a "re-birth," the weight of suffering can become a source of power and vitality. Such rebirths are characterized by a simple progression. First, the recognition of an innate problem — "a sense," James writes, "that there is *something wrong with us* as we naturally stand." Second, "*we are saved from the wrongness* by making proper connection with the higher powers."

Modern studies confirm the salutary effect of faith on depression. For example, one study of 271 religious and nonreligious adults in treatment for depression found that the former had an edge in their recovery, largely because their beliefs gave them something that depression tends to strip away — hope. A meta-analysis of depression and spirituality came to a similar conclusion, with two important caveats. First, what psychologists call "negative religious coping" — blaming God for one's trouble or refusing to deal with difficulties while taking refuge in religious activities — is associated with higher levels of depressive symptoms. Second, "extrinsic motivation" — doing outwardly pious things for the sake of show — was found to do little good. The benefit lies in "intrinsic motivation," the thirst for connection to something beyond the self. If one seeks belief merely to feel better, that very interest in self-advantage might well keep belief and its benefits at bay.

As a young man, Lincoln saw how religion could ameliorate life's blows. Joshua Speed remembered Lincoln saying that the most ambitious man could see every hope fail, but the earnest Christian could never fail, because fulfillment lay beyond life on earth. "When I knew him," Speed said, "in early life . . . he had tried hard to be a believer, but his reason could not grasp and solve the great problem of redemption as taught." Although Lincoln's doubts have often been mistaken for lack of interest in religious matters, the reverse is probably true. Many of history's greatest believers have also been the fiercest doubters. "It's hard to imagine what religious tradition would be," says the scholar Jennifer Michael Hecht, author of *Doubt: A History*, "if there weren't people looking up and saying that they disagreed with what had come before."

According to Isaac Cogdal, who talked theology with Lincoln and Herndon in their law office, "His mind was full of terrible Enquiry." The inquiry seems to have intensified around points of stress in Lincoln's life, like his breakdown in 1841, when Speed's mother recommended the Bible as the "best cure for the 'Blues'" and Lincoln agreed, "could one," he said, "but take it according to the truth." After Eddie Lincoln's death in 1850, a recently arrived minister in Springfield, the Reverend James Smith, conducted the boy's funeral. Smith often visited the Lincoln home at the corner of Eighth and Jackson. Like Lincoln, Smith had been a skeptic, but after he converted to Christianity, he published a book, *The Christian's Defense,* that aimed to draw other freethinkers into his flock. According to Smith, Lincoln read his book and found it convincing. "He examined the Arguments as a lawyer who is anxious to reach the truth investigates testimony," Smith recounted. "The result was the announcement by himself that the argument in favor of the Divine Authority and inspiration of the Scripture was unanswerable." The Lincolns later rented a pew at Smith's First Presbyterian Church — which reserved them space for services but did not bind them to accept the church's creed, as membership would. This arrangement, which Lincoln repeated in Washington, nicely represented his relationship with traditional religion in his mature years. He visited, but he didn't move in.

One difference between his ideas and the dominant Christian ones is worth close attention. Lincoln discounted the notion that sin could be wiped out through confession or repentance. "Lincoln maintained," said William Herndon, "that God could not forgive; that punishment has to follow the sin." This view fitted with both the stern, unforgiving God of Calvinism, with which Lincoln had been raised, and the mechanistic notion of a universe governed by fixed laws. But unlike the Calvinists, who disclaimed any possibility of grace for human beings not chosen for that fate, Lincoln did see a chance of improvement. And unlike some fatalists, who renounced any claim to a moral order, Lincoln saw how man's reason could discern purpose even in the movement of a vast machine that grinds and cuts and mashes all who interfere with it. Just as a child learns to pull his hand from a fire when it is hot, people can learn when they are doing something that is not in accord with the wider, unseen order. To Lincoln, Herndon explained, "suffering was medicinal & educational." In other words, it could be an agent of growth.

After Lincoln's election in 1860 and the crisis that followed, what he described as a "process of crystallization" began in his mind on the subject of faith. The burden of his work brought home to him a visceral and fundamental connection with something greater than he. When friends said they feared his assassination, he said, "God's will be done. I am in his hands." He repeatedly called himself an "instrument" of a larger power — which he sometimes described as the people of the United States, and other times as God — and said he had been charged with "so vast, and so sacred a trust" that "he felt that he had no moral right to shrink; nor even to count the chances of his own life, in what might follow."

The next turning point came with Willie Lincoln's death in February 1862. Mary Lincoln said that, though Lincoln "was a religious man always," his ideas about "hope" and "faith" began to change, by which she probably meant hope and faith in the afterlife. After Willie was interred, Lincoln went several times to look at his body in its tomb. He asked an army officer, "Did you ever dream of a lost friend & feel that you were having a direct communion with that friend & yet a consciousness that it was not a reality?" The man said yes; he thought "all may have had such an experience." Lincoln said, "So do I dream of my boy Willie," sobbing and shaking with emotion. In this vulnerable period, Lincoln was influenced by the Reverend Phineas D. Gurley, whose Presbyterian church he attended. In his eulogy over Willie, Gurley preached that "in the hour of trial" one must look to "Him who sees the end from the beginning and doeth all things well." With confidence in God, Gurley said, "our sorrows will be sanctified and made a blessing to our souls, and by and by we shall have occasion to say with blended gratitude and rejoicing, 'It is good for us that we have been afflicted.'" Lincoln asked Gurley to write out a copy of the eulogy. In the trials ahead, he would hold to this idea as if it were a life raft.

Lincoln's humility certainly brought him comfort. "There was something touching," said the journalist Noah Brooks, "in his childlike and simple reliance upon Divine aid, especially when in such extremities as he sometimes fell into . . . he more earnestly than ever sought that strength which is promised when mortal help faileth." One time Lincoln said, in Brooks's hearing, "I am very sure that if I do not go away from here a wiser man, I shall go away a better man, for having learned here what a very poor sort of man I am." It was all the more powerful that Lincoln said this cheerfully.

Yet Lincoln's spiritual view did not relieve him of responsibility. Every day presented scores of decisions — on personnel, on policy, on the movement of troops and the direction of executive departments. So much of what today is delegated to political staffs and civil servants then required a direct decision from the president. He controlled patronage, from the embassy in China to the post office in St. Louis. He personally reviewed every case of a soldier sentenced to death. In all these matters he had to exercise his judgment in accordance with law, custom, prudence, and compassion. The paradox is that, as much as his attention focused on an unseen realm, Lincoln's emphasis remained strictly on the material world of cause and effect. "These are not . . . the days of miracles," he said, "and I suppose it will be granted that I am not to expect a direct revelation." Lincoln did not expect God to take him by the hand. On the contrary, he said, "I must study the plain physical facts of the case, ascertain what is possible and learn what appears to be wise and right."

Typical of "sick souls" in the way he turned, from a sense of wrongness, to a power greater than he, Lincoln was also an original theological thinker. For centuries, settlers on the North American continent had been assured that they were special in God's eyes. They were the "City upon a Hill," in John Winthrop's phrase, decidedly chosen, like the Israelites of old. Lincoln turned this on its head when he said, "I shall be most happy indeed if I shall be an humble instrument in the hands of the Almighty, and of this, his almost chosen people, for perpetuating the object of that great struggle." The country, Lincoln said, was *almost* chosen — that is, *not yet* chosen, not *in fact*, but *very close to being*, chosen. Out of that phrase emerged a strain of Lincoln's thinking that grew stronger and clearer as his presidency wore on. As others invoked the favor of God, Lincoln opened a dynamic space between mortal works and divine intention. Among his papers, after his death, his secretaries found this undated statement that has come to be known as the "Meditation on the Divine Will."

> The will of God prevails — In great contests
> each party claims to act in accordance with
> the will of God. Both <u>may</u> be, and one
> <u>must</u> be wrong. God can not be <u>for</u>, and
> <u>against</u> the same thing at the same time.
> In the present civil war it is quite possible
> that God's purpose is something different from
> the purpose of either party — and yet the human
> instrumentalities, working just as they do, are of
> the best adaptation to effect this

After this first passage, the handwriting grows shakier; the words practically tremble with the thoughts they express. First, Lincoln crossed out the last word he had written.

> ~~this~~ His purpose. I am
> almost ready to say this is probably true — that
> God wills this contest, and wills that it shall
> not end yet — By his mere quiet power, on the minds
> of the now contestants, He could have either <u>saved</u>
> or <u>destroyed</u> the Union without a human cont-
> est — Yet the contest began — And having begun
> He could give the final victory to either side
> any day — Yet the contest proceeds —

Lincoln's clarity came in part from his uncertainty. It is hard to overestimate just how unusual this was. Most religious thinkers, explains the historian of religion Mark Noll in *America's God,* not only assumed God's favor but assumed they could read His will. Of course, both assumptions often were no more than a high-minded statement of partisan interests. A fantastic outpouring of religious expression came with the beginning of hostilities. Julia Ward Howe's "Battle Hymn of the Republic" captured the mood in the North:

> Mine eyes have seen the glory of the coming of the Lord:
> He is trampling out the vintage where the grapes of wrath are stored;
> He hath loosed the fateful lightning of His terrible swift sword:
> His truth is marching on.

As these lyrics made the rounds of Union troops, southern soldiers fashioned their own God's army. The seal of the Confederacy contained the inscription *Deo Vindice* — God Will Vindicate. When the Rebels fared well in early fighting, they plainly saw God's hand.

Lincoln cut straight to the contradiction of both sides' assuming that God was on their side. "Both may be, and one must be wrong." No one — not he, not Julia Ward Howe, not Thomas "Stonewall" Jackson, that pious and fierce southern warrior — knew just what God intended. "We must work earnestly in the best light He gives us," Lincoln wrote, "trusting that so working still conduces to the great ends He ordains." Once a minister remarked to Lincoln something along the lines of "I hope the Lord is on our side." Lincoln said he didn't agree, adding, in substance, "I hope we are on the Lord's side."

"How was it," asks Mark Noll, "that this man who never joined a church and who read only a little theology could, on occasion, give expression to profound theological interpretations of the War between the States?" Viewing Lincoln through the lens of his melancholy, we see one cogent explanation: he was always inclined to look at the full truth of a situation, assessing both what could be known and what remained in doubt. When times were hard, he had the patience, endurance, and vigor to stay in that place of tension. With this in mind, we return to the summer of 1863, to the time when Lincoln found comfort in the Book of Job. It is instructive that he would turn to Job in a moment of darkness, for it is about the value of questioning one's faith, even to the point of emotional agony.

As the story goes, God has gathered his angels around him, and he boasts of his pious servant Job. Satan scoffs at this, saying that Job's piety merely reflects his good fortune. To settle the argument, God permits Satan to take away Job's possessions, kill his children, and afflict him with boils. Job at first struggles to stay pious, then lashes out in anger at God and demands to know the reason for his afflictions. Finally God rewards Job, praising his skepticism and his demands for the truth, while punishing those who tried to comfort Job with the usual bromides. Faith, the story suggests, means getting worked up, asking tough questions. Commenting on the Book of Job, the prominent nineteenth-century theologian Mark Rutherford wrote, "God is great, we know not his ways. He takes from us all we have, but yet if we possess our souls in patience, we *may* pass the valley of the shadow, and come out in sunlight again."

Lincoln probably saw the parallels: Job lost his family. Lincoln lost his child, many friends, and vast numbers of soldiers in his charge. Job lost his great estate. Lincoln, in a real sense, had lost his country, for by 1863 the war was no longer about preserving the Union; it was about building something new. What distinguished Lincoln was his willingness to cry out to the heavens in pain and despair, and then turn, humbly and determinedly, to the work that lay before him.

After the battle at Gettysburg, the project of burying the dead became a major public work. An attorney named David Wills headed up the effort, planning a dedication ceremony and securing the services of Edward Everett to deliver a formal oration. Two and a half weeks before the ceremony, Wills wrote to Lincoln requesting that, after the oration, he "formally set apart these grounds to their Sacred use by a few appropriate remarks." Wills's idea of the cemetery's "sacred use" was to hold dead bodies. Lincoln would pay homage to that conventional notion of sacred, then articulate his own. Mary Lincoln would remark that he "felt religious More than Ever about the time he went to Gettysburg." And indeed, the speech he gave was filled with his own brand of religious sentiment, though the only mention of the deity came with "this nation under God." The holy entity Lincoln discussed at Gettysburg was a national idea. This speech, probably as widely read as any piece of prose in history, is nevertheless worth repeating, for it rewards renewed attention.

> Four score and seven years ago our fathers brought forth on this continent, a new nation, conceived in Liberty, and dedicated to the proposition that all men are created equal.
>
> Now we are engaged in a great civil war, testing whether that nation, or any nation so conceived and so dedicated, can long endure. We are met on a great battle-field of that war. We have come to dedicate a portion of that field, as a final resting place for those who here gave their lives that that nation might live. It is altogether fitting and proper that we should do this.
>
> But, in a larger sense, we can not dedicate — we can not consecrate — we can not hallow — this ground. The brave men, living and dead, who struggled here, have consecrated it, far above our poor power to add or detract. The world will little note, nor long remember what we say here, but it can never forget what they did here. It is for us the living, rather, to be dedicated here to the unfinished work which they who fought here have thus far so nobly advanced. It is rather for us to be here dedicated to the great task remaining before us — that from these honored dead we take increased devotion to that cause for which they gave the last full measure of devotion — that we here highly resolve that these dead shall not have died in vain — that this nation, under God, shall have a new birth of freedom — and that government of the people, by the people, for the people, shall not perish from the earth.

In the fall of 1863, it had been nine years since Lincoln tied his political philosophy to the Declaration of Independence's expression of innate equality. At Gettysburg, he began by declaring that sentiment the core principle of the republic. If the Union triumphed under his leadership, so would triumph the idea of equality and natural rights. We take this bold interpretation for granted, which is a measure of its astonishing success. "The Civil War *is* to most Americans," Garry Wills writes, "what Lincoln wanted it to *mean.*"

Lincoln's determination to effect this meaning was wrapped up in humility. It is an irony often remarked upon that such a renowned piece of rhetoric as the Gettysburg Address argues for its own insignificance. It is another irony that many more people today know what Lincoln *said* at Gettysburg than what the soldiers *did* there. This says something important about the spirit of the piece and of the man. While it was "fitting and proper," Lincoln said, to perform the standard rites and dedicate a cemetery, in a larger sense, the living were the ones who needed to be dedicated by the memory of soldiers who gave their lives for an idea.

If the speech has the ring of truth, that's partly because Lincoln walked his talk. He is an example of what William James calls the "ripe fruits of religion" — also called saintliness and enlightenment. Earlier I described it as transcendent wisdom. People who are guided by a sense of something larger than themselves will look past the petty concerns of the self — the wounded pride that comes from personal insult, for example, or the wish to seem stronger or better than other people. "Magnanimities once impossible," James writes, "are now easy; paltry conventionalities and mean incentives once tyrannical hold no sway." Lincoln clearly operated in this spirit. He said, "I shall do nothing in malice. What I deal with is too vast for malicious dealing." Even political opponents saw Lincoln's compassion. The oft-quoted remark from Frederick Douglass, that Lincoln was the first white man of power who did not manifest superiority, was not a political endorsement but an acknowledgment that a man with whom he often disagreed had a good heart. The many stories of Lincoln pardoning soldiers, eagerly seeking excuses when he had to, are no less valid as an indication of his character for having become a biographical cliché. One instance in which Lincoln refused a pardon also bears the mark of empathy, as Lincoln instructed the prisoner, who had been convicted of slave trading, to cease his appeals and prepare for the "awful change" that awaited him.

Lincoln's letters exhibit patience and grace. When General David Hunter wrote to him protesting his "banishment" to Kansas, described himself as "very deeply mortified, humiliated, insulted and disgraced," and suggested that his only "sin" was in executing an ill-advised presidential order, Lincoln wrote this response: "Yours of the 23rd. is received; and I am constrained to say it is difficult to answer so ugly a letter in good temper." The president had no censure for Hunter's actions but only for the "flood of grumbling despatches and letters I have seen from you." Explaining that no insult had been intended by sending him to Kansas, which Lincoln held to be an important and honorable position, the president continued, "I have been, and am sincerely your friend; and if, as such, I dare to make a suggestion, I would say you are adopting the best possible way to ruin yourself." Lincoln then sent the letter by private messenger, instructing that the note be given to Hunter only when he was in a good mood.

Though he often protested about people who came to see him out of greed, Lincoln said that he appreciated the chance to do kindnesses. Joshua Speed once watched as Lincoln heard from two distressed women, the mother and wife of a man in prison for resisting the draft. When he granted their request, the mother said she would meet Lincoln in heaven. "I am afraid with all my troubles," Lincoln answered, "I shall never get there, but if I do, I will find you. That you wish me to get there is the best wish you could make for me." When the women left, Speed said, "Lincoln, with my knowledge of your nervous sensibility it is a wonder that such scenes as this don't kill you." "I am very unwell," Lincoln replied. But he said the scene Speed had just witnessed "is the only thing I have done to day which has given me any pleasure . . . That old lady was no counterfeit." "Speed," Lincoln added, "die when I may, I want it said of me by those who know me best that I always plucked a thistle and planted a flower where I thought a flower would grow."

Late 1863 and early 1864 gave Lincoln a respite. General Grant's success in opening the Mississippi River dealt a huge blow to the Confederacy, which was now cut in half. And Grant, a humble, hard-driving character like Lincoln, proved to be the general that the president had been waiting for. The famous quip about Grant, that he looked "as if he had determined to drive his head through a brick wall, and was about to do it," aptly described a man who had lived through much pain and was ready for more. When Lincoln made him commander of the whole war effort, leadership of the Western Department fell to General Sherman, whose bouts of mania and depression had nearly derailed his career early in the war, but who proved himself skillful and ruthless. All three men agreed that only brutal aggression could subdue the rebellion. By June 16, 1864, the war had gone on for more than three years, and Lincoln acknowledged its toll. "War, at the best, is terrible, and this war of ours, in its magnitude and in its duration, is one of the most terrible. It has deranged business, totally in many localities, and partially in all localities. It has destroyed property, and ruined homes; it has produced a national debt and taxation unprecedented, at least in this country. It has carried mourning to almost every home, until it can almost be said that the 'heavens are hung in black.'" And yet, Lincoln continued, "we accepted this war for an object, a worthy object, and the war will end when that object is attained. Under God, I hope it never will until that time."

But that summer, it seemed as if the object would not be reached. Grant's campaign against Lee in Virginia was desperately slow and produced the worst carnage of the war. Resentments in the North ran high. Though Lincoln was nominated again by his party, he heard from the New York political boss Thurlow Weed in early August that his election was an "impossibility." Weed identified the problem: "The People are wild for Peace. They are told that the President will only listen to terms of Peace on condition Slavery be 'abandoned.'" The influential editor Horace Greeley wanted to find another Republican candidate to take Lincoln's place.

Lincoln would neither back down nor step aside. He had seized slaves, under his war powers, as property. Yet, he said emphatically, they were to be freed, forever, as men. Without permanent freedom, he argued, the original purpose of the seizure would be negated. "Negroes, like other people, act upon motives," he explained. "Why should they do any thing for us, if we will do nothing for them? If they stake their lives for us, they must be prompted by the strongest motive — even the promise of freedom. And the promise being made, must be kept." Knowing that military emancipation was only a stopgap, Lincoln saw that truly delivering on the promise would mean an amendment to the Constitution forbidding slavery, which he would live to see passed by both houses of Congress and ratified by the states.

Earlier in his career, Lincoln had countenanced continuing bondage for the sake of the Union and its idea. He now argued for freedom on the same principle. Having often bowed to racist prejudice, he now poked his finger in its eye. He looked forward to the day when peace would come, "and come to stay; and so come as to be worth the keeping in all future time . . . And then, there will be some black men who can remember that, with silent tongue, and clenched teeth, and steady eye, and well-poised bayonet, they have helped mankind on to this great consummation; while, I fear, there will be some white ones, unable to forget that, with malignant heart, and deceitful speech, they have strove to hinder it."

Lincoln couldn't have given his opponents a larger opening for the November 1864 election. The Democrats made George McClellan their nominee. The general, who still had his commission though no active command, supported the war but opposed emancipation. His party, however, embraced a strong Copperhead element that wanted to see an immediate armistice and a negotiated peace. The nation faced a stark choice between a party unambiguously for Union with freedom and one united against freedom and mixed on the Union. O. H. Browning said it was all over, writing in a condescending note that he had never expected much from his old friend. "I thought he might get through," Browning wrote, "as many a boy has got through college, without disgrace and without knowledge; but I fear he is a failure."

Lincoln saw how slim were his chances. "This morning," he wrote on August 23, "as for some days past, it seems exceedingly probable that this Administration will not be re-elected. Then it will be my duty to so co-operate with the President elect, as to save the Union between the election and the inauguration; as he will have secured his election on such ground that he can not possibly save it afterwards." Lincoln also laid plans, in the event of his loss, to encourage slaves to flee across Union lines to freedom while they had the chance.

On August 18 and 22, Lincoln spoke to two groups of soldiers who were on their way home to Ohio. Expecting that he, too, was going to be sent home, he took care to frame the consequences of the coming election. "I wish it might be more generally and universally understood," he said on the eighteenth, "what the country is now engaged in. We have, as all will agree, a free Government, where every man has a right to be equal with every other man. In this great struggle, this form of Government and every form of human right is endangered if our enemies succeed. There is more involved in this contest than is realized by every one. There is involved in this struggle the question whether your children and my children shall enjoy the privileges we have enjoyed. I say this in order to impress upon you, if you are not already so impressed, that no small matter should divert us from our great purpose."

For all his emotion, Lincoln rarely injected personal details into his public remarks; the reserved reference to "my children" went further than usual. On August 22 he went further than that: "It is not merely for to-day, but for all time to come that we should perpetuate for our children's children this great and free government, which we have enjoyed all our lives. I beg you to remember this, not merely for my sake, but for yours. I happen temporarily to occupy this big White House. I am a living witness that any one of your children may look to come here as my father's child has. It is in order that each of you may have through this free government which we have enjoyed, an open field and a fair chance for your industry, enterprise and intelligence; that you may all have equal privileges in the race of life, with all its desirable human aspirations. It is for this the struggle should be maintained." Even in a kind of self-pronounced political eulogy, Lincoln reflected on his own extraordinary story *not* to claim sympathy but precisely the opposite, to diminish himself next to the goal that embraced every American, then and in the future.

In early September, General Sherman captured Atlanta, and overnight everything changed. Suddenly the end of the war seemed in sight and Lincoln had a commanding political position. In the election, Lincoln won fifty-five percent of the popular vote and captured all but three of the loyal states. Afterward, the military struggle took on the air of a denouement. Grant chased the southern armies to the point of near surrender. Sherman, who had said that the moment the war stopped he would do his enemies any personal kindness, began his punishing march to the sea, intended to make southern civilians feel the pinch of war.

By March 4, Lincoln's second inauguration, northern victory could be expected. The president had ample reason to boast about the success. Instead, in his address he quickly passed over the "progress of our arms, upon which all else chiefly depends" and steered straight into the storm that had engaged his attention for so long: the role of God in the Civil War. He spelled out the argument of the "Meditation on the Divine Will," that with both sides claiming God's favor, one must be wrong, and both might be wrong. When the fighting began, he said, "neither party expected for the war the magnitude or the duration which it has already attained. Neither anticipated that the cause of the conflict might cease with, or even before, the conflict itself should cease. Each looked for an easier triumph, and a result less fundamental and astounding."

The question was, what should be made of the fundamental and astounding conflict? What was its common lesson? Lincoln ventured an answer, which he framed rhetorically to make it both an argument and a question. He began by quoting the Book of Matthew: "Woe unto the world because of offenses! for it must needs be that offenses come; but woe to that man by whom the offense cometh." In other words, it is inevitable that people will do wrong, but wrongdoers can expect to be punished. He continued:

If we shall suppose that American slavery is one of those offenses which, in the providence of God, must needs come, but which, having continued through his appointed time, he now wills to remove, and that he gives to both North and South this terrible war, as the woe due to those by whom the offense came, shall we discern therein any departure from those divine attributes which the believers in a living God always ascribe to him? Fondly do we hope — fervently do we pray — that this mighty scourge of war may speedily pass away. Yet, if God wills that it continue until all the wealth piled by the bondsman's two hundred and fifty years of unrequited toil shall be sunk, and until every drop of blood drawn by the lash shall be paid by another drawn with the sword, as was said three thousand years ago, so still it must be said, "The judgments of the Lord are true and righteous altogether."

Both North and South were responsible for "American slavery," Lincoln argued. Justice would be served if both sides were punished for it. And the scales of justice might be righted only with something approaching a national apocalypse. It was a stark case, but why did Lincoln make it? His purpose was surely not narrowly political. When Thurlow Weed complimented Lincoln on the speech, calling it "the most pregnant and effective use to which the English Language was ever put," Lincoln thanked him and said he expected the speech to "wear as well as — perhaps better than — any thing I have produced; but I believe it is not immediately popular. Men are not flattered by being shown that there has been a difference of purpose between the Almighty and them. To deny it, however, in this case, is to deny that there is a God governing the world. It is a truth which I thought needed to be told; and as whatever of humiliation there is in it, falls most directly on myself, I thought others might afford for me to tell it."

The key word was humiliation. Lincoln knew the tendency of victors in a grueling conflict was to seek vengeance, and of the vanquished to turn bitter. He argued that both sides should bear in mind their shared wrong and see their common opportunity. He concluded: "With malice toward none; with charity for all; with firmness in the right, as God gives us to see the right, let us strive on to finish the work we are in; to bind up the nation's wounds; to care for him who shall have borne the battle, and for his widow, and his orphan — to do all which may achieve and cherish a just and lasting peace among ourselves, and with all nations."

These words were a peroration, not just to the speech but to Lincoln's whole career. The cause worth struggling for went beyond any partisan or temporal sense of right or wrong. There was a supreme right that all people should work for, regardless of what agony or joy it brought in the short term. Hindrances to that goal might be frustrating or excruciating, but the goal could be defeated only if the people forsook it. Moreover, while achievements could bring the country closer to the goal, they would forever fall short of its full realization. Mortal works were imperfect, but were dignified insofar as they reached, worked, and suffered for perfection.

"Malice toward none" was hardly a popular slogan. Consider the words of Henry Ward Beecher, as popular and influential in his day as Billy Graham has been in his. "I charge the whole guilt of this war," Beecher said in 1864, "upon the ambitious, educated, plotting political leaders of the South . . . A day will come when God will reveal judgment, and arraign at his bar these mighty miscreants." Beecher looked forward to the day when "these most accursed and detested of all criminals" would be "caught up in black clouds full of voices of vengeance and lurid with punishment" and "plunged downward forever in an endless retribution." "Endless retribution" — now there was a phrase that people would rally behind. What Lincoln sought to forestall would in fact come to pass. A vengeful reconstruction policy, the backlash it provoked, and the failure to provide adequately for the well-being of four million freed slaves had ramifications that would last to the present day. The pain of the Civil War sank into many fields.

Attuned to that pain, Lincoln enjoyed, in the final weeks of his life, the sights of peace and victory. On April 4, 1865, he returned from a tour of Richmond, which had just been evacuated by Confederate officials. Secretary of the Interior James Harlan was struck by the change in him. "That indescribable sadness which had previously seemed to be an adamantine element of his very being, had been suddenly exchanged for an equally indescribable expression of serene joy as if conscious that the great purpose of his life had been achieved . . . yet there was no manifestation of exultation, or ecstasy. He seemed the very personification of supreme satisfaction." On April 11, 1865, Lincoln addressed a crowd on the White House lawn. "We meet today not in sorrow," he told them, "but in gladness of heart."

He would taste this gladness only briefly. In the crowd stood the dashing young actor John Wilkes Booth. In his speech, Lincoln discussed the case of Louisiana, where an argument was under way over whether freed blacks would have the right to vote. Lincoln said he favored suffrage for the sizable population of educated blacks and for Union soldiers. Booth recoiled at the prospect of what he called "nigger citizenship," and he said, "Now, by God, I'll put him through. That is the last speech he will ever make."

In admiring Lincoln's spirit we risk lionizing him as a man. We would do well to remember the humble determination with which he lived his final day. On the morning of April 14, Lincoln woke up around 7 A.M., put on his slippers, and read a few pages of the Bible. He had breakfast with his family, did some paperwork, and visited the War Department before his cabinet gathered at eleven. General Grant joined the meeting and gave details of the surrender at Appomattox. Lincoln asked what terms he had given the common soldiers. "I told them," Grant said, "to go back to their homes and families, and they would not be molested, if they did nothing more." Lincoln liked the sound of that.

Grant said that he soon expected word from Sherman. With the surrender of Lee's army, Sherman's contest remained the last open front of the war. Lincoln hoped to hear from him, too, and he anticipated good news. The reason, he said, was a recurring dream, which he'd had the night before. Lincoln had a long-standing interest in dreams. He spoke of them, interpreted them, and sometimes acted on them. "Think you better put 'Tad's' pistol away," he had written his wife in June 1863. "I had an ugly dream about him." While he was in Richmond, he had a dream that the White House was burning, and he sent Mrs. Lincoln back home. But it fit with the times that, on April 14, he thought his dream was a good omen. In it, he was floating away on some vast and indistinct expanse toward an unknown shore. The strange thing was, Lincoln said, the dream was always followed by a great change or disaster. The group chatted about that, speculating on what change might be in store. "I think it must be from Sherman," Lincoln said.

It was Good Friday, and government offices closed at noon. In the afternoon, Lincoln took a carriage ride with his wife. "I never saw him so supremely cheerful — his manner was even playful," she said. "Dear Husband," she said to him, "you almost startle me by your great cheerfulness." "We must both, be more cheerful in the future," he answered. "Between the war and the loss of our darling Willie, we have both been very miserable." Earlier in the week, the two had talked about plans for after the end of his second term. Lincoln said he wanted to see California. And he'd always said that he planned to go back to Springfield and practice law.

When he returned to the White House, Lincoln found two old friends from Illinois walking across the White House lawn. "Come back, boys, come back," he called. The two men, General Isham N. Haynie and Richard Oglesby, complied. Now the governor of Illinois, Oglesby had five years before organized the meeting of state Republicans in Decatur, where Lincoln became known as the rail-splitter. The men spent an hour together. Lincoln read aloud four chapters from *Petroleum Nasby*, continuing even after he was called for dinner. Finally, his guests got up to leave. "I'd much rather swap stories than eat," Lincoln said. At dinner with Mary, Tad, and Robert, Lincoln said he was worn out. Afterward, he walked to the War Department with his bodyguard, William H. Crook. Crook said that Lincoln walked slowly and seemed "more depressed than I had ever seen him." At the War Department, Lincoln talked briefly with Stanton, dropping his arm over the secretary's shoulders. There was still no word from Sherman; everyone was waiting for news. On the way back, Lincoln told Crook to go home for the night.

At the White House, the president spent a few minutes working on papers. At some point that day, he inspected the case of a soldier named Patrick Murphy, who had deserted one regiment and joined another under an assumed name. Murphy had been found guilty and sentenced to be shot, but the court-martial recommended that his sentence be commuted because he was mentally ill. On the side of the case paper, Lincoln wrote, "This man is pardoned, and hereby ordered to be discharged from the service."

A stream of visitors had commenced, but Lincoln had plans to go out. It had been announced in the morning papers. He told his guard that he wanted to keep the plans, because the people expected it. He told his wife that if he stayed home he would have no rest. He dressed and put on his coat and hat. In his pockets he had a penknife, two pairs of spectacles, a Confederate five-dollar bill, and some newspaper clippings, among them a letter from the English reform leader John Bright praising Lincoln's "grand simplicity of purpose." As he stepped out onto the White House grounds, Congressman Isaac Arnold approached. "Excuse me now," Lincoln said to Arnold as he climbed into his carriage. "I am going to the theatre. Come and see me in the morning."

Epilogue

FOUR YEARS AGO, on a lark, I went to spend a weekend with the Association of Lincoln Presenters, who were having their annual convention in Beckley, West Virginia. Of the several hundred members, forty-four Lincolns showed up that year — men dressed in black suits, with stovepipe hats and beards shaved above the chin. Some of them were short and thin, some were tall and hulking. Some had real beards with gray hair, others had false beards made of black hair. One of the Lincolns was in a wheelchair, with an oxygen tank. One looked like Elvis Presley dressed up as Lincoln — sideburns, sunglasses, everything but the gold lamé.

I went to Beckley because I thought I could learn something from these men that wasn't in books. For the same reason, over the years I've traveled to all the important Lincoln sites, from his birthplace outside Hodgenville, Kentucky, to Ford's Theatre in Washington. I held in my hands the letters he wrote to Joshua Speed and stood on the dais where he delivered the "House Divided" speech. I saw the bullet that killed him, a .41-caliber lead musket ball, its pieces held together with wire, behind glass at the National Museum of Health and Medicine. I took notes on all kinds of details with no apparent connection to my topic. Did you know that Lincoln liked popcorn, and oysters, and a good strong cup of coffee? It's true.

These curiosities served to remind me of something that was clear to me at the beginning of this journey but that, as I moved through it, could sometimes get cloudy. What drew me to the story of Lincoln's melancholy at the start was a sense of connection to him as a person. This man whom I had grown up to think of as a marble statue came alive for me when I first learned about how he suffered, and how he talked about it. I wanted to learn the full story and share it with other people. Doing that meant doing the work of history — lots of time in libraries, filling out call slips, going through manuscript boxes, working the photocopying machine. The difference between the initial sense of interest I had and the work it took to bring it to life was perhaps like the difference between admiring a house and trying to build one. But of course it's living in the house that makes building it worthwhile. And it's the connection we have to figures in history that makes it worth learning about them. Whether the connection is moral, emotional, intellectual — or, okay, sexual — it can change who we are. Certainly, spending seven years with Lincoln has changed me. I suspect it will continue to. With good stories, and with wise people, the buds of contact keep blooming.

My own connection with Lincoln is personal and specific, but his story offers lessons that we can share. I am left, then, at the end of seven years of study, wanting to articulate the living wisdom that Lincoln's life contains.

To start, the essence of this story is that it *is* a story, not a theory or a principle or a program. It unfolds over time, through peaks and valleys, with conflict and change. The outline of the story appeared to me early in my research. It took much longer to realize its subtleties, some of which, I'm sure, still elude me. Nevertheless, the book is structured according to the three major stages that I've observed in Lincoln's life. I refer to them as fear, engagement, and transcendence.

"Fear" comes from the first word in an age-old definition of melancholia: "fear and sadness without cause." To be more precise, you could say "without *apparent* cause, or *disproportionate* to apparent cause." While this story is about melancholy throughout, the first part illustrates its dark heart, the querulous, dissatisfied, doubting experience often marked by periods of withdrawal and sometimes by utter collapse. The letter Lincoln wrote on January 23, 1841 — rather, its ninety concluding words — perfectly articulates the first stage. Spare, direct, and forceful, it gets to the core of depression, as the Gettysburg Address does the core of the American experiment:

> I am now the most miserable man living. If what I felt were distributed to the whole human family there would not be one happy face on the earth. I must die or be better it appears to me. I awfully forebode I shall not. The matter you speak of on my account you may attend to as you

see fit, as I fear I shall be unable to attend to business. If I could be myself, I would rather stay here with Judge Logan. I can write no more.

This is what it's like: to feel not only miserable but the most miserable;
to feel a strange, muted sense of awful power; to believe plainly that either the misery must end or life will — and yet to fear the misery will not
end. A deeply intimate letter, it is also ice cold. No stories are told, no explanations offered, no thoughts reported from his tortured mind — not
even particular feelings. The letter is like a skeleton. Any miserable person who awfully forebodes he shall never be better could add his or her
own flesh. Lincoln got to the pure concentrate. The fact that he spoke
thus, not to a counselor or dear friend but to his law partner, indicates
how relentlessly he insisted on acknowledging his fears. Through the first
stage of his melancholy, he drove deeper and deeper into his pain, hovering over what, according to Albert Camus, is the only serious question
human beings have to deal with. He asked whether he could live, whether
he could face life's misery, and the first stage ended when he decided that
he must.

I call the second stage "engagement" because the word, for me, captures the essence of Lincoln's melancholy in his middle years. Whereas
the first stage is characterized largely by his own private experience, the
second stage has him turning to the world around him. From *whether* he
could live, he turned to *how* he *would* live. Building bridges out from his
lonely self, he engaged with the psychological culture of his time, trying
to make himself emotionally and mentally, investigating who he was,
what he could do to change, and what he could only accept and endure.
Some strategies were apparent — the temple of reason became his place
of refuge; humor and poetry gave him relief. Throughout, his work kept
him connected to the world around him, and he went at it dutifully,
manfully. Still, throughout this stage, questions remained paramount. In
large part because of the trials of his depressions, Lincoln knew what he
wanted to live for, but for years he suffered without any clear prospect of
how he would achieve it. He continued to plod ahead, even as clarity
about *why* eluded him. He lived with paradox: showing in full force both
resignation and defiance, pathos and humor, fear and hope.

Before describing Lincoln's third act, we should note that these stages
resonate with the arc of stories throughout time — the descent, ordeal,
and return of the hero's journey; the crisis, struggle, and resolution of
spiritual awakenings. But they also shed light on the mundane experi-

ence of day-to-day lives, in which our suffering can be felt and acknowl-edged, then kept in check while we engage and endure, and, finally drawn on for insight or wisdom. The elegance of Lincoln's story is that it suggests, in its structure, a sense of order and proportion.

For example, depressed people are often unable to get out of bed, feel-ing a kind of paralysis that seems physical and involuntary, even though, on some level, it's known to be mental and volitional. Truly, for those in thrall to mental agony, as Andrew Solomon has observed, merely going to brush one's teeth can feel like a Herculean task. A common argument today has two people standing over the bed. One says, "He can't help it. He has an illness and should be treated with deference." The other dis-putes this, muttering, "He just needs a swift kick in the butt."

Lincoln's story allows us to see that both points may be true. First, when overcome by mental agony, he allowed himself to be overcome, and for no small time. He let himself sink to the bottom and feel the scrape. Those who say that we must *always* buck up should see how Lin-coln's time of illness proved also to be a time of gestation and growth. Those who say we must *always* frame mental suffering in terms of illness must see how vital it was that Lincoln roused himself when the time came. How might Lincoln have endangered his future, and his potential, had he denied himself the reality of his suffering? How, too, might he have stagnated had he not realized that life waits for those who choose to live it?

When a depressed person does get out of bed, it's usually not with a sudden insight that life is rich and valuable, but out of some creeping sense of duty or instinct for survival. If collapsing is sometimes vital, so is the brute force of will. To William James we owe the insight that, in the absence of real health, we sometimes must act *as if* we are healthy. Buoyed by such discipline and habit, we might achieve actual well-being. As Lincoln advised a grumbling general who felt humiliated at having only three thousand men under his command, "'Act well your part, there all the honor lies.' He who does *something* at the head of one Regiment, will eclipse him who does nothing at the head of a hundred." Two dec-ades before he wrote these words, after the winter of a great depression, Lincoln understood doing *something* to be as simple as going to work, or just making preparations for it, which he gamely advised Joshua Speed to do if his "mind were not right." In the small battles of life, brushing one's teeth, taking a walk — these can be movements in preparation for victory.

A key feature of Lincoln's story is that in this middle stage, while his labors were picayune, he kept sight of a grand potential. "It is *much* for the young to know," he said in his eulogy to Zachary Taylor in 1850, "that treading the hard path of duty, as he trod it, *will* be noticed, and *will* lead to high places." Lincoln said this at a time when his own faith had been sorely tested — for all he knew, his dreams would come to nothing. But the faith itself led him to tread the hard path with a sense of purpose, adjusting to reality but never quite settling. He feared that he would not, but trusted that he would, finally find his way. When he did, everything he had lived through had its purpose.

In mythical stories, a character undertakes a journey, receiving at every step totems that, at the time, have no clear value but at the end turn out to provide the essential tools for a final struggle. We can see this in Lincoln's journey. In the first stage, he asked the big questions. Why am I here? What is the point? Without the sense of essential purpose he learned by asking these questions, he may not have had the bedrock vision that governed his great work. In the second stage, he developed diligence and discipline, working for the sake of work, learning how to survive and engage. Without the discipline of his middle years, he would not have had the fortitude to endure the disappointments that his great work entailed. In the third stage, he was not just working but doing the work he felt made to do, not only surviving but living for a vital purpose. Yet he constantly faced the same essential challenges that had been presented to him throughout. All through his career fighting the extension of slavery, and all through his presidency, he faced painful fear and doubt — indeed, he faced it on an awful scale. But he repeatedly returned to a sense of purpose; from this purpose he put his head down to work at the mundane tasks of his job; and with his head down, he glanced up, often enough, at the chance to effect something meaningful and lasting. We justly look upon the transcendence of his final days with admiration, noticing the amazing balance between earthly works and self-dissolution. But even then, he was a product of his journey.

The overarching lesson of Lincoln's life is one of wholeness. Knowing that confidence, clarity, and joy are possible in life, it is easy to be impatient with fear, doubt, and sadness. If one desires to "stir up the world," it is easy to be impatient with work for the sake of work. Yet no story's end can forsake its beginning and its middle. Perhaps in the inspiration of Lincoln's end we can receive some fortitude and instruction about all that it took for him to get there, and all that it continues to take. In *The*

Life of Poetry, Muriel Rukeyser writes that the "images of history" can "reach us imaginatively." She continues: "The life of Jesus; the life of Buddha; the life of Lincoln, or Gandhi, or Saint Francis of Assisi — these give us the intensity that should be felt in a lifetime of concentration, a lifetime which seems to risk the immortal meanings every day . . . These lives, in their search and purpose, offer their form, offer their truths. They reach us as hope." The hope is not that suffering will go away, for with Lincoln it did not ever go away. The hope is that suffering, plainly acknowledged and endured, can fit us for the surprising challenges that await.

Of all the paradoxes of Lincoln's life, none is more powerful than the fact that the man who would come to be known throughout the world — from American schoolrooms to the tribal councils of the Caucasus Mountains — was deeply mysterious to the people who knew him best. "Those who have spoken most confidently of their knowledge of his personal qualities," wrote the Pennsylvania Republican Alexander McClure, "are, as a rule, those who saw least of them below the surface." After more than two decades of studying Lincoln, following thirty years of direct contact, William Herndon wrote in 1887 to a friend, "In one of your letters you ask me this question in substance — 'Do you think that Lincoln wished to be known — *thoroughly known*' and to which I answer emphatically — No — he was a hidden man and wished to keep his own secrets. As I trail the man step by step, like a dog trails a fox I find many new *spots* — many new *holes* — much to admire and much to regret. It nearly kills me in my old age to persist in my search."

Four years later, Herndon returned to a theme that had intrigued and puzzled him for decades. "Let me say to you," he wrote to a young man interested in Lincoln, "that he had *a double consciousness* — if not a treble consciousness. First he was a terribly gloomy — sad man at times — 2dly he was at times full of humor — 'joky' — witty & happy. Gloom & sadness were his predominant state — 3dly at times he was neither sad nor humorous, but was simply in a pleasant mood — ie he was not in a gloomy nor a mirthful fit — *was kindly thoughtful*, not serious ever — a state of thought & good feeling united for the moment . . . This last state was not of long duration. Lincoln was a curious — mysterious — quite an incomprehensible man. Do not think that I exaggerate." Just three weeks later, Herndon died.

Perhaps the mystery is that Lincoln joined qualities that, though we well understand that they exist separately, confound us when united.

There is something so real about this union that it awakens what is real in us when we encounter it. Yet there is something mystical in it, and distant. "I am sure," said Ralph Waldo Emerson in his eulogy of Lincoln, "if this man had ruled in a period of less facility of printing, he would have become mythological in a very few years, like Aesop or Pilpay, or one of the Seven Wise Masters." Searching and struggling with the real records of his life, we try to see him as a real man. As we ruminate, finally, on the lessons of his life, we try to remove it from the airy realms of myth and bring it into the reality of our lives. I have struggled to do this. I've looked for the grand meanings with a telescope aimed at the night sky. But my vision often failed me, and the nights often got cloudy, and I took refuge, always, in the details — the black walnut and honey locust trees that made up the rails Lincoln split as a young man; the brown ink and trembling hand on the "Meditation on Divine Will"; the way that, when he told a story, he planted his feet on the ground, lifting his right leg slightly, then throwing it over his left leg as he laughed uproariously.

When I went to Beckley, West Virginia, to join the Association of Lincoln Presenters at their annual convention, my mind was full of big questions. These men who dressed up as Lincoln day after day, did they *feel* something? Could they help me *see* something as abstract as melancholy? But from the moment I arrived, my mission went awry. I hadn't realized that I'd be the only civilian. The Lincolns didn't know what to make of me. They kept asking, "Are you a new Lincoln?" I tried to explain why I was there, but I didn't really know myself, and "I'm writing a book" didn't seem to satisfy the men in black who were hovering around me in the lobby of the Country Inn and Suites. Finally, when Jim Sayre, a veteran presenter from Lawrenceburg, Kentucky, said to me, "Are you a new Lincoln?" I muttered something about not having had time to get my outfit together. "Come on, then," Jim said, and he took me upstairs to lend me his spare. I put on the white shirt ("Wal-Mart special," Sayre said), clipped on the flat bow tie, and pulled on the black trousers. "Always travel with a spare," Sayre said. I said okay, and put on the hat.

I spent the weekend wandering around the convention's events, learning what I could. I gazed up to look for the meaning of it all, but kept stumbling and going back to the details. Did you know that Lincoln wore top hats of silk for fine occasions and of beaver for everyday? It's true, the rain rolls right off beaverskin. Maybe I expected a group of eccentrics, but it was a pretty ordinary convention. The Lincolns talked about who was getting which gigs and how much they paid. Reenactments and conventions are good. Weddings pay well, and you get a good feed. The staple of their work, of course, is visits to schools. Just as book writers wonder how to interest television and radio shows, who help them interest readers, the Lincolns constantly look to interest teachers, who will put them in front of rooms full of children.

Near the end of the weekend, I sat down on the hotel's porch and had a talk with Cranston "Bud" Green, from Versailles, Missouri. He was seventy-six years old. He had come to the convention fresh from open-heart surgery, and he walked with a slight stoop, leaning on his sassafras cane. After I had suited up, most of the Lincolns assumed I was one of them and started right in with the unsolicited advice — mainly, "There's good work for beardless Lincolns." But when Bud Green asked me what I was doing there, I told him I was writing a book on Lincoln's depression. "I have manic depression," he said. He told me about growing up during the Great Depression, raising Christmas trees and working as a pitchman at fairs. He told me about the time, many years later, when he pulled off an interstate and checked into a motel intending to hang himself. Then he thought of his kids and steered his car back on the road. When he finished the story, suffering lingered in the air between us. I asked him, "Does being Lincoln help?" He answered me quickly: "Yes, it helps. But it can hurt, too. It hurts when the teachers don't call."

Maybe trying to find meaning in our ordinary lives by learning about Lincoln is as absurd as dressing up in the kind of clothes he wore, but in that moment I felt the connection. A man I didn't know had the courage to tell me that he suffered, and he had the power to tell me what he was after. Lincoln might be far away and gone, but something runs unbroken through the present and the past. Bud Green wants the teachers to call; I want NPR to call, and *The Oprah Winfrey Show*. On April 14, Lincoln wanted Sherman to call, and while he waited, he told his cabinet about a dream he'd had the night before.

February 24, 2005

AFTERWORD

NOTES

BIBLIOGRAPHY

ACKNOWLEDGMENTS

INDEX

Afterword

"What Everybody Knows":
A Historiography of Lincoln's Melancholy

As GRAND AND IMMOVABLE as history can seem, it comes to us through ordinary people who make mistakes even as they make progress. This explains, in short, how a subject such as Lincoln's melancholy could be neglected and obscured for many decades, and how, more recently, it has been excavated and restored to its rightful place as an important aspect of his life and character.

The first biographical works on Lincoln came from his contemporaries, who for the most part looked upon his depression with frank curiosity. It seemed not a matter of shame but an intriguing aspect of his character, and indeed an aspect of his grand nature. These works, we should say, did not dwell inordinately on the melancholy. Nor did most of them seek to extract its essence by using medical theory or philosophy. They tended, rather, to note the facts of Lincoln's gloomy nature, usually in a straightforward manner, and move on.

The man who studied the melancholy most closely — because he studied everything about Lincoln closely — was William Henry Herndon, Lincoln's law partner from 1844 to 1861. Technically, the partnership continued until Lincoln's death in April 1865. Soon after that, Herndon began to solicit material from men and women who had known Lincoln. By mid-November 1866, he had collected roughly four hundred testimonials, plus original letters, newspaper clippings, and court files. Herndon hired a clerk to have his "Lincoln Record" copied out by hand. He had the copied items bound in leather in three legal-size volumes. He placed them in a bank vault. "If I die," he wrote, "the record is safe."

It wasn't theft or fire or flood that threatened the record's legacy, but a war over Lincoln's memory, fueled in part by changing ideas about mental health and illness. The first battles began when Herndon attempted to connect Lincoln's profound suffering as a young man to his genius as a mature leader. Instead he set in motion a chain of events that would not only obscure the connection for later generations but cause Lincoln's melancholy to practically disappear.

Herndon loved Lincoln and thought history should have a full knowledge of him. He detested hagiography, the kind of biography that treats a subject with glassy-eyed reverence. Herndon had known Lincoln as a man with human strengths and frailties. The full story of his life, he argued, would not diminish but magnify appreciation of his excellence. In any case, he believed that, as a practical matter, what was covered up by Lincoln's friends would be set upon by his enemies. "Is any man so insane," he wrote to a mutual friend of the late president, "as to suppose that any truth concerning Lincoln will be hid and buried out of human view? Folly! The best way is to tell the whole truth and let it burn up lies. Lincoln is above reproach, thank God; let no one fear to have all the truth about him brought clearly to light."

Early in his research, Herndon began to hear from people who had lived with Lincoln at New Salem, where, when he was twenty-six, he had collapsed in depression. It had something to do with his law studies, Herndon heard. And it came right after the death of a young woman named Ann Rutledge. Herndon eventually gathered testimony from twenty-four people on this matter. Most of them had seen Lincoln's breakdown firsthand; all were connected to his intimates at New Salem. Seventeen of them said, at least, that Lincoln had grieved to an unusual degree after Rutledge's death, and many considered that he had had a brush with insanity. Herndon wrote on June 8, 1865, "I have been searching for *the facts* & *truths* of Lincoln's life — not fictions — not fables — not floating rumors, but *facts* — *solid facts* & *well attested truths* . . . From such an investigation . . . I am satisfied, in connection with my own knowledg of Mr L. for 30 years, that Mr L's whole early life *remains to be written*."

In the late 1860s, William Herndon had graying black hair and a bushy beard. He was, a reporter noted, "disposed to shut one eye for accuracy in conversation, his teeth discolored by tobacco, and over his angular features, which suggest Lincoln's in ampleness and shape, the same half-tender melancholy." A curious man and a voracious reader, Herndon aspired to be what we now call a public intellectual. He gobbled up works on philosophy, theology, and psychology. He described Lincoln as a "realist rather than an idealist." As in many things, Herndon was the opposite, living in the airy realm of thought. He had decided to "write & publish the *subjective* Mr

Lincoln — 'the inner life' of Mr L. . . . a short little thing — giving him in his passions — appetites — & affections — perceptions — memories — judgements — understanding — will, acting under & by motives, *just* as he lived, breathed — ate & laughed in this world, clothed in flesh & sinew — bones & meat."

Herndon worked fiercely to find and depose key witnesses. Among other coups, he conducted a rare interview with Lincoln's aged stepmother. Trained as a lawyer, Herndon knew how to get information out of people. If he had to pay for help, he did so. When he received some morsel, he responded with more questions. At the end of each interview, he'd read back his notes, make corrections, and ask for a confirming signature. But cogent narrative was not Herndon's strength. "I sincerely wish I were a competent, a great man to write my friend's life," he wrote. "I have not got the capacity to write much at best and not that much well." When he did speak out about what he'd learned, he did it hastily. He hurried, in part, because he feared that the stories he was uncovering would fall into the hands of a malicious or ignorant writer and be made into a scandal. He began a series of lectures in Springfield on Lincoln's mind and character. He made arrangements to give a lecture on November 16, 1866, at the courthouse, that would deal with the subject of Lincoln's prostration after Ann Rutledge's death.

Later generations would miss the fact that Herndon's interpretation of Lincoln's first breakdown must be seen apart from the evidence he had collected. The latter, as is typical of basic evidence, was full of opinions, imperfect memories, vivid details, and conflicting narrative lines, each distinguished by the character of the witness, his or her proximity to Lincoln at important moments, and so on. The interpretation, as with nearly all historical accounts, was the synthesis of and extrapolation from that material by a single mind. It was also the product of a flowery, effusive style, full of sweeping claims and long discursions. In the November 16 lecture, Herndon revealed an important fact of Lincoln's biography: his first serious depression. But he also created a shroud of confusion around it, first by identifying an ostensible cause — that "Lincoln loved Anna Rutledge better than his own life" — and second by claiming that the grief over her loss was a major factor in his lifelong melancholy. It was a fire, Herndon said, that forged in Lincoln his mature character. "Lincoln first came to himself, after so great grief," Herndon wrote. Crushed by Rutledge's death, "he thought and reflected on man and woman, the transient and permanent — love, duty, nature, destiny, the past, present, and the future — of God."

Impatient with Herndon's rhapsodic prose, reporters plucked from the lecture its core sensation: that Lincoln had loved this village girl, and that her death played a major role in his life. The *New York Times* reported that the materials "concerning MR. LINCOLN and MISS RUTLEDGE . . . are exceedingly interesting and throw much light on phases of MR. LINCOLN's character, and especially on the melancholy and abstracted mood which so many of his friends have observed, and which no one hitherto has attempted to explain." Note that Lincoln's melancholy was considered an established fact, on which new light was sought.

Early works on Lincoln, including Francis Carpenter's *Six Months in the White House,* published in 1866, gave significant attention to his moods. People were hungry to understand them. It made sense to people that some secret cause lay in his past. "I would like to have you write me what the skeleton was with Lincoln," one old colleague wrote Herndon. "What gave him that peculiar melancholy? What cancer had he inside? . . . I always thought there was something but never knew what." Now Herndon had provided an answer, and on the strength of it a legend took shape. In April 1867, the journalist Caroline Dall, who was friendly with Herndon, published a piece in the *Atlantic Monthly* that declared Lincoln's love for Rutledge to be "the key to his whole life." Had she and Lincoln married, Dall said, he would never have gone into politics. "He would have tasted the cup of happiness, and it would have been enough."

From the start, opinions of Lincoln's widow played a role in the Ann Rutledge legend. Mary Lincoln had never been a national darling, and after she left the White House she became something of a national villain. As early as 1865 or 1866, her own sister Elizabeth Edwards said, "Mary Lincoln has had much to bear, though she don't bear it well. She has acted foolishly — unwisely and made the world hate her."

Much of her unwise behavior had to do with money. Convinced that she was nearly a pauper, "scarcely removed from want," even after her husband's estate was settled at $110,000 (roughly $1.9 million in modern terms), she demanded money from Congress — imperiously, many thought — so that she could live in a style that befitted her. When she didn't get it, she dreamed up a scheme to sell some of her gowns and jewels. She got mixed up with a pair of hucksters who put these goods on public display and planned a traveling show to which they would charge admission. At their encouragement, she wrote letters suggesting that certain politicians should help lest she charge them with corruption. Then the *New York World* published these letters and the affair blew up in Mary Lincoln's face. Accusations flew that she had stolen public property from the White House, padded expense accounts, and dealt out patronage, expecting recompense. Newspapers assailed her — a "dreadful woman," said the *Republican* of Springfield, Massachusetts, who "persists in forcing her repugnant individuality before the world." The *New York Citizen* called the affair "one of the most humiliating revelations in the social life of our country," and urged that "Mrs. Lincoln, for the honor of the country, should be silenced at whatever cost."

Herndon didn't mention Mary Lincoln in his lecture of November 1866. But the implication was clear enough. He said that her husband, after Ann Rutledge's death, "*never* addressed another woman, in my opinion, 'yours affectionately'; and generally and characteristically abstained from the use of the word '*love*.'" He noted that some in New Salem believed that if Lincoln and Rutledge had married, he would have become "a purely domestic man," as he needed some "whip and spur" to push him into politics. Finally, he quoted Lincoln as saying, in 1835, that his heart lay buried in Rutledge's grave. Herndon made his view explicit in a private letter. "Mr. Lincoln was a sad, gloomy, and melancholic man," he wrote. This temperament sprang chiefly from "his organism, his make-up and his constitution," but his "original nature" was intensified by several events, including "the untimely death of Ann Rutledge, and his unfortunate marriage to Miss Mary Todd, and the hell that came of it."

It is not at all clear, as many scholars assume, that Lincoln's widow and his former law partner had always hated each other. In fact, Herndon had more sympathy for Mary Lincoln than most, insisting repeatedly that her husband bore much of the responsibility for the quality of their marriage. As late as August 1866, Herndon and Mrs. Lincoln were on cordial terms. That month, after he requested an interview, she sent a fulsome response, recalling "my beloved husband's truly affectionate regard for you" and assuring Herndon that he was "cherished with the sincerest regard by my sons & myself." She added, "I have been thinking for some time past that I would like to see you & have a long conversation," and she sat for an interview in September 1866.

After Herndon's lecture, however, the widowed First Lady was at his throat, calling him a "dirty dog" and alleging that her husband had worked with him only out of pity. She told one of Lincoln's colleagues to shut Herndon up, threatening vaguely, "It will not be *well with him* — if he makes the least disagreeable or false allusion in the future. *He* will be closely watched." Mary Lincoln allowed that Lincoln may have had some romance in his early days. "But as my husband was *truth itself*," she wrote, "and as he always assured me, he had cared for no one but myself . . . I shall assuredly remain firm in my conviction — that *Ann Rutledge*, is a myth . . . Nor did his life or his joyous laugh, lead one to suppose his heart, was in any unfortunate woman's grave — but in the proper place with his loved wife & children."

The rivalry between William Herndon and Mary Lincoln would shape Lincoln studies for much of the next century; its effects still linger. Ann

Rutledge was just one piece of it. Herndon believed, perhaps naively, that he could write his friend's life fully and honestly, "*just* as he lived, breathed." He wanted to discuss openly Lincoln's unorthodox religious views, his domestic life, and his melancholy. Mary Lincoln wanted to paint an idyllic portrait of her family and marriage. Amazingly, decades after all of Lincoln's friends and family had passed away, the stories told by William Herndon would be shot from the sky, to be replaced by those preferred by Mary Lincoln.

Soon after he completed his "Lincoln Record," Herndon got into deep financial trouble. An off-and-on heavy drinker who had been sober for years — including the period in which he gathered his biographical materials — he fell off the wagon. Desperate for cash, he sold the rights to his record to Ward Hill Lamon, a lawyer who had worked with Lincoln in Illinois and who later became his marshal for the District of Columbia. Lamon was estranged from the Republicans after the war and grew close to a prominent Democratic family, to whose son, a partisan journalist named Chauncey Black, he turned over Herndon's materials, to ghostwrite a book. Thus did the stories Herndon had collected first appear between hard covers. *The Life of Abraham Lincoln,* by Ward Hill Lamon, appeared in 1872. The book cited Herndon throughout, eliding the interviewer (who himself had considerable personal knowledge of Lincoln) with the many other sources he had drawn upon. Black remained truly a ghost: to this day, the work is discussed as though Lamon really wrote it.

The book kicked up a huge storm. In addition to a lengthy account of the Rutledge romance, it reported that Lincoln's mother was illegitimate and that Lincoln dissented from orthodox Christianity. Among the copious evidence Herndon had on this matter was a statement from Mary Lincoln — from their interview of September 1866 — that Lincoln was not a "technical Christian." This quite reasonable statement was nevertheless shocking at the time. Herndon became embroiled in a knockdown fight with several prominent preachers who undertook to defend Lincoln against what they regarded as his apostasy. Mary Lincoln sided with the preachers — she said she'd been misquoted — which further deepened the split between her and Herndon, upon whom all kinds of attacks descended, portraying him as a drunk, a liar, and a madman.

In the 1880s, William Herndon sobered up and began to correspond with an ambitious Indiana college boy named Jesse Weik. The two soon joined forces to prepare a biography. Herndon offered raw material — from memory and from the originals of his "Lincoln Record" — which Weik polished and embellished. The book, *Herndon's Lincoln: The True Story of a Great Life,* was published in 1889, two years before Herndon died.

Here, too, the ghostwriter played a much larger role than is generally acknowledged.

Two decades after Herndon had gathered his materials, he had to decide how to narrate Lincoln's tortured winter of 1840–1841. As we have seen, many details of the aborted romance of that season remain obscure. Several witnesses agreed that Abraham Lincoln and Mary Todd had been engaged, then split, and that he had an extended collapse. But when did they split? Who initiated it? What was going on with Lincoln when he declared himself "the most miserable man living"? It is problematic that, faced with such vexing questions, writers often choose a version of events based on the material in front of them, and tell it without admitting any doubts, as though they were omniscient. When evidence gives only the bare bones, many histories treat the past like a well-dressed pageant, where everyone is in full costume and the author is in a front-row seat. Herndon sometimes took such an approach. Weik pushed the text even further from the facts.

In an early interview, Mary Lincoln's sister Elizabeth Edwards had said, according to Herndon's notes, "Lincoln and Mary were Engaged — Every thing was ready & prepared for the marriage — Even to the Supper &c —. Mr L failed to meet his Engagement — Cause insanity." Later, she repeated this story to a journalist. "Arrangements for wedding had been made," the writer's notes read, "— even cakes had been baked — but L. failed to appear . . . Mary was greatly mortified by L's strange conduct." In fact, no one else remembered that a wedding had actually been set, nor has a marriage license been found. On the other hand, Elizabeth Edwards was hardly a dubious witness. No one was closer to Mary Todd at the time.

Herndon made the aborted wedding the centerpiece of his story. In a draft, he described the event, adding a few colorful details, such as the bride waiting nervously for the groom, the guests departing one by one. And he assigned it a date, "about January '41" — a reasonable guess, all the more so for acknowledging doubt. Jesse Weik elaborated further, having the nervous bride fiddle with the flowers in her hair, then withdraw in grief to her room. Most important, Weik placed the wedding on a specific day. Plucking a phrase from a letter Lincoln wrote a year and a half later, Weik decided that the aborted ceremony had been set for "that fatal first," January 1, 1841. At the time, it probably seemed a reasonable extrapolation from the facts — the sort of leap often made by historical writers. It would have important implications, however, as future generations seized on the mistake to try to wipe away the truth of the whole period in Lincoln's life.

Though Lincoln was widely eulogized after his death and became the subject of many articles and books in the late nineteenth century, it was only in the early twentieth century that he became an American demigod. By then, adults who had lived and suffered through the Civil War had mostly died. Whites looked to Lincoln as a symbol of national reconciliation. African Americans looked to him as a symbol of their liberty and equality. And a huge wave of immigrants — about fifteen million of whom arrived between 1890 and 1914 — revered him as a symbol of American pluck and possibility. In this era, memorials to honor Lincoln were being built in Washington, D.C. (with a statue modeled on an enthroned Zeus), and on the site of his birth in Kentucky. Lincoln Logs became a popular toy.

A second generation took over Lincoln biography, prominent among them the journalist Ida Tarbell, the poet Carl Sandburg, the minister William Barton, and the former senator Albert Beveridge. Lincoln's intimates — including Herndon, Speed, and Mary Lincoln — had died, which meant biographers had to rely on the printed record, though they hunted up surviving acquaintances of Lincoln and their children. The accounts of this era gave considerable space to his melancholy, because it was obviously a big part of Lincoln's life and because it played to the popular understanding of Lincoln as a "man of sorrows" who faced great internal and external difficulties and endured them, emerging as meek, forceful, and grand. The Standard Oil Company published a pamphlet on the seventy-fifth anniversary of Gettysburg: *Abraham Lincoln: Man of Suffering*. In the 1920s, a homily called "The Failure" started to appear in magazines. It listed Lincoln's setbacks: "Lost job in 1832. Defeated for state legislature in 1832. Failed in business in 1833. Sweetheart died in 1835. Had nervous breakdown in 1836. Defeated for Speaker in 1838," and so on. The point was that just as Lincoln had passed through hardship to greatness, ordinary people could do the same. (This list is still a staple of popular culture, appearing on inspirational business posters and in the original *Chicken Soup for the Soul*; of course it's posted on numerous Web sites.) For a sense of the attitude toward mental trouble in this era, consider that in 1919, when President Woodrow Wilson had a stroke, which news his aides believed was unsuitable for public consumption, they sent the president's physician to tell reporters that he was suffering from "nervous exhaustion" that required rest for "a considerable time." The two-deck banner headline in the *New York Times* the next day read: PRESIDENT SUFFERS NERVOUS BREAKDOWN, TOUR CANCELED; SPEEDING BACK TO WASHINGTON FOR A NEEDED REST.

In the 1920s and 1930s, people scarcely distinguished the facts of Lincoln's melancholy from the twin myths of his love for Ann Rutledge and his dreadful marriage to the woman now known as "Mary Todd Lincoln." Indeed, the dismal career of the president's widow continued to cast a shadow. She had watched two of her children die while her husband was alive; she was with Lincoln when he was killed. Then Tad, the youngest boy, died in 1871, at age eighteen. By then, the former First Lady's mental illness was well enough understood that the *Illinois State Journal* of Springfield reported that "her conduct has greatly distressed her friends and relatives in this city and the most charitable construction they can put on her strange course is that she is insane." In 1875, Robert Todd Lincoln, the one son who lived to adulthood, committed his mother to an asylum. She spent four months as a patient at Bellevue Place, in Batavia, Illinois, and lived her final years in isolation.

In the Progressive Era, the nation was busy exalting its sixteenth president, and it needed a love interest for the narrative — his widow would not do. Instead she became a shrewish antihero, the foil of the patient, humble, and inspiring Great Emancipator. The story that Lincoln had bolted from an actual wedding gained wide circulation. And Ann Rutledge became one of the most famous characters in the country. After all, hadn't Lincoln loved her? Hadn't he gone nearly mad at her death and cherished her memory all his life? In 1915, Edgar Lee Masters's popular *Spoon River Anthology,* poems in the form of monologues from the dead, included one for Ann that canonized the legend's astonishing claims:

> Out of me unworthy and unknown
> The vibrations of deathless music;
> "With malice toward none, with charity for all."
> Out of me the forgiveness of millions toward millions,
> And the beneficent face of a nation
> Shining with justice and truth.
> I am Anne Rutledge who sleep beneath these weeds,
> Beloved in life of Abraham Lincoln,
> Wedded to him, not through union,
> But through separation.
> Bloom forever, O Republic,
> From the dust of my bosom!

Ann Rutledge had become nothing less than the martyred mother of the nation. In Petersburg, Illinois, a new graveyard installed her remains in a central plot, with Masters's epitaph on the gravestone — fiction having created a new reality. A few miles away, New Salem was rebuilt, with help from William Randolph Hearst, as a kind of shrine to the Lincoln-Rutledge romance. From 1930 to 1940, three motion pictures on Lincoln — D. W. Griffith's *Abraham Lincoln,* John Ford's *Young Mr. Lincoln,* and *Abe Lincoln in Illinois,* based on the hit Broadway play by Sherwood Anderson — featured her and young Abe. In 1937, the Baltimore & Ohio Railroad introduced a new passenger train to join the "Abraham Lincoln" on its Chicago–St. Louis line, the "Ann Rutledge." (Amtrak still uses the name.)

Biographers also embraced the story. Ida Tarbell, the chief authority on Lincoln in the late nineteenth and early twentieth centuries, described a melancholy Lincoln living in the "shadow of Ann Rutledge's death." Perhaps the apogee of the legend, in terms of serious biography, came in 1926 when Carl Sandburg, in his two-volume work *Abraham Lincoln: The Prairie Years*, described Ann Rutledge as a "quiet soft bud of a woman," a "slim girl with corn-silk hair" who made Lincoln tremble when he so much as looked at her. After her death and his collapse, Sandburg wrote that it took weeks for "an old-time order" to come back to Lincoln, "only it was said that the shadows of a burning he had been through were fixed in the depths of his eyes, and he was a changed man keeping to himself the gray mystery of the change."

In this same era, students of Lincoln saw the need for a thorough study of Lincoln's mental life, one that would separate the wheat from the chaff and illuminate established facts with expert testimony. In the early 1920s, a physician named W. A. Evans, who wrote a column for the *Chicago Tribune*, received several letters from a distant relative of Lincoln who had information about mental illness in the family of Lincoln's uncle. Dr. Evans forwarded them to a Lincoln scholar of the time, William E. Barton, writing, "I hope you will seriously consider doing the 'Mind of Lincoln.' It is needed and I do not know of anyone in the country who can do it so well as you." Barton seized on the lead and ended up writing several articles based on the material he received from the relative, Berenice Lovely. But soon this material, like so much other good data, would be lost amid the ruins of the Ann Rutledge legend.

The legend crested and fell along with the stock market. In 1928, the *Atlantic Monthly* began publishing a collection of letters between Lincoln and Rutledge, along with diary entries from a close friend of the couple, narrating their doomed romance. After brief inspections, both Tarbell and Sandburg called the letters genuine. The *Atlantic's* editor, Ellery Sedgwick, had been charmed by the owner of the letters, a California actress named Wilma Frances Minor, who said she had found them in an old family trunk. But the letters were obvious fakes. They contained childish misspellings (a lame attempt to simulate early-nineteenth-century prose) and glaring anachronisms (references to Kansas before the state existed). Complaints came after the first installment appeared in December 1928, but Sedgwick dug in his heels and published the second and third installments in January and February 1929. Finally Minor explained that her mother, a spiritualist, had contacted Lincoln and Rutledge from the grave, with Minor herself transcribing the results. "I would die on the gallows that the spirit of Ann and Abe were speaking through my mother and me," Minor said.

The Minor affair ended up ushering in the third era of Lincoln studies.

First the story had been controlled by Lincoln's friends (and their ghost-writers). Then the popular historians had taken over. Now the reins passed to professional historians, a burgeoning group emerging from new Ph.D. programs (a creation of the late nineteenth and early twentieth centuries). University-trained historians tended to look askance at the amateurs who had come before them. For the professionals in the Lincoln field, the Ann Rutledge story was a perfect example of what had gone wrong. For years they had been aching to knock it down, and the *Atlantic Monthly* threw a hanging curve. Paul Angle, a graduate of the master's program in history at the University of Illinois and the executive secretary of the Lincoln Centennial Association, did the honors for the historical guild. In the April 1929 *Atlantic*, he exposed the Minor letters as fakes. Perhaps more important, he used his piece to scold amateurs who tried to write history. The baton had been taken by a new generation.

In the 1930s and 1940s, professional historians assembled a complete edition of Lincoln's writings, among other reference works, and produced scholarly books on many aspects of his life. Chief among these scholars was a professor at the University of Illinois at Urbana-Champaign, James Garfield Randall. In 1911, when he received his Ph.D. in history, graduate study in the United States was in its adolescence. He grew up with the field and became a towering figure — "the greatest Lincoln scholar of all time," declares *The Abraham Lincoln Encyclopedia*. Randall was an apostle for, and an arbiter of, high standards in scholarship. His early work focused on constitutional history, but he turned to Lincoln in the late 1920s and early 1930s. The country was drowning in Lincoln material, Randall said in a 1934 lecture, but any "careful scholar" could see "gaps, doubts, prevalent misconceptions, unsupported interpretations, and erroneous assumptions." Randall began his own biography, which would eventually reach three volumes (the last one finished by a colleague after Randall's death).

Randall's wife, Ruth Painter Randall, had long helped with his research and writing. Their partnership would have a big influence on the scholarly and popular understanding of Abraham Lincoln in the second half of the twentieth century. The title of her memoir sheds light on their relationship: *I, Ruth: Autobiography of a Marriage; The Self-Told Story of the Woman Who Married the Great Lincoln Scholar, James G. Randall, and Through Her Interest in His Work Became a Lincoln Author Herself.* When her husband undertook his full-scale biography, she recounts, he asked her to prepare a chapter on the Lincolns' marriage. "I well remember the next contributing incident," she wrote. It was February 14, 1944, and she and her husband were sitting in the parlor of their five-room apartment in Urbana. He was sixty-two years old, a short man with iron-gray hair and a broad smile. He wore a three-piece suit with a watch in his vest pocket and his Phi Beta

Kappa key on the chain. She had white hair with soft curls. She spoke with a slight drawl, a remnant of Roanoke, Virginia, where she grew up and where she met Professor Randall. They began to date several years after his first wife died, and married several years after that. In 1944, they had been married twenty-six years.

On this Valentine's Day, the Randalls were listening to the radio. Suddenly the program changed to a holiday presentation of a popular drama: the romance between Ann Rutledge and Abraham Lincoln. Professor Randall got up, walked over to the radio, and snapped it off. He told his wife that the original interviews and letters collected by Herndon had just been purchased by the Library of Congress. For decades they had been privately held, and only one biographer since Jesse Weik had been allowed to use them. Randall had already assigned his star graduate student, a Mississippi native named David Herbert Donald, to produce a biography of Herndon for his dissertation. That night, Randall wrote in his diary, "I gave the wife a new assignment . . . suggested she might go after the subject of Lincoln and Ann Rutledge."

From that assignment came an appendix in Randall's second volume, *Lincoln the President,* titled, "Sifting the Ann Rutledge Evidence" — a piece not credited to, but apparently written by, Ruth Painter Randall. ("It is very largely her work," J. G. Randall wrote of the appendix, in a private letter.) It is a seminal work in Lincoln studies, not only because it served to demolish the traditional romance but because it did so by attacking its foundation in Herndon's records. The professional historians — "scientific historians," they sometimes called themselves — distrusted what they called "reminiscence" and what has recently been received more favorably as "oral history." The fact that Herndon took down the memories of people in 1866 about events that happened in 1835 already made his records suspect. Herndon, moreover, had come to symbolize to the professional historians all that they disliked about amateur history. David Herbert Donald's biography of Herndon portrayed him as a drunkard and a dreamer. Herndon's records were, Ruth Painter Randall wrote, a grab bag of "misty" memories given by "old settlers" who had been "induced under suggestion, or psychological stimulus." In other words, Herndon had coaxed people to remember things that probably never happened, then embellished their memories in his notes.

Why would Herndon do it? To Ruth Painter Randall, the motive was clear: he "disliked and feared Mary Lincoln" and wished to embarrass her and undermine her significance. For the same reason, he sought to mar her marriage to Lincoln, beginning with a fiction about a failed wedding and continuing with a twisted tale that, during their courtship, Lincoln loved another woman; that Mary had flirted with other men; that Lincoln, tortured by doubt over his obligations and desires, collapsed into a profound depression. As a matter of fact, these elements are attested to by a wide array of sources. But in Randall's version it was just another part of Herndon's "frame-up" of Mary Lincoln. The truth, Randall argued, was that Lincoln never loved another woman, nor did he doubt his love for Todd. On the contrary, when Lincoln found her, his life took on "a joyous new focus and vitality"; he walked in a "golden haze." Then, owing to her family's opposition, the engagement was broken off amicably, peacefully, on January 1, 1841. As a result, Lincoln suffered "emotional agony": "This sweet, newly discovered world was shattered. Mr. Lincoln had barely tasted the joy of having someone of his very own to love when that joy was taken from him, leaving him in a gray and flavorless world."

Having attacked Herndon for his use of reminiscence, Ruth Painter Randall now used it herself. But where Herndon had relied on memories to illuminate a period with scarce contemporary material, Randall dismissed not only recollections from many sources but a bevy of contemporary documents. She called them the made-up stories of "gossiping tongues." She preferred an explanation by the son of Ninian and Elizabeth Edwards, which he gave sixty-some years after the events in question, which took place when he was an infant. "I wish I had a better — that is, a more direct — source," Randall admitted privately, but she used it anyway.

The first two volumes of J. G. Randall's *Lincoln the President* were published in 1945 to great fanfare. The *Saturday Review* put Randall on its cover, his face superimposed over Lincoln's. The biography was a major work by a revered scholar. But the core ideas of Randall's books — for example, that the Civil War could have been avoided and that abolitionists had exaggerated the risk of slavery's spread — had less long-term influence than two chapters ghostwritten by his wife. Almost overnight, the Ann Rutledge "myth," as it became known, was excised from the record. In a 1952 Lincoln biography, Benjamin Thomas decried that Lincoln's romance with Ann Rutledge was a "legend for which no shred of contemporary evidence has been found." Most scholars, he said, found it "improbable and reject utterly its supposed enduring influence on Lincoln." That same year, Ralph McGill wrote an *Atlanta Constitution* column that dealt — rather judiciously — with Ann Rutledge and promptly received a letter from James Harvey Young, a professor of history at Emory University and a former student of Randall's. "Romantic mythology surrounding the lives of our great men, I suppose, can never be completely dispelled by the work of scholars," Young began. Noting "Herndon's hatred for Mrs. Lincoln," he explained, "Out of this animosity and his strange views of what history needed to do for Lincoln's early career, Herndon created the myth of the Ann Rutledge romance and, by the use of leading questions, elicited from

New Salem old-timers what has passed for evidence, giving the tale a seeming validity. If, because of Herndon, mythology has overstressed the role of Ann, so too, also because of Herndon, mythology has been unduly harsh with Mary."

This letter sums up fairly well what happened over the next four decades, as scholars not only accepted that Ann Rutledge was a "myth" but used the fact as an index of professional rigor. In their haste to fall into line, none disputed or even checked the work attributed to J. G. Randall. The "greatest Lincoln scholar of all time" had passed his edict, and it would be adhered to strictly. What happened next is best explained in the words of Randall himself. Cited in the Introduction of this book, the passage bears repeating here: "What happens over and over is that a certain idea gets started in association with an event or figure. It is repeated by speakers and editors. It soon becomes a part of that superficial aggregation of concepts that goes under the heading 'what everybody knows.' It may take decades before a stock picture is even questioned as to its validity."

Beginning in the late 1940s and early 1950s, "everybody knew" that the Rutledge story was a myth. Scholarly works — and, soon, the popular works that took their cues from them — mentioned Ann Rutledge only to take a jab at Herndon. A 1972 edition of Mary Lincoln's letters, for example, noted that "Herndon's cruelest offense against Mrs. Lincoln was his invention of the Ann Rutledge romance." It became conventional wisdom that his interviews were not trustworthy. In a book on Lincoln's legislative career, the future U.S. senator Paul Simon declaimed, "Herndon did not hesitate to change interviews to make them fit his preconceived theories." The most radical charge had become accepted as fact.

It is a sad fact that the momentum of a necessary correction often sweeps away valuable substance along with errors. The cliché "throwing the baby out with the bath water" applies. The myth of how Ann Rutledge's death shaped Lincoln's whole life, and the fictional dross, such as her specter hovering over his shoulder at Gettysburg, ought well to have been shucked, and the Randalls and their colleagues did it. But they threw out the baby. Beginning in the late 1940s, for about the next forty years, no discussion took place of Lincoln's breakdown in his mid-twenties. The whole thing was assigned the status of myth. With that leg kicked from under the table, the evidence of how he began to manifest his melancholy in the late 1830s slid off and crashed to the floor.

And in what would prove the final blow to the subject of Lincoln's melancholy, the second breakdown was squeezed to a pittance. Ruth Painter Randall, in *Mary Todd Lincoln: Biography of a Marriage* and other books and articles, made Herndon's invention of the failed wedding the symbol of the poor widow maligned by the vicious lawyer. Now scholars took note that the wedding story had been concocted, passing over the other material from that winter with a yawn. Yes, Lincoln had been depressed, but only because he and Mary Todd had split up. It was a discrete episode with a simple cause and a happy ending. As Ruth Painter Randall had explained, "All the evidence is that Lincoln's condition was that of severe mental distress with accompanying effects upon his health, that the interrupted courtship was the cause of it, and that he was making a conscious and deliberate effort towards restoration of a normal life."

A word in that sentence opens the door to a crucial and heretofore unexplored aspect of the Randalls' campaign against William Herndon. The campaign, as we have seen, was waged on grounds of proper historical method. To be sure, this played a significant role in the minds of the husband-and-wife team, though not so much as they claimed. There was another factor in their work, however, that can be understood only by seeing the vexing intersection of history and psychology, and the ferocious battle that began in the early twentieth century over whether certain historical figures were "normal" or "ill."

The late nineteenth century saw the birth of experimental psychology and the spread of secular "moral therapies," an increase in asylums and other healing centers, and advances in the study of the brain. Psychology and psychiatry had come into their own. Sigmund Freud developed psychoanalysis, and Emil Kraepelin, Freud's great rival, created a diagnostic system for mental disorders (the forerunner of the *Diagnostic and Statistical Manual*). To Freud and his protégés can be traced modern psychotherapy, to Kraepelin and his followers, biological psychiatry.

As earthshaking as these individual developments were, they were mere tremors compared to the single idea that joined together all psychologists and psychiatrists. For millennia — from Aristotle to Descartes to Kant — scientists and philosophers had agreed that the human psyche was, at its core, a mystery. Aspects of it could be understood, but in the end humans would have to adjust to a reality beyond their ability to know. The new psychologists argued that the mind could be understood, its ailments repaired, and its ordinary functions fine-tuned.

In this new psychology tension arose between the experimental method — which sought universal truths by impartial study of large numbers of people — and individual observation, which admitted of uniqueness and idiosyncrasy. Freud, whose bravado knew few bounds, wanted both to write the laws of human nature and to show how they played out in the lives of unique figures. Thus he turned to history, subjecting Leonardo da Vinci to a postmortem psychoanalysis. In October 1909, Freud wrote to his colleague Carl Jung that "the riddle of Leonardo da Vinci's character has suddenly become transparent to me." He added, "Biography, too, must become ours."

Just as mesmerism, in the early nineteenth century, originated in Vienna and flowered in the United States, so too did Freudian psychoanalysis. After Freud's famous lectures at Clark University in 1909 — coincidentally, the centennial of Lincoln's birth — the new psychology became all the rage. And many new analysts, spending their days with patients on couches, turned at night to psychobiography. Lincoln, of course, was a prime subject. In 1922, Nathaniel Stevenson's *Lincoln: An Account of His Personal Life, Especially of Its Springs of Action as Revealed and Deepened by the Ordeal of War* drew on the typical Freudian motifs, as when Stevenson asserted that the "ghost" of Lincoln's father was always "lurking somewhere, waiting to seize upon him, when his energies were in ebb." It was only a matter of time before psychobiographers assigned diagnostic labels. In 1931, Dr. A. A. Brill, the editor and translator of *The Basic Writings of Sigmund Freud* and the top psychoanalyst in America, told the American Psychiatric Association that Lincoln had a "schizoid manic personality, now and then harassed by schizoid manic moods." In substance, the paper he presented was a recitation of familiar Lincoln stories. But the clinical language he used provoked a storm of protest. A Brooklyn physician accused Brill of "blaspheming the memory of the immortal dead." Thereafter, writers would be forced to take a stand: Was Lincoln "normal" or "ill"?

In the early thirties, when J. G. Randall began his work on Lincoln, he received the galleys of *Lincoln: A Psycho-Biography*, by the well-known New York analyst L. Pierce Clark. In his seminal 1934 lecture, Randall cited Clark's book in his second paragraph as an example of the dross that passed for history. From then on, he made clear his strong dislike of psychobiography. And here we find an explanation for the deep hostility that the Randalls and their colleagues had for Lincoln's law partner. J. G. Randall wrote in his introduction to *Lincoln the President*, "Herndon was a self-made psychoanalyst long before that somewhat modern art became known." In her chapter on the Ann Rutledge evidence Ruth Painter Randall repeatedly linked Herndon in a pejorative way to Freudian psychiatry: his writing style was "soaring psychoanalysis with glowing language"; the Rutledge story "appealed to all the sentimentalizing and psychoanalyzing impulses of Herndon's nature"; he added his "irrepressible contribution of psychoanalysis" to it. "Herndon," she elaborated, "was a rough-hewn man, given to drunkenness and certain mental quirks. He was firmly convinced, as he often asserted, that he could read people's minds and that he knew what was truth by his own power of intuition. The result was that he usually believed what he wanted to believe."

These attacks made a silly caricature of a complex man. It is true that Herndon believed in his intuition, and he believed he learned things about people, Lincoln included, by being in close proximity to them. It is also true that he fell into some excesses of fancy — none more marked than the original Ann Rutledge lecture. But on the whole, his career as a student of Lincoln was marked by a dedication to trustworthy facts. His bold conclusions were balanced with humility. Just weeks before he died, Herndon said that he'd spent his whole life trying to understand Lincoln but that he was "mysterious, quite an incomprehensible man." If anything, the tension in Herndon between the fruits of intuition (not "clairvoyance") and the fruits of research makes for a good case study of the tension that inevitably inflicts biographers. The irony is that, failing to see that tension, and making Herndon into a caricature, the Randalls committed the very violations of which they accused Herndon. Intoxicated with their own powers of intuition, they went well beyond the evidence at hand.

To some extent, it is an inherent flaw of biography that, in order to wrestle a figure onto the page, three dimensions get turned into two. Rough spots are ironed out. Minor conflicts are magnified to suit the needs of a dramatic narrative. There is good reason to speak of "Herndon's Lincoln" or "Sandburg's Lincoln," because the real man can only be approximated in any of these works, and the imagination of the biographer obviously plays a large role. J. G. Randall and Ruth Painter Randall, for all their keen insights, had a glaring blind spot when it came to the sadness and pain in Lincoln's life. Ruth Painter Randall probably put her finger on the origin of the blind spot when she wrote that, in Lincoln's time, "the mental climate was quite different then from what it is now: it was considered quite the thing to do, in writing a friend, to dwell on one's emotions without restraint and even analyze them to what seems at present a ridiculous extent. Few today would let themselves go to the extent that Abraham did in writing his law partner three weeks after the parting from Mary 'I am now the most miserable man living. I must die or be better. I awfully forebode I shall not. If what I felt were distributed to the entire human family, there would not be one happy face on the earth.'" Historians tell stories from material they take seriously, and perhaps — influenced by the repressed style of the time — she did not take melancholy seriously.

The irony is that, by casting aside actual evidence as "ridiculous" or "small-town gossip" or "invented," the Randalls ensured that Lincoln's inner life would be little studied by serious historians. The 1940s and 1950s were a golden era for the introduction of basic evidence on Lincoln into the public domain. In 1947, the Library of Congress opened access to the papers that had been held by Robert Todd Lincoln. Herndon's papers also became available for inspection. Diaries from the Lincoln period poured into the public realm. This could have been the time to consolidate the gains, turn aside the faults of the previous century, and build a study on solid sources. Instead, with the two breakdowns virtually eliminated from the canon, there was no foundation on which to build an evidence-driven story.

Thus was the subject left to the psychoanalysts. In the 1957 work *Lincoln's Emotional Life*, Dr. Milton Shutes made no effort to discuss the substance of Lincoln's early depressions, and mentioned Herndon only to dismiss him. His interest was in Lincoln's childhood: "There are many unanswerable questions. For example: whether an overlong weaning caused too great mother dependence; or whether the father took the mother's attention away too soon, leaving an angry baby with rebellious feelings of mother privation and father jealousy." These were important questions only if one assumes — as does Freudian theory — that adult neurosis springs from childhood trauma in general, and Oedipal tensions in particular.

It has always been trouble for psychobiographers that so little is known about Lincoln's early childhood. But for several decades prominent authors made do by wringing blood from stones. Dr. Edward J. Kempf produced, in 1965, a three-volume "analytical biography of a great mind," indiscriminately mixing serious evidence and obviously bogus stories, such as the claim that Lincoln's father once slaughtered Abraham's pet pig, leaving the boy traumatized and, as Kempf explained, "conditioned to resent, more intensely than normal, unnecessary violations of human and animal rights, to hate tyrannical injustice, and to be deeply inclined to see life as a tragic fatalist."

Another type of psychobiography found insight in the close reading of reliable texts. Lincoln's 1838 Lyceum speech, in which he warned of the "towering genius" who could be satisfied only by dictatorship, proved fodder for a famous 1962 essay by Edmund Wilson, which concludes, "It is evident that Lincoln has projected himself into the role against which he is warning." This view of a young Lincoln seized with guilt and ambition influenced George Forgie, who found Lincoln displacing these characteristics onto Stephen Douglas (whom he then "murders" politically to expiate his own guilt), and Dwight Anderson, who found Lincoln to be the "bad son." Anderson had a new take on Lincoln's well-known White House dream in which he saw a dead president lying in state. This president wasn't Lincoln, Anderson declared, but George Washington, who "haunted him [Lincoln] like Banquo's ghost."

The best regarded of the literary psychobiographies, *Lincoln's Quest for Union* by Charles Strozier, distinguished itself by finding evidence of the Oedipus complex in Lincoln, hidden in plain sight. In one of his brief memoirs, Lincoln had described (in the third person) how he once shot a wild turkey when his father was away from the farm, but never after "pulled a trigger on any larger game." In Lincoln's sketch, this passage was followed by a report of the death of Lincoln's mother — which juxtaposition Strozier found highly significant. Lincoln, he argued, felt guilty about shooting the turkey, a "symbolic way of communicating unconscious feelings" of guilt over his mother's death, for which "he felt somehow responsible." Strozier went on: "Lincoln wished his father away because he wanted to possess the mother. He could only realize the wish, however, by appropriating the magical power of the father's gun as he struggled to beat out his father in competition for the mother. At some point, he must have felt victorious in that struggle, but the gun he appropriated proved more deadly than anticipated, for with it he killed the helpless turkey . . . In the confusion of mourning his mother's death, Lincoln thus seemed to construct an unconscious explanation for her loss that 'explained' her death in terms of punishment for his own earlier forbidden sexual wishes. As punishment for his love, she died." Strozier had worked wonders, fitting Lincoln's life into Freud's model for the origin of melancholia, when repressed feelings in the wake of a loved one's death prevent healthy mourning.

Though historians argued fiercely about these works, the methods of psychobiography — the liberal use of Freudian jargon, the casual assignment of formal diagnoses, and the imputation of specific meanings to ambiguous episodes — became widespread in history and journalism. The basic assumption of psychotherapy, that the adult personality is rooted in childhood trauma, became conventional wisdom. Meanwhile, historians viewed the private lives of public figures in new ways. Richard Nixon's presidency, as David Greenberg has shown in *Nixon's Shadow,* was a turning point, as Nixon convinced many reasonable people that the mental life of an elected official was relevant to a study of his leadership. After that, little was out of bounds.

It's not coincidental that a new attitude toward the private lives of public figures coincided with a new era in psychology. With a huge increase in psychiatric diagnoses, the advent of blockbuster drugs, and the mainstreaming of psychotherapy, new interest emerged in the depression of historic figures. References to Lincoln's depression became common. On February 12, 1998, the federal Substance Abuse and Mental Health Services Administration issued a press release saying that from the time he was a teenager, Abraham Lincoln "lived with what today some people think might have been depression and bipolar disorder." This heavily qualified sentence was followed by the claim that "Abraham Lincoln is an inspiration to everyone who is living with depression and/or bipolar disorder." Dozens of newspapers picked up the story. "Depression Hounded Abe," ran the headline in the *Pittsburgh Post-Gazette*. The *Albany Times Union* asked, "Is Honest Abe to be remembered now as Moody Abe?" In June 1999, in the first-ever White House Conference on Mental Health, Donna Shalala, the secretary of health and human services, began by quoting Lincoln, "a man known to have suffered bouts of depression." That fall, a full-page ad in *Behavioral Health Management* — part of a public service campaign sponsored by Eli Lilly, the maker of Prozac — showed a picture of Lincoln standing next to a height chart, drawn over with prison bars. "There are some people who think those with mental illness should be locked up and kept from society," the ad reads. "Obviously, there is a flaw in that thinking."

As the environment became suited for an open treatment of Lincoln's depression, the material with which to do so came back into view. The rebirth of oral history played a large role. The Work Projects Administration's interviews with African Americans in the 1920s and 1930s proved a prize cache of material. In the 1960s, a graduate of the WPA's Federal Writers' Project, Studs Terkel, started to collect his interviews with ordinary people into books. The resurgence of the field was marked by the founding, in 1966, of the Oral History Association, which celebrates "the oldest type of historical inquiry, predating the written word, and one of the most modern, initiated with tape recorders in the 1940s and now using 21st-century digital technologies."

This set the stage for the fourth major period in Lincoln studies. In the 1980s, a number of scholars began, without each other's knowledge, to reconsider oral histories of Lincoln in general, and the evidence of Herndon's informants in particular. One was Douglas Wilson, a professor of English at Knox College in Galesburg, Illinois. A scholar of Thomas Jefferson's literary career, Wilson decided in early 1988 to write an essay comparing Jefferson's reading (which was famously voracious) with Abraham Lincoln's (famously selective). Seeking primary sources on Lincoln's reading, Wilson soon discovered that one of the few people who had investigated the subject firsthand was William Henry Herndon. He learned that Herndon's original "Lincoln Record" — now called the Herndon-Weik Collection at the Library of Congress — was available, albeit in a microfilm version of Herndon's original handwritten scratchings, plus the letters Herndon received from his correspondents. Wilson requested the fifteen reels of microfilm by interlibrary loan and began to read through them on his old plastic microfilm machine.

Like all good scholars of his era, Wilson knew, as he recalls, "that the Ann Rutledge story was a myth, that some people still believed it, but that it wasn't true." Over four months, he read all the original letters and interviews. He remembers saying to himself, "What's wrong with this? I don't see what's wrong with this." When he finished, he went to J. G. Randall's *Lincoln the President,* David Herbert Donald's *Lincoln's Herndon,* and Ruth Painter Randall's *Mary Todd Lincoln.* "Their arguments just weren't convincing — not to someone who had just read the original material," Wilson says. "And I could see at a glance how biased Mrs. Randall was and how selectively she used her evidence against Herndon. The same was true of Donald when he treated the Herndon records." Wilson discussed his work with Rodney Davis, a historian at Knox College and an authority on early-nineteenth-century Illinois. Wilson proposed that they collaborate on a project to annotate and publish the Herndon records. Davis was at first skeptical. "I was trained to think of reminiscence as nuclear waste," he says. "It was the kind of thing that you didn't pay close attention to. But then Doug got into the Ann Rutledge business, and I must say I was overwhelmed with the weight of the testimony."

That same year, 1988, John Y. Simon, a Civil War historian and the editor of the Ulysses S. Grant papers, gave a lecture on the Ann Rutledge story at a Lincoln conference. His idea had been to review the legend that had been properly cast out of the canon. But he had the same experience as Wilson, and his paper — the first one to publicly question the Randalls' treatment of Ann Rutledge — created a sensation. Meanwhile, a historian at Connecticut College named Michael Burlingame had dug deep into not only Herndon's interviews but a vast array of long-neglected primary sources on Lincoln's character, relationships, and psychological experience. Burlingame, too, had been educated with a dim view of Herndon's material. "But when I examined the records for myself, I saw: these aren't the unreliable memories of old codgers drooling on their walkers and making up stories." Rather, Burlingame approached each interview and each memory as a separate historical resource with its own mix of problems and merits. His 1994 book, *The Inner World of Abraham Lincoln,* included much new evidence.

Burlingame has now edited and brought out ten volumes of primary material, including the never before published interviews conducted by Lincoln's White House secretary John G. Nicolay for a biography. (He has more source material ready for publication but has suspended work while he finishes a multivolume, cradle-to-grave biography of Lincoln.) In 1998, Rodney Davis and Douglas Wilson brought out *Herndon's Informants: Interviews, Letters, and Statements on Abraham Lincoln.* This is an edited and carefully annotated volume of Herndon's original "Lincoln Record," which is now understood to be one of the first oral history projects, if not the first. The same year, Wilson's *Honor's Voice: The Transformation of Abraham Lincoln* offered a thorough treatment of Lincoln's life from 1831 to 1842, drawing on the Herndon records and other material.

As it happened, just as *Herndon's Informants* and *Honor's Voice* were being published, I ran across a reference to Lincoln's melancholy in *On Suicide: Great Writers on the Ultimate Question*. The book contained an excerpt from the sociologist Harold Kushner's work on suicide, *Self-Destruction in the Promised Land*. In the excerpt, Kushner considered the cases of two historical figures who were suicidal. Meriwether Lewis almost certainly did kill himself. Lincoln considered self-destruction but, Kushner argued, employed adaptive mechanisms that turned the episode into an instrument of growth.

I was amazed by the story. I wondered why I hadn't heard about it before, and if it meant that fresh work could be done on the subject. I assumed the answer would be no, but I put the question to Lincoln scholars. I wrote first to David Herbert Donald, whose prize-winning *Lincoln* was my introduction to the subject. Donald replied with an encouraging note, the first of many welcoming gestures from the giants on whose shoulders I clambered. Andrew Delbanco, the editor of *The Portable Lincoln*, invited me to a series of lectures, "The Anatomy of American Melancholy" (now published as *The Real American Dream*), which opened my eyes to the literary and intellectual culture of the nineteenth century. John Sellers, the curator of Lincoln material at the Library of Congress, gave me a beginner's reading list and invited me to an annual symposium sponsored by the Lincoln Association of the Mid-Atlantic (now the Abraham Lincoln Institute). There, on March 28, 1998, I heard lectures by Burlingame and Wilson, both of whom addressed new findings of primary material by and about Lincoln; by Thomas Lowry, a retired psychiatrist, who with his wife, Beverly Lowry, had recently uncovered hundreds of previously unknown documents in Lincoln's hand in the National Archives; and by Cullum Davis, editor of the Lincoln Legal Papers, a monumental effort to publish 100,000 primary documents on Lincoln's legal career on CD-ROM.

I see now that I stumbled upon Lincoln's melancholy at the precise moment when my interest could be pursued. The combination of newly discovered material and old material made easily accessible in edited and annotated volumes has been a boon to the field. The past seven years has also seen a massive body of material posted online, including *The Collected Works of Abraham Lincoln* and the Lincoln papers at the Library of Congress, in which much of his incoming correspondence can be found, in addition to originals of many of his major works. With these advantages, conditions are as conducive as ever for building a study on the foundation of primary sources. Works on Lincoln in recent years bear the mark of increased appreciation for the firsthand observations of his life. At the same time, we've seen an increase in narrowly focused studies, some of which pluck out bits and pieces from the Lincoln record to assemble a cartoon portrait of modern fantasies.

While this study proceeds from a modern interest and sensibility, my purpose has been to understand as clearly as possible the way Lincoln lived, suffered, and grew. Whenever possible, in the source notes that follow I have referred to the letters, interviews, and sketches that draw out the words of people who knew Lincoln, who felt his presence in a room, and who saw the flash of his blue-gray eyes.

Notes

Names

AL: Abraham Lincoln
WHH: William Henry Herndon

Books

CWL: Roy P. Basler, ed., *The Collected Works of Abraham Lincoln.* 9 vols.
Day by Day: Earl Schenck Miers, ed., *Lincoln Day by Day: A Chronology, 1809–1865.* 3 vols.
Herndon's Informants: Douglas L. Wilson and Rodney Davis, eds., *Herndon's Informants: Letters, Interviews, and Statements about Abraham Lincoln.*
Herndon's Lincoln: William H. Herndon and Jesse W. Weik, *Herndon's Lincoln: The True Story of a Great Life.* 3 vols.
Hidden Lincoln: Emanuel Hertz, ed., *The Hidden Lincoln: From the Letters and Papers of William H. Herndon.*
Intimate Memories: Rufus Rockwell Wilson, ed., *Intimate Memories of Lincoln.*
Lincoln among His Friends: Rufus Rockwell Wilson, ed., *Lincoln among His Friends: A Sheaf of Intimate Memories.*
Lincoln Observed: Michael Burlingame, ed., *Lincoln Observed: The Civil War Dispatches of Noah Brooks.*
Lincoln Papers: David C. Mearns, ed., *The Lincoln Papers.* 2 vols.
MTL, Life and Letters: Justin G. Turner and Linda Levitt Turner, eds., *Mary Todd Lincoln: Her Life and Letters.*
An Oral History: Michael Burlingame, ed., *An Oral History of Abraham Lincoln: John G. Nicolay's Interviews and Essays.*
Recollected Words: Don E. Fehrenbacher and Virginia Fehrenbacher, eds., *Recollected Words of Abraham Lincoln.*
Reminiscences of Abraham Lincoln: Allen Thorndike Rice, ed., *Reminiscences of Abraham Lincoln by Distinguished Men of His Time.*

Manuscript Collections

Barton Papers: William E. Barton Papers, University of Chicago
Davis Papers: David Davis Papers, Illinois State Historical Library

Hardin Papers: Hardin Family Papers, Chicago Historical Society
Herndon-Weik Ms.: William H. Herndon and Jesse W. Weik Manuscripts, Library of Congress
Holland Papers: Josiah G. Holland Papers, New York Public Library
Randall Papers: James G. and Ruth Painter Randall Papers, Library of Congress
Tarbell Papers: Ida B. Tarbell Papers, Allegheny College

Institutions

ISHL: Illinois State Historical Library (now the Abraham Lincoln Presidential Library)
LSC: Lincoln Studies Center, Knox College

Full bibliographical information is given on the first reference; subsequently, last names and abbreviated titles are used. Full citations for most sources can be found in the Bibliography, excluding newspapers. Primary sources are identified where possible. Where titles or dates are given for published letters or interviews, they follow the form in the particular publication. For example, Lincoln's letters and speeches follow the titles and dates used in the *Collected Works*.

In a work of this sort, based on research from diverse sources and accumulated over many years, facts may have been omitted and errors committed. Amplifications or corrections of textual or source material will be gratefully received, included in future editions, and posted at www.lincolnsmelancholy.net/errata.html. Send e-mails to corrections@shenk.net.

INTRODUCTION

1 *In early May 1860:* Details of the wigwam and convention are drawn from Wayne C. Temple, "Lincoln's Fence Rails," *Journal of the Illinois State Historical Society* 47 (Spring 1954): 20–34; Richard J. Oglesby, statement to J. McCan Davis, *Lincoln among His Friends,* 191–94 (originally published as "Origin of the Lincoln Rail as Related by Governor Oglesby," *Century Magazine,* June 1900, 271–75); Jane Martin Johns, *Personal Recollections of Early Decatur, Abraham Lincoln, Richard J. Oglesby, and the Civil War* (Decatur, Ill.: Decatur Chapter, Daughters of the American Revolution, 1912), 79–82; William E. Baringer, *Lincoln's Rise to Power* (Boston: Little, Brown, 1937), 180–86; and Johnson to WHH, 1865–66, *Herndon's Informants,* 462.
"to tease expectation": Johnson to WHH, 1865–66, *Herndon's Informants,* 462.
Lincoln was crouched: ibid.
"aroused me again": AL to Jesse W. Fell, enclosing autobiography, December 20, 1859, *CWL,* vol. 3, 512.
2 *"the most convincing":* Robert S. Harper, *Lincoln and the Press* (New York: McGraw-Hill, 1951), 46–47.
lifted him up on their shoulders: Johnson to WHH, 1865–66, *Herndon's Informants,* 463.
failed to rate a mention: James M. McPherson, *Battle Cry of Freedom: The Civil War Era* (New York: Oxford University Press, 1988), 219.
"I am not in a position": AL to Norman B. Judd, February 9, 1860, *CWL,* vol. 3, 517.
managing the convention: Oglesby headed up the committee to provide the convention meeting place. Baringer, *Lincoln's Rise to Power,* 181, citing *Chicago Press & Tribune,* April 23, 1860.
Oglesby had decided: Johns, *Personal Recollections of Early Decatur,* 80. John Hanks

claimed that he came up with the idea. John Hanks to *Illinois State Chronicle*, reprinted in the *Cincinnati Rail Splitter*, August 15, 1860.

3 *"Lincoln's name"*: *Lincoln among His Friends*, 186.
"I then thought him": Johnson to WHH, 1865–66, *Herndon's Informants*, 463.

4 *"I'm not very well"*: Milton H. Shutes, *Lincoln and the Doctors: A Medical Narrative of the Life of Abraham Lincoln* (New York: Pioneer Press, 1933), 74.
"No element": Henry C. Whitney, *Life on the Circuit with Lincoln* (Boston: Estes and Lauriat, 1892), 139.
"His melancholy dripped": *Herndon's Lincoln*, vol. 3, 588.
"There can be no new": Merrill D. Peterson, *Lincoln in American Memory* (New York: Oxford University Press, 1994), 97, citing Noah Brooks, "The Final Estimate of Lincoln," *New York Times*, February 12, 1898.
Lincoln once noted: AL, "Second Lecture on Discoveries and Inventions," February 11, 1859, *CWL*, vol. 3, 362.

5 *"What happens over and over"*: J. G. Randall, *Lincoln the President*, 2 vols. (New York: Dodd, Mead, 1945), vol. 1, viii.

6 *"like nuclear waste"*: Rodney Davis, interview with author, August 21, 2003.
"Evidence is then unearthed": Randall, *Lincoln the President*, vol. 1, viii.

7 *"Ridiculous"*: Ruth Painter Randall, draft ms., Randall Papers.

8 *Affecting more than 100 million people*: These statistics are drawn from *Mental Health: A Report of the Surgeon General* (Rockville, Md.: U.S. Department of Health and Human Services, 1999); Michael Hogan, keynote address, *Nineteenth Annual Rosalynn Carter Symposium on Mental Health Policy*, 4; and Gregg Easterbrook, *The Progress Paradox: How Life Gets Better While People Feel Worse* (New York: Random House, 2003), 163–66.
"peculiar misfortune": AL to Joshua F. Speed, February 25, 1842, *CWL*, vol. 1, 280.

1. THE COMMUNITY SAID HE WAS CRAZY

11 *the principal factors*: S. Nassir Ghaemi, *The Concepts of Psychiatry: A Pluralistic Approach to the Mind and Mental Illness* (Baltimore: Johns Hopkins University Press, 2003), 216.
a person who has: *Diagnostic and Statistical Manual of Mental Disorders: DSM-IV* (Washington, D.C.: American Psychiatric Association, 1994), 342.
His parents: See the portraits of Thomas Lincoln and Nancy Hanks Lincoln in Mark Neely, *The Abraham Lincoln Encyclopedia* (New York: McGraw-Hill, 1982), 184, 187.

12 *"was kindness, mildness, tenderness"*: John Hanks, interview with WHH, 1865–66, *Herndon's Informants*, 454.
"intellectual, sensitive and somewhat sad": WHH to Jesse W. Weik, January 19, 1886, *Hidden Lincoln*, 139.
"to border on the serious — reflective": Thomas L. D. Johnston, interview with WHH, 1866, *Herndon's Informants*, 533.
"often got the 'blues'": Robert H. Browne, *Abraham Lincoln and the Men of His Time: His Cause, His Character, and True Place in History, and the Men, Statesmen, Heroes, Patriots, Who Formed the Illustrious League about Him*, 2 vols. (Chicago: Blakely-Oswald, 1907), vol. 1, 82–83.
"a deranged mind": William H. Townsend, *Lincoln and the Bluegrass: Slavery and Civil War in Kentucky* (Lexington: University of Kentucky Press, 1955), 19, citing *Lincoln v. O'Nan et al.*, December 10, 1810, file 215, Fayette Circuit Court.

mood swings: Berenice V. Lovely to William E. Barton, June 26, 1921, Barton Papers.
strong physical resemblance: William E. Barton, "Why Lincoln Was Sad," *Dearborn Independent,* August 28, 1926, 22.
"Lincoln characteristics": A. R. Simmons to William E. Barton, March 7, 1923, Barton Papers.
Mary Jane Lincoln: Admissions Book, Illinois Hospital for the Insane, Record #2715, May 23, 1867, Illinois State Archives. The complete record reads, "Mary J. Lincoln / Hancock County Aged 39 — Single — native of Kentucky / Insane thirteen years — Cause unknown / Not thought to be hereditary — Not suicidal / Her father was cousin to Abraham Lincoln and she has features much like his / Parmelia Lincoln (sis) Carthage." In the margin it reads, "August 30/88 . . . Sent to LaHarpe / Telegraph to Hezekiah Lincoln — La Harpe, Hancock Co. Ills."
"the disease is with her hereditary": The jury's findings are given on a printed form, with blank spaces for the particulars of the case, which have been written in by hand (shown here in italics): "We, the undersigned, Jurors in the case of *Mary Jane Lincoln* alleged to be insane, having heard the evidence in the case, are satisfied that said *Mary Jane Lincoln* is insane, and is a fit person to be sent to the Illinois State Hospital for the Insane; that *she* is a resident of the State of Illinois and County of *Hancock;* that *her* disease is of *thirteen years* duration; that the cause is supposed to be — *no cause made known to the Jury;* that the disease is with *her* hereditary; that *she* is NOT subject to Epilepsy, and that *she* is free from vermin, or any infectious disease, and that *she* is *not* a pauper, and that these proceedings are had in strict accordance with the Statutes of the State of Illinois relating to the Insane." Hancock County Court, "Verdict of Jury in the Matter of Mary Jane Lincoln Alleged to Be Insane," May 17, 1867, Illinois State Archives.
"suffered from all the nervous disorders known": Berenice V. Lovely to W. A. Evans, April 21, 1921, Barton Papers.

13 *"the Lincoln horrors":* Berenice V. Lovely to William E. Barton, May 14, 1922, Barton Papers. "Family historian" is my term for Lovely, not an official designation.
"The genes confer only susceptibility": Ghaemi, *The Concepts of Psychiatry,* 217.
climate and diet: Jennifer Radden, *The Nature of Melancholy: From Aristotle to Kristeva* (New York: Oxford University Press, 2000), 65.
harsh life events: David B. Cohen, *Out of the Blue: Depression and Human Nature* (New York: W. W. Norton, 1994), 36.
Lincoln's early life: The best sources on Lincoln's childhood are his own autobiographical sketches. See AL to Jesse W. Fell, enclosing autobiography, December 20, 1859, *CWL,* vol. 3, 511–12, and AL, "Autobiography Written for John L. Scripps," c. June 1860, *CWL,* vol. 4, 60–68.
Eventually, the disease: Neely, *The Abraham Lincoln Encyclopedia,* 184.
"No announcement strikes the members": Louis A. Warren, *Lincoln's Youth: Indiana Years, Seven to Twenty-one, 1816–1830* (New York: Appleton, 1959), 52.
"When the individual": James Maxwell, Jr., *A Memoir of the Diseases Called by the People the Trembles and the Sick Stomach or the Milk Sickness As They Appear in the Virginia Military District in the State of Ohio* (Louisville, 1841), 16.

14 *For two to six months:* Michael Burlingame, *The Inner World of Abraham Lincoln* (Urbana: University of Illinois Press, 1994), 95.
dirty and poorly clothed: A. H. Chapman to WHH, September 8, 1865, *Herndon's Informants,* 99.
"sad, if not pitiful": While on his way to see his stepmother in 1861, Lincoln "became more or less reminiscent," recalled Augustus H. Chapman, who accompanied him, "adverting frequently to family affairs. He spoke in the most affectionate way of his

stepmother, characterizing her as the best friend he ever had. He alluded to the sad, if not pitiful condition of his father's family at the time of the marriage to his stepmother and described the wholesome change in the children due to her encouragement and advice." Jesse W. Weik, *The Real Lincoln: A Portrait* (Cambridge: Riverside Press, 1922), 293.

14 *Sarah Lincoln had a sharp mind:* John Hanks to Jesse W. Weik, June 12, 1887, *Herndon's Informants,* 615. For a biography of Sarah Lincoln, see Neely, *The Abraham Lincoln Encyclopedia,* 130.

gave birth to a stillborn child: A. H. Chapman to WHH, September 8, 1865, *Herndon's Informants,* 100.

"We went out and told Abe": Warren, *Lincoln's Youth,* 82.

his father helped him along: Allen C. Guelzo, *Abraham Lincoln: Redeemer President* (Grand Rapids, Mich.: Erdmans, 1999), 34.

"Abe read all the books": Sarah Bush Lincoln, interview with WHH, September 8, 1865, *Herndon's Informants,* 107.

For generations, Lincoln men: The definitive genealogical source on Lincoln's ancestors is Waldo Lincoln, *History of the Lincoln Family: An Account of the Descendants of Samuel Lincoln of Hingham, Massachusetts, 1637–1920* (Worcester, Mass.: Commonwealth Press, 1923).

15 *"Lincoln was lazy":* Dennis Hanks, interview with WHH, September 8, 1865, *Herndon's Informants,* 104.

Lower levels of support: See, for example, Benjamin Shaw et al., "Emotional Support from Parents Early in Life, Aging, and Health," *Psychology and Aging* 19, no. 1 (2004): 4–12.

one out of four infants died: Facts on mortality in Lincoln's time are drawn from Kenneth J. Winkle, *The Young Eagle: The Rise of Abraham Lincoln* (Dallas: Taylor Trade Publications, 2001), 14–15, and "Public Health and Technology During the 19th Century," Institute for Learning Technologies, Columbia University, www.ilt.columbia .edu/projects/bluetelephone/html/health.html, March 31, 2005.

He spent a lot of time alone: Sarah Bush Lincoln, interview with WHH, September 8, 1865, *Herndon's Informants,* 108.

"Lincoln would Chide us": Nathaniel Grigsby, interview with WHH, September 12, 1865, *Herndon's Informants,* 114.

"contending that an ants life": Matilda Johnston Moore, interview with WHH, September 8, 1865, *Herndon's Informants,* 109.

mounted a stump: ibid., 110.

16 *would flock around him:* Nathaniel Grigsby, interview with WHH, September 12, 1865, *Herndon's Informants,* 114.

no money or connections: Lincoln famously described himself at this time as a "strange, friendless, uneducated, penniless boy." AL to Martin S. Morris, March 26, 1843, *CWL,* vol. 1, 320.

a wrestling match: For a detailed account of this episode, see Douglas L. Wilson, *Honor's Voice: The Transformation of Abraham Lincoln* (New York: Knopf, 1998), 19–43.

when he recited the poetry: John McNamar to WHH, November 25, 1866, *Herndon's Informants,* 420.

Lincoln looked like a yokel: James Short to WHH, July 7, 1865, *Herndon's Informants,* 72.

"He became popular": Jason Duncan to WHH, late 1866–early 1867, *Herndon's Informants,* 539.

"mainly due to his personal popularity": John T. Stuart, interview with John G. Nicolay, June 23, 1875, *An Oral History,* 10–11.

"a success which gave me more pleasure": AL to Jesse W. Fell, enclosing autobiography, December 20, 1859, *CWL,* vol. 3, 512.

"I never saw Mr Lincoln": George M. Harrison to WHH, late summer 1866?, *Herndon's Informants,* 330.

"Certainly, he was the best natured": Elizabeth Abell to WHH, February 15, 1867, *Herndon's Informants,* 556–57.

17   *"Boys, if that is all":* J. Rowan Herndon to WHH, May 28, 1865, in *Herndon's Informants,* 8.

Lincoln won the election easily: Wilson, *Honor's Voice,* 151.

"the secrets of that science": Ted Widmer, *Martin Van Buren* (New York: Times Books, 2005), 32–33.

all but five percent of the men: Winkle, *The Young Eagle,* 131; table, 122.

"studied with nobody": AL, "Autobiography Written for John L. Scripps," c. June 1860, *CWL,* vol. 3, 65.

"all his folks": L. M. Greene, interview with James Quay Howard, May 1860, *Lincoln Papers,* vol. 1, 156.

"Mr. Lincoln believed": O. H. Browning, interview with John G. Nicolay, June 17, 1875, *An Oral History,* 6–7.

"Every man is said to have": AL, "Communication to the People of Sangamo County," March 9, 1832, *CWL,* vol. 1, 8–9.

18   *Seeing him despondent:* Jason Duncan to WHH, late 1866–early 1867, *Herndon's Informants,* 540.

"procured bread, and kept soul and body together": AL, "Autobiography Written for John L. Scripps," c. June 1860, *CWL,* vol. 3, 65.

"let the whole thing go": James Short to WHH, July 7, 1865, *Herndon's Informants,* 74.

"somewhat injured his health": Mentor Graham, interview with WHH, May 29, 1865, *Herndon's Informants,* 11.

"read hard — day and night": Isaac Cogdal, interview with WHH, 1865–66, *Herndon's Informants,* 441.

"He became emaciated": Henry McHenry, interview with WHH, May 29, 1865, *Herndon's Informants,* 14.

19   *Lincoln visited her often:* See, for example, John Jones, statement for WHH, October 22, 1866, in *Herndon's Informants,* 387.

the weather turned cold: William Petersen, *Lincoln-Douglas: The Weather As Destiny* (Springfield, Ill.: Charles C. Thomas, 1943), 62–64.

he couldn't bear the idea: Elizabeth Abell to WHH, February 15, 1867, *Herndon's Informants,* 557.

"As to the condition": Henry McHenry to WHH, January 8, 1866, *Herndon's Informants,* 155.

"told Me that he felt": Mentor Graham, interview with WHH, April 2, 1866, *Herndon's Informants,* 242.

"Mr Lincolns friends": William G. Greene, interview with WHH, May 30, 1865, *Herndon's Informants,* 21.

"Lincoln was locked up": Hardin Bale, interview with WHH, May 29, 1865, *Herndon's Informants,* 13.

"That was the time": Elizabeth Abell to WHH, February 15, 1867, *Herndon's Informants,* 557.

19 *The myths and countermyths:* A recent treatment of the Ann Rutledge affair is John
   Evangelist Walsh, *The Shadows Rise: Abraham Lincoln and the Ann Rutledge Legend*
   (Urbana: University of Illinois Press, 1993).

20 *"The effect upon Mr Lincoln's mind":* Robert B. Rutledge to WHH, c. November 1,
   1866, *Herndon's Informants,* 383.
   "I did not know": James Short to WHH, July 7, 1865, *Herndon's Informants,* 73.
   "It's not the large things": Cohen, *Out of the Blue,* 76, citing Charles Bukowski, "The
   Shoelace."
   "Lincoln bore up": John Hill to WHH, June 6, 1865, *Herndon's Informants,* 23.

21 *"quite melancholy for months":* George U. Miles to WHH, March 23, 1866, *Herndon's
   Informants,* 236.
   a major depressive episode: DSM, 320–27.
   "What helps make the case": Kay Redfield Jamison, interview with author, October 6,
   1998.
   typical age for a first episode: S. Nassir Ghaemi, interview with author, March 11, 2004.

22 *"Most of the Marfanologists":* Victor A. McKusick, interview with author, October 18,
   2000. The Marfan story came to prominence with an article by Harold Schwartz,
   "Abraham Lincoln and the Marfan Syndrome," *Journal of the American Medical Association* 187, no. 7 (February 15, 1964): 473–79. For the contrary view, see John K.
   Lattimer, "Lincoln Did Not Have the Marfan Syndrome," *New York State Journal of
   Medicine* 81 (November 1981): 1805–13. The leading Lincoln scholar Gabor Boritt,
   with Adam Boritt, once weighed in with a paper titled "The President Who Was
   to Die in 1866," but the question remains open in many minds. McKusick, with
   others, has long wanted to conduct a DNA test, which would almost certainly
   answer the question. But he hasn't been granted permission to work with what he
   considers the "gold standard" samples of Lincoln's DNA, which are controlled by
   the National Museum of Health and Medicine, an agency of the Department of
   Defense. For an account of the DNA debate, see Philip R. Reilly, *Abraham Lincoln's
   DNA and Other Adventures in Genetics* (Cold Spring Harbor, N.Y.: Cold Spring
   Harbor Laboratory Press, 2002), 3–13. More interesting than the Marfan question,
   Reilly argues, is whether a DNA test might establish Lincoln's vulnerability to de-
   pression.
   At least one study: Karen Wolk, e-mail to author, December 17, 2004. Wolk referred
   me to K. F. Peters et al., "Living with Marfan Syndrome II: Medication Adherence
   and Physical Activity Modification," *Clinical Genetics* 60 (2001): 283–92, and K. F.
   Peters et al., "Living with Marfan Syndrome III: Quality of Life and Productive
   Planning," *Clinical Genetics* 62 (2002): 110–20.
   what psychiatrists call hypomania: "A Hypomanic Episode is defined as a distinct period during which there is an abnormally and persistently elevated, expansive, or irritable mood that lasts at least 4 days . . . This period of abnormal mood must be accompanied by at least three additional symptoms from a list that includes inflated
   self-esteem or grandiosity (nondelusional), decreased need for sleep, pressure of
   speech, flight of ideas, distractability, increased involvement in goal-directed activities or psychomotor agitation, and excessive involvement in pleasurable activities
   that have a high potential for painful consequences. If the mood is irritable rather
   than elevated or expansive, at least four of the above symptoms must be present."
   DSM, 335.
   alternate between depressed: ibid., 337.
   "he appeared to enjoy life rapturously": Robert L. Wilson to WHH, February 10, 1866,
   Herndon's Informants, 205. Sadly, Wilson doesn't date his conversation with Lincoln,

but he indicates that Lincoln's practice of forbearing to carry a knife was of no small duration. Lincoln kept up the practice, Wilson said, "as long as I was intimately acquainted with him" and "previous to his commencement of the practice of the law." Lincoln didn't begin to practice law until March 1837, eighteen months after Ann Rutledge died.

23 *more than half will have a second:* DSM, 341.
major depressive disorder: ibid., 339.
two episodes of major depression: ibid., 342.
The phrase "clinical depression": Clinical depression is a catch phrase meaning a depression significant enough to merit diagnosis or treatment by a clinician. The term does not appear in the *DSM-IV* description of depressive disorders.

24 *"In virtually any other":* William Styron, *Darkness Visible: A Memoir of Madness* (New York: Random House, 1990), 44.
Florence Nightingale: "Ailment of Nurse Nightingale Is Diagnosed," Associated Press, May 3, 2003.
"epidemic hysteria, with conversion symptoms": David M. Harley, "Explaining Salem: Calvinist Psychology and the Diagnosis of Possession," *American Historical Review* 110, no. 2 (April 1996): 329.
"life story" perspective: Ghaemi, *The Concepts of Psychiatry*, 14.
"To restore the human subject": Oliver Sacks, *The Man Who Mistook His Wife for a Hat* (New York: Vintage, 1996), xviii–xix.

25 *"alterations in thinking, mood":* The full definitions: "Mental health — the successful performance of mental function, resulting in productive activities, fulfilling relationships with other people, and the ability to adapt to change and to cope with adversity; from early childhood until late life, mental health is the springboard of thinking and communication skills, learning, emotional growth, resilience, and self-esteem. Mental illness — the term that refers collectively to all mental disorders. Mental disorders are health conditions that are characterized by alterations in thinking, mood, or behavior (or some combination thereof) associated with distress and/ or impaired functioning." *Mental Health: A Report of the Surgeon General — Executive Summary* (Rockville, Md.: U.S. Department of Health and Human Services, 1999), vii.

2. A FEARFUL GIFT

26 *"melancholy resentment":* Stanley Crouch, "Black Like Huck: Revisiting Twain in the Age of Oprah," *New York Times Magazine*, June 6, 1999.
"melancholy suspicion": Andrew Delbanco, *The Real American Dream: A Meditation on Hope* (Cambridge: Harvard University Press, 1999), 23.
"the agony and sweat": William Faulkner, acceptance speech, Nobel Prize in literature, Stockholm, Sweden, December 10, 1950, http://nobelprize.org/literature/ laureates/1949/faulkner-speech.html, March 27, 2005.
"Why is it that all men": Radden, *The Nature of Melancholy*, 57, citing Aristotle (or a follower of Aristotle), "Problems Connected with Thought, Intelligence, and Wisdom," in *Problems* (c. second century B.C.E.)

27 *The sorrowful, existentially anxious:* Radden, *The Nature of Melancholy*, 48.
The burden: Jennifer Radden, "Melancholy and Melancholia," in David Michael Levin, ed., *Pathologies of the Modern Self: Postmodern Studies on Narcissism, Schizophrenia, and Depression* (New York: New York University Press, 1972), 231–50.

27 *Springfield might have seemed:* For a portrait of Springfield, see Paul Angle, *"Here I Have Lived": A History of Lincoln's Springfield, 1821–1865* (Chicago: Abraham Lincoln Book Shop, 1971; orig. 1935). The goods mentioned are drawn from advertisements in the *Sangamo Journal* in the early 1840s.

28 *"every thing that the country needed":* Joshua F. Speed, *Reminiscences of Abraham Lincoln and Notes of a Visit to California* (Louisville: John P. Morton, 1884), 21.

He had green eyes so light: "Gray" was the common description. AL to Jesse W. Fell, enclosing autobiography, December 20, 1859, *CWL*, vol. 3, 511.

Speed was twenty-two years old: Remarkably, no thorough biography exists on Joshua Speed, a gaping hole in the literature on Lincoln and his time. For now, the best works are Robert L. Kincaid, *Joshua Fry Speed: Lincoln's Most Intimate Friend* (Harrogate, Tenn.: Lincoln Memorial University, 1943), and Gary Lee Williams, "James and Joshua Speed: Lincoln's Kentucky Friends," Ph.D. thesis, Duke University, 1971.

"if my experiment here as a lawyer": Details about Speed's store, and Lincoln's exchange with Speed there, come from two accounts: Joshua F. Speed, statement for WHH, by 1882, *Herndon's Informants*, 588–91, and Speed, *Reminiscences*, 21–22.

"He was a sad looking man": WHH statement, Herndon-Weik Ms.

"constitutional melancholy": O. H. Browning, interview with John G. Nicolay, June 17, 1875, *An Oral History*, 6–7.

"a settled form of melancholy": Ida M. Tarbell, *Abraham Lincoln and His Ancestors* (Lincoln: University of Nebraska Press, 1977; orig. 1924), 226–27.

29 *"I could not have slept tonight":* Joshua F. Speed, statement for WHH, by 1882, *Herndon's Informants*, 590.

There were other stories: See, for example, Jesse K. Dubois, interview with WHH, December 1, 1888, *Herndon's Informants*, 718.

"In many things he was sensitive": Mary Owens Vineyard to WHH, July 22, 1866, *Herndon's Informants*, 262.

"Men at once, at first blush": *Herndon's Lincoln*, vol. 3, 473–74.

30 *"The contest on this Bill":* Robert L. Wilson to WHH, February 10, 1866, *Herndon's Informants*, 204.

"He told me that he was whipped": Jesse K. Dubois, interview with John G. Nicolay, July 4, 1875, *An Oral History*, 30–31.

"vied with each other": WHH to C. O. Poole, January 5, 1886, *Hidden Lincoln*, 123.

"Well, I will tell you": William Butler, interview with John G. Nicolay, June 1875, *An Oral History*, 22–23. For a discussion of Butler's reliability, see Wilson, *Honor's Voice*, 171, 346–7n.1.

Lincoln owned and used: Stewart Winger, *Lincoln, Religion, and Romantic Cultural Politics* (DeKalb: Northern Illinois University Press, 2003), 53.

"Each has its advantages": Francis Lieber, ed., *Encyclopaedia Americana* (Philadelphia: Carey, Lea & Carey, 1829–1847), vol. 12, 174.

31 *"A fitful stain of melancholy":* Edgar Allan Poe, "The Assignation," in Philip Van Doren Stern, ed., *The Portable Edgar Allan Poe* (New York: Penguin Books, 1973), 205.

Lord Byron was all the rage: For an excellent treatment of Lincoln's interest in Byron, see Wilson, *Honor's Voice*, 190–93.

"Sorrow is Knowledge": Frank D. McConnell, ed., *Byron's Poetry* (New York: W. W. Norton, 1978), 125.

a favorite of Lincoln's: Wilson, *Honor's Voice*, 191. For the text of this poem, see ibid., citing Ernest Hartley Coleridge, ed., *The Poetical Works of Lord Byron* (New York: Scribner, 1905), 146.

"age of Introversion": Ralph Waldo Emerson, "The American Scholar," August 31,

1837, in Brooks Atkinson, ed., *The Complete Essays and Other Writings of Ralph Waldo Emerson* (New York: Modern Library, 1950), 60.

twice as many women as men: "Nearly twice as many women (12.0 percent) as men (6.6 percent) are affected by a depressive disorder each year." National Institutes of Mental Health, "The Numbers Count: Mental Disorders in America, 2001," www .nimh.nih.gov/publicat/numbers.cfm#5, August 29, 2004, citing D. A. Regier et al., "The De Facto Mental and Addictive Disorders Service System," *Archives of General Psychiatry* 50, no. 2 (1993): 85–94.

"Men are not supposed": Terrence Real, *I Don't Want to Talk about It: Overcoming the Secret Legacy of Male Depression* (New York: Fireside, 1998), 23.

32 *While only half as many:* Kay Redfield Jamison, *Night Falls Fast: Understanding Suicide* (New York: Knopf, 1999), 46. Men, Jamison writes, "may have a more aggressive and volatile component to their depression" and "are also less likely to seek medical help for psychiatric problems" (46–47).

"halve themselves": Real, *I Don't Want to Talk about It,* 23.

"human, redeeming, ambiguous": Radden, *The Nature of Melancholy,* 48.

physical strength and athletic prowess: For example, Lincoln was an impressive wrestler and, according to James Short, could lift "1000 pounds of shot by main strength." James Short to WHH, July 7, 1865, *Herndon's Informants,* 74.

vowed to whip anyone: Herndon's Lincoln, vol. 1, 195–96.

"That gives me the hypo": AL to Mary S. Owens, May 7, 1837, *CWL,* vol. 1, 79.

"Whenever I find myself": Herman Melville, *Moby-Dick* (New York: Penguin Books, 1980; orig. 1851), 21.

33 *"Take my word for it":* ibid., 82–83.

"I have suffered so much": Joshua F. Speed to Mary L. Speed, February 2, 1841, Speed Family Papers, University of Louisville Archives.

Lincoln later used: For example, see *Recollected Words,* 9.

"to break or subdue": Webster's Dictionary, 1895.

"Lovely Boy" and "Dearly Beloved": E. Anthony Rotundo, *American Manhood* (New York: Basic Books, 1993), 56–57.

"You know my desire to befriend": AL to Joshua F. Speed, February 13, 1842, *CWL,* vol. 1, 269.

34 *no par in his life:* For example, John Hay and John G. Nicolay, Lincoln's White House secretaries, wrote that "Speed was the only — as he was certainly the last — intimate friend that Lincoln ever had." John Hay and John G. Nicolay, *Abraham Lincoln: A History,* 10 vols. (New York: Century, 1890), vol. 1, 193.

"No two men": Joshua F. Speed to Josiah G. Holland, June 22, 1865, Holland Papers.

"the peculiar misfortune": AL to Joshua F. Speed, February 25, 1842, *CWL,* vol. 1, 280.

"like the rich fruit": Joshua F. Speed to Mary L. Speed, October 31, 1841, Filson Historical Society.

"excessive pleasure": AL to Joshua F. Speed, February 13, 1842, *CWL,* vol. 1, 269.

"outing": "Abe Lincoln's Home Town Outraged at His 'Outing,'" *Independent,* June 27, 1999. Other headlines included: "Ready to Rewrite Lincoln's Love Life?" *Ottawa Citizen,* July 5, 1999; "All They Did Was Sleep, Say Lincoln's Straight Shooters," *Courier Mail* (Queensland, Australia), May 17, 1999; "Maybe He Wasn't Honest about Everything," *Oregonian,* May 12, 1999.

Kramer has since quietly: Larry Kramer, interview with author, June 11, 2003.

Lincoln measured a "5": C. A. Tripp, *The Intimate World of Abraham Lincoln* (New York: Free Press, 2005), 20.

"I to your assistance": Macbeth, act 3, scene 1.

35 *"anxious":* "anxious" and "anxiously" appear 193 times in the *Collected Works.*

35 *deprecating what would follow:* For example: "Having resolved to write to some of your mother's family and not having the express permission of anyone of them to do so, I have had some little difficulty in determining on which to inflict the task of reading what I now feel must be a most dull and silly letter," AL to Mary Speed, September 27, 1841, *CWL,* vol. 1, 259.

straw, horsehair, and feather: Elizabeth Cater, "The History of the Real Mattress and Base Co," August–October 1999, www.realbeds.com.au/b_h.html, March 20, 2005.

Not only families: As the historian Christine Stansell writes, "Travelers piled in with each other at inns; siblings routinely shared beds; women friends often slept with each other as readily on an overnight visit as they took their tea together in the kitchen — and sometimes displaced husbands to do so. Civil War soldiers 'spooned' for comfort and warmth (and Civil War reenactors now do the same for accuracy's sake)." Christine Stansell, "What Stuff!" *New Republic,* January 17, 2005.

Jonathan Ned Katz: Two articles by Katz serve to introduce male-male sexuality in the nineteenth century: "Coming to Terms: Conceptualizing Men's Erotic and Affectional Relations with Men in the United States, 1820–1892," and "'Homosexual' and 'Heterosexual': Questioning the Terms," both in Martin Duberman, ed., *A Queer World: The Center for Lesbian and Gay Studies Reader,* 216–35, 177–80. For the quotation beginning "I do start" and for the origin of "homosexual" and "heterosexual," see "Coming to Terms," 216–17. The point that these words are relatively new is not pedantic. Rather, it raises the broader issue of what Katz calls our "epistemological hubris and ontological chutzpah," which "prevent us from understanding the varieties of sexuality and gender within their own social structure and time . . . Though presented to us as words marking an external fact of nature, the terms 'homosexual' and 'heterosexual' constitute a normative sexual ethic, a sexual-political ideology, and one historically specific way of categorizing the relationships of the sexes." They "also arise out of and help maintain a historically specific way of socially ordering gender and eroticism. 'Heterosexual' and 'homosexual' refer to groups, identities, and even behaviors and experiences that are time-limited, specifically modern phenomena, contingent on a peculiar institutional structuring of masculinity, femininity, and lust." Katz, "'Homosexual' and 'Heterosexual,'" 177–78.

36 *'there wasn't a line in the sand':* E. Anthony Rotundo, interview with author, October 21, 2001. See also Rotundo, *American Manhood,* 75–91. In his chapter "Youth and Male Intimacy," Rotundo writes of young men in the early to mid-nineteenth century: "Friendship was based on intimacy, on a sharing of thought and emotion. The friend was now a partner in sentiment as well as action. While boys had little interest in 'the social feelings of the heart,' young men like Daniel Webster [and like Lincoln and Speed] cultivated those same emotions. The gentle (even 'feminine') emotions of the heart replaced the rough aggressions of boyhood. Young men might even express their fondness for each other in affectionate physical gestures. All together, these friendships inverted familiar patterns of male behavior — they were intimate attachments that verged on romance" (75). See also Roy Morris, Jr., *The Better Angel: Walt Whitman in the Civil War* (New York: Oxford University Press, 2000), 133, 150.

Speed also slept: Speed told Herndon that in 1839 and 1840 he was "keeping a pretty woman in this City." Joshua F. Speed, interview with WHH, January 5, 1889, *Herndon's Informants,* 719. According to Abner Y. Ellis, Lincoln had "many opportunities" to be with prostitutes "while in Company with J.F.S. and Wm B two old rats in that way." Abner Y. Ellis, statement for WHH, c. January 23, 1866, *Herndon's Informants,* 171.

Lincoln may well have slept: John T. Stuart told WHH that during the Black Hawk War he and Lincoln "went to the hoar houses." John T. Stuart, interview with WHH, 1865–66, *Herndon's Informants*, 719. For his part, Speed told a story to William Herndon about the "pretty woman" he was keeping. Herndon's notes read: "Lincoln desirous to have a *little* said to Speed — 'Speed, do you know where I can get *some*; and in reply Speed said — 'Yes I do, & if you will wait a moment or so I'll send you to the place with a note. You cant get *it* without a note or by my apperance.' Speed wrote the note and Lincoln took it and went to see the girl — handed her the note . . . Lincoln told his business and the girl, after some protestations, agreed to satisfy him. Things went on right — Lincoln and the girl stript off and went to bed." But trouble arose when Lincoln found out the charge would be five dollars, when he had only three. "Lincoln went out of the house, bidding the girl good evening and went to the store of Speed, saying nothing . . . Speed had occasion to go and see the girl in a few days, and she told him just what was said and done." Joshua F. Speed, interview with WHH, January 5, 1889, *Herndon's Informants*, 719.

"The twentieth-century tendency": Carroll Smith-Rosenberg, "The Female World of Love and Ritual: Relations Between Women in Nineteenth-Century America," in *Disorderly Conduct: Visions of Gender in Victorian America* (New York: Knopf, 1985), 58–59. This essay, originally in the journal *Signs* in 1975, is a classic in the study of nineteenth-century same-sex relationships. "An abundance of manuscript evidence," Smith-Rosenberg writes, "suggests that eighteenth- and nineteenth-century women routinely formed emotional ties with other women. Such deeply felt same-sex friendships were casually accepted in American society. Indeed, from at least the late eighteenth through the mid-nineteenth century, a female world of varied and yet highly structured relationships appears to have been an essential aspect of American society. These relationships ranged from the supportive love of sisters, through the enthusiasms of adolescent girls, to sensual avowals of love by mature women" (59). Letters cited by Smith-Rosenberg show not only an emotional intensity but also a sensual and physical longing.

"If I was asked what it was": Speed, *Reminiscences*, 34.

"I was fresh from Kentucky": ibid., 17–18.

37 *"If ever I feel the soul":* AL, "Speech on the Sub-Treasury," December [26], 1839, *CWL*, vol. 1, 178.

"left the stump literally whipped": Wilson, *Honor's Voice*, 199, citing *Illinois State Register*, November 23, 1839.

"Lincoln did not come up": Joseph Gillespie to WHH, January 31, 1866, *Herndon's Informants*, 181.

"peculiarly embarassing": AL, "Speech on the Sub-Treasury," December [26], 1839, *CWL*, vol. 1, 159.

"Well, I made a big speech": AL to John T. Stuart, January 20, 1840, *CWL*, vol. 1, 184.

he felt destined: WHH to Ward Hill Lamon, February 25, 1870, *Hidden Lincoln*, 68. "Mr. Lincoln told me that his ideas of something burst in him in 1840 . . . This was the exact time that his convictions developed into a religious fervor. He always had a conviction more or less of ruin. This sprang from his physical organization, as I think, and yet it grew on him all his life — so he told me, often spoke of it to me in my office and on the circuit when we traveled together."

One theory of evolutionary psychology: A good introduction to evolutionary psychology and depression is "The Evolution of Depression — Does It Have a Role?" *All in the Mind*, with Natasha Mitchell and guests Drs. Edward Hagen, Paul J. Watson, and Daniel Nettle, April 3, 2004. A transcript is available at www.abc.net.au/rn/science/

mind/stories/s1261369.htm. An authoritative work on evolutionary psychology is Robert Wright, *The Moral Animal: Evolutionary Psychology and Everyday Life* (New York: Pantheon, 1994).

39 *"If destruction be our lot"*: AL, "Address Before the Young Men's Lyceum of Springfield, Illinois," January 27, 1838, *CWL*, vol. 1, 108.

According to Joshua Speed: In a brief interview with Herndon in early June 1865, Speed mentioned, and Herndon noted, "Lincoln on Suicide — about 1840 — see journal 1840." Herndon apparently queried Speed for more, and Speed replied, in September 1866: "My recollection is that the Poem on Suicide was written in the Spring of 1840 or Summer of 1841. It was published in the Sangamo Journal soon after it was written." Six years after this interview, Herndon reported to his colleague Ward Hill Lamon, "As to the Lincoln poem on suicide, I found out from Speed that it was written in 1838, and I hunted up the *Journal* and found where the poem was, what day published, etc., etc., but someone had cut it out — supposed to be Lincoln. I could never find another copy, and so there is an end of that." Joshua F. Speed, interview with WHH, by June 10, 1865, *Herndon's Informants*, 30; Joshua F. Speed to WHH, September 13, 1866, ibid., 337; and WHH to Ward Hill Lamon, February 25, 1870, *Hidden Lincoln*, 67.

Two questions arise. First, why did Speed associate the poem with three separate periods and what do these periods have in common? The answer may lie not in Lincoln's life but in Speed's. In 1838, in the spring of 1840, and in the summer of 1841, Speed went on lengthy trips away from Springfield. He may well have remembered that Lincoln had written and/or published the poem when he was away, and that he saw it only upon his return. The second question — did someone really cut the poem out of the newspaper? — endures. There is at least one other example of Lincoln material being excised. The R. G. Dun & Company Collection, in the Baker Library at Harvard Business School, contains field reports sent, beginning in 1841, to the Mercantile Agency — later R. G. Dun & Co., the forerunner of Dun & Bradstreet. These reports, used by businesses and merchants to size up potential clients and partners, often contained gossip and hearsay. The entry on Lincoln would be fascinating. But as the historian Scott Sandage found when he studied one of the record books, the contents had been scraped off the page, apparently with a razor blade. *Born Losers: A History of Failure in America* (Cambridge: Harvard University Press, 2005), 156–58.

One reason: Ward Hill Lamon's *The Life of Abraham Lincoln* (Lincoln: University of Nebraska Press, 1999; orig. 1872), 241, places the suicide poem sometime in 1841. *Herndon's Lincoln*, in a passage apparently written by Jesse W. Weik, followed Lamon's date (vol. 1, 216).

recently an independent scholar: For an announcement of the find and a cogent analysis of the poem, see Richard Lawrence Miller, "Lincoln's 'Suicide' Poem: Has It Been Found?" *For the People: The Newsletter of the Abraham Lincoln Association* 6 (Spring 2004): 1.

40 *William Styron*: "As one who has suffered from the malady in extremis yet returned to tell the tale, I would lobby for a truly arresting designation. 'Brainstorm,' for instance, has unfortunately been preempted . . . Told that someone's mood disorder has evolved into a storm — a veritable howling tempest in the brain, which is indeed what a clinical depression resembles like nothing else — even the uninformed layman might display sympathy." Styron, *Darkness Visible*, 37–38.

"The single most": Edwin S. Shneidman, *The Suicidal Mind* (New York: Oxford University Press, 1996), 59.

"that intensity of thought": AL to Joshua F. Speed, January 3, 1842, *CWL*, vol. 1, 265.

41 *But the context points:* To these points, made by Richard Lawrence Miller, it should be added that "The Suicide's Soliloquy" shifts radically in tone at the end, tipping from subdued and controlled language into something wilder, even desperate. This is characteristic of Lincoln's work in the late 1830s and early 1840s, including his 1838 Lyceum address, his 1839 speech on the state bank, and his 1842 temperance lecture. *A number of scholars:* Joshua Wolf Shenk, "Eureka Dept.: The Suicide Poem," *The New Yorker,* June 14–21, 2004.
   "The idea of Hell": Shneidman, *The Suicidal Mind,* 158.
42 *"Depression is the most difficult":* S. Nassir Ghaemi, interview with author, June 8, 2004.

3. I AM NOW THE MOST MISERABLE MAN LIVING

43 *Countless works:* For one short treatment of this traditional view, see *CWL,* vol. 1, 228–29n.3. "Lincoln was absent from the legislature January 13 to 19 because of illness of a psychopathic nature, brought on in all probability by what he later would refer to as 'that fatal first of Jany. '41' . . . General agreement has been reached among modern scholars to the effect that on this date Lincoln asked to be released from his engagement to Mary Todd . . . Lincoln underwent misery of no mild variety as the result, not merely of his own indecision and instability, but also of his awareness that he was the cause of an injury to Mary Todd no less severe and humiliating than his own."
   "that fatal first of Jany. '41": AL to Joshua F. Speed, March 27, 1842, *CWL,* vol. 1, 282.
44 *state's population tripled:* Drew E. VandeCreek, "Frontier Settlement," on LincolnNet, http://lincoln.lib.niu.edu/frontier.html, February 21, 2005.
   Stoking the fires: For the political and economic mechanics behind the internal improvements scheme and the debt crisis that followed, see Paul Simon, *Lincoln's Preparation for Greatness: The Illinois Legislative Years* (Norman: University of Oklahoma Press, 1965), 48–54, 151–56, 173–78, 182–88, 225–27, 232–36. Also useful is Newton Bateman, ed., *Historical Encyclopedia of Illinois and History of Sangamon County* (Springfield, Ill.: Sangamon County Genealogical Society, 1987). Except where otherwise noted, the details to follow are drawn from these texts. One picayune note: the body of the law authorized $10.25 million in bonds, but $500,000 was added to this in separate canal bonds.
   wanted to be the DeWitt Clinton: Joshua F. Speed, interview with WHH, 1865–66, *Herndon's Informants,* 476.
   scores of banks failed: Of 729 banks with charters in 1837, 194 were forced to close their doors. Peter L. Rousseau, "Jacksonian Monetary Policy, Specie Flows, and the Panic of 1837," Working Paper No. 00-W04R, January 2000, rev. June 2001, Department of Economics, Vanderbilt University.
   endure the short-term pain: AL, "Report and Resolutions Introduced in Illinois Legislature in Relation to Purchase of Public Lands," January 17, 1839, *CWL,* vol. 1, 135–38.
   "without benefit of clergy": AL to John Stuart, January 20, 1840, *CWL,* vol. 1, 184.
45 *His colleagues frankly:* Orville H. Browning to John J. Hardin, January 14, 1841, Hardin Papers.
   "In short, arriving": Wilson, *Honor's Voice,* 223.
   nine cases: Jean H. Baker, *Mary Todd Lincoln: A Biography* (New York: W. W. Norton, 1987), 90.
   "with great diffidence": AL, "Remarks in Illinois Legislature Amending a Bill Providing Interest on State Debt," December 4, 1840, *CWL,* vol. 1, 216.

45 *But in a maneuver:* For a firsthand account of the inglorious window jump, see Joseph Gillespie to WHH, January 31, 1866, *Herndon's Informants,* 187–88. For a concise treatment of the politics of the affair, see Willard L. King, *Lincoln's Manager, David Davis* (Cambridge: Harvard University Press, 1960), 40–41.

"appeared to enjoy": Simon, *Lincoln's Preparation for Greatness,* 229, citing *Illinois State Register,* December 12, 1840.

46 *pack the state courts:* To deprive Whigs of their majority on the state Supreme Court, the Democrats added five justices to the court and, to boot, abolished the circuit courts, where Whigs were plentiful. Stephen A. Douglass, Lincoln's nemesis, took one of the new Supreme Court seats. The court-packing bill passed by just one vote. "Had Lincoln been himself," argues Willard L. King, "it probably would not have passed." King, *Lincoln's Manager,* 41.

"It can not be": AL to Andrew McCormick, January 1841?, *CWL, First Supplement, 1832–1865* (New Brunswick, N.J.: Rutgers University Press, 1974), 5–6. McCormick's name was alternately spelled with an *i* and an *a.*

"I made a point of honor": Lincoln gave the details of this courtship in a letter to Eliza Browning, from which the quotations in this paragraph are drawn. AL to Mrs. Orville H. [Eliza] Browning, April 1, 1838, *CWL,* vol. 1, 117–19.

47 *"Mr. Lincoln and Mr. Speed":* Elizabeth Edwards, interview with WHH, 1865–66, *Herndon's Informants,* 623.

Mary Todd: See Baker, *Mary Todd Lincoln,* 74–79, for the circumstances of her arrival, and Baker, 51, for a physical description.

"if there were several": Presley Judson Edwards, memoirs, 1898, Chicago Historical Society.

"She could make a bishop": Katherine Helm, *The True Story of Mary, Wife of Lincoln: Containing the Recollections of Mary Lincoln's Sister Emilie, Mrs. Ben Hardin Helm: Extracts from Her War-time Diary, Numerous Letters and Other Documents Now First Published by Her Niece, Katherine Helm* (New York: Harper, 1928), 81.

ambitious woman: Elizabeth and Ninian Edwards, interview with WHH, July 27, 1887, *Herndon's Informants,* 623.

According to Mrs. Edwards: Elizabeth Todd Edwards, interview with WHH, 1865–66, *Herndon's Informants,* 443.

Henry Clay: Ruth Painter Randall, *Mary Lincoln: Biography of a Marriage* (Boston: Little, Brown, 1953), 23.

Todd often said: Elizabeth Edwards, interview with WHH, 1865–66, *Herndon's Informants,* 443.

courtship in the early nineteenth century: See Ellen K. Rothman, *Hands and Hearts: A History of Courtship in America* (New York: Basic Books, 1984).

48 *"a matrimonial pledge":* Baker, *Mary Todd Lincoln,* 87–88.

"She darted after him": Joshua F. Speed, interview with WHH, 1865–1866, *Herndon's Informants,* 474.

"She had taken a fancy": O. H. Browning, interview with John G. Nicolay, June 17, 1875, *An Oral History,* 1.

According to a variety: O. H. Browning, interview with John G. Nicolay, June 17, 1875, *An Oral History,* 1–2; Ninian Edwards, interview with WHH, September 22, 1865, *Herndon's Informants,* 133; Elizabeth Edwards, interview with WHH, 1865–66, *Herndon's Informants,* 443–44; Jane D. Bell to Ann Bell, January 27, 1841, Wilson, *Honor's Voice,* 237; Joshua F. Speed, interview with WHH, 1865–66, *Herndon's Informants,* 475.

wry, self-assured: This description is drawn from Matilda Edwards's own letters in the Edwards Papers, Knox College Library, and from a statement by Edwards's niece

Alice Edwards Quigley, March 22, 1935, in Harry O. Knerr, "Abraham Lincoln and Matilda Edwards," copy in Tarbell Papers.

"like the wind at play": Joshua F. Speed to Eliza J. Speed, March 12, 1841, ISHL.

stayed in the Edwards home: Elizabeth Edwards, interview with WHH, 1865–66, *Herndon's Informants*, 443.

"a most interesting young lady": Mary Todd to Mercy Ann Levering, December 1840, *MTL, Life and Letters*, 19.

"became very much attached": O. H. Browning, interview with John G. Nicolay, June 17, 1875, *An Oral History*, 1–2.

49   *Todd was still encouraging*: For Mary Todd's links to Stephen Douglass, see Wilson, *Honor's Voice*, 218, 238–40, 244; for Edwin ("Bat") Webb, 228, 243–44; for Joseph Gillespie, 222.

"She has a great many Beaus": Jane D. Bell to Ann Bell, January 27, 1841, Wilson, *Honor's Voice*, 237.

"flirtations with [Stephen] Douglas": Elizabeth and Ninian W. Edwards, interview with WHH, *Herndon's Informants*, July 27, 1887, 623.

"My beloved husband": Mary Lincoln to Josiah G. Holland, December 4, 1865, *MTL, Life and Letters*, 293.

"when it comes to women": AL to Mary Owens, August 16, 1837, *CWL*, vol. 1, 94.

"Went to see 'Mary'": Joshua F. Speed, interview with WHH, 1865–66, *Herndon's Informants*, 475, 477.

50   *"Miss Todd released Lincoln"*: Ninian Edwards, interview with WHH, September 22, 1865, *Herndon's Informants*, 133.

"The world had it": Elizabeth Todd Edwards, interview with WHH, 1865–66, *Herndon's Informants*, 443–44.

"His conscience troubled him": O. H. Browning, interview with John G. Nicolay, June 17, 1875, *An Oral History*, 1.

"Lincoln went Crazy": Joshua F. Speed, interview with WHH, 1865–66, *Herndon's Informants*, 475.

51   *"went Crazy as a Loon"*: Ninian W. Edwards, interview with WHH, September 22, 1865, *Herndon's Informants*, 133.

"gave me more pleasure": AL to Joshua F. Speed, March 27, 1842, *CWL*, vol. 1, 282.

52   "Lincoln's, lincoln green": Mary Todd to Mercy Ann Levering, December 1840, *MTL, Life and Letters*, 21.

"will return on Monday": Cyrus Edwards to Nelson G. Edwards, December 29?, 1840, Edwards Family Collection, Knox College Library. Wilson, *Honor's Voice*, 355n.1, notes that the postmark is faint but December 29 can clearly be seen under a microscope.

53   *"You know I am never sanguine"*: AL to John T. Stuart, January 20, 1840, *CWL*, vol. 1, 184.

54   *father had died*: James Speed to Joshua F. Speed, April 1, 1840, Filson Historical Society.

the price of hemp: R. L. Troutman, "Aspects of Agriculture in the Ante-Bellum Bluegrass," *Filson Club History Quarterly* 45 (1971): 166–67.

"tottering concern": The quotations from Speed in this paragraph and the next are from Joshua F. Speed to Mary L. Speed, February 2, 1841, Speed Family Papers, University of Louisville Archives, transcription by B. Ballantine and P. Lassiter.

fifty-plus slaves: When John Speed, Joshua's father, died in 1840, he owned fifty-seven persons. His will assigned fifteen slaves to his wife and four each to his children. Pen Bogert, slave data on John Speed, in the vertical file, "Farmington — African Americans," Filson Historical Society Library, 1997.

54   "Mr Speed's *ever changing heart*": Mary Todd to Mercy Levering, December 1840, *MTL, Life and Letters,* 20.
"*policy reasons*": Ninian Edwards, interview with WHH, September 22, 1865, *Herndon's Informants,* 133.

55   "*I am sure I have seen*": Samuel J. Hayes to Helen Hayes, July 24, 1837, Samuel J. Hayes Collection, Illinois Historical Survey.
After a respite: Petersen, *Lincoln-Douglas: The Weather As Destiny,* 74. Petersen, a physician, gathered weather data from military bases in Illinois and linked Lincoln's breakdowns in 1835 and 1840–1841 with the sharp drops in temperature in both periods. Though turgid prose makes his theory inaccessible, Petersen's basic point, that weather affects people's emotional states, resonates with common sense and recent clinical investigations into seasonal affective disorder, or SAD. "SAD was first noted before 1845, but was not officially named until the early 1980's. As sunlight has affected the seasonal activities of animals (i.e., reproductive cycles and hibernation), SAD may be an effect of this seasonal light variation in humans. As seasons change, there is a shift in our 'biological internal clocks' or circadian rhythm, due partly to these changes in sunlight patterns. This can cause our biological clocks to be out of 'step' with our daily schedules. The most difficult months for SAD sufferers are January and February." National Mental Health Association, "Seasonal Affective Disorder," www.nmha.org/infoctr/factsheets/27.cfm, March 31, 2005. For a clinical treatment of the condition and its response to light therapy, see N. E. Rosenthal et al., "Seasonal Affective Disorder: A Description of the Syndrome and Preliminary Findings with Light Therapy," *Archives of General Psychiatry* 41 (1984): 72–80. A year after this breakdown, Lincoln wrote that his friend Joshua Speed should be aware of his "*exposure to bad weather . . .* which my experience clearly proves to be verry severe on defective nerves."
Lincoln's friend David Davis: "Would that I could give you all a hearty shake of the hand," Davis wrote on January 19, 1841. "My spirits would undoubtedly raise several degrees this cold day — for you must know that I am writing with the thermometer several degrees below zero. I have been out riding two days this winter when the severity of the cold was greater than had ever before been known in this Succer State." King, *Lincoln's Manager,* 40, citing Davis to William P. Walker, January 19, 1841.
political nightmare: After all the wrangling in December 1840, the Assembly authorized the issuance of special bonds to pay the interest due on January 1, 1841. The state made its next payment as well, but then defaulted. "Four years after the passage of the measure," writes Paul Simon, "Illinois had a debt of $15,000,000, and Illinois bonds were selling for 15 cents on the dollar . . . The state debt kept climbing. By 1853 the debt had reached almost $17,000,000. Not until 1857 was the state able to pay even the interest on the bonds. Not until 1882 were the bonds finally paid — forty-five years after the passage of the measure and seventeen years after Lincoln's death." *Lincoln's Preparation for Greatness,* 52. See also Governor Thomas Ford, *A History of Illinois from Its Commencement as a State in 1818 to 1847,* annotations and introduction by Rodney Davis (Urbana: University of Illinois Press, 1995; orig. 1854), 144, and Theodore C. Pease, *The Frontier State, 1818–1848* (Urbana: University of Illinois Press, 1987), 228–29.

56   *In Victorian America:* "Throughout most of Lincoln's life," writes Thomas F. Schwartz, "New Year celebrations were closer to the festivities we associate with Christmas." People exchanged gifts, including books published for the occasion, with titles like *The Gift for 1841.* Thomas F. Schwartz, "Santa Abraham?" *For the People: The Newsletter of the Abraham Lincoln Association* 1, no. 4 (Winter 1999): 6.
leap year of 1840: Baker, *Mary Todd Lincoln,* 90.

One is a young woman: Sarah Rickard Barret to WHH, August 3, 1888, *Herndon's Informants,* 664.

he might have contracted syphilis: WHH to Jesse W. Weik, January 1891, *Hidden Lincoln,* 259. See also Wilson, *Honor's Voice,* 127–29.

as many as half of the men: Baker, *Mary Todd Lincoln,* 88.

typical feature of hypochondriasis: Benjamin Rush, *Medical Inquiries and Observations upon the Diseases of the Mind* (New York: New York Academy of Medicine, 1962; orig. 1812), 5.

Whatever the reasons: For an account of Lincoln's known whereabouts in January 1841, see *Day by Day,* vol. 1, 151–53.

57 *his "indisposition":* "Mr. Lincoln has recovered from his indisposition," the *Register* reported on January 29, 1841, "and has attended the House for more than a week past, during which time he made no minority report, although he attended every meeting of the committee of Investigation."

"two Cat fits and a Duck fit": Martinette Hardin to John J. Hardin, January 22, 1841, Hardin Papers.

"He has grown much worse": Edwin Webb to Orville H. Browning, January 17, 1841, Orville Hickman Browning Papers, Illinois Historical Survey.

several hours a day: H. W. Thornton to Ida Tarbell, December 21, 1895, Tarbell Papers.

"hypochondriaism": AL to John T. Stuart, January 20, 1840, *CWL,* vol. 1, 228.

"how are the mighty fallen!": James C. Conkling to Mercy Ann Levering, January 24, 1841, typescript in ISHL.

"Poor fellow, he is in rather": Jane D. Bell to Ann Bell, January 27, 1841, in Wilson, *Honor's Voice,* 237. This letter was also printed in the *Lincoln Herald* 50, no. 4 (December 1948–February 1949): 47, but that text omitted a final fragment. Wilson draws his text from a copy in the Randall Papers.

58 *"desolating tortures":* Daniel Drake, "History of Two Cases of Burn, Producing Serious Constitutional Irritation," *Western Journal of the Medical and Physical Sciences* 4 (April–June 1830): 48–60, 53. Drake's conclusion resonates with a famous critical remark on nineteenth-century psychopharmacology by Dr. Oliver Wendell Holmes. In an 1860 lecture at the Massachusetts Medical Society, Holmes stated that, with a few exceptions, if "the whole materia medica, *as now used,* could be sunk to the bottom of the sea, it would be all the better for mankind, — and all the worse for the fishes." H. Wayne Morgan, *Drugs in America: A Social History, 1800–1980* (Syracuse, N.Y.: Syracuse University Press, 1982), 1.

hypochondriasis became the term: Stanley W. Jackson, *Melancholia and Depression* (New Haven: Yale University Press, 1986), 37.

Medical Inquiries: What follows, unless otherwise specified, is drawn from Rush, *Medical Inquiries,* 74–134.

"direct and drastic interferences": Robert C. Fuller, *Alternative Medicine in American Religious Life* (New York: Oxford University Press, 1989), 13–14.

elephant tamers: Rush, *Medical Inquiries,* 193.

59 *Arsenic and strychnine:* Fuller, *Alternative Medicine,* 14.

Doctors approved: Norbert Hirschhorn, Robert G. Feldman, and Ian A. Greaves, "Abraham Lincoln's Blue Pills: Did Our Sixteenth President Suffer from Mercury Poisoning?" *Perspectives in Biology and Medicine* 44, no. 3 (Summer 2001): 315–22.

Since it binds: Hirschhorn, Feldman, and Greaves write: "Regardless in what form or route it enters the body, mercury is eventually metabolized to mercuric chloride — 'corrosive sublimate' — which preferentially binds to the central nervous system and kidneys; thus mercury's toxicity is mainly revealed by neurobehavioral disorders or renal failure. Because mercury is excreted from the body only slowly, over months to years, one can suffer chronic poisoning by taking mercury in small, regular amounts that build up body stores faster than excreted. Once mercury is absorbed, the signs and symptoms of poisoning are reliably predictable." This article argues that Lincoln's use of mercury adversely affected him both physically and emotionally. Studies have found that two thirds of people using mercury become "irritable, anxious, and hostile to the point of sudden rages and even violence." The treatment used for depression in Lincoln's time also produced depression, along with increased "emotional lability and hypersensitivity." Ibid., 325–26.

59 *"It would be worth much"*: Joshua F. Speed to WHH, November 30, 1866, *Herndon's Informants*, 430.

60 *"Benjamin Franklin of the West"*: Charles D. Aring, "Daniel Drake and Medical Education," *Journal of the American Medical Association* 254, no. 15 (October 18, 1985): 2120.
"the long and frightful train": Daniel Drake, *Discourse on Intemperance* (Cincinnati: Locker & Reynolds, 1828), 21.

61 *He found his own case*: Details of the burn story and quotations from Daniel Drake that follow are from Drake, "History of Two Cases of Burn," 48–60.
"the medicine of the mind": Rush, *Medical Inquiries*, 103.

62 *"I have, within the last"*: AL to John Stuart, January 20, 1841, *CWL*, vol. 1, 228.
"From the deplorable": AL to John Stuart, January 23, 1841, *CWL*, vol. 1, 229. I have examined the original letter in the ISHL with Kim Bauer, the library's curator of Lincoln manuscripts. On beige paper, about six inches wide and ten inches high, it is written with a rich blue ink, probably from an indigo die, Bauer said. The first part of the letter, which dispassionately recites recent political news, is written in small, neat script. The handwriting grows larger and messier at the top of the second page. Then there is a long, slightly smeared dash. "He's obviously laboring a little bit when he finishes this letter," Bauer said. "Possibly he left and came back. I don't know if he left, but he stopped. You can see that the writing changes." Indeed, beginning with the words "For not giving you a general summary of news, you *must* pardon me," the ink gets significantly darker, as though the heaviness of the moment took physical expression in the pressure Lincoln exerted with his pen.
worst of the cold weather lifted: Jane D. Bell to Ann Bell, January 27, 1841, in Wilson, *Honor's Voice*, 237.
"You see by this": AL to John T. Stuart, February 3, 1841, *CWL, First Supplement, 1832–1865*, 6.
his "embrigglement": Wilson, *Honor's Voice*, 231. This word is attributed to Jesse K. Dubois in Milton Hay to John Hay, February 8, 1887, "Recollection of Lincoln: Three Letters of Intimate Friends," *Bulletin of the Abraham Lincoln Association* 25 (December 1931): 9.
"hanging about — moody": Turner R. King, interview with WHH, 1865–66, *Herndon's Informants*, 464.
"sick head ache and hypo": Joshua F. Speed to Mary L. Speed, February 2, 1841, Speed Family Papers, University of Louisville Archives.
"All feeling is dead and dust": Joshua F. Speed to Eliza Speed, March 12, 1841, ISHL.
another attack of the hypo: Wilson, *Honor's Voice*, 245, citing Joshua F. Speed to William Butler, May 18, 1841.

63 *posting overseas*: Claude Moore Fuess, *Daniel Webster*, 2 vols. (Boston: Little, Brown, 1930), vol. 2, 94n.2, citing John T. Stuart to Daniel Webster, March 5, 1841, in the private collection of Wilson Olney.
"the gay world": Mary Todd to Mercy Levering, June 1841, *MTL, Life and Letters*, 27.

In a move: Ninian Edwards, interview with WHH, September 22, 1865, *Herndon's Informants,* 133.

"moody & hypochondriac": Joshua F. Speed to WHH, January 12, 1866, *Herndon's Informants,* 158.

Approaching it from Bardstown Road: The description of Farmington, and Lincoln's experiences there, unless otherwise noted, are drawn from the author's tour of the estate and from Kincaid, *Joshua Fry Speed;* "Lincoln Talked to Uncle and Joshua Made Love," *Louisville Courier-Journal,* February 13, 1938; and AL to Mary Speed, September 27, 1841, *CWL,* vol. 1, 259–61.

saddle of mutton: Mildred Bullitt to Tom [?], January 2, 1861, Bullitt Papers, Filson Historical Society.

peaches and cream: AL to Mary Speed, September 27, 1841, *CWL,* vol. 1, 261.

65 *Anthony Storr:* Anthony Storr, *Solitude: A Return to the Self* (New York: Ballantine Books, 1988), 33–34, 62.

"If architects want to strengthen": Victor Frankl, *Man's Search for Meaning* (New York: Washington Square Press, 1985; orig. 1946), 127–28.

"irrepressible desire": Speed, *Reminiscences,* p. 39.

"desired to live for": Joshua F. Speed to WHH, February 7, 1866, *Herndon's Informants,* 196. For more on the sources for this exchange, see note on pages 288–89.

4. A SELF-MADE MAN

69 *"It does not depend on the start":* Stephen T. Logan, interview with John G. Nicolay, July 6, 1875, *An Oral History,* 38.

"self-made man": Simon, *Lincoln's Preparation for Greatness,* 231, citing *Quincy Whig,* January 1, 1841. "Abraham Lincoln of Sangamon is emphatically a man of high standing," the paper declared, "being about six feet four in his stockings, slender, and loosely built. He is, I suppose, over 30 years old, has been in the legislature repeatedly, and was run as one of the Whig electors in the late election. Mr. L. is a self-made man, and one of the ablest, whether a lawyer or legislator, in the State. As a speaker, he is characterized by a sincerity, frankness and evident honesty calculated to win attention and gain the confidence of the hearer."

In Lincoln's time: Winkle, *The Young Eagle,* 125, 133–34. For more on the advent of "self-made" men, see Joyce Appleby, "New Cultural Heroes in the Early National Period," in Thomas L. Haskell and Richard F. Teichgraeber, eds., *Culture of the Market: Historical Essays* (New York: Cambridge University Press, 1993), 163–88.

71 *"What hath God wrought":* For an account of this message, sent on May 24, 1844, see Jill Lepore, *A Is for American: Letters and Other Characters in the Newly United States* (New York: Knopf, 2002), 152. The code is from the Web site of the Australian Centre for the Moving Image, www.acmi.net.au. Various sources give different capitalization and punctuation. By the time of the Civil War, the United States had 50,000 miles of telegraph line and 1,400 stations. For more on the culture generated by the telegraph, see Tom Standage, *The Victorian Internet: The Remarkable Story of the Telegraph and the Nineteenth Century's On-Line Pioneers* (London: Weidenfeld and Nicolson, 1998).

the church had censored: See Edward S. Reed, *From Soul to Mind: The Emergence of Psychology from Erasmus Darwin to William James* (New Haven: Yale University Press, 1997).

9 A.M. on October 23, 4004 B.C.: Sir John Lightfoot, an eminent Hebrew scholar at

Cambridge, gave this date after a thorough study of Scriptures. See Andrew D. White, *A History of the Warfare of Science with Theology in Christendom* (New York: D. Appleton, 1897), 9.

71 *Then geologists:* For a discussion of geology's role in the early-nineteenth-century intellectual landscape — and Lincoln's interest in the subject — see Guelzo, *Redeemer President,* 108. The major work was Charles Lyell's *Principles of Geology,* published in three volumes from 1830 to 1833.

Lincoln became a proponent: Herndon's *Lincoln,* vol. 3, 438.

"in which a people reshapes": Fuller, *Alternative Medicine,* 19–20, citing William McLoughlin, *Revivals, Awakenings and Reform* (Chicago: University of Chicago Press, 1978).

72 *"Human beings need to organize":* Delbanco, *The Real American Dream,* 1.

the independent self: For an excellent treatment of the ethos of the mid-nineteenth century, see ibid., 47–80.

"Individualism is a novel expression": Alexis de Tocqueville, *Democracy in America.* The text of this classic work is online at the University of Virginia's Hypertext Projects. The quotation appears in vol. 2, sec. 2, "Of Individualism in Democratic Countries," http://xroads.virginia.edu/~HYPER/DETOC/ch2_02.htm, April 1, 2005. For more on the emergence of individualism, see Winkle, *Young Eagle,* 125.

73 *"Push along. Push hard":* Illinois State Journal, January 8, 1853.

later portrayed as a shiftless: For a concise treatment of the historiography on Thomas Lincoln, see Neely, *The Abraham Lincoln Encyclopedia,* 187–88.

satisfied with his life: Nathaniel Grigsby, interview with WHH, September 12, 1865, Herndon's Informants, 113. "Thomas Lincoln was not a lazy man — but a tinker[?] — a piddler — always doing but doing nothing great — was happy — lived easy — & contented. had but few wants and Supplied these."

"I could scarcely believe": F. B. Carpenter, *The Inner Life of Abraham Lincoln: Six Months at the White House* (Lincoln: University of Nebraska Press, 1995; orig. *Six Months at the White House with Abraham Lincoln,* 1866), 96–98.

74 *He could visit New Orleans:* AL traveled to the Crescent City when he was nineteen and twenty-two. AL, "Autobiography Written for John L. Scripps," c. June 1860, *CWL,* vol. 4, 62–63.

Lawyers made it so: In the famous phrase of the historian Charles Sellers, lawyers were the "shock troops of capitalism," creating and enforcing the mechanisms of a market economy. See Charles Sellers, *The Market Revolution: Jacksonian America, 1815–1846* (New York: Oxford University Press, 1991), 47.

"I want in all cases to do right": AL to Mary S. Owens, August 16, 1837, *CWL,* vol. 1, 94.

"Honest Abe": Lincoln first got the nickname after judging horse races in New Salem in the early 1830s. Douglas L. Wilson, "Young Man Lincoln," paper presented at Gettysburg College, Gettysburg, Pa., September 1999.

"physical assets and strength of character": ibid.

"let the whole thing go": James Short to WHH, July 7, 1865, Herndon's Informants 74.

75 *"I feel like a failure":* Sandage, *Born Losers,* 5.

"We never knew a man": Illinois State Journal, January 8, 1853.

"the mass of men": Henry David Thoreau, *Walden,* in Carl Bode, ed., *The Portable Thoreau* (New York: Penguin Books, 1982), 263.

"I cannot help counting": Sandage, *Born Losers,* 1.

"Many of his friends feared": Robert B. Rutledge to WHH, c. November 1, 1866, Herndon's Informants, 383.

"The Doctors say": Jane D. Bell to Ann Bell, January 27, 1841, in Wilson, *Honor's Voice*, 237.

"more persons are attacked": Pliny Earle, *Visit to Thirteen Asylums for the Insane in Europe* (Philadelphia: Dobson, 1841), 127.

76 *dominant thinking on inheritance*: See Charles Rosenberg, "The Bitter Fruit: Heredity, Disease, and Social Thought," in *No Other Gods: On Science and American Social Thought* (Baltimore: Johns Hopkins University Press, 1976), 25–53.

"agreeable enough to people": Unless otherwise noted, quotations on asylums are from David J. Rothman, *The Discovery of the Asylum: Social Order and Disorder in the New Republic* (Boston: Little, Brown, 1971), 112–16, 126, 130.

77 *"We might at first refuse"*: C. B. Hayden, "On the Distribution of Insanity in the United States," *Southern Literary Messenger* 10, no. 3 (March 1844): 178–81.

visit from Dorothea Dix: In the summer of 1846, Dix stopped at Springfield during a three-month tour of Illinois, in which she inspected the conditions of the state's mentally ill. She returned to the capital in December 1846. In January 1847 she submitted a report on the state's insane and urged the legislature to commission an asylum. David L. Lightner, ed., *Asylum, Prison, and Poorhouse: The Writings and Reform Work of Dorothea Dix in Illinois* (Carbondale: Southern Illinois University Press, 1999), 1, 8, 103.

78 *"These fears"*: Lauren Slater, interview with author, August 24, 2001.

"rather a bright lad": AL to Andrew Johnston, April 18, 1846, *CWL*, vol. 1, 377–78. For the text of the poem, see *CWL*, vol. 1, 384–85. I made a great effort to learn more about Matthew Gentry, to little avail. I did find that he was the oldest of eight children, with three brothers and four sisters. Born around 1806, he married Hetty Fisher on March 18, 1827. They had no children. ("Family Group Sheet" on the children of James Gentry, Sr., and Elizabeth Hornbeck, on file at the Spencer County Public Library, Rockport, Indiana.) Matthew was clearly alive in 1844, when Lincoln saw him "lingering in this wretched condition." He had probably died by 1850; the census of that year made no mention of him. According to the *History of Warrick, Spencer, and Perry Counties Indiana* (Chicago: Goodspeed Bros., 1885), under the entry for James Gentry, Sr., Matthew died at his father's home.

79 *His first cousin Mordecai Lincoln*: Facts on Mordecai Lincoln here are drawn from Berenice V. Lovely to William Barton, October 18, 1921, Barton Papers; Walter B. Stevens, *A Reporter's Lincoln*, edited by Michael Burlingame (Lincoln: University of Nebraska Press, 1998; orig. 1916), 217–24; Robert W. McClaughrey, "Mordecai Lincoln and His Dog Grampus," in *Intimate Memories*, 55–58; and Mordecai's own letters and notes in the Barton Papers.

"quite attached": *Intimate Memories*, 56.

5. A MISFORTUNE, NOT A FAULT

81 *Separate Baptism*: Guelzo, *Redeemer President*, 36.

82 *"out-Calvined Calvin"*: William E. Barton, *The Life of Abraham Lincoln*, 2 vols. (Indianapolis: Bobbs-Merrill, 1925), vol. 2, 460. Bound to have an effect in any case, for Abe Lincoln the impact of such messages was amplified because he had scant exposure to other points of view. Even after he learned to read, for years he had access to only two books, the Bible and John Bunyan's *Pilgrim's Progress*. In a sketchbook that contains his earliest known writing, he copied a verse from the Calvinist hymn writer Isaac Watts, which began, "Time what an empty vaper 'tis . . ." *CWL*, vol. 1, 1.

82 *"acedia":* The victim, Cassian said, "frequently gazes up at the sun, as if it was too slow in setting, and so a kind of unreasonable confusion of mind takes possession of him like some foul darkness, and makes him idle and useless for every spiritual work." According to Cassian, many elders considered that acedia was the "noonday demon" of Psalm 90. Andrew Solomon took this phrase as the title for his award-winning book. Cassian's description of the disease is in Radden, *The Nature of Melancholy,* 71–72. For the way acedia blended with melancholy, see Solomon, *The Noonday Demon: An Atlas of Depression* (New York: Scribner, 2001), 287. For the requirement of penitence and confession, see Jackson, *Melancholia and Depression,* 69.

"Some Devil is often very Busy": Radden, *The Nature of Melancholy,* 165, citing Cotton Mather, *The Angel of Bethesda* (1724).

"For the godly": Harley, "Explaining Salem," 310.

He recited: "Burns helped him to be an infidel as I think — at least he found in Burns a like thinker and feeler." James H. Matheny, interview with WHH, by March 2, 1870, *Herndon's Informants,* 577.

He carried around: Herndon's Lincoln, vol. 3, 439–40.

hurt Lincoln politically: James H. Matheny (interview with WHH, November 1866, *Herndon's Informants,* 432) said that his father "with all his soul hated to vote for him because he heard that Lincoln was an infidel . . . Many Religious — Christian whigs hated to vote for Lincoln on that account." This was no secret to Lincoln. In 1837, he noted that a political opponent had gone around asking people if they "ever heard Lincoln say he was a deist." AL, "Second Reply to Adams," October 19, 1837, *CWL,* vol. 1, 106. By 1843, Lincoln knew that some people refused to vote for him for Congress because they heard he was a deist. AL to Martin S. Morris, March 26, 1843, *CWL,* vol. 1, 320.

When Lincoln put his ideas: John Hill to WHH, June 27, 1865, *Herndon's Informants,* 61–62.

83 *a kind of august tradition:* This discussion relies heavily on Susan Jacoby, *Freethinkers: A History of American Secularism* (New York: Metropolitan Books, 2004), especially 4–5, 19, 32, 35–36, 63–64.

Dozens of new Christian sects: Louis Menand, *The Metaphysical Club* (New York: Farrar, Straus and Giroux, 2001), 80, citing Nathan O. Hatch, *The Democratization of American Christianity* (New Haven: Yale University Press, 1989), 3–4.

84 *"heavenly black eyes":* AL to Joshua F. Speed, January 3?, 1842, *CWL,* vol. 1, 266.

"In the winter of 40 & 41": Joshua F. Speed to WHH, November 30, 1866, *Herndon's Informants,* 430.

"Feeling, as you know I do": AL to Joshua F. Speed, January 3?, 1842, *CWL,* vol. 1, 265–66.

85 *"almost crazy":* Susan P. Bullitt to John C. Bullitt, April 8, 1841, Bullitt Family Papers, Filson Historical Society.

87 *disease wasn't a product:* Here I draw principally from Robert C. Fuller, *Alternative Medicine,* 20, 23, 30–31, and from Fuller's *Mesmerism and the American Cure of Souls* (Philadelphia: University of Pennsylvania Press, 1982), 31, 44.

H. L. Mencken joked: George H. Douglas, *H. L. Mencken, Critic of American Life* (Hamden, Conn.: Archon Books, 1978), 87.

"a profound stir": Sophie Bledsoe Herrick, "The First Lincoln Baby and a Friend's Sound Advice," *Intimate Memories,* 61–62, reprinting articles from *Century Magazine* (March 1892) and *Methodist Review* (October 1915). The story that follows is drawn entirely from Herrick. Is her version reliable? A young child at the time, she almost

certainly heard the story from her father, who in his later years became a bitter political opponent of Lincoln's. Yet it's hard to imagine that the story was made up to slight Lincoln, for any slight intended would fall just as heavily, if not more so, on Bledsoe himself. Furthermore, I have examined Herrick's other work and judge her to be a credible source.

88 *"Mrs. B":* Though described by Herrick as a boarder at the Globe Tavern, this unidentified woman resembles Sarah Beck, the house's owner and proprietor.

per capita consumption: W. J. Rorabaugh, *The Alcoholic Republic: An American Tradition* (New York: Oxford University Press, 1981), 10. Rorabaugh points out that "after reaching this peak, consumption fell sharply under the influence of the temperance movement, and since 1840 its highest levels have been under 2 gallons — less than half the rate of consumption in the 1820s" (10). Though Lincoln connected the cessation of drink to good health, a strong tradition connected good health to drinking. "At the beginning of the eighteenth century, tradition taught, and Americans, like Englishmen and Europeans, universally believed, that rum, gin, and brandy were nutritious and healthful. Distilled sprits were viewed as foods that supplemented limited and monotonous diets, as medications that could cure colds, fevers, snakebites, frosted toes, and broken legs, and as relaxants that would relieve depression, reduce tension, and enable hardworking laborers to enjoy a moment of happy, frivolous camaraderie" (23). Lincoln probably had in mind the healthful aspects of alcohol — along with the fun — when he wrote, of the old view of alcohol, "It is true, that even *then*, it was known and acknowledged, that many were greatly injured by it; but none seemed to think the injury arose from the *use* of a *bad thing*, but from the *abuse* of a *very good thing.*" AL, "Temperance Address," February 22, 1842, *CWL,* vol. 1, 274.

89 *"in the thundering tones":* AL, "Temperance Address," February 22, 1842, *CWL,* vol. 1, 271–79.

"Old School" Calvinism: Allen C. Guelzo, "Abraham Lincoln and the Doctrine of Necessity," *Journal of the Abraham Lincoln Association* 18 (Winter 1997), http://jala.press .uiuc.edu/18.1/guelzo.html, March 31, 2005.

"There is but one thing": AL to Mary Speed, September 27, 1841, *CWL,* vol. 1, 261.

"If from all these causes": AL to Joshua F. Speed, January 3?, 1842, *CWL,* vol. 1, 265.

90 *"you are safe":* AL to Joshua F. Speed, February 13, 1842, *CWL,* vol. 1, 269–70.

"not to some false and ruinous": AL to Joshua F. Speed, January 3?, 1842, *CWL,* vol. 1, 265.

she had taken ill: Mrs. William C. Bullitt to John Bullitt, February 9, 1842, Bullitt Family Papers, Filson Historical Society.

"The death scenes": AL to Joshua F. Speed, February 3, 1842, *CWL,* vol. 1, 267–68.

91 *"There's a divinity":* Herndon's Lincoln, vol. 3, 436. This phrase is from *Hamlet,* act 5, scene 2.

like billiard balls: This was a popular metaphor among scientists and philosophers explaining the "doctrine of necessity." See, for example, William Godwin, *Enquiry Concerning Political Justice,* Book IV: Operation of Opinion in Societies, Individuals; Chapter VIII: Inferences from the Doctrine of Necessity. http:// dwardmac.pitzer.edu/Anarchist_Archives/godwin/pj4/pj4_8.html, April 1, 2005.

"His idea was that": Herndon's Lincoln, vol. 3, 597.

"I once contended": ibid., 438.

"strikes and cuts": WHH to Jesse W. Weik, February 25, 1887, Hidden Lincoln, 181.

"what I understand is called": AL, "Handbill Replying to Charges of Infidelity," July 31, 1846, *CWL,* vol. 1, 382.

91 *"Virtually all of the major"*: Guelzo, "Abraham Lincoln and the Doctrine of Necessity," http://jala.press.uiuc.edu/18.1/guelzo.html, para. 15.

92 *"watchmaker God"*: Jacoby, *Freethinkers*, 4.
    "The universal sense of mankind": AL, "Temperance Address," February 22, 1842, *CWL*, vol. 1, 275.
    "The truth is": AL to Joshua F. Speed, July 4, 1842, *CWL*, vol. 1, 289.

93 *"It made a deep impression"*: Joshua F. Speed to WHH, September 17, 1866, *Herndon's Informants*, 342. When Mrs. Speed requested a photograph of Lincoln as president, he wrote on it: "For Mrs. Lucy G. Speed from whose pious hands I accepted the present of an Oxford Bible Twenty years ago." Joshua F. Speed to WHH, December 6, 1866, *Herndon's Informants*, 500.
    "priest ridden": This quote is from a letter that appeared in the *Beardstown Chronicle* on November 1, 1834. Though it was signed "Samuel Hill," a shopkeeper in New Salem, Douglas L. Wilson argues persuasively that Lincoln was the author. "Abraham Lincoln Versus Peter Cartwright," *Lincoln Before Washington: New Perspectives on the Illinois Years* (Urbana: University of Illinois Press, 1997), 55–73.
    "Tell your mother": AL to Mary Speed, September 27, 1841, *CWL*, vol. 1, 261.
    James professed himself: Louis Menand writes of James, "Although he believed in the legitimacy of the religious response to the universe, he was never able to attain its consolation himself. All his efforts to make contact with God, or to enter into what he could regard as a spiritual state of mind, were unsuccessful. 'My personal position is simple,' he wrote two years after the publication of *The Varieties of Religious Experience* to one of the book's critics. 'I have no living sense of commerce with a God.' And then, in an understatement: 'I envy those who have, for I know that the addition of such a sense would help me greatly.'" Louis Menand, "William James and the Case of the Epileptic Patient," *New York Review of Books*, December 17, 1998, citing William James to James H. Leuba, April 17, 1904.
    "He always seemed to deplore": Albert T. Bledsoe, review of Ward Hill Lamon's *Life of Abraham Lincoln,* in *Southern Review* (April 1873). Reprinted in *Lincoln among His Friends*, 483–84.

94 *"intense anxiety and trepidation"*: AL to Joshua F. Speed, February 25, 1842, *CWL*, vol. 1, 280.
    "How miserably things seem": ibid., 281.
    one of Benjamin Rush's prescriptions: Rush, *Medical Inquiries*, 126.

95 *"Before I resolve"*: AL to Joshua F. Speed, July 4, 1842, *CWL*, vol. 1, 288.
    "I believe now": ibid., 289.
    "for without, you would not": AL to Joshua F. Speed, October 5, 1842, *CWL*, vol. 1, 303.
    "commenced choaking & sobbing": Abner Y. Ellis, statement for WHH, January 23, 1866, *Herndon's Informants*, 173.

96 *"glooming"*: James H. Matheny, interview with WHH, May 3, 1866, *Herndon's Informants*, 251.
    "I think if I were you": AL to Joshua F. Speed, February 13, 1842, *CWL*, vol. 1, 269–70.
    This age-old prescription: Robert Burton, in his classic *Anatomy of Melancholy,* wrote, "I write of melancholy, by being busy to avoid melancholy. There is no greater cause of melancholy than idleness, no better cure than business." Courtesy of Project Gutenberg, www.gutenberg.org/etext/10800.
    "To Hell, I suppose": *Herndon's Lincoln*, vol. 2, 229.
    "Lincoln looked and acted": James H. Matheny, interview with WHH, May 3, 1866, *Herndon's Informants*, 251.
    "A. L. to Mary": Wayne C. Temple, *Abraham Lincoln: From Skeptic to Prophet* (Mahomet, Ill.: Mayhaven, 1995), 27.

6. THE REIGN OF REASON

97 *popular psychological theory:* This is a paraphrase of Daniel Walker Howe, *The Making of the American Self,* 5–6.

"It will in future": AL, "Address Before the Young Men's Lyceum of Springfield, Illinois," January 27, 1838, *CWL,* vol. 1, 115.

"most powerful moral effort": AL, "Temperance Address," February 22, 1842, *CWL,* vol. 1, 275, 279.

98 *"many of his friends feared":* Robert B. Rutledge to WHH, November 30, 1866, *Herndon's Informants,* 426. Lincoln used the same imagery when he referred to Matthew Gentry as "a human form with reason fled."

Lincoln bemoaned his inability: See AL to Mrs. Orville [Eliza] Browning, April 1, 1838, *CWL,* vol. 1, 117–19, and AL to Joshua F. Speed, July 4, 1842, *CWL,* vol. 1, 288–90.

In 1840, he once mocked: Replying to a speech by the Democrat Jesse B. Thomas, Lincoln mocked the man's past and imitated his voice and gestures, the effect being "absolutely overwhelming and withering," said an observer. *Lincoln among His Friends,* 467. Thomas scampered away in tears. Lincoln hunted him down the next day to apologize; years later, he said he still regretted it deeply. *Herndon's Lincoln,* vol. 1, 198. Lincoln's chagrin may have been compounded by knowledge that Thomas was not well mentally. He committed suicide on May 4, 1853. Bateman, *Historical Encyclopedia of Illinois,* 521. See Robert Bray, "'The Power to Hurt': Lincoln's Early Use of Satire and Invective," *Journal of the Abraham Lincoln Association,* Winter 1995, http://jala.press .uiuc.edu/16.1/bray.html, March 31, 2005.

challenged him to a duel: For a recent treatment of this incident, see Douglas L. Wilson, "Lincoln's Affair of Honor," *Atlantic Monthly,* February 1998, 64–71.

"fancy, emotion, and imagination": James H. Matheny, interview with WHH, November 1866, *Herndon's Informants,* 431–32.

"There was a strong tinge": Joseph Gillespie to WHH, January 31, 1866, *Herndon's Informants,* 185.

"You are young, and I am older": AL, "Verses: to Rosa Haggard," September 28, 1858, *CWL,* vol. 3, 203.

99 *"grossly misdiagnosed":* James McCullough, Jr., *Treatment for Chronic Depression: Cognitive Behavioral Analysis System of Psychotherapy (CBASP)* (New York: Guilford Press, 2000), 8.

"a burden which they habitually bear": Emil Kraepelin, *Manic-Depressive Insanity and Paranoia,* edited by G. M. Robertson (Edinburgh: Livingstone, 1921), 192.

100 *"rather an unladylike profession":* Mary Todd to Mercy Ann Levering, December 1840, *MTL, Life and Letters,* 21.

Once she caused: Baker, *Mary Todd Lincoln,* 81–82.

By law, she became: For one popular take on domestic expectations in the mid-nineteenth century, see Catharine Beecher, *A Treatise on Domestic Economy,* originally published in 1841.

Mary Lincoln: Jennifer Fleischner, *Mrs. Lincoln and Mrs. Keckly: The Remarkable Story of the Friendship Between a First Lady and a Former Slave* (New York: Broadway Books, 2003), 7.

their first child: For the dates of births and deaths in the Lincoln family, see "Family Record in Abraham Lincoln's Bible," November 4, 1842–April 4, 1853, *CWL,* vol. 1, 304.

a cottage at Eighth and Jackson: David Herbert Donald, *Lincoln* (New York: Simon and Schuster, 1995), 96. For a thorough treatment of Lincoln's home, see Wayne C.

Temple, *By Square and Compasses: The Building of Lincoln's Home and Its Saga* (Bloomington, Ill.: Ashlar Press, 1984).

100   *time at home shrank:* Writes Charles Strozier, "A subtle shift had occurred in the pattern of Lincoln's absences between 1843 and 1850 — they had lengthened. In the early days of his marriage he seldom stayed away more than two weeks and determinedly broke up longer trips into two- and three-week units. By 1850, however, he took five long trips that lasted one, four, four, six, and one weeks, in that order . . . The same pattern holds true for the next few years." Charles B. Strozier, *Lincoln's Quest for Union: Public and Private Meanings* (New York: Basic Books, 1982), 117, citing *Day by Day.*

an 830-mile journey: Baker, *Mary Todd Lincoln,* 108.

In the year Eddie was born: ibid. There were two main circuit trips a year, from September to January and March to June. Leonard Swett to J. H. Drummond, May 27, 1860, *Reminiscences of Abraham Lincoln.*

101   *"love him better":* James Gourley, interview with WHH, 1865–66, *Herndon's Informants,* 453.

"little engine that knew no rest": *Herndon's Lincoln,* vol. 2, 375.

"a more restless ambition": ibid., 295–96.

an unknown number were burned: Thomas F. Schwartz, the Illinois state historian, notes that the letter from AL to Mary Lincoln, June 12, 1848, was found in a "burn pile" in Springfield, as were Mary's surviving letters to her husband at that time. Interview with author, February 11, 2002. As with many Victorians, Mary Lincoln believed in destroying correspondence. She wrote to Hannah Shearer, January 1, 1860, "Let *the flames* receive this, so soon as read." *MTL, Life and Letters,* 62. Robert Todd Lincoln was known for destroying papers containing personal details, and probably did so during the decades he retained exclusive control over his father's papers. See *Lincoln Papers,* vol. 1, 121–29.

"Will you be a good girl": AL to Mary Lincoln, June 12, 1848, *CWL,* vol. 1, 477–78.

"I really wish to see you": AL to Mary Lincoln, September 22, 1863, *CWL,* vol. 6, 474.

"She was very highly strung": Helm, *The True Story of Mary, Wife of Lincoln,* 32.

102   *"As we used familiarly":* O. H. Browning, interview with John G. Nicolay, June 17, 1875, *An Oral History,* 1.

tantrums of sadness: See Jesse Dubois, undated interview with Jesse W. Weik, *Herndon's Informants,* 692, and Burlingame, *Inner World,* 273, citing WHH to Jesse Weik, January 23, 1886.

"very violent temper": John T. Stuart, interview with John G. Nicolay, June 24, 1875, *An Oral History,* 15.

"one of her nervous spells": Anna Eastman Johnson, interview with A. Longfellow Fiske, *Commonweal,* March 2, 1932, reprinted in *Intimate Memories,* 134. Johnson grew up in a house near the Lincolns'.

He kept a couch: Burlingame, *Inner World,* 272, citing Victor Kutchin to the editor of the *New York Times,* August 21, 1934, in *New York Times,* August 26, 1934. Kutchin had inherited the couch from Lincoln's friend Mason Brayman.

"If she became excited": Weik, *The Real Lincoln,* 121.

Once Mary Lincoln slapped: James Matheny, interview with WHH, January 1887, *Herndon's Informants,* 713–14.

103   *"You, no doubt":* AL to Joshua F. Speed, October 22, 1846, *CWL,* vol. 1, 390–91.

"seem to derive personal gratification": Hagop S. Akiskal, "Overview of Chronic Depressions and Their Clinical Management," in Hagop Akiskal and Giovanni B. Casson, eds., *Dysthymia and the Spectrum of Chronic Depressions* (New York: Guilford Press, 1997), 24.

"The better part of one's life": AL to Joseph Gillespie, July 13 1849, *CWL*, vol. 2, 57–58.

"Every man is proud": AL, "Address Before the Wisconsin State Agricultural Society," September 30, 1859, *CWL*, vol. 3, 475.

104   *"Now if you should hear"*: AL to Richard S. Thomas, February 14, 1843, *CWL*, vol. 1, 307.

"The people of Sangamon": AL to Martin S. Morris, March 26, 1843, *CWL*, vol. 1, 320.

Baker stepped aside: Baker had assured Lincoln he would bow out by September 1845. Edward Baker Lincoln was born on March 10, 1846. Donald W. Riddle, *Lincoln Runs for Congress* (New Brunswick, N.J.: Rutgers University Press, 1948), 78, and "Family Record in Abraham Lincoln's Bible," November 4, 1842–April 4, 1853, *CWL*, vol. 1, 304.

In the general election: Riddle, *Lincoln Runs for Congress,* 177.

"Being elected to Congress": AL to Joshua F. Speed, October 22, 1846, *CWL*, vol. 1, 390–91.

"peculiar misfortune": AL to Joshua F. Speed, February 25, 1842, *CWL*, vol. 1, 280.

"At this, my heart sank": Mill's case is discussed in Mike W. Martin, "Depression: Illness, Insight, and Identity," *Philosophy, Psychiatry, and Psychology* 6, no. 4 (1999): 271–86; citing John Stuart Mill, *Autobiography* (New York: Penguin, 1989; orig. 1873), 112.

In extreme cases: Cohen, *Out of the Blue,* 118.

105   *Just days after:* Lincoln sewed up the nomination when John J. Hardin withdrew from the race on February 16, 1846. Benjamin Thomas, *Abraham Lincoln: A Biography* (New York: Knopf, 1952), 107. He first wrote to Andrew Johnston mentioning his poetry on February 24, 1846. *CWL*, vol. 1, 366.

"heart-sickening": AL to WHH, June 22, 1848, *CWL*, vol. 1, 490.

"In this troublesome world": AL to Mary Lincoln, April 16, 1848, *CWL*, vol. 1, 465.

106   *personal favorites of Lincoln's:* Lincoln famously called Clay his "beau ideal of a statesman." AL, "First Debate with Stephen A. Douglas at Ottawa, Illinois," August 21, 1858, *CWL*, vol. 3, 29. Webster, he said, was the author of the best piece of political rhetoric he knew, the "Reply to Hayne." *Herndon's Lincoln*, vol. 3, 478.

Lincoln backed Taylor: Albert J. Beveridge, *Abraham Lincoln, 1809–1858*, 2 vols. (Boston: Houghton Mifflin, 1928), vol. 1, 441–43.

"abandoned": AL, "Remarks and Resolution Introduced in the United States House of Representatives Concerning Abolition of Slavery in the District of Columbia," January 10, 1849, *CWL*, vol. 2, 22n.4.

"political suicide": *Herndon's Lincoln*, vol. 3, 306. "In fact," writes Charles Strozier, "Lincoln had not really failed in Congress. The scholarly consensus is that he performed reasonably well for a freshman Congressman. But his own sense was one of failure. He was profoundly depressed at his inability to perform up to the level of expectation of his grandiose ambitions. Unless one appreciates how much Lincoln expected of himself, his depression seems odd and misplaced. But it is in these terms — general and psychological rather than narrowly political — that Lincoln's statements to Herndon about committing political suicide in Washington make sense." Strozier, *Lincoln's Quest for Union,* 167.

"It will now mortify me deeply": AL to Josiah M. Lucas, April 25, 1849, *CWL*, vol. 2, 43–44.

trample all my wishes: For a thorough treatment of this episode, see Thomas F. Schwartz, "An Egregious Political Blunder: Justin Butterfield, Lincoln, and Illinois Whiggery," *Journal of the Abraham Lincoln Association* 8 (1986), http://jala.press.uiuc.edu/8/schwartz.html, March 31, 2005.

106   *As a consolation:* John Stuart, interview with WHH, 1865–66, *Herndon's Informants,* 479–80. Beveridge, *Abraham Lincoln,* vol. 1, 493, points out that no official record exists that the job was offered to Lincoln.

"disgusted": Charles H. Hart to WHH, March 3, 1866, *Herndon's Informants,* 223.

107   *"As you make no mention":* AL to John D. Johnston, February 23, 1850, *CWL,* vol. 2, 76–77.

Two years later: AL to John D. Johnston, January 12, 1851, *CWL,* vol. 2, 96.

"because it appeared to me": ibid.

His son did not: Rodney Davis, "Abraham Lincoln: Son and Father," Edgar S. and Ruth W. Burkhardt Lecture Series (Galesburg, Ill.: Knox College, 1997), 11.

"open souled": Mentor Graham, interview with WHH, May 29, 1865, *Herndon's Informants,* 11.

108   *"the most secretive":* WHH to J. E. Remsberg, September 10, 1887, published by H. E. Barker, 1917, copy in ISHL.

"If he had griefs": Joseph Gillespie to WHH, December 8, 1866, *Herndon's Informants,* 507–8.

"he was not": Mary Lincoln to Josiah Holland, December 4, 1865, *MTL, Life and Letters,* 293.

"His reason and his logic": James H. Matheny, interview with WHH, November 1866, *Herndon's Informants,* 431–32.

"blue spells": Gibson William Harris, "My Recollections of Abraham Lincoln," *Farm and Fireside* 27, no. 7 (January 1, 1905): 25. Harris's recollections ran serially in the magazine between December 1, 1904, and February 15, 1905.

"That Star gazing": Abner Y. Ellis to WHH, December 6, 1866, *Herndon's Informants,* 500.

Three years later: Presley Judson Edwards, "Memoirs," n.p.

109   *"I was sitting with":* Whitney, *Life on the Circuit,* 139–40.

"One morning, I was awakened": ibid., 47–48.

"The most marked": Weik, *The Real Lincoln,* 111–12.

110   *"he might be seen":* Jonathan Birch, interview with Jesse W. Weik, *Herndon's Informants,* 727–28.

"alone in his gloom": Herndon wrote a number of times about finding Lincoln depressed in the morning. See WHH to Jesse Weik, January 11, 1886, *Hidden Lincoln,* 133–34; "Lincoln's Domestic Life," Herndon-Weik Ms.

111   *"was part of his nature":* Henry Whitney to WHH, June 23, 1887, *Herndon's Informants,* 617.

"With depression": Cohen, *Out of the Blue,* 69.

7. THE VENTS OF MY MOODS AND GLOOM

112   *the "blue mass":* Lincoln took "Blue pills — blue Mass when he had a sick head ache," a symptom linked to melancholia. Ward Hill Lamon, interview with WHH, 1865–66, *Herndon's Informants,* 466. There is a big story behind Lincoln's use of this little pill. Today depression is considered a "biological brain disease," but the blue mass aimed squarely at the guts, which a long medical tradition identified as the locus of emotional and behavioral health. Indeed, accounts of Lincoln blend reports of his constipation and his melancholy. Lamon, for example, said that when Lincoln had no "passages," he got his sick headaches. John T. Stuart attributed Lincoln's blues to the fact that his liver didn't function properly. "It did not secrete bile," he told Jesse W. Weik, "and his bowels were equally inactive. It was this that made him look

so sad and depressed. That was my notion, and I remember I talked to him about it and advised him to resort to blue-mass pills which he did. This was before he went to Washington. When I came on to Congress in 1863, he told me that for a few months after his inauguration as President he continued the pill remedy, but he was finally forced to cease because it was losing its efficacy besides making him more or less irritable." Weik, *The Real Lincoln*, 112.

James Whorton, in *Inner Hygiene: Constipation and the Pursuit of Health in Modern Society* (New York: Oxford University Press, 2000), explains that laxatives were also early antidepressants. While humoral theory has lost currency, and modern psychiatry focuses on the brain, recent research on the enteric nervous system — the "brain in the gut" — has given new credibility, and complexity, to old linkages between digestion and mood. See Michael Gershon, *The Second Brain: The Scientific Basis of Gut Instinct and a Groundbreaking New Understanding of Nervous Disorders of the Stomach and Intestines* (New York: HarperCollins, 1998).

These small round pills: Details on the blue mass and the physiology of mercury are drawn from Norbert Hirschhorn, Robert G. Feldman, and Ian A. Greaves, "Abraham Lincoln's Blue Pills: Did Our Sixteenth President Suffer from Mercury Poisoning?" *Perspectives in Biology and Medicine* 44, no. 3 (Summer 2001): 315–22, and from Norbert Hirschhorn, interviews with author, September 22, 1999, and June 3, 2002. Hirschhorn argues that mercury poisoning affected Lincoln's mood and performance.

"drank his dram": Nathaniel Grigsby, interview with WHH, September 12, 1865, *Herndon's Informants*, 112.

Corneau and Diller drugstore: The extant records of Lincoln's charge account were assembled by James T. Hickey and published in *The Collected Writings of James T. Hickey* (Springfield: Illinois State Historical Society, 1984), 220–26.

In 1899, when Merck: The list of treatments also includes several kinds of acids, alcohol, arsenic, belladonna, caffeine, camphor, cannabis, chloral hydrate ("as hypnotic"), cocaine, galvanism (i.e., therapeutic application of direct-current electricity), ignatia, morphine, musk, nitrous oxide, opium ("especially useful"), phosphorus, thyraden, Turkish baths, valerian, and zinc phosphide. *Merck's 1899 Manual of the Materia Medica: Together with a Summary of the Therapeutic Indications and a Classification of Medicaments* (New York: Merck & Co., 1899; reprint, 1999), 145–46. The list also included chloroform, which, according to the physician and Lincoln biographer Milton Shutes, Lincoln used. Shutes recounts that, as president, Lincoln once went to see a dentist to have a tooth pulled. As the doctor adjusted his forceps around the tooth, Lincoln said, "Just a minute, please!" To the dentist's surprise, he reached into his pocket for a small bottle of chloroform, took a few deep inhalations, and gave the signal to go ahead. Milton Shutes, *Lincoln and the Doctors: A Medical Narrative of the Life of Abraham Lincoln* (New York: Pioneer Press, 1933), 88.

And all medicines: For a glimpse of the pharmaceutical market in Lincoln's time, see James Harvey Young, "Marketing of Patent Medicines in Lincoln's Springfield," *Pharmacy in History* 27, no. 2 (1985): 98–102.

113 *"You flaxen men": Recollected Words*, 186.

"Your distemper must be rooted": John Charles Bucknill and Daniel H. Tuke, *A Manual of Psychological Medicine* (New York: Hafner, 1968; orig. 1858), 155. For other versions of this story, see *The Complete Works of Ralph Waldo Emerson*, vol. 8 (London, 1884), 174, and Cohen, *Out of the Blue*, 152–53.

modern research: See Robert Provine, *Laughter* (New York: Viking, 2000), 189–207. "The exploration of medicinal mirth," writes Provine, "begins with the description of laughter's physiological profile . . . Laughter is the kind of powerful, bodywide act that really shakes up our physiology, a fact that has motivated speculations about its medicinal and exercise benefits since antiquity. During vigorous laughter, we take a deep breath, throw back our head, stretch the muscles of our face, jaw, throat, diaphragm, chest, abdomen, neck, back, and sometimes the limbs, and exhale in explosive, chopped 'ha-ha-ha's. When our breath is exhausted, we often take another deep breath and start the cycle all over again." Research by William Fry has shown that for elevating heart rate, one minute of vigorous laughter is the equivalent of ten minutes on a rowing machine. In a simple sense, then, as Provine writes, "laughter may provide a gentle form of aerobic exercise." There is also a connection between humor and one's ability to manage stress. "The health-sustaining factor," Provine writes, "may not be laughter itself but how laughter and humor are used to confront life's challenges." In one study, subjects best able to describe a bloody film in a humorous way also reported the least stress in their lives. In another study, subjects were shown a film of grisly industrial accidents, then told to narrate it using either a humorous or a serious style. The humor group had lower negative affect and tension. "To be effective," Provine notes, "the humorous narrative need not be funny; it's sufficient for the subjects simply to give it a try." Perhaps the most powerful research concerns the analgesic, or pain-reducing, effect of humor. Several studies have found, for example, that people can withstand higher degrees of pain when they are being simultaneously amused.

114 *The fact that people laugh:* ibid., 201.

And it flowers in groups: ibid., 25, 45.

"The core of all humor": Glenn Collins, "Toonology: Scientists Try to Find Out What's So Funny about Humor," *New York Times,* September 28, 2004.

In a study of professional: Rhoda L. Fisher and Seymour Fisher, *Pretend the World Is Funny and Forever: A Psychological Analysis of Comedians, Clowns, and Actors* (Hillsdale, N.J.: Lawrence Erlbaum Associates, 1981).

at a house-raising: Dennis F. Hanks, interview with WHH, June 13, 1865, *Herndon's Informants,* 42.

the "country boys": Joseph Gillespie to WHH, January 31, 1866, *Herndon's Informants,* 182.

115 *"Well, it may come pretty hard":* My language here closely follows Benjamin P. Thomas, "Lincoln's Humor: An Analysis," in Michael Burlingame, ed., *"Lincoln's Humor" and Other Essays* (Urbana: University of Illinois Press, 2002), 3–22, 7.

"Thomas Lincoln . . . could beat": Dennis Hanks, June 13, 1865, *Herndon's Informants,* 37. In a campaign biography, which Lincoln read and corrected, he let stand the assertion that "from his father came that knack of story-telling, which has made him so delightful among acquaintances, and so irresistible in his stump and forensic drolleries." W. D. Howells, *Life of Abraham Lincoln* (Bloomington: Indiana University Press, 1960; orig. 1860), 20.

a region known for conspicuous talent: Joseph Gillespie to WHH, December 8, 1866, *Herndon's Informants,* 508.

Though he was saturated: Thomas, "Lincoln's Humor," 16.

"dirty and smutty": H. E. Dummer, interview with WHH, 1865–66, *Herndon's Informants,* 443.

"I can contribute nothing": Ward Hill Lamon, *Recollections of Abraham Lincoln,* edited by Dorothy Lamon Teillard (Lincoln: University of Nebraska Press, 1994), 16–17.

116 *"Do you remember the story":* Moses Hampton to AL, March 30, 1849, *Lincoln Papers,* vol. 1, 169.

"It was the wit he was after": Thomas, "Lincoln's Humor," 13.

"Fun and gravity": Abner Y. Ellis to WHH, c. January 1866, *Herndon's Informants,* 161.

"The ground work": John M. Scott to WHH, February 2, 1866, *Herndon's Informants,* 193.

"has the same effect on me": *Recollected Words,* 437–38.

"If it were not for these stories": WHH to Jesse W. Weik, November 17, 1885, *Hidden Lincoln,* 104.

117 *"in which every one present"*: Robert L. Wilson to WHH, February 10, 1866, *Herndon's Informants,* 202, 205.

"Gloom and sadness": WHH to Truman H. Bartlett, February 27, 1891, transcript by LSC, Truman Bartlett Papers, Massachusetts Historical Society.

"in special times": Ward Hill Lamon, interview with WHH, 1865–66, *Herndon's Informants,* 466.

"It was wit & joke": David Davis, interview with WHH, September 20, 1866, *Herndon's Informants,* 350–51.

"all at once burst out": Frances Todd Wallace, interview with WHH, 1865–66, *Herndon's Informants,* 485–86.

"His mirth to me": John M. Scott to WHH, February 2, 1866, *Herndon's Informants,* 193.

118 *Lincoln once told*: *Recollected Words,* 81.

"A central theme": Fisher and Fisher, *Pretend the World Is Funny and Forever,* 48.

Jackie Mason's first career: ibid., 63–64.

In court once: Thomas W. S. Kidd, address before the Bar Association of Sangamon County, April 25, 1903, *Intimate Memories,* 90.

119 *He would go to his room*: John T. Stuart, interview with WHH, December 20, 1866, *Herndon's Informants,* 519.

"repeated it over and over": ibid.

"Some of Shakespeare's plays": AL to James H. Hackett, August 17, 1863, *CWL,* vol. 6, 392.

In the fall of 1849: This story is drawn from W. J. Anderson, "Reminiscence of Abraham Lincoln," February 18, 1921, ms., Chicago Historical Society. As a boy, Anderson was a music student of Lois E. Hillis, née Newhall.

120 *Then, in 1845*: Lincoln wrote of the poem, "I met it in a straggling form in a newspaper last summer, and I remember to have seen it once before, about fifteen years ago, and this is all I know about it." AL to Andrew Johnston, April 18, 1846, *CWL,* vol. 1, 378. Maurice Boyd, *William Knox and Abraham Lincoln: The Story of a Poetic Legacy* (Denver: Sage Books, 1966), supposes that the newspaper was the *Louisville Evening Post,* citing *Lincoln Lore,* April 5, 1937.

121 *"Beyond all question"*: AL to Andrew Johnston, April 18, 1846, *CWL,* vol. 1, 378.

When he was president: Boyd, *William Knox and Abraham Lincoln,* xviii, citing James Grant Wilson, "Recollections of Lincoln," *Putnam's Magazine,* February 1909, 525. Knox died of a paralytic stroke on November 12, 1825, at thirty-six. Boyd, xxxiv.

Compare Ecclesiastes 1:9: These texts are from ibid., viii.

The last two verses: Lawrence Weldon, draft for speech, August 1, 1865, *Herndon's Informants,* 89.

Then, with his other hand: The text of Knox's poem here is reproduced from the copy Lincoln presented to Lois Newhall. Boyd, *William Knox and Abraham Lincoln.*

122 *"a reflex in poetic form"*: *Reminiscences of Abraham Lincoln,* 213.

"The music of Lincoln's thought": David J. Harkness and R. Gerald McMurtry, *Lincoln's Favorite Poets* (Knoxville: University of Tennessee Press, 1959), 42.

"For pure pathos": Carpenter, *The Inner Life of Abraham Lincoln,* 58.

The one sustained effort: For details of this trip, see *Day by Day,* vol. 1, 238.

122 *"Thinking I might aid"*: AL to Andrew Johnston, April 18, 1846, *CWL*, vol. 1, 378.
"That part of the country": AL to Andrew Johnston, February 24, 1846, *CWL*, vol. 1, 367.

123 *"If I read a book"*: Emily Dickinson to T. W. Higginson, August 16, 1870, in Thomas H. Johnson, ed., *The Letters of Emily Dickinson*, 3 vols. (Cambridge: Belknap Press of Harvard University Press, 1958), vol. 2, 473–74.
"My childhood's home": The text of Lincoln's poems is reproduced from *CWL*, vol. 1, 367–70, 378–79, and 385–86. The poems were published in the *Quincy Whig*, May 5, 1847, with the two cantos collected as "The Return," with the subtitles "Part I — Reflection" and "Part II — The Maniac." AL to Andrew Johnston, February 25, 1847, *CWL*, vol. 1, 392n.3.
Yet the typical course: A piece found in the Holland Papers, presumably written by Josiah G. Holland, begins:

> My early home! Fond memory loves
> To linger by thy hallowed shrine,
> Where joys that only childhood knows,
> Life's brightest, gayest joys were mine.

The poem meditates on the loss of "friends of my early days" and includes the image of a "lonely tomb" and a "shadowy past." But at the end, the poem resolves that these influences "shall cheer me to my latest day . . . And each intruding fear allay."

124 *"the perceptions were sometimes"*: Joseph Gillespie to WHH, January 31, 1866, *Herndon's Informants*, 185.
"The very spot": "This stanza, apparently written for this letter only, does not appear in the manuscript containing both cantos." *CWL*, vol. 1, 386n.5.

125 *"I fear I shall meet"*: WHH to Jesse W. Weik, February 6, 1887, *Hidden Lincoln*, 167.

8. ITS PRECISE SHAPE AND COLOR

126 *"What man actually needs"*: Frankl, *Man's Search for Meaning*, 127.

127 *"Lincoln was speculating"*: WHH to Ward Hill Lamon, March 6, 1870, transcription by LSC.
"Slavery is founded": AL, "Speech at Peoria, Illinois," October 16, 1854, *CWL*, vol. 2, 255.

128 *the United States elbowed:* The Gadsden Purchase in the early 1850s, by which the nation acquired additional land in present-day New Mexico and Arizona, brought America to its present borders, excluding Alaska and Hawaii.

129 *"acts of aggression and encroachment"*: John C. Calhoun, "The Southern Address," in Richard K. Crallé, ed., *The Works of John C. Calhoun*, 6 vols. (Columbia, S.C.: A. S. Johnston, 1851), vol. 6, 290–313.
The old lion: McPherson, *Battle Cry of Freedom*, 70–71.
This prompted Harriet Beecher Stowe: James M. McPherson, introduction to Harriet Beecher Stowe, *Uncle Tom's Cabin* (New York: Library of America, 1991; orig. 1852), xi.
"We went to bed one night": Albert J. Von Frank, *The Trials of Anthony Burns: Freedom and Slavery in Emerson's Boston* (Cambridge: Harvard University Press, 1998), 207.
"became the hallmark": McPherson, *Battle Cry of Freedom*, 76.
"both injustice and bad policy": AL and Dan Stone, "Protest in Illinois Legislature on Slavery," *CWL*, vol. 1, 75.

"*evil*": AL to Williamson Durley, October 3, 1845, *CWL*, vol. 1, 347.

"*the one* great *question*": Discussing the political consequences of President Taylor's death, Lincoln said, "I fear that the one *great* question of the day, is not so likely to be partially acquiesced in by the different sections of the Union, as it would have been, could Gen. Taylor have been spared to us." This refers to the debate over the Compromise of 1850, which centered on slavery. AL, "Eulogy on Zachary Taylor," July 25, 1850, *CWL*, vol. 2, 89.

130   "*raise a hell of a storm*": Beveridge, *Abraham Lincoln*, vol. 2, 182n.2, citing a conversation between Douglas and Kentucky senator Archibald Dixon.

"*[Douglas] took us by surprise*": AL, "Speech at Peoria, Illinois," October 16, 1854, *CWL*, vol. 2, 282.

131   "*safety valve*": Eric Foner, *Free Soil, Free Labor, Free Men: The Ideology of the Republican Party Before the Civil War* (New York: Oxford University Press, 1970), 27.

In part because: Beveridge (*Abraham Lincoln*, vol. 2, 67) writes, "When Lincoln came home after his first session in Congress, scarcely a town or hamlet in Illinois but was sending men and families to join the long caravans plodding across the plains toward the sunset." As the *Quincy Whig* reported on February 19, 1850: "The fever is extending and increasing . . . affecting all classes . . . young men, middle-aged and old alike."

"*If we do not exclude*": Foner, *Free Soil*, 57.

Lincoln's own Illinois: The constitution was approved by the voters in March 1848. Kathryn M. Harris, "Generations of Pride: African American Timeline," www.illinois history.gov/lib/GenPrideAfAm.htm, March 26, 2005.

The state's "black laws": James M. McPherson, *The Negro's Civil War: How American Negroes Felt and Acted During the War for the Union* (New York: Pantheon, 1965), 7, citing *Liberator*, July 13, 1860.

On his train ride home: Robert W. Johannsen, *Stephen A. Douglas* (Urbana: University of Illinois Press, 1977; orig. 1973), 451.

132   "*It is estimated*": Details of Springfield during the fair week are drawn from the *Illinois State Journal*, October 1–6, 1854.

a number of other prominent: Herndon's *Lincoln*, vol. 2, 371.

"*It was a marked face*": Horace White, "Abraham Lincoln in 1854," *Putnam's Magazine*, March 1909, 724.

133   "*You know I am never sanguine*": AL to John T. Stuart, January 20, 1840, *CWL*, vol. 1, 184.

"*The most trying thing*": Noah Brooks, "The Military Prospect," June 14, 1864 (published in the *Sacramento Daily Union*, July 9, 1864), *Lincoln Observed*, 113.

"*ornamented with beauty*": Herndon's *Lincoln*, vol. 3, 591.

134   "*learned helplessness*": Learned helplessness theory originated with research by the psychologist Martin Seligman in the late 1960s and is described in his book *Helplessness: On Depression, Development, and Death* (San Francisco: W. H. Freeman, 1975). In Seligman's experiments, dogs given shocks were found to "give up" and accept further painful stimuli, even when they had a means of escaping them. This led to the idea that depression comes about when people who had been subject to painful early experiences give up, physically and emotionally, expecting pain or dismay even when they have the opportunity to alleviate it. An interesting footnote to this experiment is that five percent of the dogs passively accepted shock without having been put through the original trauma.

"*depressive realism*": Details of this experiment are drawn largely from L. B. Alloy and L. Y. Abramson, "Judgment of Contingency in Depressed and Nondepressed Students: Sadder but Wiser?" *Journal of Experimental Psychology: General* 108, no. 4

(December 1979): 441–85. For a summary, see L. B. Alloy, "Depressive Realism: Sadder but Wiser?" *Harvard Mental Health Letter* 11 (1995): 4–5.

135 *"The perception of reality":* David A. Jopling, "'Take Away the Life-Lie . . .': Positive Illusions and Creative Self-Deception," *Philosophical Psychology* 9, no. 4 (December 1996): 525, citing Marie Johoda, *Current Concepts of Positive Mental Health* (New York: Basic Books, 1958), 6.

"major affective disorder (pleasant type)": Richard P. Bentall, "A Proposal to Classify Happiness as a Psychiatric Disorder," *Journal of Medical Ethics* 18 (1992): 94.

136 *People actively seek to filter:* As the psychologist Tom Pyszczynski points out, many influential theories come to this conclusion. Psychoanalytic theory holds that "a great deal of ordinary thought and behavior functions to keep painful or unacceptable emotions out of consciousness." Similarly, "cognitive dissonance theory" suggests that people change their ideas to bring them in line with their behavior, to reduce the tension that arises when their view of the world and their behavior are out of sync. "Terror management theory" explains many social behaviors as strategies to shield people from the anxiety that would come if they saw their real vulnerability. "The point that all of these theories have in common," Pyszczynski writes, "is that many common, nonpathological forms of social behavior function to keep unacceptable emotions out of consciousness." Tom Pyszczynski et al., "Emotional Expression and the Reduction of Motivated Cognitive Bias: Evidence from Cognitive Dissonance and Distancing from Victims' Paradigms," *Journal of Personality and Social Psychology* 64, no. 2 (February 1993): 177.

"If most of us": William T. Vollmann, *Rising Up, Rising Down: Some Thoughts on Violence, Freedom and Urgent Means* (New York: Ecco Press, 2004), 5, citing Aldous Huxley, *The Perennial Philosophy.*

"Throughout history": Peter D. Kramer, *Listening to Prozac* (New York: Viking, 1993), 165.

"The intensest light": Kay Redfield Jamison, *Touched with Fire: Manic-Depressive Illness and the Artistic Temperament* (New York: Free Press, 1993), 216.

137 *He could afford these luxuries:* Johannsen, *Stephen A. Douglas,* 211.

"thin, high-pitched falsetto": White, "Lincoln in 1854," 724.

"Thus, the thing is hid away": AL, "Speech at Peoria, Illinois," October 16, 1854, *CWL,* vol. 2, 274.

138 *"the great struggle of life":* AL to George C. Latham, July 22, 1860, *CWL,* vol. 4, 87.

"now when we have grown fat": AL to George Robertson, August 15, 1855, *CWL,* vol. 2, 318.

139 *A peaceful, lawful:* "I do not suppose that in the most peaceful way ultimate extinction would occur in less than a hundred years at the least; but that it will occur in the best way for both races in God's own good time, I have no doubt." AL, "Fourth Debate with Stephen A. Douglas at Charleston, Illinois," September 18, 1858, *CWL,* vol. 3, 181.

"There is a moral fitness": AL, "Eulogy on Henry Clay," July 6, 1852, *CWL,* vol. 2, 126.

In the world Lincoln saw: As late as 1900, no country in the world had a government elected by universal adult suffrage. At the end of the century, 119 countries — sixty-two percent of the nations in the world — had universal suffrage. Freedom House, "Democracy's Century: A Survey of Global Political Change in the 20th Century," http://freedomhouse.org/reports/century.html, March 24, 2005.

140 *"If destruction be our lot":* AL, "Address Before the Young Men's Lyceum of Springfield, Illinois," January 27, 1838, *CWL,* vol. 1, 109.

For the time being: There has been, of late, a great debate between those who assail Lincoln as a racist and those who defend him as a devoted servant of civil rights, albeit one limited by practical necessity. In fact, Lincoln considered full equality to be an absurdity. "Negro equality!" he wrote to himself at one point. "Fudge!! How long, in the government of a God, great enough to make and maintain this Universe, shall there continue knaves to vend, and fools to gulp, so low a piece of demagougeism as this." AL, "Fragments: Notes for Speeches," c. September 1859?, *CWL*, vol. 3, 399. The demagoguery lay in posing a scenario that was far from the public sentiment. All but a small minority considered the prospect of a multiracial society with full equality to be out of the question. Lincoln at times compared Negro slaves in the United States to Hebrew slaves in ancient Egypt. The fighting cry, then, was "Let my people go," not "Let my people stay on terms of equality with you."

This, to Lincoln: Lincoln used this imagery, warning in 1859 against Republicans' joining with Stephen Douglas. "All who deprecate that consummation, and yet are seduced into his support, do but cut their own throats." AL to W. H. Wells, January 8, 1859, *CWL*, vol. 3, 349.

But what Lincoln suspected: For a thorough treatment of the politics of the Kansas-Nebraska Act, see Beveridge, *Abraham Lincoln*, vol. 2, 167–217.

141 *"At that time":* Samuel C. Parks, statement for WHH, 1866?, *Herndon's Informants*, 538.

Even years later: AL to Norman Judd, December 9, 1859, *CWL*, vol. 3, 505.

When the Illinois General Assembly: For a detailed treatment of this election, see Matthew Pinsker, "Senator Abraham Lincoln," *Journal of the Abraham Lincoln Association* 14, no. 2 (Summer 1993), http://jala.press.uiuc.edu/14.2/pinsker.html, March 31, 2005.

"It was agreed that": Reminiscences of Abraham Lincoln, 21.

"I have really got it": AL to Joseph Gillespie, December 1, 1854, *CWL*, vol. 2, 290.

At various times: AL to Elihu B. Washburne, February 9, 1855, *CWL*, vol. 2, 304.

To his supporters' dismay: "I remember that judge S. T. Logan gave up Mr Lincoln with great reluctance," Joseph Gillespie recalled. "He begged hard to try him on one or two ballots more, but Mr Lincoln urged us not to risk it longer." Joseph Gillespie to WHH, September 19, 1866, *Herndon's Informants*, 344.

"cut and mortified": Joseph Gillespie to Isaac Arnold, April 22, 1880, Isaac A. Arnold Papers, Chicago Historical Society.

142 *"There is no event":* Reminiscences of Abraham Lincoln, 22.

"agony": AL to Elihu B. Washburne, February 9, 1855, *CWL*, vol. 2, 304.

"I could not . . . let": AL to William H. Henderson, February 21, 1855, *CWL*, vol. 2, 307.

143 *"This frustration of Lincoln's ambition":* Herndon's Lincoln, vol. 2, 377–78.

He had owned: Pen Bogert, slave data on Joshua F. Speed and on James Speed, in the vertical file, "Farmington — African Americans," Filson Historical Society Library, 1997.

146 *"the people of the South":* AL, "Fragment on Sectionalism," c. July 23, 1856, *CWL*, vol. 2, 351–52.

147 *"tragic optimist":* Frankl, *Man's Search for Meaning*, 162.

"abundance of man's heart": "Repeal the Missouri compromise — repeal all compromises — repeal the declaration of independence — repeal all past history, you still can not repeal human nature. It still will be the abundance of man's heart, that slavery extension is wrong; and out of the abundance of his heart, his mouth will continue to speak." AL, "Speech at Peoria, Illinois," October 16, 1854, *CWL*, vol. 2, 271.

148 *"crimes of Kansas":* Charles Sumner, "The Crime Against Kansas: The Apologies for the Crime; the True Remedy," delivered before the U.S. Senate, May 19–20, 1856. Excerpts from this famous speech are online at http://www.sewanee.edu/faculty/Willis/Civil_War/documents/Crime.html, April 1, 2005.

"While all seems dead": Herndon's Lincoln, vol. 2, 386.

149 *"With me, the race":* AL, "Fragment on Stephen A. Douglas, December 1856?, *CWL*, vol. 2, 383.

Just after President Buchanan: The case actually pitted Dred Scott against John *Sanford,* but the slave owner's name was misspelled in the records.

150 *"What does the New-York Tribune":* AL to Lyman Trumbull, December 28, 1857, *CWL*, vol. 2, 430.

"The Republican standard": Herndon's Lincoln, vol. 2, 395, citing WHH to AL, March 24, 1858.

"a veritable dodger": Herndon's Lincoln, vol. 2, p. 391.

In other words: AL, "Address at Cooper Institute, New York City," February 27, 1860, *CWL*, vol. 3, 538.

"evil genius": AL, "Second Debate with Stephen A. Douglas at Freeport, Illinois," August 27, 1858, *CWL*, vol. 3, 44.

"What will Douglas do now?": AL, "Fragments: Notes for Speeches," c. September 1859, *CWL*, vol. 3, 397–98.

151 *Two of the main:* Granville Sharp died before seeing any victories in the antislavery fight. William Wilberforce was on his deathbed when the slavery abolition bill passed the House of Commons; he died a month before it became law. See Adam Hochschild, *Bury the Chains: Prophets and Rebels in the Fight to Free an Empire's Slaves* (Boston: Houghton Mifflin, 2005).

"I can not but regard": AL, "Fragment on the Struggle Against Slavery," c. July 1858, *CWL*, vol. 2, 482.

"Whoever heard": Reminiscences of Abraham Lincoln, 303.

"strike home to the minds": Herndon's Lincoln, vol. 2, 400.

"If we could first know": AL, "'A House Divided': Speech at Springfield, Illinois," June 16, 1858, *CWL*, vol. 2, 461–62.

152 *Freeport Doctrine:* For a cogent account of this exchange, see McPherson, *Battle Cry of Freedom,* 184.

"I am after larger game": Carl Sandburg, *Abraham Lincoln: The Prairie Years,* 2 vols. (New York: Harcourt, Brace, 1926), vol. 2, 155.

153 *"when these poor tongues":* AL, "Seventh and Last Debate with Stephen A. Douglas at Alton, Illinois," October 15, 1858, *CWL*, vol. 2, 315.

"Think nothing of me": AL, "Speech at Lewistown, Illinois," August 17, 1858, *CWL*, vol. 2, 547.

"I am not, nor ever have been": AL, "Fourth Debate with Stephen A. Douglas at Charleston, Illinois," September 18, 1858, *CWL*, vol. 3, 145.

A growing number of critics: A charged presentation of Lincoln as a racist, Lerone Bennett, Jr.'s *Forced into Glory: Abraham Lincoln's White Dream* (Chicago: Johnson Publishing, 2000) tells of a Lincoln who liked "nigger" jokes, found blackface minstrel shows amusing, and defended slaveowners in court. Bennett finds Lincoln more an enemy than a friend to African Americans. For one response, see William Lee Miller, *Lincoln's Virtues: An Ethical Biography* (New York: Knopf, 2002).

154 *"There is no reason":* AL, "First Debate with Stephen A. Douglas at Ottawa, Illinois," August 21, 1858, *CWL*, vol. 3, 16.

"I am a living witness": AL, "Speech to One Hundred Sixty-sixth Ohio Regiment," August 22, 1864, *CWL*, vol. 7, 512.

"were utterly unconscious": AL, "Second Lecture on Discoveries and Inventions," February 11, 1859, *CWL*, vol. 3, 362–63.

155 *Reports of these spells:* Many of the most dramatic reports of Lincoln's gloomy spells came from men who only met him after 1854 — including, for example, Jonathan Birch, Lawrence Weldon, Joseph Wilson Fifer, and Henry C. Whitney.

What had looked like a sad: Compare Gibson Harris's view of "blue spells" in the mid-1840s, which could be easily broken by "a very slight thing," with Jonathan Birch's view in the late 1850s, of a man sitting "for hours at a time defying the interruption of even his closest friends. No one ever thought of breaking the spell by speech; for by his moody silence and abstraction he had thrown about him a barrier so dense and impenetrable no one dared to break through." Jonathan Birch, interview with Jesse Weik, 1887?, *Herndon's Informants,* 727–28.

"The pictures we see": Stevens, *Reporter's Lincoln,* 163.

"Abe Lincoln is up from Springfield": John H. Widmer, n.d., Tarbell Papers.

156 *"Biographies tend conventionally":* Menand made this point in an essay that examines a supposed crisis and recovery in the life of William James. James's biographers have long assumed that an episode of panic fear — in which, he wrote, "suddenly there fell upon me without any warning, just as if it came out of the darkness, a horrible fear of my own existence" — preceded a diary entry in which James resolved to believe in free will. The appeal of the interpretation is undeniable: James brought his youthful melancholia under the control of his "resolution and self-confidence"; he got sick and got better. However, as Menand demonstrates, no good evidence exists to link the two episodes. The conclusion was simply an assumption that one biographer (James's son) made, a second biographer (Ralph Barton Perry) repeated, and others accepted as truth. As with many melancholics, William James had many moments of relief, but no final recovery. Every February, he had what he called an "annual collapse." "The fact is," he wrote in 1901, when he was fifty-nine years old, "that my nervous system is utter trash, and always was so. It has been a hard burden to bear all these years, the more so as I have seemed to others perfectly well; and now it is on top and 'I' am under." Louis Menand, "William James and the Case of the Epileptic Patient," *New York Review of Books,* December 17, 1998.

But owing to favorable: Thomas, *Abraham Lincoln,* 194.

157 *"I never saw any man":* Whitney, *Life on the Circuit,* 27.

"The emotions of defeat": AL to John J. Crittenden, November 4, 1858, *CWL,* vol. 3, 335.

"The fight must go on": AL to Henry Asbury, November 19, 1858, *CWL,* vol. 3, 339.

"Though I now sink out of view": AL to Anson G. Henry, November 19, 1858, *CWL,* vol. 3, 339.

"I hope and believe": AL to Charles H. Ray, November 20, 1858, *CWL,* vol. 3, 342.

"You are feeling badly": AL to Norman B. Judd, November 16, 1858, *CWL,* vol. 3, 337.

"Some of you will be successful": AL, "Address Before the Wisconsin State Agricultural Society, Milwaukee, Wisconsin," September 30, 1859, *CWL,* vol. 3, 481–82.

9. THE FIERY TRIAL THROUGH WHICH WE PASS

159 *like a wire cable:* Harriet Beecher Stowe, "Abraham Lincoln," *Living Age,* January 2, 1864, 284.

"steel and velvet": A recording of Sandburg's address to a joint session of Congress on February 12, 1959, the 150th anniversary of Lincoln's birth, is available at the State University of New York at Albany's "Talking History" Web site: http://talkinghistory.org.

"My model will be": Leston Havens, *Learning to Be Human* (Reading, Mass.: Addison-Wesley, 1994), 17.

"I must, in candor": AL to Thomas J. Pickett, April 16, 1859, *CWL,* vol. 3, 377.

160 *Lincoln actually asked:* Gerald M. Capers, *Stephen A. Douglas: Defender of the Union* (Boston: Little, Brown, 1959), 182–83.

160 *"I, John Brown"*: F. B. Sanborn, *The Life and Letters of John Brown* (Boston: Roberts Brothers, 1891), 620.

"The death of no man": Facts in this paragraph follow McPherson, *Battle Cry of Freedom*, 209–11.

On Saturday, February 25: Details in this paragraph are from Harold Holzer, *Lincoln at Cooper Union: The Speech That Made Abraham Lincoln President* (New York: Simon and Schuster, 2004), 64–65.

161 *"woe-begone look"*: H. C. Bowen, "Recollections of Abraham Lincoln," *New York Independent,* February 11, 1909, 292.

a special urgency to revise: Richard C. McCormick recalled Lincoln saying that he "must review his address if it was to be delivered in New York," for what he had prepared for Beecher's church "might not be altogether appropriate to a miscellaneous political audience." Holzer, *Lincoln at Cooper Union*, 73.

162 *"unbecoming"*: Charles C. Nott, statement in George Haven Putnam, *Abraham Lincoln: The People's Leader in the Struggle for National Existence* (New York: G. P. Putnam, 1909), 220.

"I had a feeling of pity": Noah Brooks, *Abraham Lincoln and the Downfall of American Slavery* (New York: G. P. Putnam, 1894), 186–87.

"Our fathers, who framed": This quotation from Douglas, and the facts and quotations from Lincoln that follow, are in AL, "Address at Cooper Institute, New York City," February 27, 1860, *CWL*, vol. 3, 523–31.

163 *As Lincoln drew to the end*: Brooks, *Abraham Lincoln and the Downfall of American Slavery*, 186–87.

Four city newspapers: Holzer, *Lincoln at Cooper Union*, 149.

"was one of the happiest": Robert S. Harper, *Lincoln and the Press* (New York: McGraw-Hill, 1951), 46–47.

164 *Whisked off*: Holzer, *Lincoln at Cooper Union*, 152. The Athenaeum Club was on the site of the present-day Judge Building, 110 Fifth Avenue. "New York Songlines: Virtual Walking Tours of Manhattan Streets, 5th Avenue," http://home.nyc.rr.com/jkn/nysong lines/5av.htm, October 13, 2004.

"seemed a sad and lonely man": Putnam, *Abraham Lincoln*, 221.

"I am not sure": A. J. Dittenhoefer, *How We Elected Lincoln: Personal Recollections of Lincoln and Men of His Time* (New York: Harper & Brothers, 1916), 14–18.

"I have been unable": AL to Mary Lincoln, March 4, 1860, *CWL*, vol. 3, 555.

"Creativity doesn't happen": Mihaly Csikszentmihalyi, *Creativity: Flow and the Psychology of Discovery and Invention* (New York: HarperCollins, 1996), 23.

"Some of the people": ibid., 25–26.

165 *complexity*: ibid., 57.

"There is a great deal": Kay Redfield Jamison, *Touched with Fire: Manic-Depressive Illness and the Artistic Temperament* (New York: Free Press, 1993), 97.

One in-depth study . . . Another well-known study: ibid., 59–60, 72–73.

John Quincy Adams: P. C. Nagel, *John Quincy Adams: A Public Life, a Private Life* (New York: Knopf, 1997); *Charles Darwin*: John Bowlby, *Charles Darwin: A New Life* (New York: W. W. Norton, 1991); *Emily Dickinson*: Jane Donahue Eberwein, ed., *An Emily Dickinson Encyclopedia* (Westport, Conn.: Greenwood Press, 1998), 137; *Benjamin Disraeli*: Stanley Weintraub, *Disraeli: A Biography* (New York: Dutton, 1993); *William James*: Linda Simon, *Genuine Reality: A Life of William James* (New York: Harcourt Brace, 1998); *William Tecumseh Sherman*: Nassir Ghaemi, "General Sherman's Illness," unpublished ms.; *Leo Tolstoy*: Leo Nikolaevich Tolstoy, *My Confession* (New York: W. W. Norton, 1983); *Queen Victoria*: M. Reid, *Ask Sir James: Sir*

James Reid, Personal Physician to Queen Victoria and Physician-in-Ordinary to Three Monarchs (London: Hodder and Stoughton, 1987).

166   *"This had never happened before"*: Gary Hart, *Right from the Start: A Chronicle of the McGovern Campaign* (New York: Quadrangle, 1973), 255; for the Eagleton affair, 255–94. See also Gordon L. Weil, *The Long Shot: George McGovern Runs for President* (New York: W. W. Norton, 1973), and Haynes Johnson's series in the *Washington Post*, December 3–6, 1972.

When Congress was considering: David Greenberg, *Nixon's Shadow: The History of an Image* (New York: W. W. Norton, 2003), 263–64.

"Consulting a psychiatrist": ibid.

"technical terms": Hart, *Right from the Start*, 253.

"psychosis": The 1968 *Diagnostic and Statistical Manual of Mental Disorders* defined psychosis as any break with reality, including illogical thinking of the sort common in depression.

what sank him: Eagleton's electroshock had a conspicuous role in the press coverage of his revelations. The *New York Times* headline on July 26, 1972, read: "Eagleton Tells of Shock Therapy on Two Occasions."

"is continuing to feed": Jill Lawrence, "As Dean Forges Ahead, His Temperament Gets Closer Look," *USA Today*, November 12, 2003.

167   *Even as we practically drown:* Personal traits of political candidates have always been relevant, but the modern focus on "character" has taken a bizarre turn, beginning with the presidency of Richard Nixon. "The term itself," writes David Greenberg, "previously referred to a vast range of attributes desirable in a leader: courage, generosity, honesty, decency. Now, the word, as it got thrown about, took on a meaning that was at once both more narrow (in that it focused on the skeletons in one's closet) and more broad (in that it failed to distinguish between trivial and potentially dangerous shortcomings)." Greenberg, *Nixon's Shadow*, 265. As Greenberg points out, one big factor driving the change has been the nuclear threat. Before 1945, the president had serious responsibilities, but ones befitting someone with human strengths and weaknesses. In the nuclear age, the president became the man with his finger on the nuclear button, who in a moment could destroy the world.

"sometimes must have": Bob Dylan, "It's Alright, Ma (I'm Only Bleeding)," in Bob Dylan, *Lyrics 1962–1985* (New York: Knopf, 1992), 177.

"passing easily from grave to gay": Typescript of newspaper clipping, February 11, 1860, Jesse W. Fell Papers, Illinois Historical Survey. Written by Joseph J. Lewis, this piece was widely reprinted and became the basis for the first three Lincoln campaign biographies in book form. Harold K. Sage, "Jesse W. Fell and the Lincoln Autobiography," *Journal of the Abraham Lincoln Association* 3 (1981), http://jala.press.uiuc.edu/3/sage .html, March 31, 2005.

"placed him under guard": John Hill, "A Romance of Reality," *Menard Axis*, February 15, 1862, *Herndon's Informants*, 25. Hill was a political opponent of Lincoln's, which makes his conclusion all the more striking.

"Many of Lincoln's advisors": Donald, *Lincoln*, 242. Donald is the source for the quotes from Knapp (citing "Praise for the 'Most Available Candidate,'" *Journal of the Illinois State Historical Society* 71 [February 1978], 72), and Davis (citing Davis to John Wentworth, September 25, 1859, David Davis Papers, ISHL).

168   *The convention site:* "The Republican Convention of 1860," *Chicago History* 5, no. 11 (Spring 1960): 321–22.

he had locked up: Guelzo, *Redeemer President*, 243.

as Lincoln's manager: Leonard Swett, "David Davis," address to the Bar Association of Illinois, copy in Chicago Historical Society, 15–16. "It is my belief," Swett wrote, "if all the other causes had existed as they did exist, and Judge Davis had not lived, Mr. Lincoln would not have been nominated."

168 *"Things are working":* telegrams in the Abraham Lincoln Papers, Library of Congress.

169 *To prevail in November:* McPherson, *Battle Cry of Freedom,* 188.

"no nervousness": Charles S. Zane, "Lincoln As I Knew Him," *Sunset,* October 1912, 438.

"I think the chances": AL to Anson G. Henry, July 4, 1860, *CWL,* vol. 4, 82.

170 *"careworn":* Henry Villard, *Lincoln on the Eve of '61,* edited by Harold G. and Oswald Garrison Villard (New York: Knopf, 1941), 76.

"in good spirits": Charles M. Segal, ed., *Conversations with Lincoln* (New York: G. P. Putnam, 1961), 38. Weed's piece, originally published in the *New York Times,* February 14, 1932, was written in 1882, apparently from detailed notes made at the time of his interview with Lincoln.

"Let there be": AL to Lyman Trumbull, December 10, 1860, *CWL,* vol. 4, 149–50.

"If there is no struggle": Frederick Douglass, "West India Emancipation," August 3, 1857, in Robert James Branham and Philip S. Foner, eds., *Lift Every Voice: African American Oratory, 1787–1900* (Tuscaloosa: University of Alabama Press, 1998), 310, citing *Two Speeches by Frederick Douglass, One on West India Emancipation . . . and the Other on the Dred Scott Decision . . .* (Rochester, 1857).

If the losers: "No popular government," Lincoln said, "can long survive a marked precedent, that those who carry an election, can only save the government from immediate destruction, by giving up the main point, upon which the people gave the election." AL, "Message to Congress in Special Session," July 4, 1861, *CWL,* vol. 4, 440.

171 *"We must settle this question":* Michael Burlingame and John R. Turner Ettlinger, eds., *Inside Lincoln's White House: The Complete Civil War Diary of John Hay* (Carbondale: Southern Illinois University Press, 1999), 20.

"Mediocre presidents": Matthew Pinsker, interview with author, April 18, 2005.

"notions of freedom": Horace Greeley, *The American Conflict: A History of the Great Rebellion in the United States of America, 1860–64,* 2 vols. (Chicago: O. D. Case, 1866), vol. 1, 368.

"The present administration": Joseph Gillespie, "A Period of Troubled Waiting for Mr. Buchanan's Successor," *Intimate Memories,* 333. This recollection of Gillespie's, based on notes of a visit with Lincoln in January 1861, was first published in the *Cincinnati Commercial Gazette* in 1888.

On February 11, 1861: Sources for the departure scene include Villard, *Lincoln on the Eve of '61,* 71; *Illinois State Journal,* February 12, 1861; Victor Searcher, *The Farewell to Lincoln* (New York: Abingdon Press, 1965), 1, 6; and Weik, *The Real Lincoln,* 306–12.

172 *"My friends":* AL, "Farewell Address at Springfield, Illinois, A. Version," February 11, 1861, *CWL,* vol. 4, 190.

"one term in the lower house": AL, "Brief Autobiography," June 15?, 1858, *CWL,* vol. 2, 459.

He'd had barely a year: AL, "Autobiography Written for John L. Scripps," c. June 1860, *CWL,* vol. 4, 62.

"a plain working man": Stowe, "Abraham Lincoln," 283.

"The President-elect": Paul Revere Frothingham, *Edward Everett, Orator and Statesman* (Boston: Houghton Mifflin, 1925), 414.

"He was tall and ungainly": Henry Watterson, "When Douglas Held Lincoln's Hat," *Lincoln among His Friends,* 286.

173 *"A husband and wife":* AL, "First Inaugural Address — Final Text," March 4, 1861, *CWL,* vol. 4, 262–70.

"*In* your *hands*": AL, "First Inaugural Address — First Edition and Revisions," March 4, 1861, *CWL*, vol. 4, 261.

written out his suggestion: ibid., 261–62n.99.

175 *"were so great":* Helen Nicolay, "Characteristic Anecdotes of Lincoln," *Century Magazine*, August 1912, 699. Nicolay cites a letter from John G. Nicolay, dated July 3, 1861, which refers to a conversation between AL and O. H. Browning.

"the dumps," "keeled over": Sam Ward to S.L.M. Barlow, March 31, 1861, in Samuel L. M. Barlow Papers, Huntington Library. Ward, a Washington power broker, wrote: "'Abe' is getting heartily sick of 'the situation' — It is hard for the Captain of a new Steamer to 'work his passage.' On Friday he confessed to a friend of mine that he was in 'the dumps' & yesterday Mrs Lincoln told Russell that her husband had keeled over with sick headache for the first time in years." "Sick headache" likely referred to mental trouble.

"found the duty": AL, "Message to Congress in Special Session," July 4, 1861, *CWL*, vol. 4, 440.

called for 75,000 volunteers: AL, "Proclamation Calling Militia and Convening Congress," April 15, 1861, *CWL*, vol. 4, 332.

More than 620,000: This figure includes 360,000 Yankees and at least 260,000 Rebels. Notes James M. McPherson, "The number of southern civilians who died as a direct or indirect result of the war cannot be known; what can be said is that the Civil War's cost in American lives was as great as in all of the nation's other wars combined through Vietnam." *Battle Cry of Freedom*, 854.

With a spyglass: Donald, *Lincoln*, 306.

176 *Elmer Ellsworth:* See Ruth Painter Randall, *Colonel Elmer Ellsworth: A Biography of Lincoln's Friend and First Hero of the Civil War* (Boston: Little, Brown, 1960).

"Excuse me, but I cannot talk": New York Herald, May 25, 1861.

"open souled": Mentor Graham, interview with WHH, May 29, 1865, *Herndon's Informants*, 11.

177 *Lincoln called for the enlistment:* McPherson, *Battle Cry of Freedom*, 348.

"A kind of shiver": ibid., 362.

"with bowed head": Reminiscences of Abraham Lincoln, 172–74.

Baker's death smote: Noah Brooks, "Personal Recollections of Abraham Lincoln," *Harper's New Monthly Magazine*, July 1865, 228.

probably typhoid: Baker, *Mary Todd Lincoln*, 208–9.

178 *Elizabeth Keckly:* Though her book says "Keckley," she signed her name "Keckly." Fleischner, *Mrs. Lincoln and Mrs. Keckly*, 7.

"It is hard": Elizabeth Keckley, *Behind the Scenes, or, Thirty Years a Slave, and Four Years in the White House* (New York: Oxford University Press, 1988; orig. 1868), 103.

"He had a Sad Nature": LeGrand B. Cannon to WHH, October 7, 1889, *Herndon's Informants*, 679.

"look of depression": Edward Dicey, *Spectator of America*, edited by Herbert Mitgang (Athens: University of Georgia Press, 1971.; orig. *Six Months in the Federal States* [London: Macmillan, 1863], 90–92.

"sense enough to perceive": ibid., 91.

179 *hang himself from a tree:* Robert L. Wilson to WHH, February 10, 1866, *Herndon's Informants*, 206–7. Wilson is the same man to whom Lincoln confessed, in his late twenties, that he wouldn't carry a pocket knife for fear he might use it to kill himself.

"I expect to maintain": AL to William H. Seward, June 28, 1862, *CWL*, vol. 5, 292.

"The scenes on this field": McPherson, *Battle Cry of Freedom*, 413. "Shiloh," McPherson writes, "launched the country onto the floodtide of total war."

A compact, red-headed: Thomas, *Abraham Lincoln*, 284–85.

180 *"I was as nearly"*: *Recollected Words*, 137, citing Henry C. Deming, *Eulogy of Abraham Lincoln* (Hartford, Conn.: A. N. Clark, 1865).

"were it not": AL to William H. Seward, June 28, 1862, *CWL*, vol. 5, 292.

"idiot," "baboon": These and the other insults are in McPherson, *Battle Cry of Freedom*, 364.

"I am thwarted and deceived": ibid., 359.

"Perhaps McClellan's career": ibid.

Suspicious of her: Fleischner, *Mrs. Lincoln and Mrs. Keckly*, 209.

a term coined: Baker, *Mary Todd Lincoln*, 180.

But she quickly showed: R. Gerald McMurtry and Mark E. Neely, *The Insanity File: The Case of Mary Todd Lincoln* (Carbondale: Southern Illinois University Press, 1993), 5.

"that he was constantly": O. H. Browning, interview with John G. Nicolay, June 17, 1875, *An Oral History*, 3.

181 *"paroxysms of convulsive weeping"*: Randall, *Mary Lincoln*, 260.

"Mother, do you see": Keckley, *Behind the Scenes*, 104. On another occasion, Lincoln told William S. Wood, the commissioner of public buildings, that "the caprices of Mrs. Lincoln, I am satisfied, are the result of partial insanity." Wood said Lincoln "exhibited more feeling than I had believed he possessed" and pronounced his wife ill. "Is the malady beyond medical remedy to check," he asked, "before it becomes fully developed?" Michael Burlingame, ed., *At Lincoln's Side: John Hay's Civil War Correspondence and Selected Writings* (Carbondale: Southern Illinois University Press, 2000), 203, citing *Washington Sunday Gazette*, January 16, 1887.

"It was brought to him": Browning described this scene in two sources, which are combined here. The first sentence of the quotation is drawn from O. H. Browning, interview with John G. Nicolay, June 17, 1875, *An Oral History*, 3. The second sentence, beginning "I remained with" is from Browning, *The Diary of Orville Hickman Browning*, edited by Theodore Calvin Pease and J. G. Randall, 2 vols. (Springfield: Illinois State Historical Library, 1925–33), vol. 1, 542–43.

His favorites included: In 1862, *Artemus Ward, His Book* included the dispatch "How Old Abe Received the News of His Nomination." "There are several reports afloat," it begins, "as to how 'Honest Old Abe' received the news of his nomination, none of which are correct. We give the correct report."

The Official Committee arrived in Springfield at dewy eve, and went to Honest Old Abe's house. Honest Old Abe was not in. Mrs. Honest Old Abe said Honest Old Abe was out in the woods splitting rails. So the Official Committee went out into the woods, where sure enough they found Honest Old Abe splitting rails with his two boys. It was a grand, a magnificent spectacle. There stood Honest Old Abe in his shirtsleeves, a pair of leather home-made suspenders holding up a pair of home-made pantaloons, the seat of which was neatly patched with substantial cloth of a different color. "Mr. Lincoln, Sir, you've been nominated, Sir, for the highest office, Sir —." "Oh, don't bother me," said Honest Old Abe; "I took a *stent* this mornin' to split three million rails afore night, and I don't want to be pestered with no stuff about no Conventions till I get my stent done. I've only got two hundreds thousand rails to split before sundown. I kin do it if you'll let me alone." . . . In a few moments Honest Old Abe finished his task, and received the news with perfect self-possession. He then asked them up to the house, where he received them cordially. He said he split three million rails every day, although he was in very poor health.

"He offended many": *Reminiscences of Abraham Lincoln*, 447–48.

182 *"Ashley, I have"*: *Recollected Words,* 19, citing James M. Ashley, *Reminiscences of the Great Rebellion: Calhoun, Seward, and Lincoln* (n.p., 1890).

"If I listen": Speed, *Reminiscences,* 30.

"sicker'n your man": Thomas, *"Lincoln's Humor,"* 15.

"I think Jefferson Davis": Clifton Fadiman, ed., *The Little, Brown Book of Anecdotes* (Boston: Little, Brown, 1985), 358.

Lincoln said: Elton Trueblood, *Abraham Lincoln: Theologian of American Anguish* (New York: Harper & Row, 1973), 7.

"If we use defenses well": George E. Vaillant, *The Wisdom of the Ego* (Cambridge: Harvard University Press, 1993), 11.

183 *"weary, care-worn, and troubled"*: Browning, *Diary,* vol. 1, 559–60.

"The struggle of today": AL, "Annual Message to Congress," December 3, 1861, *CWL,* vol. 5, 53.

loyal Kentuckians into spasms: Joshua Speed, for example, was furious, writing Lincoln, "I have been so much disturbed since reading . . . that foolish proclamation of Fremont that I have been unable to eat or sleep." He feared it could crush the Union party in Kentucky. Joshua F. Speed to AL, September 3, 1861, Abraham Lincoln Papers, Library of Congress.

"I think to lose Kentucky": AL to Orville H. Browning, September 22, 1861, *CWL,* vol. 4, 532.

184 *By the beginning of 1862:* McPherson, *Battle Cry of Freedom,* 494.

could turn him out of office: As McPherson explains, in *Battle Cry of Freedom,* 506, "The Democrats had received 44 percent of the popular votes in the free states in 1860. If the votes of the border states are added, Lincoln was a minority president of the Union states."

"I have been anxious and careful": AL, "Annual Message to Congress," December 3, 1861, *CWL,* vol. 5, 48–49.

"is no more fit": *Douglass' Monthly,* August 1862.

At the same time: McPherson, *Battle Cry of Freedom,* 505–6.

185 *"He had given it"*: Gideon Welles, *Diary of Gideon Welles, Secretary of the Navy under Lincoln and Johnson,* 3 vols. (Boston: Houghton Mifflin, 1911), vol. 1, 70–71. For a detailed discussion of this episode, see Allen C. Guelzo, *Lincoln's Emancipation Proclamation: The End of Slavery in America* (New York: Simon and Schuster, 2004), 111–12.

"This is not a question": AL to Isaac M. Schermerhorn, September 12, 1864, *CWL,* vol. 8, 2.

On July 22: Guelzo, *Lincoln's Emancipation Proclamation,* 117–23.

"The Prest. was in deep distress": *CWL,* vol. 5, 486.

186 *"Sincere thanks"*: Hannibal Hamlin to AL, September 25, 1862, Abraham Lincoln Papers, Library of Congress.

"all that a vain man": AL to Hannibal Hamlin, September 28, 1862, *CWL,* vol. 5, 444.

"wicked, inhuman and unholy": McPherson, *Battle Cry of Freedom,* 595.

"darkened with particular pain": Burlingame, *Inner World,* 105, citing Stoddard, "White House Sketches," *New York Citizen,* September 29, 1866.

"What has God": ibid,, citing reminiscences of Andrew Curtin, governor of Pennsylvania, in William A. Mowry, "Some Incidents in the Life of Abraham Lincoln," 1913, clipping in the Harry E. Pratt Mss., University of Illinois Library, Urbana-Champaign.

187 *"sunken"* and *"deathly"*: Noah Brooks, who had met Lincoln in the 1850s in Illinois before decamping to California, went to Washington in November 1862 to report for the *Sacramento Daily Union* and found Lincoln "grievously altered . . . His hair is

grizzled, his gait more stooping, his countenance sallow, and there is a sunken, deathly look about the large, cavernous eyes, which is saddening to those who see there the marks of care and anxiety, such as no President of the United States has ever before known." *Lincoln Observed*, 13–14.

187 *"fourth-rate man"*: ibid., 24.

"Many speeches were made": Browning, *Diary*, vol. 1, 599.

"He soon came in": ibid., 603–4.

In the midst of this melee: For the timing of this visit, see David Davis to Laura Swett, December 21, 1862, Davis Papers. Davis said he had seen Lincoln "the other day."

William McCullough: Details on McCullough's life and death and his daughter's depression are from "Lincoln's Friend Miss Fanny McCullough," by Grace Cheney Wight, typescript, ISHL; Carl Haverlin, *A. Lincoln's Letter to Fanny McCullough* (Chicago: R. G. Newman, 1968); *Bloomington Daily Pantagraph*, December 12, 1862; and Don Sides, interviews with author, February 2–4, 2004.

188 *An old friend of the colonel's:* Details of Swett's encounter with Fanny McCullough are in Leonard Swett to William W. Orme, December 9, 1862, William W. Orme Papers, Illinois Historical Survey.

"pacing the floor": Laura R. Swett to David Davis, December 13, 1862, Davis Papers. Mrs. Swett described Fanny as "afflicted — crushed and I fear, broken hearted."

He had stayed: King, *Lincoln's Manager*, 76.

"The cares of this Government": David Davis to Laura Swett, December 21, 1862, Davis Papers.

"extreme pressure": AL to John A. Dix, December 22, 1862, *CWL*, vol. 6, 14.

"Dear Fanny": AL to Fanny McCullough, December 23, 1862, *CWL*, vol. 6, 16–17. An image of the letter is in Haverlin, *A. Lincoln's Letter*.

189 *Speed had voted against:* Joshua F. Speed to AL, November 14, 1860, Abraham Lincoln Papers, Library of Congress.

The owner of eleven slaves: Pen Bogert, slave data on Joshua F. Speed, in the vertical file, "Farmington — African Americans," Filson Historical Society Library, 1997.

he told Lincoln so: Speed did not date this conversation, but he would have made known his opposition to the Emancipation Proclamation after the preliminary draft of September 22, 1862, and before it was issued on January 1, 1863. It may be that the conversation took place in mid-December 1862, when Speed was in Washington and visited with Lincoln at the White House. (On December 18, Lincoln endorsed a letter by Speed written on Executive Mansion stationery, which was dated December 9. AL to Edwin M. Stanton, December 18, 1862, *CWL*, vol. 6, 10n.1.)

he reminded Speed: Speed referred to these conversations three times. The existence of multiple, complementary accounts, the intrinsic importance of the material, and its complexity — Speed is reporting both sides of an exchange that alludes to a conversation two decades before — make it worth quoting the originals at length. In his *Reminiscences* (39), Speed wrote, "In the winter of 1841 a gloom came over him till his friends were alarmed for his life. Though a member of the legislature he rarely attended its sessions. In his deepest gloom, and when I told him he would die unless he rallied, he said, 'I am not afraid and would be more than willing. But I have an irrepressible desire to live till I can be assured that the world is a little better for my having lived in it.'" In a letter to Herndon on February 7, 1866 (*Herndon's Informants*, 197), Speed wrote: "At first I was opposed to the proclamation and so told him — I remember well our conversation on the subject — he seemed to treat it as certain that I would recognize the wisdom of the act when I should see the harvest of good which would erelong glean from it — In that conversation he alluded to an incident in his life long passed, when he was so much deppressed that he almost contemplated suicide — At the time of his deep deppression — He said to me that he had done nothing to make any human being remember that he had lived — and that to connect his name with the events transpiring in his day & generation and so impress himself upon them as to link his name with something that would redound to the interest of his fellow man was what he desired to live for — He reminded me of the conversation, — and said with earnest emphasis — I believe in this measure (meaning his proclomation) my fondest hopes will be realized." Herndon apparently told Speed that Lincoln had said essentially the same thing to him. Speed replied on February 14, 1866 (*Herndon's Informants*, 213), that he was glad to learn this. "This," he added, "connected with his allusion to me after his emancipation proclamation, as that being the fulfillment of his long cherished hope should I think be incorporated in his life [i.e., biography] — It was the fulfillment a day dream long indulged in — which few men live to realize."

190   *"Fellow-citizens, we cannot escape"*: AL, "Annual Message to Congress," December 1, 1862, *CWL*, vol. 5, 537.

10. COMES WISDOM TO US

191   *"And even in our sleep"*: Agamemnon, translated by Deirdre Von Dornum. For an interesting history of the translation of this passage, see Christopher S. Morrissey, "'In Our Own Despair': Robert Kennedy, Richard Nixon, and Aeschylus' *Agamemnon*," Annual Meeting of the Classical Association of Canada, May 12, 2002. A summary of Morrissey's findings is available at http://morec.com/rfk.htm.

   "Almighty Architect": AL, "Speech on the Sub-Treasury," December [26], 1839, *CWL*, vol. 1, 178. Allen Guelzo, in *Redeemer President* (320), points out that this phrase was a favorite among freethinkers. It felicitously combines both the mechanistic notion of the universe and the traditional idea of God physically creating the world.

192   *"fire in the rear"*: McPherson, *Battle Cry of Freedom*, 591, citing Charles Sumner to Francis Lieber, January 17, 1863, in Edward L. Pierce, *Memoirs and Letters of Charles Sumner*, 4 vols. (Boston, 1877–93), vol. 4, 114.

   Lincoln hoped: In a diary entry on July 21, 1863, John Hay noted that Lincoln had a "long cherished & often expressed conviction that if the enemy ever crossed the Potomac he might have been destroyed." Burlingame and Ettlinger, *Inside Lincoln's White House*, 66.

   a third of his army: McPherson, *Battle Cry of Freedom*, 664. McPherson writes, "Lee was profoundly depressed by the outcome of his campaign to conquer a peace. A month later he offered his resignation to Jefferson Davis. 'No one,' wrote Lee, 'is more aware than myself of my inability for the duties of my position. I cannot even accomplish what I myself desire. How can I fulfill the expectations of others?' Thus said a man whose stunning achievements during the year before Gettysburg had won the admiration of the Western world" (665).

   "very happy": Burlingame and Ettlinger, *Inside Lincoln's White House*, 61.

   "grieved silently": ibid., 63.

193   *about 120 people*: Edward K. Spann, *Gotham at War: New York City, 1860–1865* (Wilmington, Del.: Scholarly Resources Books, 2002), 101.

   "oppressed," "deep distress," "My dear general": AL to George C. Meade, *CWL*, vol. 6, 328.

   "never sent": envelope in the Abraham Lincoln Papers, Library of Congress.

193 *"is in fine whack"*: John Hay to John G. Nicolay, August 7, 1863, in Michael Bur-
     lingame, ed., *At Lincoln's Side: John Hay's Civil War Correspondence and Selected
     Writings* (Carbondale: Southern Illinois University Press, 2000), 49.
     "somehow a sweet comfort": undated newspaper clipping, "Mr. Lincoln's Prayers An-
     swered," by General James F. Rusling, on file at the Lincoln Museum, Fort Wayne, In-
     diana.
     "His step was slow": Keckley, *Behind the Scenes*, 118–20.
     "Man is born broken": Eugene O'Neill, *The Great God Brown*, act 4, scene 1.
194 *"life force"*: Raymond E. Fancher, *Pioneers of Psychology* (New York: W. W. Norton,
     1979), 112–13. Fancher is my authority for the discussion of psychology's history be-
     fore Freud and Kraepelin.
     Both Kraepelin and Freud: For the ascension of these psychiatrists, I rely on Edward
     Shorter, *A History of Psychiatry: From the Era of the Asylum to the Age of Prozac* (New
     York: Wiley, 1997). For a short overview on Freud and religion from a sympathetic
     source, see "Freud and Religion," the Freud Museum, www.freud.org.uk/religion
     .html.
     "there is an unseen order": James, *The Varieties of Religious Experience*, 53.
195 *"a sense that"*: ibid., 498.
     one study of 271: Patricia E. Murphy et al., "The Relation of Religious Belief and Prac-
     tices, Depression, and Hopelessness in Persons with Clinical Depression," *Journal of
     Consulting and Clinical Psychology* 68, no. 6 (December 2000): 1102–6.
     A meta-analysis of depression: Timothy B. Smith, Michael E. McCullough, and Justin
     Poll, "Religiousness and Depression: Evidence for a Main Effect and the Moderating
     Influence of Stressful Life Events," *Psychological Bulletin* 129, no. 4 (July 2003): 614–36.
     "When I knew him": Speed, *Reminiscences*, 32.
     "It's hard to imagine": Jennifer Michael Hecht, interviewed by Krista Tippett, "A His-
     tory of Doubt," *Speaking of Faith*, Minnesota Public Radio, December 11, 2003, http:/
     /speakingoffaith.publicradio.org/programs/2003/12/11_doubt/webaudio.shtml.
     "His mind was full": Isaac Cogdal, interview with WHH, 1865–66, *Herndon's Infor-
     mants*, 441.
196 *"best cure for the 'Blues'"*: AL to Mary Speed, September 27, 1841, *CWL*, vol. 1, 261.
     After Eddie Lincoln's: Baker, *Mary Todd Lincoln*, 126.
     "He examined the Arguments": James Smith to WHH, January 24, 1867, *Herndon's In-
     formants*, 549.
     The Lincolns later rented: Ronald C. White, *Lincoln's Greatest Speech* (New York: Si-
     mon and Schuster, 2002), 130.
     "Lincoln maintained": WHH to F. Abbot, February 18, 1870, published as "Abraham
     Lincoln's Religion," *The Index*, April 2, 1870, 5–6.
     "suffering was medicinal": WHH to Ward Lamon, March 3, 1870, transcription by
     LSC.
     "process of crystallization": *Lincoln Observed*, 210–11.
197 *"God's will be done"*: B. B. Lloyd, interview with WHH, November 29, 1866, *Hern-
     don's Informants*, 426.
     "so vast, and so sacred a trust": AL, "Message to Congress in Special Session," July 4,
     1861, *CWL*, vol. 4, 440.
     "Did you ever dream": LeGrand B. Cannon to WHH, October 7, 1889, *Herndon's In-
     formants*, 679.
     "in the hour of trial": Ervin S. Chapman, *Latest Light on Abraham Lincoln* (New York:
     Fleming H. Revell, 1917), 504–6.
     "There was something touching": *Lincoln Observed*, 210–11.
     "I am very sure": ibid.

198   *"These are not . . . the days of miracles"*: AL, "Reply to Emancipation Memorial Presented by Chicago Christians of All Denominations," September 13, 1862, *CWL*, vol. 5, 420.

   "I shall be most happy": AL, "Address to the New Jersey Senate at Trenton, New Jersey," February 21, 1861, *CWL*, vol. 4, 236.

   "The will of God prevails": reproduced from the original manuscript at the John Hay Library, Brown University.

199   *Most religious thinkers*: Mark A. Noll, *America's God: From Jonathan Edwards to Abraham Lincoln* (New York: Oxford University Press, 2002), 430–32.

   "Mine eyes have seen": *Atlantic Monthly*, February 1862, 10.

   When the Rebels fared: Noll, *America's God*, 425.

   Thomas "Stonewall" Jackson: For a portrait of the cult around this fascinating figure, see Daniel W. Stowell, "Stonewall Jackson and the Providence of God," in Randall M. Miller, Harry S. Stout, and Charles Reagan Wilson, eds., *Religion and the American Civil War* (New York: Oxford University Press, 1998), 187–207.

   "We must work earnestly": AL to Eliza P. Gurney, September 4, 1864, *CWL*, vol. 7, 535.

   "I hope we are": This exchange was reported in the *Illinois State Journal*, February 2, 1864.

   "How was it": Noll, *America's God*, 426.

200   *"God is great"*: James, *The Varieties of Religious Experience*, 75, citing Mark Rutherford's *Deliverance* (London, 1885).

   "formally set apart": David Wills to AL, November 2, 1863, Abraham Lincoln Papers, Library of Congress.

201   *"felt religious More than Ever"*: Mary Lincoln, interview with WHH, September 1866, *Herndon's Informants*, 360.

   "Four score and seven": AL, "Address Delivered at the Dedication of the Cemetery at Gettysburg — Final Text," November 19, 1863, *CWL*, vol. 7, 23.

   "The Civil War is": Garry Wills, *Lincoln at Gettysburg: The Words That Remade America* (New York: Simon and Schuster, 1992), 38.

202   *"ripe fruits of religion"*: James, *The Varieties of Religious Experience*, 266.

   "Magnanimities once impossible": ibid., 262.

   "I shall do nothing in malice": AL to Cuthbert Bullitt, July 28, 1862, *CWL*, vol. 5, 346.

   The oft-quoted remark: *Reminiscences of Abraham Lincoln*, 193. For a treatment of the Lincoln-Douglass relationship, see David W. Blight, *Frederick Douglass and Abraham Lincoln: A Relationship in Language, Politics, and Memory* (Milwaukee: Marquette University Press, 2001).

   "awful change": AL, "Stay of Execution for Nathaniel Gordon," February 4, 1862, *CWL*, vol. 5, 128.

   "Yours of the 23rd. is received": AL to David Hunter, December 31, 1861, *CWL*, vol. 5, 84–85. A note on p. 85 has the contextual detail.

203   *"Speed, die when I may"*: Joshua F. Speed, interview with WHH, June 10, 1865, *Herndon's Informants*, 31. Lincoln used a similar image in his response to a serenade on November 10, 1864: "So long as I have been here I have not willingly planted a thorn in any man's bosom." *CWL*, vol. 8, 101.

   "as if he had determined": McPherson, *Battle Cry of Freedom*, 721.

   bouts of mania and depression: For a discussion of Sherman's mental tumult while commanding the Department of the Cumberland in Kentucky — which led to the *Cincinnati Commercial* headline "GENERAL WILLIAM T. SHERMAN INSANE" — see John F. Marszalek, *Sherman's Other War: The General and the Civil War Press* (Kent, Ohio: Kent State University Press, 1999), 63–93. I also benefited from reading Dr. S. Nassir Ghaemi's "General Sherman's Illness," unpublished ms.

203 *"War, at the best"*: AL, "Speech at Great Central Sanitary Fair, Philadelphia, Pennsylvania," June 16, 1864, *CWL*, vol. 7, 394–95.

204 *his election was an "impossibility"*: Thurlow Weed to William H. Seward, August 22, 1864, Abraham Lincoln Papers, Library of Congress.

The influential editor: Harper, *Lincoln and the Press*, 309, citing Horace Greeley to George Opdyke, August 18, 1864.

"Negroes, like other people": AL to James C. Conkling, August 26, 1863, *CWL*, vol. 6, 409.

"and come to stay": ibid., 410.

205 *"I thought he might"*: Thomas, *Abraham Lincoln*, 443.

"This morning, as for some days": AL, "Memorandum Concerning His Probable Failure of Re-election," August 23, 1864, *CWL*, vol. 7, 514.

Lincoln also laid plans: In a meeting with Frederick Douglass, Lincoln suggested — as Douglass recounted — "that something should be speedily done to inform the slaves in the Rebel states of the true state of affairs in relation to them and to warn them as to what will be their probable condition should peace be concluded while they remain within the Rebel lines: and more especially to urge upon them the necessity of making their escape." Douglass to AL, August 29, 1864, Abraham Lincoln Papers, Library of Congress. See also David W. Blight, *Frederick Douglass' Civil War* (Baton Rouge: Louisiana State University Press, 1989), 183–84.

"I wish it might be": AL, "Speech to the One Hundred Sixty-fourth Ohio Regiment," August 18, 1864, *CWL*, vol. 7, 504–5.

"It is not merely for to-day": AL, "Speech to the One Hundred Sixty-sixth Ohio Regiment," August 22, 1864, *CWL*, vol. 7, 512.

206 *General Sherman captured*: "The impact of this event," writes McPherson, in *Battle Cry of Freedom* (774–75), "cannot be exaggerated. Cannons boomed 100-gun salutes in northern cities. Newspapers that had bedeviled Sherman for years now praised him as the greatest general since Napoleon . . . The *Richmond Examiner* reflected glumly that 'the disaster at Atlanta' came 'in the very nick of time' to 'save the party of Lincoln from irretrievable ruin.'"

the moment the war stopped: McPherson writes of Sherman, "Like Lincoln, he believed in a hard war and a soft peace. 'War is cruelty and you cannot refine it,' Sherman had told Atlanta's mayor after ordering the civilian population expelled from the occupied city. But 'when peace does come, you may call on me for anything. Then will I share with you the last cracker.'" *Battle Cry of Freedom*, 809.

"progress of our arms": AL, "Second Inaugural Address," March 4, 1865, *CWL*, vol. 8, 332–33.

207 *"the most pregnant and effective"*: Thurlow Weed to AL, March 4, 1865, *CWL*, vol. 8, 356n.1.

"wear as well as": AL to Thurlow Weed, March 15, 1865, *CWL*, vol. 8, 356.

208 *"I charge the whole guilt"*: Noll, *America's God*, 428, citing Henry Ward Beecher, "Address at the Raising of the Union Flag over Fort Sumter," *Patriotic Addresses* (New York, 1887), 688–89.

"That indescribable sadness": Johnson Brigham, *James Harlan* (Iowa City: State Historical Society of Iowa, 1913), 338.

"We meet today not in sorrow": AL, "Last Public Address," April 11, 1865, 399.

209 *"Now, by God"*: McPherson, *Battle Cry of Freedom*, 852.

On the morning of April 14: For the events of this day, I have relied largely on W. Emerson Reck, *A. Lincoln: His Last 24 Hours* (Columbia: University of South Carolina Press, 1987). For the cabinet meeting, see 31–40.

Lincoln had a long-standing: "There was more or less superstition in his nature,"

Herndon wrote, "and, although he may not have believed implicitly in the signs of his many dreams, he was constantly endeavoring to unravel them. His mind was readily impressed with some of the most absurd superstitions." *Herndon's Lincoln,* vol. 3, 435.

"*I had an ugly dream*": AL to Mary Lincoln, June 9, 1863, *CWL,* vol. 6, 256.

While he was in Richmond: Mary Todd Lincoln, interview with WHH, September 1866, *Herndon's Informants,* 357–58.

"*I think it must be from Sherman*": There are two firsthand sources of Lincoln's conversation about his dream. Gideon Welles, Lincoln's secretary of the navy, wrote in his diary that, when the conversation turned to Sherman, Lincoln said that word "would, he had no doubt, come soon, and come favorable, for he had last night the usual dream which he had preceding nearly every great and important event of the war." In the dream, Lincoln said, "he seemed to be in some singular, indescribable vessel, and that he was moving with great rapidity" (Beale, *Diary of Gideon Welles,* 282–83). Frederick W. Seward, the son of Secretary of State William Seward, wrote, "The conversation turning upon the subject of sleep, Mr. Lincoln remarked that a peculiar dream of the previous night was one that had occurred several times in his life, — a vague sense of floating — floating away on some vast and indistinct expanse, toward an unknown shore. The dream itself was not so strange as the coincidence that each of its previous recurrences had been followed by some important event or disaster, which he mentioned. The usual comments were made by his auditors. One thought it was merely a matter of coincidences. Another laughingly remarked, 'At any rate it cannot presage a victory nor a defeat this time, for the war is over.' I suggested, 'Perhaps at each of these periods there were possibilities of great change or disaster, and the vague feeling of uncertainty may have led to the dim vision in sleep.' 'Perhaps,' said Mr. Lincoln, thoughtfully, 'perhaps that is the explanation'" (*Reminiscences of a War-Time Statesman and Diplomat* [New York: G. P. Putnam, 1916], 255).

government offices closed: Reck, *A. Lincoln,* 49.

"*I never saw him*": Mary Lincoln to Francis Bicknell Carpenter, November 15, 1865, *MTL, Life and Letters,* 284.

Lincoln said he wanted: Mary Lincoln, interview with WHH, September 1866, *Herndon's Informants,* 357–58.

"*Come back, boys, come back*": Reck, *A. Lincoln,* 49.

210 *At dinner:* Anson Henry to Mrs. Henry, April 19, 1865, Henry Papers, ISHL.

"*more depressed than I had*": Reck, *A. Lincoln,* 54–55, citing William H. Crook, *Through Five Administrations: Reminiscences of Colonel William H. Crook, Body-Guard to President Lincoln,* edited by Margarita Spalding Gerry (New York: Harper & Brothers, 1910), 67–68, 74–75, and Crook, *Memories of the White House: The Home Life of Our Presidents from Lincoln to Roosevelt,* edited by Henry Rood (Boston: Little, Brown, 1911), 40.

At the War Department: Reminiscences of Abraham Lincoln, 404.

On the way back: Reck, *A. Lincoln,* 55.

working on papers: William Pitt Kellogg, who had just been appointed by Lincoln as collector of the port of New Orleans, saw the president before he went to the theater and found him "in his room, apparently signing papers." Paul M. Angle, "The Recollections of William Pitt Kellogg," *Abraham Lincoln Quarterly* 3 (September 1945): 319–39.

"*This man is pardoned*": Records of the Judge Advocate General, National Archives, MM761.

He told his guard: Crook, *Through Five Administrations,* 67.

210　*He told his wife:* Anson Henry to Mrs. Henry, April 19, 1865, Henry Papers, ISHL.
　　In his pockets: The contents of Lincoln's pockets at his assassination were given by the Lincoln family to the Library of Congress in 1937. They can be inspected online at www.loc.gov/exhibits/treasures/trm012.html.
　　"Excuse me now": Isaac N. Arnold, *The Life of Abraham Lincoln* (Chicago, A. C. McClurg, 1909), 431.

EPILOGUE

211　*.41-caliber lead musket ball:* Edward Steers, Jr., interview with author, November 16, 2002. Steers is the author of *Blood on the Moon: The Assassination of Abraham Lincoln* (Lexington: University Press of Kentucky, 2001).
　　popcorn: Abner Y. Ellis to WHH, January 30, 1866, *Herndon's Informants,* 179.
　　oysters . . . coffee: Ward Hill Lamon, interview with WHH, 1865–66, *Herndon's Informants,* 466.
215　*"that treading the hard path":* AL, "Eulogy on Zachary Taylor," July 25, 1850, *CWL,* vol. 2, 89.
216　*"images of history":* Muriel Rukeyser, *The Life of Poetry* (New York: A. A. Wyn, 1949), 34.
　　"Those who have spoken": A. K. McClure and James A. Rawley, *Abraham Lincoln and Men of War-Times: Some Personal Recollections of War and Politics During the Lincoln Administration* (Lincoln: University of Nebraska Press, 1997; orig. 1892), 72.
　　"In one of your letters": WHH to Truman H. Bartlett, August 22, 1887, Truman Bartlett Papers, Massachusetts Historical Society, transcription by LSC.
　　"Let me say to you": WHH to Truman H. Bartlett, February 27, 1891, Truman Bartlett Papers, Massachusetts Historical Society, transcription by LSC.
217　*"if this man had ruled":* Waldo W. Braden, ed., *Building the Myth: Selected Speeches Memorializing Abraham Lincoln* (Urbana: University of Illinois Press, 1990), 32.

AFTERWORD

221　*Technically, the partnership continued:* As the often-told story goes, Lincoln went to his law office on his last afternoon in Springfield, before leaving for Washington in 1861. As he left the building, he looked up at the sign that hung outside. "Let it hang there undisturbed," he told Herndon. "Give our clients to understand that the election of a President makes no change in the firm of Lincoln and Herndon. If I live I'm coming back some time, and then we'll go right on practicing law as if nothing had ever happened." When Herndon began his biographical work on Lincoln, the sign hung there still. *Herndon's Lincoln,* vol. 3, 482–84.
　　four hundred testimonials: Douglas L. Wilson, "William H. Herndon and Mary Todd Lincoln," *Journal of the Abraham Lincoln Association* 22, no. 2 (Summer 2001), 8.
　　"If I die": WHH to Charles Hart, December 12, 1866, *Hidden Lincoln,* 51.
222　*He detested hagiography:* See Douglas L. Wilson, "William H. Herndon and the 'Necessary Truth,'" *Lincoln Before Washington,* 37–52. According to Herndon, Lincoln considered "biographies as generally written are not only misleading, but false," because they magnified good qualities and suppressed imperfections and failures. *Herndon's Lincoln,* vol. 3, 437.
　　"Is any man so insane": Joseph Fort Newton, *Lincoln and Herndon* (Cedar Rapids, Iowa: Torch Press, 1910), 292, citing WHH to Isaac N. Arnold.

Seventeen of them: Wilson, *Lincoln Before Washington,* 82.

"I have been searching": WHH to Josiah G. Holland, June 8, 1865, Holland Papers.

"disposed to shut one eye": Paul M. Angle, preface to *Herndon's Life of Lincoln: The History and Personal Recollections of Abraham Lincoln* (Boston: Da Capo Press, 1983), xxvii.

"realist rather than an idealist": *Herndon's Lincoln,* vol. 3, 435.

"write & publish the subjective*":* WHH to Josiah G. Holland, June 8, 1865, Holland Papers, transcription by LSC.

223 *knew how to get information:* Paul Angle writes, "Herndon's methods of obtaining information and the spirit which governed him in his investigations are well illustrated by the following letter to Squire Hall . . .

> Friend Hall: Will you have the kindness to copy Mr. Lincoln's bond to Johnson or your father, which I saw when I was down to see you. Copy every word, figure, and name *carefully* from top to bottom, and send to me, if you *please.* Don't fail. I want it to defend Lincoln's memory. *Please* write to me at any time you may think of anything that is *good or bad* of Mr. Lincoln, truthfully just as it happened and took place. Were any of you boys applicants for any office made to Mr. Lincoln while he was President?
>
> Hall — What is your honest opinion — Come *honest* opinion — in reference to Mr. Lincoln's love for his kind and relations generally. *Please* — friend — accommodate me.

Angle, editor's preface, *Herndon's Life of Lincoln,* xxvi–xxvii, citing WHH to Squire Hall, January 22, 1866. For more on Herndon's work, see *Herndon's Informants,* xiii–xxiv; and Wilson, *Lincoln Before Washington,* in particular, "Herndon's Legacy," "William H. Herndon and the 'Necessary Truth,'" "Abraham Lincoln, Ann Rutledge, and the Evidence of *Herndon's Informants,*" and "Abraham Lincoln and 'That Fatal First of January.'"

"I sincerely wish": WHH to Charles Hart, April 13, 1866, *Hidden Lincoln,* 32.

"I have not got the capacity": WHH to Josiah G. Holland, June 8, 1865, Holland Papers.

"Lincoln loved Anna Rutledge": William H. Herndon, *Lincoln, Ann Rutledge and the Pioneers of New Salem* (Herrin, Ill.: Trovillion, 1945), 3.

"Lincoln first came to himself": ibid., 47.

224 *"concerning* MR. LINCOLN *and* MISS RUTLEDGE*":* "Abraham Lincoln: A Curious and Interesting Romance in the Life of Mr. Lincoln," *New York Times,* November 24, 1866, 8.

"I would like to have": Leonard Swett to WHH, February 14, 1866, *Herndon's Informants,* 214.

"the key to his whole life": C. H. Dall, "Pioneering," *Atlantic Monthly,* April 1867, 10.

"Mary Lincoln has had much to bear": Elizabeth Edwards, interview with WHH, 1865–66, *Herndon's Informants,* 444.

"scarcely removed from want": Mary Lincoln to W. H. Brady, September 14, 1867, *MTL, Life and Letters,* 435.

her husband's estate: "Mr. Lincoln's Estate," *New York Times,* October 12, 1867, 1.

style that befitted her: MTL, Life and Letters, 245–46.

she dreamed up a scheme: Fleischner, *Mrs. Lincoln and Mrs. Keckly,* 305–15.

the New York World *published: MTL, Life and Letters,* 432.

Accusations flew: Fleischner, *Mrs. Lincoln and Mrs. Keckley,* 310, citing the *Pittsburgh Commercial,* October 29, 1867.

"dreadful woman": ibid., citing the *Springfield Republican,* October 15, 1867.

224 *"one of the most humiliating":* New York Citizen, October 5, 1867, copy in Randall Papers.

225 "never *addressed another woman," "whip and spur," his heart lay buried:* Herndon, *Lincoln, Ann Rutledge,* 40–41, 20, 40–41.

"Mr. Lincoln was a sad": WHH to Jesse Weik, January 30, 1887, *Hidden Lincoln,* 163–64.

It is not at all clear: One contemporary source does identify Herndon's dislike for Mrs. Lincoln. Gibson Harris, a law clerk for Lincoln and Herndon, remembered that Herndon "cherished a strong dislike for . . . Mrs. Lincoln, and of this fact made no secret to the office-clerk." Harris, "My Recollections of Abraham Lincoln," *Farm and Fireside,* December 1, 1904, 23. But all other indications of discord between the two came after their break, in the wake of Lincoln's death.

In fact, Herndon had more sympathy: "In her domestic troubles," Herndon wrote of Mary Lincoln, "I have always sympathized with her. The world does not know what she bore and the history of the bearing . . . The domestic *hell* of Lincoln's life is not all on one side." WHH to Jesse W. Weik, January 9, 1886, *Hidden Lincoln,* 131.

"my beloved husband's": Mary Lincoln to WHH, August 28, 1866, *MTL, Life and Letters,* 384.

she sat for an interview: Mary Lincoln, interview with WHH, September 1866, *Herndon's Lincoln,* vol. 2, 357–61.

"dirty dog": The quotations in this paragraph are in letters from Mary Lincoln to David Davis, March 4 and 6, 1867, *MTL, Life and Letters,* 414–16.

its effects still linger: The spread of the "gay Lincoln" thesis reflects, in part, continued fallout from the partisan fight between Herndonians and Mary-ophiles. C. A. Tripp, in *The Intimate World of Abraham Lincoln,* did all he could to discredit Herndon's evidence because the Ann Rutledge story was a thorn in his side. (By Tripp's account, Lincoln was too busy scheming to get men into bed to care anything for this village girl, let alone fall into a depression after her death.) Even more interesting, the one important scholar of the Lincolns who endorsed Tripp's book — she wrote the introduction — is Jean Baker, Mary Lincoln's biographer. The *New York Times* quoted Baker as saying that Lincoln's homosexuality would explain his difficult relationship with Mary Todd and "some of her agonies and anxieties over their relationship." "Some of the tempers emerged because Lincoln was so detached," Baker said. "But I previously thought he was detached because he was thinking great things about his court cases, his debates with Douglas. Now I see there is another explanation" (Dinita Smith, "Finding Homosexual Threads in Lincoln's Legend," *New York Times,* December 16, 2004).

226 *Soon after he completed . . . An off-and-on heavy drinker . . . Desperate for cash:* David Herbert Donald, *Lincoln's Herndon* (New York: Knopf, 1948), 247–49, 258–59.

Lamon was estranged: Rodney O. Davis, introduction to Ward Hill Lamon, *The Life of Abraham Lincoln* (Lincoln: University of Nebraska Press, 1999; orig. 1872), v–xxi.

"technical Christian": Mary Lincoln, interview with WHH, September 1866, *Herndon's Informants,* 360.

all kinds of attacks: Angle, preface to *Herndon's Life of Lincoln,* xxxi, notes that after the publication of Lamon's book, items "began to go the rounds of the press charging that he [Herndon] was a lunatic, a pauper, a drunkard, an infidel, a liar, a knave, and almost every other species of degradation."

In the 1880s, William Herndon: Donald, *Lincoln's Herndon,* 296–97.

227 *"Lincoln and Mary were Engaged":* Elizabeth Edwards, interview with WHH, 1865–66, *Herndon's Informants,* 443.

"Arrangements for wedding": Elizabeth and Ninian Edwards, interview with Jesse W. Weik, December 20, 1883, *Herndon's Informants*, 592.

nor has a marriage license: "The marriage license records of Sangamon County — which are complete — show that no license was issued to Lincoln on or before January 1, 1841." Angle, preface to *Herndon's Life of Lincoln*, xliii–xliv. Now that we know Weik dated the wedding at January 1, a new check should be made to see whether any license was issued at any time in the winter of 1840–1841.

"about January '41": "Lincoln & Mary Todd," WHH fragment, Herndon-Weik Ms., transcription by LSC.

Jesse Weik elaborated further: Herndon's Lincoln, vol. 2, 214.

228 *In this era*: For the swell of Lincoln's popularity in the Progressive Era, see Merrill D. Peterson, *Lincoln in American Memory* (New York: Oxford University Press, 1994), and Barry Schwartz, *Abraham Lincoln and the Forge of National Memory* (Chicago: University of Chicago Press, 2000). For particular treatment of the myths of Ann Rutledge, see Barry Schwartz, "Ann Rutledge in American Memory: Social Change and the Erosion of a Romantic Drama," *Journal of the Abraham Lincoln Association* 26, no. 1 (Winter 2005): 1–27.

Lincoln Logs: Lincoln Logs first appeared in 1918. Schwartz, *Abraham Lincoln and the Forge of National Memory*, 281. See also "Lincoln Logs: Toying with the Frontier Myth," *History Today* 43 (April 1993): 31–34.

In the 1920s, a homily: Peterson, *Lincoln in American Memory*, 196.

"PRESIDENT SUFFERS NERVOUS BREAKDOWN": *New York Times*, September 27, 1919.

Then Tad . . . died: Baker, *Mary Todd Lincoln*, 308.

229 *"her conduct has greatly distressed"*: MTL, *Life and Letters*, 442–43, citing *Illinois State Journal*, October 10, 1867.

In 1875, Robert Todd Lincoln: A complete account of this affair is R. Gerald McMurtry and Mark E. Neely, *The Insanity File: The Case of Mary Todd Lincoln* (Carbondale: Southern Illinois University Press, 1993).

"Out of me unworthy and unknown": Peterson, *Lincoln in American Memory*, 294–95.

a new graveyard: Ann's remains were moved in 1890, and Masters's poem was inscribed on the new stone in 1920. See Gary Erickson, "The Graves of Ann Rutledge and the Old Concord Burial Ground," *Lincoln Herald* 71 (Fall 1969): 90–107.

(Amtrak still uses the name): The "Ann Rutledge" offers daily service between Chicago and Kansas City, Missouri. "Illinois Service," www.amtrak.com, February 4, 2005.

230 *"shadow of Ann Rutledge's death"*: Tarbell, *Abraham Lincoln and His Ancestors*, 225.

"quiet soft bud of a woman": Sandburg, *Abraham Lincoln: The Prairie Years*, vol. 1, 140–41.

"an old-time order": ibid., 190.

"I hope you will seriously": W. A. Evans to William E. Barton, April 26, 1921, Barton Papers.

After brief inspections: Walsh, *The Shadows Rise*, 51. See also Don E. Fehrenbacher, "The Minor Affair: An Adventure in Forgery and Detection," in *Lincoln in Text and Context: Collected Essays* (Palo Alto, Calif.: Stanford University Press, 1987), 246–69.

"I would die on the gallows": Peterson, *Lincoln in American Memory*, 297–98.

231 *he exposed the Minor letters*: See Paul M. Angle, "The Minor Collection: A Criticism," *Atlantic Monthly*, April 1929, 516–25.

"the greatest Lincoln scholar": Neely, *The Abraham Lincoln Encyclopedia*, 255.

any "careful scholar": J. G. Randall, "Has the Lincoln Theme Been Exhausted?" *American Historical Review* 41, no. 2 (January 1936): 270–94.

231 *He was sixty-two years old:* description of the Randalls from Wayne Temple, interview with author, August 21, 2003.

232 *In 1944, they had been married:* Ruth Painter Randall, *I, Ruth: Autobiography of a Marriage* . . . (Boston: Little, Brown, 1968), 88–89.
"I gave the wife": Randall, *I, Ruth,* 165.
"It is very largely her work": James G. Randall to Francis S. Ronalds, February 3, 1945, Randall Papers.
"misty" memories: James G. Randall, *Lincoln the President,* vol. 2, 321–43.
"disliked and feared Mary Lincoln": ibid., vol. 1, 67.

233 *"a joyous new focus and vitality":* Ruth Painter Randall, *The Courtship of Mr. Lincoln* (Boston: Little, Brown, 1957), 126.
"gossiping tongues": ibid., 114–15.
"I wish I had a better": Ruth Painter Randall to Philip R. Baker, October 8, 1950, Randall Papers.
"legend for which no shred": Thomas, *Abraham Lincoln,* 51.
Ralph McGill: Copies of McGill's column, May 25, 1952, and Young's letter of the same day are in the Randall Papers.

234 *"Herndon's cruelest offense":* MTL, *Life and Letters,* 34.

236 *"the riddle of Leonardo":* Sigmund Freud, *The Freud Reader,* edited by Peter Gay (New York: W. W. Norton, 1989), 455.
"schizoid manic personality": A. A. Brill, "Abraham Lincoln as a Humorist," copy in the Tarbell Papers.
But the clinical language: The newspapers covering the affair led with Brill's diagnostic language. The Associated Press report began, "Abraham Lincoln was analyzed as a 'schizoid manic personality,' — a Dr. Jekyll and Mr. Hyde who had his baser nature under rigid control." The *New York Times* headline on June 6, 1931, was "Dr. Brill Describes Lincoln as 'Manic.'" On June 15, 1931, an English newspaper in Paris carried the headline "Several Refute Slur on Lincoln." The piece began, "Admirers of Abraham Lincoln thought that Americans would rush to defend their hero against the charge made by Professor Brill: that the famous President was 'a schizoid manic.'" A letter on June 13, 1931, to the *New York Times,* from Octavio E. Moscoso in New York, read, "In view of Dr. A. A. Brill's dissertation . . . it seems to me that perhaps there might be much to be gained — and hardly anything to lose — by choosing some of the future Presidents of the United States from among the schizoid manic instead of from among the Republicans and Democrats."
"Herndon was a self-made psychoanalyst": Randall, *Lincoln the President,* vol. 1, x.
"soaring psychoanalysis," "appealed to all," "irrepressible contribution": ibid., vol. 2, 336, 324, 322. Paul Angle may have been the first to make the link between Herndon and psychoanalysis. He wrote of Herndon, "Emotional, sentimental, steeped in New England transcendentalism, Herndon was inordinately fond of peering into the souls of his acquaintances in what would now be called psychoanalytical fashion. He was firmly convinced that truth could be got at by intuition, and he never doubted his own clairvoyant capacity." Preface to *Herndon's Life of Lincoln,* xxxviii.
"Herndon was a rough-hewn man": Randall, *Mary Lincoln,* 31.

238 *"murders" politically:* See George B. Forgie, *Patricide in the House Divided: A Psychological Interpretation of Lincoln and His Age* (New York: W. W. Norton, 1979).
"bad son": See Dwight G. Anderson, *Abraham Lincoln: The Quest for Immortality* (New York: Knopf, 1982).
"haunted him": Dwight G. Anderson, "Quest for Immortality," in Gabor S. Boritt,

ed., *The Historian's Lincoln: Pseudohistory, Psychohistory, and History* (Urbana: University of Illinois Press, 1996), 254.

239 *methods of psychobiography:* I am paraphrasing David Greenberg, *Nixon's Shadow: The History of an Image* (New York: W. W. Norton, 2003), 268–69.

240 *"a man known to have suffered":* Donna E. Shalala, "Promoting Mental Health for All Americans," White House Conference on Mental Health, Washington, D.C., June 7, 1999. www.os.dhhs.gov/news/speeches/990607.html, March 28, 2005.

"There are some people": The ad continues, "Historically, those with mental illness have made overwhelmingly important contributions to society. Sir Isaac Newton, Abraham Lincoln, Ludwig van Beethoven, Virginia Woolf, Michelangelo and Vincent van Gogh are just a few of those with mental illness who have helped move society forward. Don't hold people with mental illness back." The credits for the ad list the "NJ Association of Mental Health Agencies, a public service campaign supported by an educational grant from Eli Lilly & Co." *Behavioral Health Management* 19, no. 5 (September–October 1999).

"the oldest type": Oral History Association, "About OHA," http://omega.dickinson .edu/organizations/oha/about.html, March 23, 2005.

"that the Ann Rutledge story": Douglas L. Wilson, interview with author, August 20, 2003.

241 *"I was trained":* Rodney Davis, interview with author, August 21, 2003.

That same year: John Y. Simon, "Abraham Lincoln and Ann Rutledge," *Journal of the Abraham Lincoln Association* 11 (1990), http://jala.press.uiuc.edu/11/simon.html, March 31, 2005.

"But when I examined the records": Michael Burlingame, interview with author, August 21, 2003.

Bibliography

LIBRARIES AND ARCHIVES

Allegheny College Library, Meadville, Penn.
Bobst Library, New York University, New York, N.Y.
Bradley University, Peoria, Ill.
Chicago Historical Society, Chicago, Ill.
Cincinnati Historical Society, Cincinnati, Ohio
Cincinnati Medical Heritage Center, Cincinnati, Ohio
Cincinnati Public Library, Cincinnati, Ohio
Filson Historical Society, Louisville, Ky.
Gilder-Lehrman Institute, New York, N.Y.
Houghton Library, Harvard College, Cambridge, Mass.
Illinois Historical Survey, University of Illinois, Urbana, Ill.
Illinois State Archives, Springfield, Ill.
Illinois State Historical Library, Springfield, Ill.
Indiana Historical Society, Indianapolis, Ind.
John Hay Library, Brown University, Providence, R.I.
Knox College Library, Galesburg, Ill.
Library of Congress, Washington, D.C.
Lilly Library, University of Indiana, Bloomington, Ill.
Lincoln Library, Springfield, Ill.
Lincoln Museum, Fort Wayne, Ind.
Lincoln Studies Center, Knox College, Galesburg, Ill.
National Archives, Washington, D.C.
Newberry Library, Chicago, Ill.
New-York Historical Society, New York, N.Y.
New York Public Library, New York, N.Y.
Ohio Historical Society, Columbus, Ohio
Pearson Museum, Southern Illinois University, Springfield, Ill.
Rauner Special Collections Library, Dartmouth College, Hanover, N.H.
Southern Illinois University Medical Library, Springfield, Ill.
Spencer County Historical Society, Rockport, Ind.
University of Chicago Library, Special Collections Research Center, Chicago, Ill.
University of Kentucky, Lexington, Ky.

University of Louisville Archives and Records Center, Louisville, Ky.
Widener Library, Harvard University, Cambridge, Mass.
Williams Research Center, New Orleans, La.

INTERVIEWS

Renato Alarcon, Beverley Ballantine, Dan Bassuck, Kim Bauer, Pen Bogert, Michael Burlingame, Jimmy Carter, Rosalynn Carter, David B. Cohen, Rodney Davis, Andrew Delbanco, David Herbert Donald, Kyla Dunn, Jennifer Fleischner, Gregory Fricchione, Bud Green, Allen C. Guelzo, Wade Hall, Norbert Hirschhorn, Harold Holzer, Steven Hyman, Kay Redfield Jamison, Fenton Johnson, Stanley Kunitz, Katie MacLennan, Stefanie Markovits, Barbara Mason, Victor McKusick, Richard Lawrence Miller, Richard D. Mudd, Michael Myers, Chris Offutt, Matthew Pinsker, Jennifer Radden, Ruth Richards, E. Anthony Rotundo, Steve Rubenzer, Scott Sandage, Karl E. Scheibe, Barry Schwartz, Thomas F. Schwartz, Don Sides, John Y. Simon, Lauren Slater, John Speed, John Sackett Speed, Edward Steers, Gregory Stephens, Charles Strozier, Richard Taylor, Wayne C. Temple, Tanya Weisman, Douglas L. Wilson

BASIC LINCOLN TEXTS

Basler, Roy P., ed. *The Collected Works of Abraham Lincoln.* 9 vols. New Brunswick, N.J.: Rutgers University Press, 1953. This is the standard edition of Lincoln's works and includes all the Lincoln documents extant at publication. It is available at most good libraries and online, courtesy of the Abraham Lincoln Association and the University of Michigan, www.hti.umich.edu/l/lincoln.

Burlingame, Michael, ed. *An Oral History of Abraham Lincoln: John G. Nicolay's Interviews and Essays.* Carbondale: Southern Illinois University Press, 1996. Nicolay was Lincoln's chief White House secretary and the coauthor, with John Hay, of the first multivolume Lincoln biography. In 1875, Nicolay interviewed many close associates of Lincoln. Burlingame has published this material for the first time, with thorough annotation.

Burlingame, Michael, ed. *Lincoln Observed: The Civil War Dispatches of Noah Brooks.* Baltimore: Johns Hopkins University Press, 1998. Brooks was a Washington correspondent for the *Sacramento Daily Union,* beginning in late 1862. He said he saw President Lincoln almost every day. Burlingame has brought Brooks's dispatches together for the first time, with some letters shedding light on Lincoln.

Fehrenbacher, Don E., and Virginia Fehrenbacher, eds. *Recollected Words of Abraham Lincoln.* Palo Alto, Calif.: Stanford University Press, 1986. The Fehrenbachers assembled Lincoln quotations — what people remember him having said in conversation — describing the context, judging authenticity, and giving the original source.

Herndon, William H., and Jesse W. Weik. *Herndon's Lincoln: The True Story of a Great Life.* 3 vols. Chicago: Belford, Clarke, 1889. Herndon, Lincoln's law partner, solicited hundreds of reminiscences after Lincoln's death. In the 1880s, he teamed up with Weik, a young writer, to produce this book, which is still among the most influential and controversial works on Lincoln. The original edition is available in an electronic facsimile, published by Digital Scanning, Scituate, Mass., www.pdflibrary.com.

Hertz, Emanuel, ed. *The Hidden Lincoln: From the Letters and Papers of William H. Herndon.* New York: Viking Press, 1938. Although a complete edition of Herndon's letters on Lincoln is not yet available — the Lincoln Studies Center at Knox College has been assembling the material — Hertz is the best stopgap.

Mearns, David C., eds. *The Lincoln Papers*. 2 vols. Garden City, N.Y.: Doubleday, 1948. In 1923, Robert Todd Lincoln conveyed his father's papers to the Library of Congress, stipulating that they should be withheld from "official or public inspection or private view" until twenty-one years after his death.On July 26, 1947, the library opened the collection to scholars, and the librarian David Mearns assembled portions of the papers for publication the next year. The whole collection is now available online: http://memory.loc.gov/ammem/alhtml/malhome.html.

Miers, Earl Schenck, ed. *Lincoln Day by Day: A Chronology, 1809–1865*. 3 vols. Washington, D.C.: Lincoln Sesquicentennial Commission, 1960. These volumes assemble Lincoln's known activities on every day of his life. The chronology can be searched online, courtesy of Brown University, at www.stg.brown.edu/projects/lincoln.

Neely, Mark. *The Abraham Lincoln Encyclopedia*. New York: McGraw-Hill, 1982. Indispensable for serious researchers, this book will also interest casual students. It offers entries on all the major characters and topics in Lincoln's life, as well as biographers, collectors, historical sites, and so on.

Rice, Allen Thorndike, ed. *Reminiscences of Abraham Lincoln by Distinguished Men of His Time*. New York: Harper & Brothers, 1971; orig. 1888. Rice was editor of the *North American Review*. In the 1880s, he solicited sketches on Lincoln from distinguished figures such as Ulysses S. Grant, Frederick Douglass, and Walt Whitman.

Turner, Justin G., and Linda Levitt Turner, eds.. *Mary Todd Lincoln: Her Life and Letters*. New York: Knopf, 1972. The standard edition of Mary Lincoln's letters, woven together with a biographical narrative.

Wilson, Douglas, and Rodney Davis, eds. *Herndon's Informants: Letters, Interviews, and Statements about Abraham Lincoln*. Urbana: University of Illinois Press, 1998. A transcribed and exceptionally well-annotated volume of Herndon's "Lincoln Record," along with interviews conducted by Jesse W. Weik. The editors are codirectors of the Lincoln Studies Center at Knox College.

Wilson, Rufus Rockwell, ed. *Lincoln among His Friends: A Sheaf of Intimate Memories*. Caldwell, Ind.: Caxton Printers, 1942; *Intimate Memories of Lincoln*. Elmira, N.Y.: Primavera Press, 1945. Wilson assembled many of the best published pieces on Lincoln by people who knew him. These books are available at any good university or research library.

For more reference works, online resources, and other supplementary material, visit www.lincolnsmelancholy.com.

REFERENCE WORKS

Barnhart, Robert K., ed. *The Barnhart Concise Dictionary of Etymology*. New York: Harper-Collins, 1995.

Diagnostic and Statistical Manual of Mental Disorders: DSM-IV. Washington, D.C.: American Psychiatric Association, 1994.

Foner, Eric, and John A. Garraty, eds. *The Reader's Companion to American History*. Boston: Houghton Mifflin, 1991.

Gregory, Richard L., ed. *The Oxford Companion to the Mind*. New York: Oxford University Press, 1987.

Mental Health: A Report of the Surgeon General. Rockville, Md.: U.S. Department of Health and Human Services; Substance Abuse and Mental Health Services Administration;

Center for Mental Health Services; National Institutes of Health; National Institute of Mental Health, 1999.

Merck's 1899 Manual of the Materia Medica, Together with a Summary of Therapeutic Indications and a Classification of Medicaments: A Ready-Reference Pocket Book for the Practicing Physician. Rahway, N.J.: Merck, 1999; facsimile of first edition, 1899.

Wagner, Margaret E., Gary W. Gallagher, and Paul Finkelman, eds. *The Library of Congress Civil War Desk Reference.* New York: Simon and Schuster, 2002.

Webster, Noah. *American Dictionary of the English Language.* New York: S. Converse, 1828.

BOOKS, ARTICLES, LECTURES, AND FILMS

Akiskal, Hagop, and Giovanni B. Casson, eds. *Dysthymia and the Spectrum of Chronic Depressions.* New York: Guilford Press, 1997.

Allen, John W. *Legends and Lore of Southern Illinois.* Carbondale: Southern Illinois University Press, 1963.

Alloy, L. B. "Depressive Realism: Sadder but Wiser?" *Harvard Mental Health Letter* 11 (1995): 4–5.

Alvarez, A. *The Savage God: A Study of Suicide.* London: Weidenfeld and Nicolson, 1971.

Anbinder, Tyler. *Nativism and Slavery: The Northern Know Nothings and the Politics of the 1850s.* New York: Oxford University Press, 1992.

Anderson, Dwight G. *Abraham Lincoln: The Quest for Immortality.* New York: Knopf, 1982.

Anderson, William J. "Reminiscence of Abraham Lincoln." Ms., Chicago Historical Society, February 18, 1921.

Andrews, J. Cutler. *The North Reports the Civil War.* Pittsburgh: University of Pittsburgh Press, 1955.

Angle, Paul M. "Lincoln's First Love." *Bulletin of the Lincoln Centennial Association* 9 (December 1, 1927): 1.

———. "The Minor Collection: A Criticism." *Atlantic Monthly,* April 1929, 516–25.

———. *"Here I Have Lived": A History of Lincoln's Springfield, 1821–1865.* Chicago: Abraham Lincoln Book Shop, 1971; orig. 1935.

———. "The Recollections of William Pitt Kellogg." *Abraham Lincoln Quarterly* 3 (September 1945): 319–39.

———. *A Shelf of Lincoln Books: A Critical, Selective Bibliography of Lincolniana.* New Brunswick, N.J.: Rutgers University Press, 1946.

———, ed., with Richard G. Case. *A Portrait of Abraham Lincoln in Letters by His Oldest Son.* Chicago: Chicago Historical Society, 1968.

Appleby, Joyce. "New Cultural Heroes in the Early National Period." In Thomas L. Haskell and Richard F. Teichgraeber, eds., *Culture of the Market: Historical Essays.* New York: Cambridge University Press, 1993, 163–88.

———. *Inheriting the Revolution: The First Generation of Americans.* Cambridge: Belknap Press, 2000.

Aries, Philippe. *Centuries of Childhood.* New York: Vintage Books, 1962.

Aring, Charles D. "Daniel Drake and Medical Education." *Journal of the American Medical Association* 254, no. 15 (October 18, 1985): 2120–2.

Arnold, Isaac N. *The Life of Abraham Lincoln.* Chicago: A. C. McClurg & Co., 1909; orig. 1880.

Atkinson, Brooks, ed. *The Complete Essays and Other Writings of Ralph Waldo Emerson.* New York: Modern Library, 1950.

Baker, Jean H. *Mary Todd Lincoln: A Biography.* New York: W. W. Norton, 1987.

------. "The Lincoln Marriage: Beyond the Battle of Quotations." 38th Annual Robert Fortenbaugh Memorial Lecture, Gettysburg College, Gettysburg, Pa., 1999.

Barbee, David Rankin. "President Lincoln and Doctor Gurley." *Abraham Lincoln Quarterly* 5 (March 1948): 3.

Baringer, William E. *Lincoln's Rise to Power.* Boston: Little, Brown, 1937.

------. *A House Dividing: Lincoln as President Elect.* Springfield, Ill.: Abraham Lincoln Association, 1945.

------. *Lincoln's Vandalia.* New Brunswick, N.J.: Rutgers University Press, 1949.

Barton, William E. *The Paternity of Abraham Lincoln.* New York: George H. Doren, 1920.

------. *The Life of Abraham Lincoln.* 2 vols. Indianapolis: Bobbs-Merrill, 1925.

------. "Why Lincoln Was Sad." *Dearborn Independent,* August 28, 1926, 21–22.

------. *The Lineage of Lincoln.* Indianapolis: Bobbs-Merrill, 1929.

Barzun, Jacques. "Byron and the Byronic." *Atlantic Monthly,* August 1953, 47–52.

Bateman, Newton. "Abraham Lincoln." Address, Gadmus Club, Galesburg, Ill., 1932.

------, ed. *Historical Encyclopedia of Illinois and History of Sangamon County.* Springfield, Ill.: Sangamon County Genealogical Society, 1987.

------, and Paul Selby, eds. *Historical Encyclopedia of Illinois;* with Charles Edward Wilson, ed. *History of Coles County.* Chicago: Munsell, 1906.

Bates, David H. *Lincoln in the Telegraph Office: Recollections of the United States Military Telegraph Corps During the Civil War.* Lincoln: University of Nebraska Press, 1995.

Bates, Edward. *The Diary of Edward Bates, 1859–1866.* Washington, D.C.: U.S. Government Printing Office, 1933.

Bayne, Julia Taft. *Tad Lincoln's Father.* Lincoln, Neb.: Bison Books, 2001; orig. 1931.

Beale, Howard K., ed. *Diary of Gideon Welles, Secretary of the Navy under Lincoln and Johnson.* 3 vols. New York: W. W. Norton, 1960.

Beam, Alex. *Gracefully Insane: The Rise and Fall of America's Premier Mental Hospital.* New York: Public Affairs, 2001.

Beecher, Catharine. *A Treatise on Domestic Economy.* New York: Harper & Brothers, 1842.

Bennett, Lerone, Jr. *Forced into Glory: Abraham Lincoln's White Dream.* Chicago: Johnson Publishing, 2000.

Bentall, Richard P. "A Proposal to Classify Happiness as a Psychiatric Disorder." *Journal of Medical Ethics* 18 (1992): 94–98.

Beveridge, Albert J. *Abraham Lincoln, 1809–1858.* 2 vols. Boston: Houghton Mifflin, 1928.

Blight, David W. *Frederick Douglass and Abraham Lincoln: A Relationship in Language, Politics, and Memory.* Milwaukee: Marquette University Press, 2001.

Boritt, Gabor S. "The Voyage to the Colony of Linconia: The Sixteenth President, Black Colonization, and the Defense Mechanism of Avoidance." *Historian* 37 (1975): 619–32.

------. *Lincoln and the Economics of the American Dream.* Urbana: University of Illinois Press, 1994.

------, ed. *The Lincoln Enigma: The Changing Faces of an American Icon.* New York: Oxford University Press, 2001.

Bowen, H. C. "Recollections of Abraham Lincoln." *New York Independent,* February 11, 1909.

Boyd, Maurice. *William Knox and Abraham Lincoln: The Story of a Poetic Legacy.* Denver: Sage Books, 1966.

Braden, Waldo W., ed. *Building the Myth: Selected Speeches Memorializing Abraham Lincoln.* Urbana: University of Illinois Press, 1990.

Branham, Robert James, and Philip S. Foner, eds. *Lift Every Voice: African American Oratory, 1787–1900.* Tuscaloosa: University of Alabama Press, 1998.

Bray, Robert. "Abraham Lincoln and the Two Peters." *Journal of the Abraham Lincoln Association* 22 (Summer 2001): 27–48.

Brigham, Amariah. *Remarks on the Influence of Mental Cultivation and Mental Excitement upon Health.* Boston: Marsh, Capen & Lyon, 1833; reprinted in Gerald Grob, ed. *The Beginnings of Mental Hygiene in America: Three Selected Essays, 1833–1850.* New York: Arno Press, 1973.

Brooks, Noah. "The Final Estimate of Lincoln," *New York Times,* February 12, 1898.

———. *Washington in Lincoln's Time.* Edited by Herbert Mitgang. New York: Rinehart, 1958.

Brown, C. F. *Artemus Ward, His Book.* New York: Carleton, 1862.

Browne, Robert H. *Abraham Lincoln and the Men of His Time: His Cause, His Character, and True Place in History, and the Men, Statesmen, Heroes, Patriots, Who Formed the Illustrious League about Him.* 2 vols. Chicago: Blakely-Oswald, 1907.

Browning, Orville Hickman. *The Diary of Orville Hickman Browning.* Edited by Theodore Calvin Pease and J. G. Randall. 2 vols. Springfield: Illinois State Historical Library, 1925–33.

Bucknill, John Charles, and Daniel H. Tuke. *A Manual of Psychological Medicine.* New York: Hafner Publishing, 1968; orig. 1858.

Bullard, F. Lauriston. "When John T. Stuart Sought to Send Lincoln to South America." *Lincoln Herald* 47, nos. 3–4 (December 1945): 21–22.

Burlingame, Michael. *The Inner World of Abraham Lincoln.* Urbana: University of Illinois Press, 1994.

———. "New Light on the Bixby Letter." *Journal of the Abraham Lincoln Association* 16 (Winter 1995): 59–72.

———, ed. *Lincoln's Journalist: John Hay's Anonymous Writings for the Press, 1860–1864.* Carbondale: Southern Illinois University Press, 1998.

———, ed. *At Lincoln's Side: John Hay's Civil War Correspondence and Selected Writings.* Carbondale: Southern Illinois University Press, 2000.

———, and John R. Turner Ettlinger, eds. *Inside Lincoln's White House: The Complete Civil War Diary of John Hay.* Carbondale: Southern Illinois University Press, 1999.

Burton, Robert. *The Anatomy of Melancholy.* Edited by Holbrook Jackson. London, 1972.

Campbell, Joseph, with Bill Moyers. *The Power of Myth.* New York: Doubleday, 1988.

Camus, Albert. *The Myth of Sisyphus and Other Essays.* New York: Knopf, 1967; orig. 1955.

Capers, Gerald M. *Stephen A. Douglas: Defender of the Union.* Boston: Little, Brown, 1959.

Carlson, Eric T., Jeffrey L. Wollock, and Patricia S. Noel, eds. *Benjamin Rush's Lectures on the Mind.* Philadelphia: American Philosophical Society, 1981.

Carnegie, Dale. *Lincoln the Unknown.* New York: Century, 1932.

Carpenter, F. B. *The Inner Life of Abraham Lincoln: Six Months at the White House.* Lincoln: University of Nebraska Press, 1995; orig. *Six Months at the White House with Abraham Lincoln,* 1866.

Carruthers, Olive. *Lincoln's Other Mary.* Chicago and New York: Ziff-Davis, 1946.

Cartwright, Peter. *Autobiography.* Edited by Charles L. Wallis. Nashville, Tenn.: Abingdon Press, 1956; orig. 1856.

Casey, Nell, ed. *Unholy Ghost: Writers on Depression.* New York: Morrow, 2001.

Chapman, Ervin S. *Latest Light on Abraham Lincoln.* New York: Fleming H. Revell, 1917.

Clark, L. Pierce. *Lincoln: A Psycho-Biography.* New York: Scribner, 1933.

Cohen, David B. *Out of the Blue: Depression and Human Nature.* New York: W. W. Norton, 1994.

Coleman, Charles H. *Abraham Lincoln and Coles County, Illinois.* New Brunswick, N.J.: Scarecrow Press, 1955.

Coleridge, Ernest Hartley, ed. *The Poetical Works of Lord Byron.* New York: Scribner, 1905.

Collins, G. *The Louisville Directory for the Year 1841.* Louisville, 1841.

Collyer, Robert H. *Lights and Shadows of American Life.* Boston: Brainard, 1838.

Crain, Caleb. *American Sympathy: Men, Friendship, and Literature in the New Nation.* New Haven: Yale University Press, 2001.

Crellin, J. K. "Robert King Stone. M.D.: Physician to Abraham Lincoln." *Illinois Medical Journal* 155, no. 2 (February 1979): 97–99.

———. *Medical Care in Pioneer Illinois.* Springfield: Pearson Museum, Southern Illinois University School of Medicine, 1982.

Crook, W. H. *Through Five Administrations: Reminiscences of Colonel William H. Crook, Body-Guard to President Lincoln.* Edited by Margarita Spalding Gerry. New York: Harper & Brothers, 1910.

———. *Memories of the White House: The Home Life of Our Presidents from Lincoln to Roosevelt.* Edited by Henry Rood. Boston: Little, Brown, 1911.

Crouch, Stanley. "Black Like Huck: Revisiting Twain in the Age of Oprah." *New York Times Magazine,* June 6, 1999.

Csikszentmihalyi, Mihaly. *Creativity: Flow and the Psychology of Discovery and Invention.* New York: HarperCollins, 1996.

Current, Richard N. *Lincoln and the First Shot.* New York: J. B. Lippincott, 1963.

Cushman, Philip. *Constructing the Self, Constructing America: A Cultural History of Psychotherapy.* Boston: Addison-Wesley, 1995.

Dahlstrand, Frederick C. "Science, Religion, and the Transcendentalist Response to a Changing America." In Joel Myerson, ed., *Studies in the American Renaissance.* Charlottesville: University Press of Virginia, 1988.

Dain, Norman. *Concepts of Insanity, 1789–1865.* New Brunswick, N.J.: Rutgers University Press, 1964.

Dall, C. H. "Pioneering." *Atlantic Monthly,* April 1867, 403–16.

Dally, Peter. *Virginia Woolf: The Marriage of Heaven and Hell.* London: Robson Books, 1999.

Daniels, George H. *American Science in the Age of Jackson.* New York: Columbia University Press, 1968.

Davis, Cullom, ed. *The Public and the Private Lincoln: Contemporary Perspectives.* Carbondale: Southern Illinois University Press, 1979.

Davis, J. McCan. *How Lincoln Became President.* Springfield: Illinois Company, 1909.

Davis, Rodney O. Introduction to Ward Hill Lamon, *The Life of Abraham Lincoln.* Lincoln: University of Nebraska Press, 1999.

De Botton, Alain. *How Proust Can Change Your Life.* London: Picador, 1997.

Delbanco, Andrew. *The Death of Satan: How Americans Have Lost the Sense of Evil.* New York: Farrar, Straus and Giroux, 1995.

———. *The Real American Dream: A Meditation on Hope.* Cambridge: Harvard University Press, 1999.

Deming, Henry C. *Eulogy of Abraham Lincoln.* Hartford, Conn.: A. N. Clark, 1865.

Depaulo, J. Raymond. *Understanding Depression: What We Know and What You Can Do about It.* New York: Wiley, 2002.

Dicey, Edward. *Spectator of America.* Edited by Herbert Mitgang. Athens: University of Georgia Press, 1971; orig. *Six Months in the Federal States.* London: Macmillan, 1863.

Dickinson, Emily. *The Letters of Emily Dickinson.* 3 vols. Edited by Thomas H. Johnson. Cambridge: Harvard University Press, 1958.

———. *Final Harvest: Emily Dickinson's Poems.* Boston: Little, Brown, 1961.

Diggins, John P. *On Hallowed Ground: Abraham Lincoln and the Foundations of American History.* New Haven: Yale University Press, 2000.

Dirck, Brian R. *Lincoln & Davis: Imagining America, 1809–1865.* Lawrence: University Press of Kansas, 2001.

Dittenhoefer, A. J. *How We Elected Lincoln: Personal Recollections of Lincoln and Men of His Time*. New York: Harper & Brothers, 1916.

Donald, David Herbert. *Lincoln's Herndon*. New York: Knopf, 1948.

————. *Lincoln*. New York: Simon and Schuster, 1995.

————. *"We Are Lincoln Men": Abraham Lincoln and His Friends*. New York: Simon and Schuster, 2003.

————, ed. *Inside Lincoln's Cabinet: The Civil War Diaries of Salmon P. Chase*. New York: Longman, Green, 1954.

Drake, Daniel. *Discourse on Intemperance*. Cincinnati: Locker & Reynolds, 1828.

————. "History of Two Cases of Burn, Producing Serious Constitutional Irritation." *Western Journal of the Medical and Physical Sciences* 4 (April–June 1830): 48–60.

————. *Analytical Report of a Series of Experiments in Mesmeric Somniloquism Performed by an Association of Gentlemen with Speculations on the Production of Its Phenomena*. Louisville: F. W. Prescott, 1844.

————. *A Systematic Treatise, Historical, Etiological and Practical, on the Principal Diseases of the Interior Valley of North America, as They Appear in the Caucasian, African, Indian, and Esquimaux Varieties of Its Population*. 2 vols. Cincinnati, 1850, 1854.

————. *Pioneer Life in Kentucky: A Series of Reminiscential Letters*. Cincinnati: R. Clarke, 1870.

Duff, John J. *A. Lincoln: Prairie Lawyer*. New York: Rinehart, 1960.

Duncan, Kunigunde, and D. F. Nickols. *Mentor Graham: The Man Who Taught Lincoln*. Chicago: University of Chicago Press, 1944.

Durkheim, Emile. *Suicide: A Study in Sociology*. London: Routledge and Kegan Paul, 1952.

Dyche, Grace Locke Scripps. "John Locke Scripps, Lincoln's Campaign Biographer: A Sketch Compiled from His Letters." *Journal of the Illinois State Historical Society* 17 (October 1924): 333–51.

Dylan, Bob. *Bringing It All Back Home*. 1965. Sony 9128.

Earle, Pliny. *Visit to Thirteen Asylums for the Insane in Europe*. Philadelphia: Dobson, 1841.

Easterbrook, Gregg. *The Progress Paradox: How Life Gets Better While People Feel Worse*. New York: Random House, 2003.

Eberwein, Jane Donahue, ed. *An Emily Dickinson Encyclopedia*. Westport, Conn.: Greenwood Press, 1998.

Edwards, Presley Judson. Memoirs Written at "Oaklawn." Hillsboro, Ill., 1898. Typescript on microfilm, Chicago Historical Society.

Elliott, Carl. *Better Than Well: American Medicine Meets the American Dream*. New York: W. W. Norton, 2003.

Elms, Alan C. *Uncovering Lives: The Uneasy Alliance of Biography and Psychology*. New York: Oxford University Press, 1994.

Emerson, Ralph Waldo. *The Complete Works of Ralph Waldo Emerson*. London, 1884.

Epstein, Mark. *Thoughts Without a Thinker: Psychotherapy from a Buddhist Perspective*. New York: Basic Books, 1995.

Erickson, Gary. "The Graves of Ann Rutledge and the Old Concord Burial Ground." *Lincoln Herald* 71 (Fall 1969): 90–107.

Evans, Dylan. *Emotion: The Science of Sentiment*. New York: Oxford University Press, 2001.

Evans, G. Blakemore, ed. *The Riverside Shakespeare*. Boston: Houghton Mifflin, 1974.

Fadiman, Clifton, gen. ed. *The Little, Brown Book of Anecdotes*. Boston: Little, Brown, 1985.

Fancher, Raymond E. *Pioneers of Psychology*. New York: W. W. Norton, 1979.

Faraone, Stephen V., Ming T. Tsuang, and Debby W. Tsuang. *Genetics of Mental Disorders: A Guide for Students, Clinicians, and Researchers*. New York: Guilford Press, 1999.

Fehrenbacher, Don E. *Prelude to Greatness: Lincoln in the 1850s*. Palo Alto, Calif.: Stanford University Press, 1962.

———. *The Changing Image of Lincoln in American Historiography.* New York: Oxford University Press, 1968.

———. *Lincoln in Text and Context: Collected Essays.* Palo Alto, Calif.: Stanford University Press, 1987.

Fisher, Rhoda L., and Seymour Fisher. *Pretend the World Is Funny and Forever: A Psychological Analysis of Comedians, Clowns, and Actors.* Hillsdale, N.J.: Lawrence Erlbaum Associates, 1981.

Fleischner, Jennifer. *Mrs. Lincoln and Mrs. Keckly: The Remarkable Story of the Friendship Between a First Lady and a Former Slave.* New York: Broadway Books, 2003.

Foner, Eric. *Free Soil, Free Labor, Free Men: The Ideology of the Republican Party Before the Civil War.* New York: Oxford University Press, 1970.

———. Review of Lerone Bennett, Jr., *Forced into Glory: Abraham Lincoln's White Dream. Los Angeles Times Book Review,* April 9, 2000.

Ford, Governor Thomas. *A History of Illinois from Its Commencement as a State in 1818 to 1847.* Annotations and introduction by Rodney Davis. Urbana: University of Illinois Press, 1995; orig. 1854.

Forest, Derek. *Hypnotism: A History.* New York: Penguin, 2000.

Forgie, George B. *Patricide in the House Divided: A Psychological Interpretation of Lincoln and His Age.* New York: W. W. Norton, 1979.

Fraiberg, Selma. *The Magic Years: Understanding and Handling the Problems of Early Childhood.* New York: Scribner, 1959.

Frances, Allen, and Michael B. First. *Your Mental Health: A Layman's Guide to the Psychiatrist's Bible.* New York: Scribner, 1999.

Frankl, Victor. *Man's Search for Meaning.* New York: Washington Square Press, 1985; orig. 1946.

Freeman, Andrew A. *Abraham Lincoln Goes to New York.* New York: Coward-McCann, 1960.

Freud, Sigmund. *Leonardo da Vinci and a Memory of His Childhood.* New York: W. W. Norton, 1964.

———. *The Freud Reader.* Edited by Peter Gay. New York: W. W. Norton, 1989.

Fristad, Mary A., et al. "Psychosocial Functioning in Children after the Death of a Parent." *American Journal of Psychiatry* 150, no. 3 (March 1993): 511–13.

Frothingham, Paul Revere. *Edward Everett, Orator and Statesman.* Boston: Houghton Mifflin, 1925.

Fuess, Claude Moore. *Daniel Webster.* 2 vols. Boston: Little, Brown, 1930.

Fuller, Robert C. *Mesmerism and the American Cure of Souls.* Philadelphia: University of Pennsylvania Press, 1982.

———. *Alternative Medicine in American Religious Life.* New York: Oxford University Press, 1989.

———. *Spiritual but Not Religious: Understanding Unchurched America.* New York: Oxford University Press, 2001.

Gale, Robert L. *A Cultural Encyclopedia of the 1850s in America.* Westport, Conn.: Greenwood Press, 1993.

Gamwell, Lynn, and Nancy Tomes. *Madness in America: Cultural and Medical Perceptions of Mental Illness Before 1914.* Ithaca, N.Y.: Cornell University Press, 1995.

Gary, Ralph. *Following in Lincoln's Footsteps: A Complete Annotated Reference to Hundreds of Historical Sites Visited by Abraham Lincoln.* New York: Carroll & Graf, 2001.

Gay, Peter. *The Tender Passion: The Bourgeois Experience, Victoria to Freud.* New York: Oxford University Press, 1986.

Gershon, Michael. *The Second Brain: The Scientific Basis of Gut Instinct and a Ground-*

breaking *New Understanding of Nervous Disorders of the Stomach and Intestines.* New York: HarperCollins, 1998.

Gesell, Arnold, Louise Bates Ames, and Frances L. Ilg. *The Child from Five to Ten.* New York: Harper & Row, 1977.

Ghaemi, S. Nassir. *The Concepts of Psychiatry: A Pluralistic Approach to the Mind and Mental Illness.* Baltimore: Johns Hopkins University Press, 2003.

———, ed. *Polypharmacy in Psychiatry.* New York: Marcel Dekker, 2002.

Gibson, William Harris. "My Recollections of Abraham Lincoln." *Farm and Fireside* 28, nos. 5–10 (December 1, 1904, December 15, 1904, January 1, 1905, January 15, 1905, February 1, 1905, and February 15, 1905).

Gienapp, William E. *Abraham Lincoln and Civil War America.* New York: Oxford University Press, 2002.

Godwin, William. *Enquiry Concerning Political Justice.* London, 1793.

Goff, John S. *Robert Todd Lincoln: A Man in His Own Right.* Norman: University of Oklahoma Press, 1969.

Goldsmith, Barbara. *Other Powers: The Age of Suffrage, Spiritualism, and the Scandalous Victoria Woodhull.* New York: Knopf, 1998.

Goodheart, Annette. *Laughter Therapy: How to Laugh about Everything in Your Life That Isn't Really Funny.* Santa Barbara, Calif.: Less Stress Press, 1994.

Grant, Ulysses S. *Memoirs and Selected Letters.* New York: Library of America, 1990.

Greenberg, David. *Nixon's Shadow: The History of an Image.* New York: W. W. Norton, 2003.

Grimsley, Elizabeth Todd. "Six Months in the White House." *Journal of the Illinois State Historical Society* 19 (October 1926–January 1927).

Grinnell, Josiah Bushnell. *Men and Events of Forty Years: Autobiographical Reminiscences of an Active Career from 1850 to 1890.* Boston: D. Lothrop, 1891.

Grob, Gerald N. *From Asylum to Community: Mental Health Policy in Modern America.* Princeton, N.J.: Princeton University Press, 1991.

———. *The Mad among Us: A History of the Care of America's Mentally Ill.* New York: Free Press, 1994.

Guelzo, Allen C. "Abraham Lincoln and the Doctrine of Necessity." *Journal of the Abraham Lincoln Association* 18 (Winter 1997): 57–81.

———. *Abraham Lincoln: Redeemer President.* Grand Rapids, Mich.: Erdmans, 1999.

———. "Holland's Informants: The Construction of Josiah Holland's *Life of Abraham Lincoln.*" *Journal of the Abraham Lincoln Association* 23 (Winter 2002): 1–54.

———. *Lincoln's Emancipation Proclamation: The End of Slavery in America.* New York: Simon and Schuster, 2004.

Gunn, John C. *Gunn's* Domestic Medicine: *A Facsimile of the First Edition.* Knoxville: University of Tennessee Press, 1986; orig. *Domestic Medicine, or, Poor Man's Friend in the Hours of Affliction, Pain, and Sickness,* 1830.

Gurley, Phineas Densmore. *Man's Projects and God's Results.* Washington, D.C.: W. Ballantyne, 1863.

Hall, Calvin S. *A Primer of Freudian Psychology.* Cleveland: World Publishing, 1954.

———, and Vernon J. Nordby. *A Primer of Jungian Psychology.* New York: Taplinger, 1973.

Haltunen, Karen. *Confidence Men and Painted Women: A Study of Middle-Class Culture in America.* New York: Oxford University Press, 1989.

Harkness, David J., and R. Gerald McMurtry. *Lincoln's Favorite Poets.* Knoxville: University of Tennessee Press, 1959.

Harley, David M. "Explaining Salem: Calvinist Psychology and the Diagnosis of Possession." *American Historical Review* 110, no. 2 (April 1996): 307–30.

Harper, Robert S. *Lincoln and the Press.* New York: McGraw-Hill, 1951.

Harris, Kathryn M. "Generations of Pride: African American Timeline." Illinois State Historical Library, www.illinoishistory.gov/lib/GenPrideAfAm.htm.

Harrison, Lowell Hayes. *Lincoln of Kentucky.* Lexington: University of Kentucky Press, 2000.

Hart, Gary Warren. *Right from the Start: A Chronicle of the McGovern Campaign.* New York: Quadrangle, 1973.

Hatch, Nathan O. *The Democratization of American Christianity.* New Haven: Yale University Press, 1989.

Havens, Leston. *Learning to Be Human.* Reading, Mass.: Addison-Wesley, 1994.

Haverlin, Carl. *A. Lincoln's Letter to Fanny McCullough.* Chicago: R. G. Newman, 1968.

Hay, John, and John G. Nicolay. *Abraham Lincoln: A History.* 10 vols. New York: Century, 1890.

Hay, Logan. "Lincoln in 1841–1842." *Abraham Lincoln Quarterly* 2 (September 1942): 114–26.

Hayden, C. B. "On the Distribution of Insanity in the United States." *Southern Literary Messenger* 10, no. 3 (March 1844): 178–81.

Hayward, Rhodri. "Demonology, Neurology, and Medicine in Edwardian Britain." *Bulletin of the History of Medicine* 78, no. 1 (Spring 2004): 37–58.

Helm, Katherine. *The True Story of Mary, Wife of Lincoln: Containing the Recollections of Mary Lincoln's Sister Emilie, Mrs. Ben Hardin Helm: Extracts from Her War-time Diary, Numerous Letters and Other Documents Now First Published by Her Niece, Katherine Helm.* New York: Harper, 1928.

Herndon, William H. *Lincoln, Ann Rutledge and the Pioneers of New Salem.* Herrin, Ill.: Trovillion, 1945; orig. "Abraham Lincoln, Miss Ann Rutledge, New Salem, Pioneering and the Poem," November 16, 1866.

———, and Jesse W. Weik. *Herndon's Lincoln: The True Story of a Great Life.* 3 vols. Chicago: Belford, Clarke, 1889.

Hickey, James T. "The Lincolns' Globe Tavern: A Study in Tracing the History of a Nineteenth-Century Building." *Journal of the Illinois State Historical Society* 56 (Winter 1963): 629–53.

———. *The Collected Writings of James T. Hickey.* Springfield: Illinois State Historical Society, 1984.

Hill, Douglas W. "Henry Clay Whitney: A Reliable Source for Lincoln Research?" *Lincoln Herald* 102, no. 4 (Winter 2000): 177–84.

Hillman, James. *The Soul's Code: In Search of Character and Calling.* New York: Bantam Books, 1997.

Hirschhorn, Norbert, and Robert G. Feldman. "Mary Lincoln's Final Illness: A Medical and Historical Reappraisal." *Journal of the History of Medicine and Allied Sciences* 54, no. 4 (1999): 511–42.

———, Robert G. Feldman, and Ian A. Greaves. "Abraham Lincoln's Blue Pills: Did Our Sixteenth President Suffer from Mercury Poisoning?" *Perspectives in Biology and Medicine* 44, no. 3 (Summer 2001): 315–22.

Hogan, Michael. Keynote address, *Nineteenth Annual Rosalynn Carter Symposium on Mental Health Policy,* November 5–6, 2003. Atlanta: Carter Center, 2004.

Holland, J. G. *Life of Abraham Lincoln.* Springfield, Mass.: G. Bill, 1866.

Holzer, Harold. *Lincoln Seen and Heard.* Lawrence: University Press of Kansas, 2000.

———. *Lincoln at Cooper Union: The Speech That Made Abraham Lincoln President.* New York: Simon and Schuster, 2004.

———, ed. *Dear Mr. Lincoln: Letters to the President.* Reading, Mass.: Addison-Wesley, 1993.

———, ed. *The Lincoln-Douglas Debates: The First Complete, Unexpurgated Text.* New York: HarperCollins, 1993.

———, ed. *The Lincoln Mailbag: America Writes to the President, 1861–1865.* Carbondale: Southern Illinois University Press, 1998.

———, ed. *Lincoln As I Knew Him: Gossip, Tributes, and Revelations from his Best Friends and Worst Enemies.* Chapel Hill, N.C.: Algonquin Books, 1999.

Horgan, John. *The Undiscovered Mind: How the Human Brain Defies Replication, Medication, and Explanation.* New York: Free Press, 1999.

Horine, Emmet Field. "Daniel Drake and the Missing Lincoln Letter." *Manuscripts* 9 (Winter 1957): 31–34.

———. *Daniel Drake, 1785–1852: Pioneer Physician of the Midwest.* Philadelphia: University of Pennsylvania Press, 1961.

Horwitz, Tony. *Confederates in the Attic: Dispatches from the Unfinished Civil War.* New York: Pantheon Books, 1998.

Houser, M. L. *Abraham Lincoln, Student: His Books.* Peoria, Ill.: Edward Jacob, 1932.

Howe, Daniel Walker. *The Political Culture of the American Whigs.* Chicago: University of Chicago Press, 1979.

———. *The Making of the American Self: Jonathan Edwards to Abraham Lincoln.* Cambridge: Harvard University Press, 1997.

———, ed. *Victorian America.* Philadelphia: University of Pennsylvania Press, 1976.

Howells, W. D. *Life of Abraham Lincoln.* Bloomington: Indiana University Press, 1960; orig. 1860.

Huxley, Aldous. *The Perennial Philosophy.* New York: Harper & Brothers, 1945.

Illich, Ivan. *Medical Nemesis: The Expropriation of Health.* New York: Bantam Books, 1977.

Inge, M. Thomas, ed. *Handbook of American Popular Culture.* Westport, Conn.: Greenwood Press, 1989.

Jackson, Stanley W. *Melancholia and Depression: From Hippocratic Times to Modern Times.* New Haven: Yale University Press, 1986.

———. *Care of the Psyche: A History of Psychological Healing.* New Haven: Yale University Press, 1999.

Jacksonville State Hospital: The First Psychiatric Institution in Illinois. Springfield: Southern Illinois University Press, 1982.

Jacoby, Susan. *Freethinkers: A History of American Secularism.* New York: Metropolitan Books, 2004.

Jaffa, Harry V. *Crisis of the House Divided: An Interpretation of the Lincoln-Douglas Debates.* Chicago: University of Chicago Press, 1982.

———. *A New Birth of Freedom: Abraham Lincoln and the Coming of the Civil War.* Lanham, Md.: Rowman & Littlefield, 2000.

James, William. *The Varieties of Religious Experience: A Study in Human Nature.* New York: Modern Library, 1928; orig. 1902.

Jamison, Kay Redfield. *Touched with Fire: Manic-Depressive Illness and the Artistic Temperament.* New York: Free Press, 1993.

———. *An Unquiet Mind: A Memoir of Moods and Madness.* New York: Vintage Books, 1996.

———. *Night Falls Fast: Understanding Suicide.* New York: Knopf, 1999.

Johannsen, Robert W. *Stephen A. Douglas.* Urbana: University of Illinois Press, 1977; orig. 1973.

Johns, Jane Martin. *Personal Recollections of Early Decatur, Abraham Lincoln, Richard J. Oglesby, and the Civil War.* Decatur, Ill.: Decatur Chapter, Daughters of the American Revolution, 1912.

Johoda, Marie. *Current Concepts of Positive Mental Health*. New York: Basic Books, 1958.

Jones, Edgar DeWitt. *Lincoln and the Preachers*. New York: Harper & Brothers, 1948.

Jopling, David A. "'Take Away the Life-Lie . . .': Positive Illusions and Creative Self-Deception." *Philosophical Psychology* 9, no. 4 (December 1996): 525–44.

Juettner, Otto. *Daniel Drake and His Followers*. Cincinnati: Harvey Publishing, 1909.

Kaplan, Bert. *The Inner World of Mental Illness: A Series of First-Person Accounts of What It Was Like*. New York: Harper & Row, 1964.

Katz, Jonathan Ned. "Coming to Terms: Conceptualizing Men's Erotic and Affectional Relations with Men in the United States, 1820–1892" and "'Homosexual' and 'Heterosexual': Questioning the Terms." In Martin Duberman, ed. *A Queer World: The Center for Lesbian and Gay Studies Reader*. New York: New York University Press, 1997.

Kaufman, Marc. "Profiles Offer a Peek Inside the Presidential Psyche." *Washington Post*, August 7, 2000.

Kaysen, Susanna. *Girl, Interrupted*. New York: Turtle Bay Books, 1993.

Kazin, Alfred. *God and the American Writer*. New York: Knopf, 1997.

Keckley, Elizabeth. *Behind the Scenes, or, Thirty Years a Slave, and Four Years in the White House*. New York: Oxford University Press, 1988; orig. 1868.

Kempf, Edward. *Abraham Lincoln's Philosophy of Common Sense: An Analytical Biography of a Great Mind*. 3 vols. New York: New York Academy of Sciences, 1965.

Kincaid, Robert L. *Joshua Fry Speed: Lincoln's Most Intimate Friend*. Harrogate, Tenn.: Lincoln Memorial University, 1943.

———. "Joshua Fry Speed: Lincoln's Confidential Agent in Kentucky." *Lincoln Herald* 55, no. 3 (Fall 1953): 2–10.

King, Willard L. *Lincoln's Manager, David Davis*. Cambridge: Harvard University Press, 1960.

Klein, Allen. *The Healing Power of Humor: Techniques for Getting Through Loss, Setbacks, Upsets, Disappointments, Difficulties, Trials, Tribulations, and All That Not-So-Funny Stuff*. Los Angeles: J. P. Tarcher, 1989.

Klein, Donald F., and Paul H. Wender. *Understanding Depression: A Complete Guide to Its Diagnosis and Treatment*. New York: Oxford University Press, 1993.

Kocsis, Daniel, and Daniel N. Klein, eds. *Diagnosis and Treatment of Chronic Depression*. New York: Guilford Press, 1995.

Kotre, John, and Elizabeth Hall. *Seasons of Life: Our Dramatic Journey from Birth to Death*. Boston: Little, Brown, 1990.

Kraepelin, Emil. *Manic-Depressive Insanity and Paranoia*. New York: Arno Press, 1976; orig. 1921.

Kramer, Peter. *Listening to Prozac*. New York: Viking, 1993.

Kunhardt, Philip B., Philip B. Kunhardt III, and Peter W. Kunhardt. *Lincoln: An Illustrated Biography*. New York: Knopf, 1992.

Kushner, Howard I. *Self-Destruction in the Promised Land: A Psychocultural Biology of American Suicide*. New Brunswick, N.J.: Rutgers University Press, 1989.

Lamon, Ward Hill. *The Life of Abraham Lincoln*. Lincoln: University of Nebraska Press, 1999; orig. 1872.

Lande, R. Gregory. *Madness, Malingering, and Malfeasance: The Transformation of Psychiatry and the Law in the Civil War Era*. Washington, D.C.: Brassey's, 2003.

Laughlin, Clara E. "The Last Twenty-four Hours of Lincoln's Life." *Ladies' Home Journal*, February 1909.

Lawrence, Jill. "As Dean Forges Ahead, His Temperament Gets Closer Look." *USA Today*, November 12, 2003.

Ledoux, Joseph E. *The Emotional Brain: The Mysterious Underpinnings of Emotional Life*. New York: Simon and Schuster, 1996.

Lee, Hermione. *Virginia Woolf*. New York: Knopf, 1997.

Leech, Margaret. *Reveille in Washington, 1860–1865*. New York: Carroll & Graf, 1942.

Lepore, Jill. *A Is for American: Letters and Other Characters in the Newly United States*. New York: Knopf, 2002.

Lewis, C. S. *The Problem of Pain*. San Francisco: HarperSanFrancisco, 1996; orig. 1940.

————. *A Grief Observed*. London: Faber & Faber, 1964.

Lewis, Lloyd. *Myths after Lincoln*. New York: Press of the Readers Club, 1941.

Lightner, David L., ed. *Asylum, Prison, and Poorhouse: The Writings and Reform Work of Dorothea Dix in Illinois*. Carbondale: Southern Illinois University Press, 1999.

Lincoln, Waldo. *History of the Lincoln Family: An Account of the Descendants of Samuel Lincoln of Hingham, Massachusetts, 1637–1920*. Worcester, Mass.: Commonwealth Press, 1923.

Linder, Usher F. *Reminiscences of the Early Bench of Illinois*. Chicago: Chicago Legal News, 1879.

Lloyd, Carol. "Was Lincoln Gay?" *Salon*, May 3, 1999.

Loudon, Irvine, ed. *Western Medicine: An Illustrated History*. New York: Oxford University Press, 1997.

Lowry, Thomas P. *Don't Shoot That Boy! Abraham Lincoln and Military Justice*. Boston: Da Capo Press, 1999.

Luthin, Reinhard H. *The First Lincoln Campaign*. Gloucester, Mass.: P. Smith, 1964; orig. 1944.

Mansfield, Edward D. *Memoirs of the Life and Services of Daniel Drake, M.D., Physician, Professor, and Author*. Cincinnati: Applegate, 1855.

Markle, Donald E. *The Telegraph Goes to War: The Personal Diary of David Homer Bates*. Hamilton, N.Y.: Edmonston Publishing, 2003.

Marshall, H. P. "Interesting Diagnosis of Melville's Mind." In Brian Higgins and Hershel Parker, eds., *Critical Essays on Melville's* Pierre; or, The Ambiguities. Boston: G. K. Hall, 1983.

Marszalek, John F. *Sherman's Other War: The General and the Civil War Press*. Kent, Ohio: Kent State University Press, 1999.

Martin, Mike W. "Depression: Illness, Insight, and Identity." *Philosophy, Psychiatry, and Psychology* 6, no. 4 (1999): 271–86.

Masur, Louis P. *1831: Year of Eclipse*. New York: Hill and Wang, 2001.

Matheny, Lorenzo. "An Inaugural Dissertation on Fever, As It Appeared in Illinois in 1835." Diss., Transylvania University, February 20, 1836. Copy in Illinois State Historical Library.

Maxwell, James, Jr. *A Memoir of the Diseases Called by the People the Trembles and the Sick Stomach or the Milk Sickness As They Appear in the Virginia Military District in the State of Ohio*. Louisville, 1841.

Maynard, Nettie Colburn. *Was Abraham Lincoln a Spiritualist? Or, Curious Revelations from the Life of a Trance Medium*. Philadelphia: Rufus C. Hartranft, 1891.

McClure, A. K., and James A. Rawley. *Abraham Lincoln and Men of War-Times: Some Personal Recollections of War and Politics During the Lincoln Administration*. Edited by James A. Rawley. Lincoln: University of Nebraska Press, 1997; orig. 1892.

McConnell, Frank D., ed. *Byron's Poetry*. New York: W. W. Norton, 1978.

McCullough, James, Jr. *Treatment for Chronic Depression: Cognitive Behavioral Analysis System of Psychotherapy, CBASP*. New York: Guilford Press, 2000.

McCutcheon, Marc. *The Writer's Guide to Everyday Life in the 1800s*. Cincinnati: Writer's Digest Books, 1993.

McLoughlin, William. *Revivals, Awakenings and Reform*. Chicago: University of Chicago Press, 1978.

McMurtry, Larry. *Crazy Horse*. New York: Viking, 1999.

McMurtry, R. Gerald, and Mark E. Neely. *The Insanity File: The Case of Mary Todd Lincoln*. Carbondale: Southern Illinois University Press, 1993.

McPherson, James M. *The Negro's Civil War: How American Negroes Felt and Acted During the War for the Union*. New York: Pantheon Books, 1965.

———. *Battle Cry of Freedom: The Civil War Era*. New York: Oxford University Press, 1988.

———. *Abraham Lincoln and the Second American Revolution*. New York: Oxford University Press, 1992.

Mearns, David C. "Thayer's Pioneer Boy: A Second and Harder Look." *Quarterly Journal of Current Acquisitions of the Library of Congress* 13 (1955–1956): 129–34.

Mellon, James, ed. *The Face of Lincoln*. New York: Bonanza Books, 1979.

Melville, Herman. *Moby-Dick*. New York: W. W. Norton, 1967; orig. 1851.

Menand, Louis. "William James and the Case of the Epileptic Patient." *New York Review of Books*, December 17, 1998.

———. *The Metaphysical Club*. New York: Farrar, Straus and Giroux, 2001.

Miles, Mary Leighton. "The Fatal First of January." *Journal of the Illinois State Historical Society* 20, no. 1 (April 1927).

Mill, John Stuart. *A System of Logic, Raciocinative and Inductive: Being a Connected View of the Principles of Evidence, and Methods of Scientific Investigation*. London: J. W. Parker, 1843.

———. *Autobiography*. New York: Penguin, 1989; orig. 1873.

Miller, Alice. *The Drama of the Gifted Child*. New York: Basic Books, 1981.

Miller, John, ed. *On Suicide: Great Writers on the Ultimate Question*. San Francisco: Chronicle Books, 1992.

Miller, Randall M., Harry S. Stout, and Charles Reagan Wilson, eds. *Religion and the American Civil War*. New York: Oxford University Press, 1998.

Miller, Richard Lawrence. "Lincoln's 'Suicide' Poem: Has It Been Found?" *For the People: The Newsletter of the Abraham Lincoln Association* 6 (Spring 2004): 1.

Miller, William Lee. *Lincoln's Virtues: An Ethical Biography*. New York: Knopf, 2002.

Mills, Charles K. *Benjamin Rush and American Psychiatry*. New York, 1886.

Minor, Wilma Francis. "Lincoln the Lover." *Atlantic Monthly*, December 1928–February 1929.

Mitgang, Herbert, ed. *Abraham Lincoln: A Press Portrait*. New York: Fordham University Press, 2000.

Monaghan, Jay. "Was Abraham Lincoln Really a Spiritualist?" *Journal of the Illinois State Historical Society* 34 (June 1941): 209–32.

Morgan, H. Wayne. *Drugs in America: A Social History, 1800–1980*. Syracuse, N.Y.: Syracuse University Press, 1982.

Morris, Roy, Jr. *The Better Angel: Walt Whitman in the Civil War*. New York: Oxford University Press, 2000.

Myers, Michael. *When Physicians Commit Suicide: Reflections of Those They Leave Behind*. Videotape. Vancouver, B.C.: Media Services, St. Paul's Hospital and University of British Columbia, 1998.

Nagel, P. C. *John Quincy Adams: A Public Life, a Private Life*. New York: Knopf, 1997.

Neely, Mark. *The Last Best Hope on Earth: Abraham Lincoln and the Promise of America*. Cambridge: Harvard University Press, 1993.

Neugeboren, Jay. *Imagining Robert: My Brother, Madness, and Survival: A Memoir*. New York: Morrow, 1997.

———. *Transforming Madness: New Lives for People Living with Mental Illness*. Berkeley: University of California Press, 2001.

Nevins, Allen. *The War for the Union*. 4 vols. New York: Scribner, 1959–1971.

Newton, Joseph Fort. *Lincoln and Herndon*. Cedar Rapids, Iowa: Torch Press, 1910.

Nicolay, Helen. *Lincoln's Secretary: A Biography of John G. Nicolay*. New York: Longmans, Green, 1949.

Niederhoffer, Reida E. "The Milk Sickness: Drake on Medical Interpretation." *Journal of the American Medical Association* 254, no. 15 (October 18, 1985): 2123–5.

NIMH Genetics Workgroup. "Genetics and Mental Disorders." NIH publication no. 98-4268. Rockville, Md.: National Institute of Mental Health, 1998.

Noll, Mark A. *America's God: From Jonathan Edwards to Abraham Lincoln*. New York: Oxford University Press, 2002.

Norbury, Frank B. "Dorothea Dix and the Founding of Illinois' First Mental Hospital." *Journal of the Illinois State Historical Society* 92 (Spring 1999): 13–29.

Oates, Stephen B. *With Malice Toward None: The Life of Abraham Lincoln*. New York: Harper & Row, 1977.

Onstot, T. G. *Pioneers of Menard and Mason Counties*. Forest City, Ill., 1902.

Otteson, Ann I. "A Reconstruction of the Activities and Outbuildings at Farmington, an Early Nineteenth Century Hemp Farm." *Filson Club Quarterly* 59, no. 4 (October 1985).

Paine, Thomas. "Predestination" and "The Age of Reason." In M. D. Conway, ed., *The Writings of Thomas Paine*. 20 vols. New York: G. P. Putnam, 1896.

Paul, Annie Murphy. *The Cult of Personality: How Personality Tests Are Leading Us to Mislabel Our Children, Mismanage Our Companies, and Misunderstand Ourselves*. New York: Free Press, 2004.

Pease, Theodore C. *The Frontier State, 1818–1848*. Urbana: University of Illinois Press, 1987.

Perris, C. S. Holmgren, L. von Knorring, and H. Perris. "Parental Loss by Death in the Early Childhood of Depressed Patients and of Their Healthy Siblings." *British Journal of Psychiatry* 148 (1986): 165–69.

Peters, K. F., et al. "Living with Marfan Syndrome II: Medication Adherence and Physical Activity Modification." *Clinical Genetics* 60 (2001): 283–92.

———. "Living with Marfan Syndrome III: Quality of Life and Productive Planning." *Clinical Genetics* 62 (2002): 110–20.

Petersen, William. *Lincoln-Douglas: The Weather As Destiny*. Springfield, Ill.: Charles C. Thomas, 1943.

Peterson, Merrill D. *Lincoln in American Memory*. New York: Oxford University Press, 1994.

Pfeffer, Cynthia R. *Severe Stress and Mental Disturbance in Children*. Arlington, Va: American Psychiatric Publishing, 1996.

Pinsker, Matthew. "Senator Abraham Lincoln." *Journal of the Abraham Lincoln Association* 14, no. 2 (Summer 1993): 1–22.

———. *Lincoln's Sanctuary: Abraham Lincoln and the Soldiers' Home*. New York: Oxford University Press, 2003.

Plummer, Mark A. *Lincoln's Rail Splitter: Governor Richard J. Oglesby*. Urbana: University of Illinois Press, 2001.

Poe, Edgar Allan. "The Assignation." In Philip Van Doren Stern, ed., *The Portable Edgar Allan Poe*. New York: Penguin Books, 1973, 205.

Pond, Fern Nance. "Intellectual New Salem in Lincoln's Day." Address, Lincoln Memorial University, Harrogate, Tenn., February 12, 1938.

Porter, Roy. *Blood and Guts: A Short History of Medicine*. New York: W. W. Norton, 2002.

———. *Flesh in the Age of Reason*. New York: Allen Lane, 2003.

———, ed. *The Cambridge Illustrated History of Medicine*. Cambridge, England: Cambridge University Press, 1996.

Pratt, Harry E. *The Personal Finances of Abraham Lincoln*. Springfield, Ill.: Abraham Lincoln Association, 1943.

———. *Concerning Mr. Lincoln: In Which Abraham Lincoln Is Pictured As He Appeared to Letter Writers of His Time.* Springfield, Ill.: Abraham Lincoln Association, 1944.

Prince, Morton. "Roosevelt As Analyzed by the New Psychology." *New York Times,* March 24, 1912.

Provine, Robert. *Laughter.* New York: Viking Press, 2000.

Putnam, George Haven. *Abraham Lincoln: The People's Leader in the Struggle for National Existence.* New York: G. P. Putnam, 1909.

Pyszczynski, Tom, et al. "Emotional Expression and the Reduction of Motivated Cognitive Bias: Evidence from Cognitive Dissonance and Distancing from Victims' Paradigms." *Journal of Personality and Social Psychology* 64, no. 2 (February 1993): 177–86.

Radden, Jennifer. "Melancholy and Melancholia." In David Michael Levin, ed., *Pathologies of the Modern Self: Postmodern Studies on Narcissism, Schizophrenia, and Depression.* New York: New York University Press, 1972, 231–50.

———. *The Nature of Melancholy: From Aristotle to Kristeva.* New York: Oxford University Press, 2000.

Radford, Victoria, ed. *Meeting Mr. Lincoln: Firsthand Recollections of Abraham Lincoln by People, Great and Small, Who Met the President.* Chicago: Ivan R. Dee, 1998.

Randall, James G. "Has the Lincoln Theme Been Exhausted?" *American Historical Review* 41, no. 2 (January 1936): 270–94.

———. *Lincoln the President.* 2 vols. New York: Dodd, Mead, 1945.

———. *Lincoln the President: Midstream.* New York: Dodd, Mead, 1953.

———. "Historianship." *American Historical Review* 58, no. 2 (January 1953): 249–64.

———, and Richard Nelson Current. *Lincoln the President: Last Full Measure.* Urbana: University of Illinois Press, 2000.

Randall, Ruth Painter. *Mary Lincoln: Biography of a Marriage.* Boston: Little, Brown, 1953.

———. *Lincoln's Sons.* Boston: Little, Brown, 1955.

———. *The Courtship of Mr. Lincoln.* Boston: Little, Brown, 1957.

———. *Lincoln's Animal Friends: Incidents about Abraham Lincoln and Animals, Woven into an Intimate Story of His Life.* Boston: Little, Brown, 1958.

———. *Colonel Elmer Ellsworth: A Biography of Lincoln's Friend and First Hero of the Civil War.* Boston: Little, Brown, 1960.

———. *I, Ruth: Autobiography of a Marriage; The Self-Told Story of the Woman Who Married the Great Lincoln Scholar, James G. Randall, and Through Her Interest in His Work Became a Lincoln Author Herself.* Boston: Little, Brown, 1968.

Rankin, Henry B. *Personal Recollections of Abraham Lincoln.* New York: G. P. Putnam, 1916.

———. *Intimate Character Sketches of Abraham Lincoln.* Philadelphia: J. B. Lippincott, 1924.

Rathbone, Benson Godfrey (Lord Charnwood). *Abraham Lincoln.* New York: Holt, 1916.

Raveis, Victoria H., Karolynn Siegel, and Daniel Karus. "Children's Psychological Distress Following the Death of a Parent." *Journal of Youth and Adolescence* 28, no. 2 (1999): 165–80.

Real, Terrence. *I Don't Want to Talk about It: Overcoming the Secret Legacy of Male Depression.* New York: Fireside, 1998.

Reck, W. Emerson. *A. Lincoln: His Last 24 Hours.* Columbia: University of South Carolina Press, 1987.

Reed, Edward S. *From Soul to Mind: The Emergence of Psychology from Erasmus Darwin to William James.* New Haven: Yale University Press, 1997.

Reep, Thomas P. *Lincoln at New Salem.* Petersburg, Ill.: Old Salem League, 1927.

Reinhart, Mark S. *Abraham Lincoln on Screen: A Filmography, 1903–1998.* Jefferson, N.C.: McFarland, 1999.

Reynolds, David S. *Beneath the American Renaissance: The Subversive Imagination in the Age of Emerson and Melville.* New York: Knopf, 1988.

————. *Walt Whitman.* New York: Oxford University Press, 2005.

Riddle, Donald W. *Lincoln Runs for Congress.* New Brunswick, N.J.: Rutgers University Press, 1948.

————. *Congressman Abraham Lincoln.* Urbana: University of Illinois Press, 1957.

Robb, Graham. *Strangers: Homosexual Love in the Nineteenth Century.* New York: W. W. Norton, 2004.

Robert, Brian. *American Alchemy: The California Gold-Rush and Middle-Class Culture.* Chapel Hill: University of North Carolina Press, 2000.

Rose, Phyllis. *Parallel Lives: Five Victorian Marriages.* New York: Knopf, 1983.

Rosenberg, Charles E. *The Cholera Years: The United States in 1832, 1849, and 1866.* Chicago: University of Chicago Press, 1962.

————. *No Other Gods: On Science and American Social Thought.* Baltimore: Johns Hopkins University Press, 1976.

Ross, James. *The Life and Times of Elder Reuben Ross.* Nashville: McQuiddy, 1977; orig. 1882.

Rothman, David J. *The Discovery of the Asylum: Social Order and Disorder in the New Republic.* Boston: Little, Brown, 1971.

Rothman, Ellen K. *Hands and Hearts: A History of Courtship in America.* New York: Basic Books, 1984.

Rotundo, E. Anthony. *American Manhood: Transformations in Masculinity from the Revolution to the Modern Era.* New York: Basic Books, 1993.

Rousseau, Peter L. "Jacksonian Monetary Policy, Specie Flows, and the Panic of 1837." Working Paper No. 00-W04R, January 2000, rev. June 2001, Department of Economics, Vanderbilt University; forthcoming, *Journal of Economic History.*

Rubenzer, Steven J., Thomas R. Faschingbauer, and Deniz S. Ones. "Assessing the U.S. Presidents Using the Revised NEO Personality Inventory." *Assessment* 7, no. 4 (December 2000): 403–20.

Runco, Mark A., and Ruth Richards, eds. *Eminent Creativity, Everyday Creativity, and Health.* Greenwich, Conn.: Ablex, 1997.

Rush, Benjamin. *Medical Inquiries and Observations upon the Diseases of the Mind.* New York: New York Academy of Medicine, 1962; orig. 1812.

Sacks, Oliver W. *Seeing Voices: A Journey into the World of the Deaf.* Berkeley: University of California Press, 1989.

————. *The Man Who Mistook His Wife for a Hat.* New York: Vintage, 1996.

Sage, Harold K. "Jesse W. Fell and the Lincoln Autobiography." *Journal of the Abraham Lincoln Association* 3 (1981).

Sanborn, F. B. *The Life and Letters of John Brown.* Boston: Roberts Brothers, 1891.

Sandage, Scott. *Deadbeats, Drunkards, and Dreamers: A Cultural History of Failure in America, 1819–1893.* Diss., Rutgers University, October 1995.

————. *Born Losers: A History of Failure in America.* Cambridge: Harvard University Press, 2005.

Sandburg, Carl. *Abraham Lincoln: The Prairie Years.* 2 vols. New York: Harcourt, Brace, 1926.

————. *Abraham Lincoln: The War Years.* 4 vols. New York: Harcourt, Brace, 1939.

————. "Address Before a Joint Session of Congress," February 12, 1959. Audio stream at www.talkinghistory.org.

————, and Paul M. Angle. *Mary Lincoln: Wife and Widow.* New York: Harcourt, Brace, 1932.

Saum, Lewis O. *The Popular Mood of Pre–Civil War America.* Westport, Conn.: Greenwood Press, 1980.

Scheibe, Karl E. *The Drama of Everyday Life.* Cambridge: Harvard University Press, 2000.

Schwartz, Barry. "Postmodernity and Historical Reputation: Abraham Lincoln in Late-Twentieth-Century Imagination." *Social Forces* 77, no. 1 (September 1998): 63–103.

———. *Abraham Lincoln and the Forge of National Memory.* Chicago: University of Chicago Press, 2000.

Schwartz, Thomas F. "'An Egregious Political Blunder': Justin Butterfield, Lincoln, and Illinois Whiggery." *Journal of the Abraham Lincoln Association* 8 (1986): 9–19.

———. "Santa Abraham?" *For the People: The Newsletter of the Abraham Lincoln Association* 1, no. 4 (Winter 1999): 6.

Scripps, John Locke. *Life of Abraham Lincoln.* Edited by Roy P. and Lloyd A. Dunlap. Bloomington: Indiana University Press, 1961.

Searcher, Victor. *Lincoln's Journey to Greatness: A Factual Account of the Twelve-Day Inaugural Trip.* Philadelphia: John C. Winston, 1960.

Segal, Alan F. *Life after Death: A History of the Afterlife in the Religions of the West.* New York: Doubleday, 2004.

Seligman, Martin E. P. *Helplessness: On Depression, Development, and Death.* San Francisco: W. H. Freeman, 1975.

———. *Learned Optimism.* New York: Knopf, 1991.

Sellers, Charles. *The Market Revolution: Jacksonian America, 1815–1846.* New York: Oxford University Press, 1991.

Senning, John P. "The Know Nothing Movement in Illinois." *Journal of the Illinois State Historical Society* 7 (1914): 7–33.

Seward, Frederick W. *Seward at Washington, as Senator and Secretary of State: A Memoir of His Life, with Selections from His Letters, 1861–1872.* New York: Derby & Miller, 1891.

Shapiro, Henry D., and Zane L. Miller, eds. *Physician to the West: Selected Writings of Daniel Drake on Science and Society.* Lexington: University Press of Kentucky, 1970.

Shaw, Albert. *Abraham Lincoln: The Year of His Election.* New York: Review of Reviews Corp., 1929.

Shaw, Benjamin, et al. "Emotional Support from Parents Early in Life, Aging, and Health." *Psychology and Aging* 19, no. 1 (2004): 4–12.

Sheehan, Susan. *Is There No Place on Earth for Me?* New York: Vintage Books, 1983.

Shneidman, Edwin S. *The Suicidal Mind.* New York: Oxford University Press, 1996.

Shorter, Edward. *From Paralysis to Fatigue: A History of Psychosomatic Illness in the Modern Era.* New York: Free Press, 1992.

———. *A History of Psychiatry: From the Era of the Asylum to the Age of Prozac.* New York: Wiley, 1997.

Shutes, Milton H. *Lincoln and the Doctors: A Medical Narrative of the Life of Abraham Lincoln.* New York: Pioneer Press, 1933.

———. *Lincoln's Emotional Life.* Philadelphia: Dorrance, 1957.

Simon, John Y. "Abraham Lincoln and Ann Rutledge." *Journal of the Abraham Lincoln Association* 11 (1990): 13–34.

Simon, Paul. *Lincoln's Preparation for Greatness: The Illinois Legislative Years.* Norman: University of Oklahoma Press, 1965.

Simonton, Dean Keith. *Genius, Creativity and Leadership: Historiometric Inquiries.* Cambridge: Harvard University Press, 1984.

Sklar, Kathryn Kish. *Catharine Beecher: A Study in American Domesticity.* New Haven: Yale University Press, 1973.

Slater, Lauren. *Welcome to My Country.* New York: Random House, 1996.

———. *Prozac Diary.* New York: Random House, 1998.

———. *Lying: A Metaphorical Memoir.* New York: Random House, 2000.

———. *Opening Skinner's Box: Great Psychological Experiments of the Twentieth Century.* New York: W. W. Norton, 2004.

Smith, James D., III. "James Smith: Cumberland Presbyterian Minister, 1798–1871." Cumberland Presbyterian Center, www.cumberland.org/hfcpc/minister/SmithJ.htm, February 22, 2005.

Smith, Jeffery. *Where the Roots Reach for Water: A Personal and Natural History of Melancholia*. New York: North Point Press, 1999.

Smith, L. M. *The Great American Crisis: Cause and Cure of the Rebellion Embracing Phrenological Characters and Pen-and-Ink Portraits of the President, His Leading Generals and Cabinet Officers; Together with an Appendix on the Slavery Controversy, in Which Is Submitted a Novel Plan for the Full and Final Adjustment of This Vexed Question.* Cincinnati: Johnson, Stephens, 1862.

Smith-Rosenberg, Carroll. "The Female World of Love and Ritual: Relations Between Women in Nineteenth-Century America." In *Disorderly Conduct: Visions of Gender in Victorian America*. New York: Knopf, 1985.

Solomon, Andrew. *The Noonday Demon: An Atlas of Depression*. New York: Scribner, 2001.

Spalding, Mattingly. *Biography of a Kentucky Town: An Historical, Cultural, and Literary Study of Bardstown*. Baltimore, 1942.

Speed, James. *James Speed: A Personality*. Louisville: J. M. Morton, 1914.

Speed, Joshua F. *Reminiscences of Abraham Lincoln and Notes of a Visit to California: Two Lectures*. Louisville: John P. Morton, 1884.

Stakelberg, Count S. "Tolstoi Holds Lincoln World's Greatest Hero." *New York World*, February 12, 1909.

Standage, Tom. *The Victorian Internet: The Remarkable Story of the Telegraph and the Nineteenth Century's On-Line Pioneers*. London: Weidenfeld and Nicolson, 1998.

Stansell, Christine. "What Stuff!" *New Republic*, January 17, 2005.

Starcevic, Vladan, and Don R. Lipsitt, eds. *Hypochondriasis: Modern Perspectives on an Ancient Malady*. New York: Oxford University Press, 2001.

Stearns, Peter, and Jan Lewis, ed. *An Emotional History of the United States*. New York: New York University Press, 1998.

Stephen A. Douglas and the American Union. Exhibition catalogue, Department of Special Collections, University of Chicago Library, February–June 1994.

Stephens, Gregory. *On Racial Frontiers: The New Culture of Frederick Douglass, Ralph Ellison, and Bob Marley*. New York: Cambridge University Press, 1999.

Stern, Philip Van Doren. *The Life and Writings of Abraham Lincoln*. New York: Random House, 1940.

Stevens, Walter. *A Reporter's Lincoln*. Edited by Michael Burlingame. Lincoln: University of Nebraska Press, 1998; orig. 1916.

Stoddard, William O. "White House Sketches." *New York Citizen*, September 29, 1866.

———. *Inside the White House in War Times: Memoirs and Reports of Lincoln's Secretary*. Edited by Michael Burlingame. Lincoln: University of Nebraska Press, 2000; orig. 1890.

Storr, Anthony. *The Dynamics of Creation*. New York: Atheneum, 1985; orig. 1972.

———. *Churchill's Black Dog, Kafka's Mice, and Other Phenomena of the Human Mind*. New York: Grove Press, 1988.

———. *Solitude: A Return to the Self*. New York: Ballantine Books, 1988.

———. *Feet of Clay: A Study of Gurus*. London: HarperCollins, 1996.

Stowe, Harriet Beecher. *Uncle Tom's Cabin; or, Life among the Lowly*. New York: Vintage Books, 1991; orig. 1852.

———. "Abraham Lincoln." *Living Age*, January 2, 1864, 282–84.

Stowell, Daniel W. "Stonewall Jackson and the Providence of God." In Randall M. Miller, Harry S. Stout, and Charles Reagan Wilson, eds., *Religion and the American Civil War*. New York: Oxford University Press, 1998, 187–207.

————. *In Tender Consideration: Women, Families, and the Law in Abraham Lincoln's Illinois.* Urbana: University of Illinois Press, 2002.

Strozier, Charles B. *Lincoln's Quest for Union: Public and Private Meanings.* New York: Basic Books, 1982.

————. *Apocalypse: On the Psychology of Fundamentalism in America.* Boston: Beacon Press, 1994.

Styron, William. *Darkness Visible: A Memoir of Madness.* New York: Random House, 1990.

Swett, Leonard. "David Davis." Address, Bar Association of Illinois, copy in Chicago Historical Society.

Tarbell, Ida M. *The Early Life of Abraham Lincoln.* New York: A. S. Barnes, 1974; orig. 1896.

————. *The Life of Abraham Lincoln.* New York: Doubleday & McClure, 1900.

————. *Abraham Lincoln and His Ancestors.* Lincoln: University of Nebraska Press, 1977; orig. *In the Footsteps of the Lincolns,* 1924.

Taylor, Richard S. Review of Douglas L. Wilson and Rodney O. Davis, eds., *Herndon's Informants: Letters, Interviews, and Statements about Abraham Lincoln;* Douglas L. Wilson, *Lincoln Before Washington: New Perspectives on the Illinois Years;* and Douglas L. Wilson, *Honor's Voice: The Transformation of Abraham Lincoln. Journal of the Abraham Lincoln Association* 21 (Summer 2000): 44–68.

Teillard, Dorothy Lamon, ed. *Recollections of Abraham Lincoln.* Lincoln: University of Nebraska Press, 1994.

Temple, Sunderine W., and Wayne C. Temple. *Illinois' Fifth Capitol.* Springfield, Ill.: Phillips Brothers, 1988.

Temple, Wayne C. "Lincoln's Fence Rails." *Journal of the Illinois State Historical Society* 47 (Spring 1954): 20–34.

————. *By Square and Compasses: The Building of Lincoln's Home and Its Saga.* Bloomington, Ill.: Ashlar Press, 1984.

————. *Lincoln's Connections with the Illinois and Michigan Canal, His Return from Congress in '48, and His Invention.* Springfield: Illinois Bell, 1986.

————. *Abraham Lincoln: From Skeptic to Prophet.* Mahomet, Ill.: Mayhaven Publishing, 1995.

————. *"The Taste* Is *in My Mouth a Little . . .": Lincoln's Victuals and Potables.* Mahomet, Ill.: Mayhaven Publishing, 2004.

Thayer, William Makepeace. *The Pioneer Boy and How He Became President.* Boston: Walker, Wise, 1863.

Thomas, Benjamin. *Portrait for Posterity: Lincoln and His Biographers.* New Brunswick, N.J.: Rutgers University Press, 1947.

————. *Abraham Lincoln: A Biography.* New York: Knopf, 1952.

————. *Lincoln's New Salem.* Carbondale: Southern Illinois University Press, 1954.

————. *"Lincoln's Humor" and Other Essays.* Edited by Michael Burlingame. Urbana: University of Illinois Press, 2002.

————, and Harold M. Hyman. *Stanton: The Life and Times of Lincoln's Secretary of War.* New York: Knopf, 1962.

Thoreau, Henry David. *Walden.* In Carl Bode, ed., *The Portable Thoreau.* New York: Penguin Books, 1982.

Tolstoy, Leo. *My Confession; and, The Spirit of Christ's Teaching.* New York: T. Y. Crowell, 1887.

Townsend, George Alfred. *The Real Life of Abraham Lincoln: A Talk with Mr. Herndon, His Late Law Partner.* New York: Bible House, 1867; orig. in *New York Tribune,* January 25, 1867.

Townsend, William H. *Lincoln and His Wife's Hometown.* Indianapolis: Bobbs-Merrill, 1929.

———. *Lincoln and the Bluegrass: Slavery and Civil War in Kentucky.* Lexington: University of Kentucky Press, 1955.

Trietsch, James M. *The Printer and the Prince: A Study of the Influence of Horace Greeley upon Abraham Lincoln as Candidate and President.* New York: Exposition Press, 1955.

Tripp, C. A. "The Strange Case of Isaac Cogdal." *Journal of the Abraham Lincoln Association* 23, no. 1 (Winter 2002): 69–78.

———. *The Intimate World of Abraham Lincoln.* New York: Free Press, 2005.

Troutman, R. L. "Aspects of Agriculture in the Ante-Bellum Bluegrass." *Filson Club History Quarterly* 45 (1971): 166–67.

Trueblood, Elton. *Abraham Lincoln: Theologian of American Anguish.* New York: Harper & Row, 1973.

Vaillant, George E. *Adaptation to Life.* Boston: Little, Brown, 1977.

———. *The Wisdom of the Ego.* Cambridge: Harvard University Press, 1993.

VandeCreek, Drew E. "Frontier Settlement." LincolnNet, http://lincoln.lib.niu.edu/frontier.html, February 21, 2005.

Van Natter, Francis Marion. *Lincoln's Boyhood: A Chronicle of His Indiana Years.* Washington, D.C.: Public Affairs Press, 1963.

Venable W. H. *Beginning of Literary Culture in the Ohio Valley.* Cincinnati: Robert Clarke, 1891.

Verduin, Paul H. "Brief Outline of the Joseph Hanks Family." In Wilson and Davis, eds., *Herndon's Informants: Letters, Interviews, and Statements about Abraham Lincoln,* 779–83.

Vidal, Gore. *Lincoln: A Novel.* New York: Random House, 1984.

Villard, Henry. *Lincoln on the Eve of '61: A Journalist's Story.* Edited by Harold G. and Oswald Garrison Villard. New York: Knopf, 1941.

Wallace, David Foster. *Everything and More: A Compact History of ∞.* New York: W. W. Norton, 2003.

Walsh, John Evangelist. *The Shadows Rise: Abraham Lincoln and the Ann Rutledge Legend.* Urbana: University of Illinois Press, 1993.

Warren, Louis A. *Lincoln's Parentage and Childhood.* New York: Century, 1926.

———. *Lincoln's Youth: Indiana Years, Seven to Twenty-one, 1816–1830.* New York: Appleton, 1959.

Waterfield, Robin. *Hidden Depths: The Story of Hypnosis.* New York: Brunner Routledge, 2003.

Waugh, John C. *Reelecting Lincoln: The Battle for the 1864 Presidency.* New York: Crown, 1997.

Weaver, John Calvin. *Daniel Drake: A Pioneer Physician of the West.* New York: Medical Journal and Record, 1928.

Weik, Jesse W. *The Real Lincoln: A Portrait.* Cambridge: Riverside Press, 1922.

Weil, Gordon L. *The Long Shot: George McGovern Runs for President.* New York: W. W. Norton, 1973.

Weil, Simone. *Waiting for God.* New York: Harper & Row, 1973; orig. 1951.

Weintraub, Stanley. *Disraeli: A Biography.* New York: Dutton, 1993.

Welles, Gideon. *Diary of Gideon Welles, Secretary of the Navy under Lincoln and Johnson.* 3 vols. Boston: Houghton Mifflin, 1911.

Werner, Emmy E., and Ruth S. Smith. *Overcoming the Odds: High Risk Children from Birth to Adulthood.* Ithaca, N.Y.: Cornell University Press, 1992.

———. *Journeys from Childhood to Midlife: Risk, Resilience, and Recovery.* Ithaca, N.Y.: Cornell University Press, 2001.

White, Andrew D. *A History of the Warfare of Science with Theology in Christendom.* New York: D. Appleton, 1897.

White, Horace. *Abraham Lincoln in 1854*. Springfield, Ill., 1908.

———. "Abraham Lincoln in 1854." *Putnam's Magazine*, March 1909.

White, Ronald C. *Lincoln's Greatest Speech: The Second Inaugural*. New York: Simon and Schuster, 2002.

Whitman, Walt. *Complete Poetry and Selected Prose*. Edited by James E. Miller, Jr. Boston: Houghton Mifflin, 1959.

Whitney, Henry C. *Life on the Circuit with Lincoln*. Boston: Estes and Lauriat, 1892.

Whorton, James C. *Inner Hygiene: Constipation and the Pursuit of Health in Modern Society*. New York: Oxford University Press, 2000.

———. *Nature's Cures: The History of Alternative Medicine in America*. New York: Oxford University Press, 2002.

Whybrow, Peter C. *A Mood Apart: Depression, Mania, and Other Afflictions of the Self*. New York: Basic Books, 1997.

Widmer, Ted. *Martin Van Buren*. New York: Times Books, 2005.

Williams, Gary Lee. "James and Joshua Speed: Lincoln's Kentucky Friends." Master's thesis, Duke University, 1971.

Wills, Garry. *Lincoln at Gettysburg: The Words That Remade America*. New York: Simon and Schuster, 1992.

———. "What Is a Just War?" *New York Review of Books*, November 18, 2004.

Wilson, Douglas L. *Lincoln Before Washington: New Perspectives on the Illinois Years*. Urbana: University of Illinois Press, 1997.

———. *Honor's Voice: The Transformation of Abraham Lincoln*. New York: Knopf, 1998.

———. "Lincoln's Affair of Honor." *Atlantic Monthly*, February 1998, 64–71.

———. "Young Man Lincoln." Paper, Gettysburg College, September 1999.

———. "William H. Herndon and Mary Todd Lincoln." *Journal of the Abraham Lincoln Association* 22, no. 2 (Summer 2001): 1–26.

Wilson, Edmund G. "Abraham Lincoln." In *Patriotic Gore: Studies in the Literature of the American Civil War*. New York: Oxford University Press, 1962.

Wilson, Forrest. *Crusader in Crinoline: The Life of Harriet Beecher Stowe*. Westport, Conn.: Greenwood Press, 1941.

Wilson, James Grant. "Recollections of Lincoln." *Putnam's Magazine*, February 1909.

Winger, Stewart. "Lincoln's Economics and the American Dream: A Reappraisal." *Journal of the Abraham Lincoln Association* 22 (Winter 2001): 51–80.

———. *Lincoln, Religion, and Romantic Cultural Politics*. DeKalb: Northern Illinois University Press, 2003.

Winkle, Kenneth J. *The Young Eagle: The Rise of Abraham Lincoln*. Dallas: Taylor Trade Publications, 2001.

Wolf, William J. *The Almost Chosen People: A Study of the Religion of Abraham Lincoln*. Garden City, N.Y.: Doubleday, 1959.

Wright, Robert. *The Moral Animal: Evolutionary Psychology and Everyday Life*. New York: Pantheon, 1994.

Young, James Harvey. "Marketing of Patent Medicines in Lincoln's Springfield." *Pharmacy in History* 27, no. 2 (1985): 98–102.

Zall, P. M. *Abe Lincoln Laughing: Humorous Anecdotes from Original Sources by and about Abraham Lincoln*. Berkeley: University of California Press, 1982.

Zane, Charles. "Lincoln As I Knew Him." *Sunset*, October 1912, 430–38.

Acknowledgments

It's probably not possible to thank every person who has supported me in the work of making this book, but — reader be warned — I'm going to try.

I bow first to my brother David Shenk, without whose encouragement I could scarcely have begun this project and without whose support I certainly would never have finished. With David, my brother Jon Shenk has shown me how to tell stories with compassion and close attention. My love and thanks to Jon and David; to Alex Beers and Bonni Cohen; to Mom and Dad; to Grandma Shenk; to Uncle Lou and Aunt Sarah; to Sidney Cohen and Betty Ann Shenk; to Lucy, Henry, Abraham, and Anabel; to Jason and Jessica Esterkamp and Abbe Cohen; to Bill Shenk, Chuck and Joyce Shenk, Phillip and Angela Wolf; to Lila Heymann, Claire Heymann, Joan Heymann-Bergmann, and Patrick Bergmann; to Stacy and David Fisher, Michael Shenk, Alyssa Shenk, Ben Genshaft, and Andrea Beth Shenk; to Amy Wolf, Dean Volk, Rebecca Hea, Roland Hea, and Suzanne Wolf; and to the Greenes, the Beerses, the Roths, the Roy Cohens, and the Stan Cohens.

At Harvard College, Pat C. Hoy II taught me all I could learn in a classroom about writing, Steven Biel nurtured my interest in history, and Bill Kovach showed me that reporters could put bad guys in jail. At the *New Republic*, Martin Peretz and Andrew Sullivan gave me my first job and a chance to learn from a brilliant circle of writers, including Leon Wieseltier, Michael Kinsley, Hanna Rosin, Michael Lewis, and Robert Wright. Charles Peters at the *Washington Monthly* paid me to edit and study under more great talents, including Jonathan Alter, Katherine Boo, Matthew Cooper, Gregg Easterbrook, Paul Glastris, Nicholas Lemann, Jon Meacham, Matthew Miller, and Timothy Noah. After a too brief stay at the Washington bureau of *The Economist* — where I learned how to write in an English accent from Daniel Franklin, Sebastian Mallaby, Zanny Minton Beddoes, and

Yvonne Ryan — James Fallows and Steven Waldman trained me further at *U.S. News & World Report*. To Jim and Steve and to my colleagues at *U.S. News*, including Amy Bernstein, Lincoln Caplan, Erica Goode, and Joannie Fischer, I tender thanks.

My fellow editors at the *Harvard Crimson* — including Brian Hecht, Jonathan Cohn, Phil Pan, Maggie Tucker, Joe Mathews, Mary Louise Kelley, Ira Stoll, and Dante Ramos — are my gold standard for camaraderie. I am especially grateful for the friendship of John Cloud, Julian Barnes, Ivan Oransky, and David Plotz. My *Monthly* coeditors, Amy Waldman and Gareth Cook, showed me how to work well under intense pressure. I was guided by their spirit, though sorely missing Gareth's sock, in the final push to finish this manuscript. Thanks also to Amanda Bichsel Cook and Daniel Franklin.

In my first, daunting days in New York City, I found shelter in the warmth of a group who will be known to history as "the grinders." Thanks to Eve Grubin, whose contributions to the proposal linger still in this manuscript, Tara Goodrich, Susie Greenebaum, Jessica Bacal, and Arielle Eckstut. Thanks also to Joey Bacal and David Henry Sterry. Clara Jeffery edited my first long-form essays for *Harper's Magazine* with patience and impeccable good sense. The great Nell Casey helped me articulate my own melancholy, included in her anthology *Unholy Ghost*. Nell also introduced me to a circle of creative provocateurs at Stories at the Moth, where Joey Xanders turned my artistic life inside out and right side up. Dan Kennedy has helped me keep Joey's lessons alive, and has constantly tutored me in the tricky business of staying humble and purposeful. To Nell, Joey, and Dan — all my love. My thanks also to those who keep the flame lit at the Moth, including George Dawes Green, Lea Thau, Catherine Burns, Jenifer Hixson, and my fellow members of the board of directors: Alexander Roy, Mark Baltazar, Tony Hendra, Jeffrey Rudell, Margaret Braun, Anne Maffei, and Roger Skelton.

A fellowship from the Mental Health Program at the Carter Center, the project of Rosalynn Carter, helped me research and write a book proposal. Many times afterward, when my faith began to flag, a word of encouragement would come from Mrs. Carter — or an invitation to Atlanta — and buck me up. The Carter Center feels like this book's home, and I am anxious to deliver it there. My profound gratitude to Rosalynn Carter, Jimmy Carter, and the mental health program staff, including Gregory Fricchione, Thomas H. Bornemann, Lei Ellingson, Rebecca Palpant, Lynne Randolph, and Valrie Thompson. Kay Redfield Jamison, my fellowship adviser, helped me begin my mental health research. Jennifer Radden greatly aided that work and introduced me to Nassir Ghaemi, a key consultant for this project. Thanks also to Lauren Slater, Norbert Hirschhorn, Barbara Mason,

Kyla Dunn, Craig Troxclair, Shie Rozow, Donnell Stern, Richard Simon, and Ruth Richards.

Among the historians who have personally helped me, I am most deeply indebted to Douglas Wilson, Rodney Davis, and Michael Burlingame, who not only did the work I could build upon but welcomed me warmly as an informal student and as a colleague. Scott A. Sandage was hugely helpful with the culture of Lincoln's time and the politics of our own. Thanks also to Jennifer Fleischner, Allen C. Guelzo, David Herbert Donald, Harold Holzer, Richard Lawrence Miller, Jonathan H. Mann, Matthew Pinsker, David Greenberg, Jonathan Ned Katz, Andrew Delbanco, Molly Murray, Anthony Rotundo, Thomas F. Schwartz, Don Sides, John Y. Simon, Thomas Lowry, Richard Taylor, Kenneth Winkle, Michael F. Bishop, Wayne C. Temple, Sharon Wilson, Norma Davis, Paul Verduin, Margaret Westman, Phyllis Rose, Brooks D. Simpson, Ted Widmer, Bud Green, Jim Sayre, and all my fellow members of the Association of Lincoln Presenters.

History is built on manuscripts, and the keepers of historical papers do a crucial job with little acclaim. Thanks to John Hoffman and James M. Cornelius at the Illinois Historical Survey, Cheryl Schnirring and Kim Bauer at the Abraham Lincoln Presidential Library, Jay Satterfield and his staff at the University of Chicago Library, Carolyn Texley and Cindy VanHorn at the Lincoln Museum, Pen Bogert and everyone at the Filson Historical Society, Ada Hubbard at the Hancock County Historical Society, Ed Russo at the Lincoln Library in Springfield, John Daly at the Illinois State Archives, and Jane Westenfeld at Allegheny College. Special thanks to Beverley Ballantine, an authority on the family of Judge John Speed of Farmington. Thanks also to Dan Weinberg and Sylvia Castle-Dahlstrom at the Abraham Lincoln Bookshop. For shelter on my travels, thanks to Kitty Miller, Kristen Graham, Katherine Marsh, and Ralph Muhs.

In my six years of teaching at the New School University, and my one semester at New York University, I have had hundreds of students, and to them I say: You taught me well. Thanks to Robert Polito, Jackson Taylor, Deborah Landau, Luis Jaramillo, and everyone at the New School Writing Program, and to the faculty and staff of the NYU Expository Writing Program.

Bruce Feiler helped me get this book off the ground and has been sharp and generous throughout. In the long slog of drafting the manuscript, I benefited from several months of intense work with Stephen Hubbell. My agent, Tina Bennett, and her assistant, Svetlana Katz, have been a great team at Janklow and Nesbit. Thanks also to Anne Seiwerath, Lori Glazer, Laurence Cooper, and everyone at Houghton Mifflin. Tyler Rudick, Mary Fratini, Kayte VanScoy, Rebecca Segall, Summer Lynne Block, Hazen Allen, and Joe Dempsey have helped me with research. Kim Cutter helped me finish. For encouragement and assistance, thanks to Frank Rich, Scott Stossel, Curtis Fox, Warren St. John, Dean Olsher, Deborah C. Kogan, Eric Alterman, Coleman Hough, Stephen Smith, Eric Konigsberg, Eric Pape, Rich Garella, Annie Murphy Paul, Cindy Chupack, Dennis J. Drabelle, Ernest Drucker, Jennifer Bluestein, Chloe Breyer, David Carr, John and Molly Aboud, Chris Decherd, Greg Kamalier, Easy Klein, Emily Marcus, Debra Marquart, Amy Meeker, Jim Nelson, Rosie O'Donnell, Kaja Perina, Tony Salvatore, Jennifer Lehr, John Lehr, John Seabrook, Virginia Heffernan, Hilit Shifman, Carmine Starnino, Naseem Surhio, Nina Collins, Alison Conte, Tom de Kay, Michaela Murphy, Francesca Ortenzio, Maud Casey, James Kornbluh, Matt Aselton, Julia Rothwax, Megan Olden, Pari Chang, Meredith Tucker, Nina Davenport, Nell Eisenberg, Suzanne Smalley, Eve Pomerance, Stacy Abramson, Rosemary Hutzler, Garrett Hongo, D. J. Waldie, Nick Paumgarten, Mia Morgan, Rosalie Fay Barnes, Rebecca Wolff, Alissa Shipp, Elizabeth Kadetsky, Gersh Kuntzman, Greg Walloch, Gretchen Rubin, Julie Subrin, Michael Descoteau, Kira Pollack, Libby Garland, Lucinda Rosenfeld, Jenny Carchman, Ken Kurson, Kees deMooy, Chris Offutt, Karen Latuchie, Chris Desser, Naomi Lifschitz, Micki McGee, Rosalind Solomon, Nick Flynn, A. M. Homes, Fenton Johnson, Tom Judd, and the Cake Man. Thanks to the staff and patrons of the MacDowell Colony, Yaddo, and the Blue Mountain Center, where portions of this book were written.

Among those who have tended to my mental and spiritual health over the past seven years are Richard "Emotions Are Like Jelly Beans" Chefetz, Paula Eagle, Julie Holland, Antonio Burr, Sally Frances, Andrew Tartasky, Jill Blakeway, Shauna Kanter, Warren Moe, Oliver Williams, Matthew Riechers, Rabbi Burt Siegel, and Ricardo Cruciani. Thanks also to the Mankind Project and to Dave Lambert, Bob Handelman, Adam Zuckerman, Chris Bowen, Mark Menges, Richard Dirksen, Brigham Sweet, Alain Hunkins, Lenn Snyder, Jay Hodgson, Mark Boal, and Matt Sislowitz.

Thanks to all my friends. Janalyn Glascock, Traci Freeman, Michael J. O'Grady, the Holzman-Meranus family, the Boracks, the Barons, Geri Mailender, Alison Hiller Harmon, Christopher Hawthorne, Rachel Fine, Steve Silberman, Keith Karraker, Andrew Shuman, Sara Dickerman, Crispin Roven, Daniela Raz, Jenny Mayher, Ashvin Pande, Maura Swan, Courtney Williams, Cullen Gerst, Elizabeth Scarboro, Adam Goodheart, Gary Bass, Kelly A. E. Mason, Rachel Greene, Elizabeth Wollman, Emily Adcock, Amy Kaufman, Jennifer Senior, Jane Jaffin, Jeff Whelan, Austin Bunn, Eva Zuckerman, Christopher Heine, Anne Marxer, Tessa Blake, Ian Williams, Bill Werde, Suzanne Clores, Elisabeth Subrin, Elizabeth Miller, Jainee McCarroll, Jennifer Pitts, Jennifer Szalai, Jesse Drucker, Jill Birnbaum, Joseph Braude, Kathleen Leisure, Michael Kadish, Nina Siegal, Noah Robischon, Pamela Paul, Patty Griffin, Sarah Haberman, Anna Schuleit, Alex Forman, Hannah Tinti, Laurie Sandell, and David Petersen.

Though I have met him only in my dreams, no artist has helped me more or pushed me harder than Bruce Springsteen. If anyone knows the Boss, for God's sake would you send him this book?

For several years, I have cloistered myself in work and kept up only with a group of dearly appreciated friends. Ted Rose is my man on the mountain, on the ocean, and in the city. Jesse Upton is my man in Fort Greene. Adam Piore is my Donald Kaufman. Bliss Broyard has gone with me to colonies and libraries and offices and helped me keep faith at every step. Dr. Ari Handel has hashed out every struggle in this book with me, sometimes while sweating profusely. Mark Wiedman is my secretary of the treasury. Andy Allbee has shown me the path of the superior man. Brooke Delaney is going with me from stage one to stage two. Sara Lamm picked me up and took me out for ice cream. Rachel Lehmann-Haupt made me beef stew with raspberries. I love you all. Pop the corks.

In memory: Sol A. Shenk, Bertha "Bébé" Wolf, Rabbi Sidney Wolf, Philippe Wamba, Rosemary Quigley, Jack Roth, and Daniel Bassuck.

Without Eamon Dolan, this book would never have crossed the threshold from idea to reality. To my great editor, I offer great thanks and the prize piece from my collection of Lincoln kitsch — a sterling silver spoon with the Gettysburg Address inscribed on the bowl.

I am grateful, finally, to Abraham Lincoln. "The fight must go on."

Index